Henry Gee

The Elizabethan Clergy and the Settlement of Religion

1558-1564

Henry Gee

The Elizabethan Clergy and the Settlement of Religion
1558-1564

ISBN/EAN: 9783337128647

Printed in Europe, USA, Canada, Australia, Japan

Cover: Foto ©ninafisch / pixelio.de

More available books at **www.hansebooks.com**

THE
ELIZABETHAN CLERGY
AND
THE SETTLEMENT OF RELIGION

HENRY GEE

HENRY FROWDE, M.A.
PUBLISHER TO THE UNIVERSITY OF OXFORD

LONDON, EDINBURGH, AND NEW YORK

THE
ELIZABETHAN CLERGY
AND THE
SETTLEMENT OF RELIGION
1558–1564

BY

HENRY GEE, B.D., F.S.A.
CO-EDITOR OF 'DOCUMENTS ILLUSTRATIVE OF ENGLISH CHURCH HISTORY'

WITH ILLUSTRATIVE DOCUMENTS AND LISTS

Oxford
AT THE CLARENDON PRESS
1898

Oxford
PRINTED AT THE CLARENDON PRESS
BY HORACE HART, M.A.
PRINTER TO THE UNIVERSITY

RICHARDO · WATSON · DIXON

ECCLESIAE · SS · TRINITATIS · CARLIOLENSIS

CANONICO

QVI

INTEGROS · HISTORIAE · FONTES

ADIRE

ET · QVAE · INDEFESSO · LABORE · INVENERIT

SINE · IRA · AC · STVDIO · REFERRE · SOLITVS

EXEMPLVM · IVNIORIBVS · PRAEBVIT

HOC · TENTAMEN · QVANTVLVMVCNQVE

AD · HISTORIAM · SAECVLI · XVI · ILLVSTRANDAM

GRATO · ANIMO

DEDICO

PREFACE

ONE of the most useful services that can be rendered at the present time to English Ecclesiastical History is to turn the microscope on disputed points in the light of our constantly increasing means of information. We now possess in the British Museum, the Public Record Office, the Bishops' Registries, and elsewhere, an easily accessible store of contemporary documents for medieval and modern history; so that it should not be difficult to settle finally many still doubtful questions, and to test traditions hitherto accepted on insufficient evidence.

The primary object of the present work is to investigate the treatment of the clergy at the beginning of Elizabeth's reign, and to estimate the number deprived for refusing, by reason of their papal sympathies, to conform to the settlement of religion then made. I began by trying to discover the actual numbers of those deprived. The figures accepted by English Church writers vary between one hundred and eighty-nine and four hundred. Roman Catholic authorities, on the other hand, have asserted with Rishton that 'the better part of the clergy followed in the footsteps of their prelates: very many of them, high dignitaries in the Church, were either thrown into prison or banished the realm [1].' In attempting a solution of this problem, I was led at the outset to trace all the modern lists to that of Nicholas Sanders, compiled

---

[1] Sanders, *Anglican Schism*, Eng. Tr. by D. Lewis, p. 261.

about 1570. A very slight examination of his work, however, proved that his figures were inaccurate and misleading; and accordingly, after a preliminary survey of contemporary writers, I set to work to discover what there might be in the way of strictly coeval and official sources of information. It soon became evident that, despite pretty general objections to the new *régime*, very few of the clergy were deprived at the commencement of the reign; and it therefore seemed expedient to extend the inquiry over a longer period. I then determined to make 1564 my limit, since in that year and until 1570 nonconformity appeared to be due to Puritan rather than to Roman sympathies. I soon found that I must take into account not merely the bare number of those deprived, but the general attitude of the clergy towards the settlement of religion, together with some survey of the means taken to gain their adherence or to inflict punishment upon those who persisted in their opposition. As I went through the Domestic State Papers, the Patent Rolls, the Exchequer Records, &c., my research gradually brought to light many facts connected with the Visitation of 1559, the work of the Ecclesiastical Commissioners, the operation of the Penal Laws, and other matters which Strype and his successors had not been in a position to see so clearly. In the end it seemed worth while to set out these facts in detail in chronological order. I therefore place before the reader, in sequence of time, what I have been able to collect, within the limits indicated, with regard to the methods and operation of the Settlement, so far as the clergy are concerned. The result of the direct inquiry into the number of clergymen deprived for Papal sympathies between 1558 and 1564 is to some extent negative, but the evidence seems to warrant my conclusion that it cannot have greatly exceeded two hundred. Further, I believe that I have proved the leniency with which the penal laws were at that time administered, in the face of the opposite assertion commonly made by Roman Catholic writers. Severity was to come; but not until later events made it, as the Government thought, necessary. Until 1570 the penal laws were not generally enforced. In the six years now under review the number of persons imprisoned, whether clerical or lay, was small; and those returned into the King's Bench as excommunicate were likewise comparatively few.

My thanks are due to the Archbishop of Canterbury for permission to transcribe manuscripts at Lambeth, and to the Bishop of London and the Bishop of Bristol for their countenance and suggestions. I have also to thank many others who have assisted me in various ways: in fact it is only at the end of my task that I realize how wide is my indebtedness even in such a comparatively small investigation as the present. First, I must mention my friend Mr. W. J. Hardy, F.S.A., with whom as collaborator I originally intended to write the book. To my regret, his other engagements have only permitted him to supply the first draft of the chapter on the deprivation of the bishops. Mr. Hardy has found time, however, to give me much advice with regard to the tracing of documents, and he has read the proof-sheets with me. The use of the editorial 'we' throughout the work is, indeed, due to our proposed partnership; and having begun with it I retained it to the end. I must also return special thanks to the Bishops' Registrars, who showed me the utmost courtesy, and allowed free access to such documents as I wished to see; to Canon Dixon of Warkworth for much counsel, and for accepting the dedication of the book, though he is in no way responsible for its contents; to Mr. G. H. Overend, F.S.A., of the Public Record Office, whose help is ever ready to all those who consult him; to Mr. William Page, F.S.A., whose sane judgement is a constant support to his friends ; to Mr. S. Wayland Kershaw, F.S.A., whose kindness is well known to all frequenters of the Lambeth Palace Library; to Mr. C. W. Moule, Fellow and Librarian of Corpus Christi College, Cambridge, who, at much personal inconvenience I fear, gave me more than one opportunity of consulting the Parker MSS.; to Mr. F. B. Bickley of the British Museum, who has afforded me constant help ; to the Rev. George Hennessy, whose unique knowledge of London Diocesan Registers has been ungrudgingly placed at my disposal ; to Chancellor Lecke of Lincoln, Canon Church of Wells, and Canon Edmondes of Exeter, who gave me all facilities for consulting the Chapter Acts in their custody ; and especially to Miss Ethel Stokes, whose accurate transcription and orderly work has put me in possession of some lists and other documents which I was unable to find time to copy for myself.

HENRY GEE.

SUMMARY OF CONTENTS

CHAPTER I.

ELIZABETH'S FIRST PARLIAMENT.

THE authorities expected opposition from the clergy to any change in the *status quo*, p. 2. First signs of change, p. 2. Protest of the clergy when Parliament assembled in January, 1559, p. 3. Introduction of the Supremacy Act in the Commons, p. 4. The original bill in the Lords, p. 4. The bill annexed passes the Lords (with the original bill), and goes to the Commons, p. 5. The bill annexed passes the Commons, p. 5. A new bill is introduced; reasons for dropping the old one, p. 5. The most material points of the final Act enumerated, p. 7. The passage of the Uniformity Act through the Houses, p. 7. The penal provisions of the Uniformity Act, p. 8. Conclusion of the first parliament, p. 9.

Illustrative Documents: i. The Supremacy Act (1 Eliz. cap. 1). ii. The Uniformity Act (1 Eliz. cap. 2).

CHAPTER II.

THE DEPRIVATION OF THE BISHOPS.

Action before Parliament sat, p. 30. The Bishops in Parliament, p. 31. The Westminster Disputation involves some of the Bishops in trouble, p. 31. First proceedings against the Bishops after May 8, 1559, p. 33. Action under the Commission of May 23, p. 34. The oath tendered to Justices and Judges in June, p. 35. The Bishops again examined, p. 35. Deprivations after July 7, p. 36. Deaths of four of the Bishops, p. 38.

Illustrative Document: Commission to the Privy Council to administer the Oath.

CHAPTER III.

ARRANGEMENTS FOR A ROYAL VISITATION.

The clergy as a body are reluctant, p. 41. Deliberation of Cecil and his advisers, p. 42. Scheme for a royal visitation, p. 42. The writ of visitation, p. 44. Probable discussions as to the method of visitation, p. 44. Departure of the cloistered clergy, p. 45.
Illustrative Documents: i. The Royal Injunctions of 1559 collated with those of Edward VI. ii. Articles of Inquiry, 1559.

CHAPTER IV.

ROYAL VISITATION OF THE NORTHERN PROVINCE, 1559.

Arrangements complete in July, 1559, p. 71. Names of the Visitors for the North, p. 71. Part taken by the Visitors named, p. 72. Issue of writs of prohibition, p. 73. Summary of the duties of the Visitors, p. 73. Narrative of the Visitation, p. 74. At Nottingham, p. 74. Returns furnished by Churchwardens, &c., p. 76. Southwell and Halifax, p. 76. Proceedings at York, p. 77. Form of the Oath subscribed, p. 77. Deprivations at York, p. 78. Diocese of Durham, p. 79. Diocese of Carlisle, p. 80. Appointment of Assessors, p. 80. Diocese of Chester, p. 81. Conclusion of the Northern Visitation, p. 82.
Illustrative Documents: i. Names of absentees from the Visitation. ii. Letters Patent directing the Northern Visitation.

CHAPTER V.

ROYAL VISITATION OF THE SOUTHERN PROVINCE.

Our materials for the Southern Visitation, p. 94. (1) London, Norwich, and Ely, p. 94. Places of Session in London, p. 95; Norwich, p. 96; Ely, p. 97. (2) Oxford, Lincoln, Peterborough, Coventry, and Lichfield, p. 97. (3) Salisbury, Bristol, Exeter, Bath and Wells, Gloucester, p. 98. Route of the Western Visitors, p. 100. (4) Canterbury, Rochester, Winchester, Chichester, p. 100. (5) Welsh dioceses with Hereford and Worcester, p. 101. Signatories in the Southern Visitation, p. 101.
Illustrative Document: Alphabetical list of extant subscriptions.

CHAPTER VI.

ROYAL VISITATION OF THE UNIVERSITIES, 1559.

The Oxford Visitation as described by Wood, p. 130. Number of the deprived at Oxford, p. 131. The Cambridge Visitation, p. 132.
Illustrative Documents: i. The writ of Visitation for Cambridge and Eton, June, 20, 1559. ii. Oxford University Deprivations, 1559. iii. Cambridge University Deprivations, 1559.

CHAPTER VII.

THE FIRST ECCLESIASTICAL COMMISSION, 1559-1562.

Distinction between the Visitation and the Commission, p. 137. The Supremacy Act contemplates such a commission, p. 137. First hint of the Commission, p. 138. Duties of the Commission, p. 139. Its special connexion with London, p. 139. Loss of Records of the Commission, p. 140. It was to sit in November, 1559, p. 140. Suspension of the Visitations in October, p. 141. A new writ issued to the Commission, p. 142. Proceedings in November, 1559, p. 142. The recusants deprived, p. 143. Proceedings with the deprived bishops, p. 144. Other prisoners at this time, p. 145.
Illustrative Documents: i. Writ for the issue of the Permanent Commission, July 19, 1559. ii. Writ of October 20, 1559, for administering the Oath. iii. Supplementary list of signatures, November, 1559.

CHAPTER VIII.

THE METROPOLITICAL VISITATION OF 1560-1.

Settlement of sees in the interval, December 1559-March 1560, p. 156. The Supremacy Oath not strictly tendered during the interval before the Metropolitical Visitation, p. 157. State of the North to April, 1560, p. 158. Parker inhibits the Southern Bishops from visiting, May, 1560, p. 158. His commissions issued in August, p. 158. Further Commissioners, 1560, p. 159. Object of this Visitation, p. 160. Revival of the Visitation for other dioceses, 1561, p. 161. Scory's letters, p. 161. Importance of Scory's letters, p. 162. Visitation of Eton, p. 162. Proceedings of Horne, June, 1561, p. 162. Further action of Horne, p. 163. Summary, p. 163.

CHAPTER IX.

NORTHERN COMMISSIONS DURING 1561 AND 1562.

State of conformity during the vacancy of the Northern dioceses. p. 165. The sees at last filled up, 1561, p. 166. Issue of a commission to administer the Oath, May 5, 1561, p. 166. Episcopal visitations and reports, p. 167. i. Best, p. 167. ii. Pilkington, p. 168. General effect of the Commission for 1561, p. 169. The laity largely escape the oath, p. 169. Instructions for the Council of the North, 1562, p. 170. Summary of the position, December, 1562, p. 171.

Illustrative Document: Commission to administer the Oath in the North, May 5, 1561.

CHAPTER X.

THE SECOND ECCLESIASTICAL COMMISSION, 1562.

A new Commission in 1562, p. 174. First proceedings under the new Commission, p. 175. Restraint and surveillance of recusants, p. 175. Other duties of the new Commission, p. 176. Summary of the work of the Commissions, 1559-1562, p. 177.

Illustrative Documents: i. Official abstract of the writ of July 20, 1562. ii. Recusants which are abroad and bound to certain places.

CHAPTER XI.

THE PENAL LAWS OF ELIZABETH'S SECOND PARLIAMENT, 1563-4.

Fears of Papal sympathy, p. 186. A new bill for the assurance of the Supremacy, p. 187. Comparison with 1 Eliz. cap. 1, p. 188. Two chief points: i. Papal sympathy, p. 188. ii. Oath of Allegiance, p. 188. The special severity of the Act as regards the oath, p. 189. The new stage indicated by this Act, p. 189. Spiritual censures and the writ *De Excommunicato Capiendo*, p. 190. The most important points in the Act, p. 191. These two Acts are not pressed severely, p. 192. The imprisoned Bishops in relation to this legislation, p. 192. Scott escapes, p. 192. Bonner and Watson, p. 193. The Emperor intercedes for the Bishops, p. 193. Release of the Bishops from the Tower, p. 194. The Emperor's second letter and the Queen's reply, p. 194. Bonner and the oath, 1564, p. 195. Sequel as regards the other Marian Bishops, p. 195.

Bishop Poole, p. 196. In review the Assurance Act was pressed in a few cases only, p. 196. The same assertion holds good for the other Act, p. 197. A possible explanation for clerical acquiescence at this time, p. 198. The Privy Council inquire as to the Justices, 1564, p. 199. No Commission yet issued under the Assurance Act. p. 201. Our limit reached, November, 1564, p. 201.

Illustrative Documents: i. Assurance of Supremacy Act (5 Eliz. cap. 1). ii. Act for the due execution of the writ *De Excommunicato Capiendo.*

CHAPTER XII.

THE DEPRIVED CLERGY: ESTIMATES OF HISTORICAL WRITERS.

Estimates in modern histories of the number deprived, p. 217. Strype's three lists, p. 217. (*a*) D'Ewes', p. 217. (*b*) Cotton MS. Titus C. 10, f. 172, p. 218. Comparison of this list with that in Camden's *Annals*, p. 218. Origin of Camden's list in Sanders' *De Visibili Monarchia*, p. 219. Clerke's criticism of Sanders, p. 220. Justification of such criticism, p. 221. (*c*) Cardinal Allen, p. 222. Origin of Allen's list, p. 222. The list in Tierney's *Dodd*, and its origin, p. 223. Criticism of Tierney's list, p. 224. General conclusion about the lists, p. 224.

Illustrative Documents: i. The list of Nicolas Sanders, 1571. ii. The Summary in *Ad Persecutores Anglos*, 1583. iii. The Summary in J. Bridgwater's *Concertatio Ecclesiae Anglicanae*, 1588. iv. The list of Dodd as corrected by Tierney, 1839.

CHAPTER XIII.

THE DEPRIVED CLERGY: EVIDENCE OF REGISTERS.

An investigation of the Registers is necessary, p. 236. Nature and extent of their evidence, p. 236. Supplementary evidence at Lambeth, and in Bishops' Certificates, and Crown Presentations, p. 237. The list of deprived resulting from these combined materials, p. 238. This list needs careful pruning, p. 238. The method of its reduction, p. 239. The result of this process, p. 239. Objections considered. i. Incompleteness of the registers, p. 241. ii. The large number of men ordained, p. 242. iii. The case of curates, p. 243. iv. The asserted probability of resignation for conscience sake, p. 243. Conclusion, p. 247.

CHAPTER XIV.

SUMMARY OF THE INQUIRY.

Facts established: Initial hostility of the clergy, p. 248. The basis of the settlement, p. 248. Royal Visitation, 1559, p. 248. First Ecclesiastical Commission established, 1559, p. 249. Metropolitical visitation of the South, 1560-1, p. 249. Visitation of the North, 1561, p. 250. New Ecclesiastical Commission, July 20, 1562, p. 250. Penal Statutes of 1563, p. 250. Sanders' list of the deprived, p. 250. Evidence of Registers, &c., p. 251.

APPENDIX I. Lists of Clergymen deprived, 1558-1564, p. 252.

APPENDIX II. List of Institutions after deprivation, 1558-1564, p. 271.

APPENDIX III. Further continuation of these lists, 1564-1570, p. 288.

INDEX, p. 293.

CHRONOLOGICAL TABLE

1558.

Nov. 17 . . . Accession of Queen Elizabeth.
Dec. 14 . . . Watson's sermon at the Funeral of Queen Mary.
Dec. ? . . . . Conferences held at Sir T. Smith's house.
Dec. 27 . . . Proclamation to repress preaching.

1559.

Jan. 23 . . . Parliament assembles.
Jan. 24 . . . Convocation meets.
Jan. 25 . . . First session of Parliament.
? . . . . Protest of Convocation.
Feb. ? . . . . Bourne deprived of the Presidency of Wales.
Feb. 15 . . . Original Bill of Supremacy drawn up.
Feb. 16 . . . Uniformity Bill read in the Commons.
Feb. 21 . . . First reading of Supremacy Bill in the Commons.
Feb. 28 . . . The bill sent up to the Lords.
Feb. 28 } The bill read twice.
March 13 }
March 15, 17, 18 } Readings of the bill annexed in the Lords.
March 20, 21, 22 } Readings of the bill annexed in the Commons.
March. 31 . The Westminster Disputation begins.
April 3 . . . Some of the Bishops before the Queen.
April 4 . . . Bishops White and Watson sent to the Tower.
April 10, 12, 13 } New Supremacy Bill read in the Commons.
April 15, 17, 25 } New Supremacy Bill read and the proviso annexed in the Lords.
April 18, 19, 20 } Uniformity Bill read in the Commons.

b

April 26, 27   Debate and reading of Supremacy Bill in the Commons.
April 26, 27, 28 }   Uniformity Bill read in the Lords.
April 28, 29. Final readings of Supremacy Bill in the Lords.
May 8 . . . . Parliament prorogued. The Bishops forbidden to leave London.
May 23 . . .   Commission to the Privy Council to administer the oath.
May 30 . . .   Deprivation of Bonner.
June . . . . . Injunctions and articles of inquiry ready.
June . . . . . The oath administered to Justices of the peace.
June . . . . . Departure of the cloistered clergy.
June 20 . . . Commission to visit Cambridge and Eton issued.
June 24 . . . The Prayer Book comes into use.
June 24 . . . Issue of writs for royal visitation.
June 26 . . . Deprivation of Bishops Oglethorpe, Scott, Bayne, Pates, Goldwell, White and Watson.
June ? . . . . Commencement of the Oxford visitation.
July 7 . . . . Deprivation of Heath and Thirlby.
July 19 . . . Issue of writ for Ecclesiastical Commission.
July 20 . . . Tunstall comes to London.
Aug. 8 . . .   Commencement of the Cambridge visitation.
Aug. 10 . . . Deprivation of Morgan and Turberville.
Aug. 11 . . . Commencement of the London visitation.
Aug. 22 . . . Commencement of the Northern visitation.
Sept. 9 . . . Commission to Tunstall and others to consecrate Parker.
Sept. 21 . . . The visitors in the diocese of Durham.
Sept. 28. . . Deprivation of Tunstall.
Oct. 3 . . . . The visitors in the diocese of Carlisle.
Oct. 9 . . . . The visitors in the diocese of Chester.
Oct. ? . . . . Suspension of the visitations.
Nov. 1-7 . .   Meeting of the Ecclesiastical Commission in London.
Nov. 15 ? . . Deprivation of recusants by the Commissioners.
Nov. 18. . .   Death of Tunstall and Bayne.
Dec. 17. . .   Consecration of Parker.
Dec. 21 . . . Consecration of Grindal (London), Cox (Ely), Sandys (Worcester), Meyrick (Bangor).
Dec. 23 . . . Death of Bishop Morgan.
Dec. 31. . .   Death of Oglethorpe.

1560.

Jan. 21 . . . Consecration of Young (St. Davids), Bullingham (Lincoln), Jewel (Salisbury), Davies (St. Asaph).
Feb. 27 . . . Commission for administering the oath in the Palatinate of Chester.

March 24 . . Consecration of Guest (Rochester), Berkeley (Bath and Wells), Bentham (Coventry and Lichfield).
April . . . . Bonner imprisoned in the Marshalsea.
May . . . . . Watson and Pates sent to the Tower.
May . . . . . Heath and Thirlby sent to the Tower.
May 13 . . . Scott imprisoned in the Fleet.
May 17 . . . Parker inhibits Scory from visiting.
June 18 . . Turberville and Bourne sent to the Tower.
Aug. 8 . . . Parker issues five commissions for visitation.
Sept. 8 . . . Commission issued to Jewel for visitation of Salisbury diocese.
Sept. 11 . . . Commission issued for Rochester and Canterbury dioceses.
Nov. . . . . Parker directs the southern bishops to send in returns.
Dec. 3. . . . Commission issued for the visitation of Gloucester.
Dec. 19 . . . Commission for visitation of Peterborough diocese.

1561.

Feb. 18 . . . Commission for visitation of Worcester diocese.
March 2. . . Consecration of Pilkington (Durham), and Best (Carlisle). Translation of Young to York.
April 24 . . Commission for visitation of Oxford diocese.
May 4 . . . Consecration of Downham (Chester).
May 5 . . . . Issue of a Commission to administer oath in the North.
June . . . . . Horne visits Winchester diocese.
July . . . . . Best visits Carlisle diocese.
Aug. 22 . . . Commission for the visitation of Eton.
Sept. . . . . Horne visits certain Colleges in Oxford.

1562.

July 20 . . . Commission for trying religious offences in the Palatinate of Chester.
July 20 . . . A new Ecclesiastical Commission issued.
Aug. 6 . . . The Commission directs the Bishops to make returns of recusancy.
Nov. . . . . Instructions on Uniformity to the Council of the North.

1563.

Jan. 12 . . . Meeting of Elizabeth's Second Parliament.
            Meeting of Convocation.
Jan. 28 . . . Petition of the Commons for penal legislation.
Feb. 15, 20 . Second and third readings in Commons of Assurance of Supremacy Bill.

Feb. 25 . . First reading of the Assurance Bill in the Lords.
March 1, 3 . Second and third readings.
April 9 . . . The Bill for writ *De Excommunicato* passed.
April 10. . . The Assurance and *De Excommunicato* Bills receive Royal Assent.
May. . . . . The oath tendered to Bonner and Watson.
July . . . . . Outbreak of the Plague.
Sept. 6. . . . The Bishops in the Tower liberated.
Sept. 24 . . . The Emperor appeals to the Queen.

1564.

April . . . . Letter of Dennum to Cecil.
April 26 . . . The oath again adminstered to Bonner.
October. . . The Council directs a return of the Justices.

THE ELIZABETHAN CLERGY AND THE SETTLEMENT OF RELIGION

CHAPTER I.

ELIZABETH'S FIRST PARLIAMENT.

DURING the five years of Queen Mary's reign a large number of clergymen were deprived in England and Wales[1]. Fresh institutions were in most cases[2] made to the cures thus left vacant. In this way, when Elizabeth came to the throne on November 17, 1558, she found a small body of regulars[3] and a large number[4] of seculars, whom we may regard as more or less sincerely attached to the existing state of the church. That they would have

<small>CHAP. I
The authorities expected opposition from the clergy to any change in the *status quo*.</small>

---

[1] See the Rev. W. H. Frere's *Marian Reaction in its relation to the English Clergy*. He says (p. 74): 'It is quite clear that the Marian deprivations amount to a great upheaval which, for the time at least, altered the whole *personnel* of the clergy in a way unequalled either before or since.'

[2] But study of the registers and of such returns as we have e. g. for the Diocese of Ely (Add. MS. 5813. f. 78), combined with incidental mention of vacancies in the Zurich letters and elsewhere (see below, p. 82, *note* 2), makes it abundantly clear that for various reasons a certain number of benefices were vacant at the beginning of Elizabeth's reign.

[3] Under Queen Mary certain religious houses had been restored, but the number of monks and friars does not appear to have been considerable, and it probably included many who were not in orders. Sanders in his *De Visibili Monarchia*, Book VII, gives very few names of dispossessed monks. Cf. Dixon, iv. 617.

[4] No exact estimate of numbers has been drawn up. On Camden's authority (trans. 1625, p. 30) it has usually been said that there were 9,400 clergy. His original words, however, are *promotiones ecclesiasticae*, and, as the registers show, one man often held two, three, or even more of such *promotiones*.

CHAP. I

First signs of change.

little sympathy with any alteration in the *status quo* may readily be assumed. For the present, the services and the *personnel* of the church remained undisturbed, but the known sympathies of the Queen, and her chief advisers, must have led all men to look for extensive alterations before long. Such alterations, indeed, must have been contemplated by the responsible authorities from the very moment that Elizabeth came to the throne. It is equally clear from a state paper which belongs to the beginning of the reign that strong opposition to change was expected by the Privy Council from the bishops and clergy in possession [1].

The first sign which bespoke the policy to follow, was given before the end of the year, when at Sir T. Smith's house in Westminster those conferences were begun in which the Prayer Book was revised in readiness for the approaching session of Parliament [2]. No special Commission, it is true, was issued for this revision, but from the antecedents of those engaged upon it, the probable result of the work must have been easy to predict. It is scarcely likely that the fact of these conferences failed to transpire. Meanwhile the Protestant party in England being reinforced from abroad began to put themselves very much in evidence, and a good deal of unwise preaching was heard. The other party were not backward. In consequence of this a proclamation was issued on December 27, which silenced all preaching for the time, and postponed any alteration of service with the exception of the Gospel and Epistle and the Ten Commandments, together with the Litany, the Lord's Prayer, and the Creed 'until consultation may be had by Parliament, by her Majesty and her three estates of this Realm [3].' A threat was added that 'if any shall

---

[1] This paper exists in Cotton MS. Julius, F. vi. It is printed by Strype in *Annals of the Reformation*, i. App. no. 4, 'What dangers may ensue upon the alteration.' It enumerates five classes, and amongst them: 'Bishops and all the clergy will see their own ruin. In confession, and preaching, and all other ways they can, they will persuade the people from it,' &c.

[2] See Cardwell, *History of Conferences* on P. B., p. 19.

[3] H. Dyson's Collection of Proclamations, f. 3.

disobediently use themselves to the breach hereof, her majesty both must and will see the same duly punished, both for the quality of the offence, and for example to all others neglecting her majesty's so reasonable commandment[1].'

Queen Elizabeth's first Parliament was summoned to meet on January 23, 1559, but actually began to sit on the 25th. On the 24th, Convocation assembled, and the unanimity of the clergy was at once evidenced by their deliberations on the preservation of existing religion. They issued in a few days a formal protest against any alteration, and in this they emphasized five particular points of doctrine[2] and practice, being instigated to do so by the Protestant tone of the Lord Keeper's speech, and the sermon of Dr. Cox at the opening of Parliament. In these articles thus drawn up, the first three deal with the doctrine of the Mass, and are a verbal reproduction of the theses disputed in 1554 at Oxford, when Cranmer, Ridley, and Latimer were condemned. These points were evidently regarded as what Strype calls 'the great κριτήριον of Popery.' The fourth emphasized the Papal Supremacy, and the fifth declared ' that the authority of handling and defining concerning the things belonging to faith, sacraments, and discipline ecclesiastical, hath hitherto ever belonged, and ought to belong only to the pastors of the church, whom the Holy Ghost for this purpose hath set in the church, and not to laymen.' It appears that all five articles were endorsed by the Universities of Oxford and Cambridge, and were laid before the House of Lords by Lord Keeper Bacon[3], with the significant exception of the last article as quoted above.

Protest of the clergy when Parliament assembles in 1559.

---

[1] This threat was frequently put into execution during the early months of 1559, as the Privy Council Acts, which survive until May, sufficiently attest. It may be said here, without proving the matter in detail, that a few of the clergy ultimately deprived and others got into trouble long before the summer of 1559; e.g. J. Gregyll, Vicar of Barking; H. Comberford, of Lichfield; T. Byrche, Vicar of Witley; J. Denton, Vicar of Spelhurst; J. Murren, Vicar of Ludgate. See *Privy Council Acts*, pp. 54. 63. Others are sent to the Fleet; ibid. 59. See also pp. 71, 77, 87, 92, and *passim*.

[2] Wilkins, iv. 179, from Parker MS. 121, f. 193.

[3] Strype, *Ann.* i. 56.

CHAP. I

Introduction of the Supremacy Act in the Commons.

Thus, at the outset, Convocation and the Universities placed themselves in opposition to the course of legislation which the new Parliament was expected to pursue.

The qualms felt by the clergy and Universities were speedily justified. It is impossible to follow in detail all the debates of Parliament when Hansard was as yet not dreamed of, but from the valuable summaries of the proceedings which we find in the Journals of the Houses, and in the admirable compendia of Sir Simonds D'Ewes, we are quite able to understand what was done. The great Act, generally known as the Supremacy Act of Elizabeth, which forms the foundation of the Elizabethan Church Settlement, and the beginning of repressive legislation, was before the two Houses of Parliament during the greater part of the session. It is quite clear from the changes introduced, and from such records of the divisions as have survived, that it was no easy business to get the bill through. If we would follow its history clearly, we should keep before us three distinct bills which may be termed the original bill, the bill annexed, and the final draft. We first hear of the original bill on February 15, when Committees of the House of Commons were appointed to draw up a bill to annex the Supremacy to the Crown. This, of course, amounted to a declaration of war against the Convocation and Universities in their present attitude. We have no particulars of the proceedings, but it appears that the bill was complete within a week, for it was read for the first time on February 21. The thought at this time was evidently to hurry the bill through, as it was read a second time the very next day (an unusually rapid progress as the fate of other bills makes clear), and a third time on Saturday, February 25. At this stage it is called 'The Bill for the Supremacy of the Churches of England and Ireland, and abolishing of the Pope of Rome.' So ended the momentous week so far as the Commons were concerned.

The original bill in the Lords.

On the first available day—Monday, February 27, the Bill was sent up to the Lords. The next day it was read a first time. At this point the Treasons Bill was allowed to take precedence of the Supremacy, and we hear no more of the latter for a fortnight, when it is read a second time on March 13. It would seem clear that a diversity of opinion had now manifested itself. What followed it is not easy to determine. It seems that the bill was on this same day referred again to certain Committees of the Commons[1]. The result, however, is clear enough, for we find that a new bill was ready within two days, the design being to annex this to the previous bill.

This new bill, or the additional provisoes, or whatever we are to call the changes made on March 13, was read a first time in the Lords on March 15. The same haste now characterizes the proceedings. This bill annexed, as we here term it, was read a second time March 17, and a third on March 18. It was now finally passed, so far as the new provisoes were concerned, and was sent down to the Commons the very same day. Meantime, also on the same day, the Lords read the original bill a third time, so that this original bill and the bill annexed were for the present concluded, so far as the Lords were concerned. The Episcopal dissentients were the Archbishop of York, the Bishops of London, Winchester, Worcester, Llandaff, Coventry, Exeter, Chester, Carlisle. The Abbot of Westminster also voted against it, and the Earl of Shrewsbury and Lord Montacute. At the next session of the Commons on Monday, March 20, the bill annexed was read a first time, on the 21st, a second, and on the 22nd, a third. On the forenoon of the same day the bill annexed was sent up to the Lords again, with a proviso which the Commons had added, and this proviso was read three times and passed by the Lords before that day's session concluded.

At this stage the combined bills ought surely to have become law. The sequel is a little perplexing, and may be given in D'Ewes' own words: 'But whether the many new additions and alterations in this foregoing bill had made some confusion in it, or that the House of Commons disliked that their bill formerly passed with them had

The bill annexed passes the Lords (with the original bill), and goes to the Commons.

The bill annexed passes the Commons.

A new bill is introduced. Reasons for dropping the old one.

[1] See D'Ewes' *Journal*, 29.

received so much reformation in the Upper House, or for what other cause I know not: most certain it is that they had no desire the said former bill should be made a perpetual law by her Majesty's royal assent; and thereupon they framed a new bill to the like purpose (in which I suppose they included also the substance of all the additions, provisoes, and amendments which the Lords had annexed to their former bill) which had its first reading in the House of Commons.... On Monday the 10th day of this instant April, being thus intitled (much differing from the title thereof here annexed, or after added, before the printed statute), viz. The Bill to avoid the usurped power claimed by any foreign potentate in this realm, and for the oath to be taken by spiritual and temporal officers.' Such is D'Ewes' hypothesis [1]. It is unfortunate that we do not possess the actual text of the original Act or the bill annexed, so that it is impossible to discover why the bill as passed on March 22 was thrown aside. Looking, however, to the fact, that several bills dealing with church matters were now before the Houses, it was resolved to drop the bill for the time being. and to incorporate some of these enactments in the final draft [2]. It may be that in consequence of the steady opposition of the Spiritual Peers, which tacitly involved that of all the clergy, it was determined to make the penalties of the Act more stringent. At all events, on April 10, the progress of the bill begins *de novo,* for on this day a new bill was brought into the Commons under the new title already mentioned by D'Ewes, viz. 'The Bill to avoid the usurped power claimed by any foreign potentate in this realm, and for the oath to be taken by spiritual and temporal officers.' The second reading took place on April 12, and the third on April 13. The title appears to have been again altered at this stage to 'The Bill for restoring the spiritual jurisdiction to the imperial crown of the realm, and abolishing foreign power.' The next day it was sent up to the Lords, and received its first reading on the 15th, and the second on the 17th. A week

---

[1] D'Ewes' *Journal,* 29. [2] Strype, *Ann.* i. 58.

elapsed during which the Uniformity Bill was occupying the attention of the Commons. On the 25th the Lords debated a new proviso for the Supremacy Bill, and read it twice. Next day the proviso was passed finally by the Lords, and the bill was read a third time by them, and sent down to the Commons. It would appear that the proviso was passed by the Lower House within the next two days, for the bill and proviso were returned once more to the Lords on the 28th. The Commons had added a proviso of their own which the Lords seem to have read twice on the day of its arrival. At last on April 29, the proviso was passed apparently without difficulty, and the Supremacy Act was complete. The royal assent was added on May 8th.

Such was the troubled passage of the measure through the Houses of Parliament. The full text will be found in the Appendix. It will be seen that the Act may be summarized as follows: it repeals certain Acts of Queen Mary, and revises some of Henry VIII (notably 25 Henry VIII. cap. 19: the Submission of the Clergy), and one of Edward VI; it annexes ecclesiastical jurisdiction to the Crown; it gives authority to appoint ecclesiastical commissioners with the most ample powers; it prescribes a Supremacy oath; it appoints penalties for refusing the oath. The most material points to be noticed for our purpose are: (1) The Oath of Supremacy; (2) The Appointment of Ecclesiastical Commissioners. By these means it is enacted that the clergy, who are already known to be opposed to alterations, are to acknowledge the Queen's Supremacy on the one hand, whilst a Commission with all the powers of Henry's Supremacy Act may at any time be appointed to manage church jurisdiction.

The most material points of the final Act enumerated.

We turn now to the history of the Elizabethan Uniformity Act. It was first heard of on February 16 in the Commons, so that the original idea was to run the Uniformity Bill more or less *pari passu* with the Supremacy Act. On the day mentioned, the bill, already drafted, was allowed its first reading; but at this juncture, when it goes by the

The passage of the Uniformity Act through the Houses.

name of the 'Bill for Common Prayer and Administering of Sacraments,' it disappears from view for two months, the Supremacy Bill thus taking precedence of it. The protest of the Convocation, and the animus which it displayed, caused the authorities, we can scarcely doubt, to take the precaution of fortifying themselves behind the Supremacy Act before they again pressed on the Uniformity Bill. In this way, the Supremacy Bill had reached its final stage before the Bill of Uniformity was again introduced. It was, then, on April 18 that the 'Bill for the Unity of the Service of the Church, and Ministration of the Sacraments' was read a first time. It would seem probable from this title that a new bill was now before the House. Passing its second reading on the next day, and its third on the day after that, the bill was brought up to the Lords on April 25, when another small change in the title is noted. This now runs: 'The Bill for Uniformity of Common Prayer, and Service in the Church, and Administration of the Sacraments.' It was read the three statutable times on three consecutive days—April 26, 27, 28. On the last day it was opposed in a speech of great vigour by Dr. Cuthbert Scott, Bishop of Chester. He gives, however, no hint of what amount of opposition existed amongst the clergy at large. Those who voted against the third reading were the Archbishop of York, the Bishops of London, Ely, Worcester, Llandaff, Coventry and Lichfield, Exeter, Chester, Carlisle, the Marquis of Winchester, the Earl of Shrewsbury, Lords Montague, Morley, Sheffield, Dudley, Wharton, Rich, North.

The penal provisions of the Uniformity Act.

Referring the reader once more to the Appendix for the text of the Act, we may here summarize the penal provisions as follows: For using any other form of Prayer after June 24, 1559, or for speaking against it or depraving it, the penalty is one year's sequestration of benefice, and six months' imprisonment for the first offence; deprivation and a year's imprisonment for a second offence; deprivation and imprisonment for life for a third offence. In order to carry out this *régime* of liturgical uniformity, the archbishops and bishops are empowered to make use of church censures; justices are to hear and determine all cases brought before them in sessions and assizes within their commission[1]; bishops may join the justices in such trials as take place within their dioceses.

Chap. I

It will be unnecessary to follow the legislation of Elizabeth's first Parliament any farther. The two important Acts for our purpose are those which have been described, and which formed the legislative basis of the settlement of religion until the second Parliament which met in 1563. The dissolution took place on May 8, 1559, after the Acts had received the royal assent. In the next chapters we shall see the steps that were taken when the settlement of religion was carried out in accordance with the Acts of Supremacy and Uniformity.

Conclusion of the first Parliament. May 8, 1559.

I.

AN ACT RESTORING TO THE CROWN THE ANCIENT JURISDICTION OF THE STATE ECCLESIASTICAL AND SPIRITUAL, AND ABOLISHING ALL FOREIGN POWER REPUGNANT TO THE SAME.

(1 ELIZABETH, CAP. I.)

[Transcr. *Statutes of the Realm*, iv. pt. i. p. 350.]

Most humbly beseech your most excellent majesty, your faithful and obedient subjects, the Lords spiritual and temporal, and the

Recital of proceedings under

---

[1] Special instructions were given to the justices in regard to their duties connected with the settlement of religion. The oath was directed to be taken by the writ of May 23 (p. 39). Accordingly, we find that the Essex magistrates took the oath at Chelmsford on June 16, under the superintendence of the lord lieutenant, the Earl of Oxford. See the earl's return, dated August 21, (S. P. Dom.), and cf. Strype's *Sir T. Smith*, p. 57. Among the duties prescribed were the following: to call three or four parishioners and to charge them to get the Prayer Book; to see that the proper service was used, or to bring the curate before the lord lieutenant; absentees from service to be presented; to give attendance on such preaching as the queen or bishops send, so long as they tarry in those parts. These duties merely carry out in detail the principle contained in the Uniformity Act concerning justices (p. 26).

Chap. I

Henry VIII and Mary in making and repealing laws dealing with ecclesiastical matters.

Commons, in this your present Parliament assembled, that where in time of the reign of your most dear father, of worthy memory, King Henry VIII, divers good laws and statutes were made and established, as well for the utter extinguishment and putting away of all usurped and foreign powers and authorities out of this your realm, and other your highness's dominions and countries, as also for the restoring and uniting to the imperial crown of this realm the ancient jurisdictions, authorities, superiorities, and pre-eminences to the same of right belonging and appertaining, by reason whereof we, your most humble and obedient subjects, from the five-and-twentieth year of the reign of your said dear father, were continually kept in good order, and were disburdened of divers great and intolerable charges and exactions before that time unlawfully taken and exacted by such foreign power and authority as before that was usurped, until such time as all the said good laws and statutes, by one Act of Parliament made in the first and second years of the reigns of the late King Philip and Queen Mary, your highness's sister, intituled an Act repealing all statutes, articles, and provisions made against the See Apostolic of Rome since the twentieth year of King Henry VIII, and also for the establishment of all spiritual and ecclesiastical possessions and hereditaments conveyed to the laity, were all clearly repealed and made void, as by the same Act of repeal more at large does and may appear; by reason of which Act of repeal, your said humble subjects were eftsoons brought under an usurped foreign power and authority, and do yet remain in that bondage, to the intolerable charges of your loving subjects, if some redress, by the authority of this your High Court of Parliament, with the assent of your highness, be not had and provided:

Repeal of Mary's Act of repeal.

May it therefore please your highness, for the repressing of the said usurped foreign power and the restoring of the rites, jurisdictions, and pre-eminences appertaining to the imperial crown of this your realm, that it may be enacted by the authority of this present Parliament, that the said Act made in the said first and second years of the reigns of the said late King Philip and Queen Mary, and all and every branch, clauses, and articles therein contained (other than such branches, clauses, and sentences as hereafter shall be excepted) may, from the last day of this session of Parliament, by authority of this present Parliament, be repealed, and shall from thenceforth be utterly void and of none effect.

And that also for the reviving of divers of the said good laws and statutes made in the time of your said dear father, it may also please your highness, that one Act and statute made in the twenty-third year of the reign of the said late King Henry VIII, intituled, An Act that no person shall be cited out of the diocese wherein he or she dwells, except in certain cases;   *Chap. I — Revival of the following statutes: 23 Hen. VIII, c. 9.*

And one other Act made in the twenty-fourth year of the reign of the said late King, intituled, An Act that appeals in such cases as have been used to be pursued to the see of Rome shall not be from henceforth had nor used, but within this realm;   *24 Hen. VIII, c. 12.*

And one other Act made in the twenty-fifth[1] year of the said late King, concerning restraint of payment of annates and firstfruits of archbishoprics and bishoprics to the see of Rome;   *23 Hen. VIII, c. 20.*

And one other Act in the said twenty-fifth year, intituled, An Act concerning the submission of the clergy to the king's majesty;   *25 Hen. VIII, c. 19.*

And also one Act made in the said twenty-fifth year, intituled, An Act restraining the payment of annates or firstfruits to the Bishop of Rome, and of the electing and consecrating of archbishops and bishops within this realm;   *25 Hen. VIII, c. 20.*

And one other Act made in the said twenty-fifth year, intituled, An Act concerning the exoneration of the king's subjects from exactions and impositions heretofore paid to the see of Rome, and for having licences and dispensations within this realm, without suing further for the same;   *25 Hen. VIII, c. 21.*

And one other Act made in the twenty-sixth year of the said late king, intituled, An Act for nomination and consecration of suffragans within this realm;   *26 Hen. VIII, c. 14.*

And also one other Act made in the twenty-eighth year of the reign of the said late king, intituled, An Act for the release of such as have obtained pretended licences and dispensations from the see of Rome;   *28 Hen. VIII, c. 16.*

And all and every branches, words, and sentences in the said several Acts and statutes contained, by authority of this present Parliament, from and at all times after the last day of this session of Parliament, shall be revived, and shall stand and be in full force and strength, to all intents, constructions, and purposes.

And that the branches, sentences, and words of the said several Acts, and every of them, from thenceforth shall and may be judged, deemed, and taken to extend to your highness, your heirs and   *The words of these statutes to apply*

---

[1] This Act, printed as 23 Hen. VIII, cap. 20, did not receive the royal assent till 25 Hen. VIII.

successors, as fully and largely as ever the same Acts, or any of them, did extend to the said late King Henry VIII, your highness's father.

And that it may also please your highness, that it may be enacted by the authority of this present Parliament, that so much of one Act or statute made in the thirty-second year of the reign of your said dear father King Henry VIII, intituled, An Act concerning precontracts of marriages, and touching degrees of consanguinity, as in the time of the late King Edward VI, your highness's most dear brother, by one other Act or statute, was not repealed; and also one Act made in the thirty-seventh year of the reign of the said late King Henry VIII, intituled, An Act that doctors of the civil law, being married, may exercise ecclesiastical jurisdiction; and all and every branches and articles in the said two Acts last mentioned, and not repealed in the time of the said late King Edward VI, may from henceforth likewise stand and be revived, and remain in their full force and strength, to all intents and purposes; anything contained in the said Act of repeal before mentioned, or any other matter or cause to the contrary notwithstanding.

And that it may also please your highness, that it may be further enacted by the authority aforesaid, that all other laws and statutes, and the branches and clauses of any Act or statute, repealed and made void by the said Act of repeal, made in the time of the said late King Philip and Queen Mary, and not in this present Act specially mentioned and revived, shall stand, remain, and be repealed and void, in such like manner and form as they were before the making of this Act; anything herein contained to the contrary notwithstanding.

And that it may also please your highness, that it may be enacted by the authority aforesaid, that one Act and statute made in the first year of the reign of the late King Edward VI, your majesty's most dear brother, intituled, An Act against such persons as shall unreverently speak against the Sacrament of the Body and Blood of Christ, commonly called the Sacrament of the altar, and for the receiving thereof under both kinds, and all and every branches, clauses, and sentences therein contained, shall and may likewise, from the last day of this session of Parliament, be revived, and from thenceforth shall and may stand, remain, and be in full force, strength, and effect, to all intents, constructions, and purposes, in such like manner and form as the same was at any time in the first year of the reign of the said late King Edward VI; any law, statute, or other matter to the contrary in any wise notwithstanding.

<small>CHAP. I</small>

And that also it may please your highness, that it may be further established and enacted by the authority aforesaid, that one Act and statute made in the first and second years of the said late King Philip and Queen Mary, intituled, An Act for the reviving of three statutes made for the punishment of heresies, and also the said three statutes mentioned in the said Act, and by the same Act revived, and all and every branches, articles, clauses, and sentences contained in the said several Acts and statutes, and every of them, shall be from the last day of this session of Parliament deemed and remain utterly repealed, void, and of none effect, to all intents and purposes; anything in the said several Acts or any of them contained, or any other matter or cause to the contrary notwithstanding.

<small>A repeal of the statute 1 & 2 Philip & Mary, c. 6, reviving the Heresy Acts.</small>

And to the intent that all usurped and foreign power and authority, spiritual and temporal, may for ever be clearly extinguished, and never to be used or obeyed within this realm, or any other your majesty's dominions or countries, may it please your highness that it may be further enacted by the authority aforesaid, that no foreign prince, person, prelate, state, or potentate, spiritual or temporal, shall at any time after the last day of this session of Parliament, use, enjoy, or exercise any manner of power, jurisdiction, superiority, authority, pre-eminence or privilege, spiritual or ecclesiastical, within this realm, or within any other your majesty's dominions or countries that now be, or hereafter shall be, but from thenceforth the same shall be clearly abolished out of this realm, and all other your highness's dominions for ever; any statute, ordinance, custom, constitutions, or any other matter or cause whatsoever to the contrary in any wise notwithstanding.

<small>All foreign authority within the queen's dominions abolished.</small>

And that also it may likewise please your highness, that it may be established and enacted by the authority aforesaid, that such jurisdictions, privileges, superiorities, and pre-eminences, spiritual and ecclesiastical, as by any spiritual or ecclesiastical power or authority have heretofore been, or may lawfully be exercised or used for the visitation of the ecclesiastical state and persons, and for reformation, order, and correction of the same, and of all manner of errors, heresies, schisms, abuses, offences, contempts, and enormities, shall for ever, by authority of this present Parliament, be united and annexed to the imperial crown of this realm.

<small>Ecclesiastical jurisdiction annexed to the crown.</small>

CHAP. 1

The queen may assign commissioners to exercise ecclesiastical jurisdiction.

And that your highness, your heirs and successors, kings or queens of this realm, shall have full power and authority by virtue of this Act, by letters patent under the great seal of England, to assign, name, and authorize, when and as often as your highness, your heirs or successors, shall think meet and convenient, and for such and so long time as shall please your highness, your heirs or successors, such person or persons being natural-born subjects to your highness, your heirs or successors, as your majesty, your heirs or successors, shall think meet, to exercise, use, occupy, and execute under your highness, your heirs and successors, all manner of jurisdictions, privileges, and pre-eminences, in any wise touching or concerning any spiritual or ecclesiastical jurisdiction, within these your realms of England and Ireland, or any other your highness's dominions or countries; and to visit, reform, redress, order, correct, and amend all such errors, heresies, schisms, abuses, offences, contempts, and enormities whatsoever, which by any manner spiritual or ecclesiastical power, authority, or jurisdiction, can or may lawfully be reformed, ordered, redressed, corrected, restrained, or amended, to the pleasure of Almighty God, the increase of virtue, and the conservation of the peace and unity of this realm, and that such person or persons so to be named, assigned, authorized, and appointed by your highness, your heirs or successors, after the said letters patent to him or them made and delivered, as is aforesaid, shall have full power and authority, by virtue of this Act, and of the said letters patent, under your highness, your heirs and successors, to exercise, use, and execute all the premises, according to the tenor and effect of the said letters patent; any matter or cause to the contrary in any wise notwithstanding.

By whom the oath of supremacy is to be taken.

And for the better observation and maintenance of this Act, may it please your highness that it may be further enacted by the authority aforesaid, that all and every archbishop, bishop, and all and every other ecclesiastical person, and other ecclesiastical officer and minister, of what estate, dignity, pre-eminence, or degree soever he or they be or shall be, and all and every temporal judge, justice, mayor, and other lay or temporal officer and minister, and every other person having your highness's fee or wages, within this realm, or any your highness's dominions, shall make, take, and receive a corporal oath upon the evangelist, before such person or persons as shall please your highness, your heirs or successors, under the great seal of England to assign and name, to accept and to take the same according to the tenor and effect hereafter following, that is to say: _{Chap. 1}

'I, *A. B.*, do utterly testify and declare in my conscience, that the queen's highness is the only supreme governor of this realm, and of all other her highness's dominions and countries, as well in all spiritual or ecclesiastical things or causes, as temporal, and that no foreign prince, person, prelate, state or potentate, has, or ought to have, any jurisdiction, power, superiority, pre-eminence, or authority ecclesiastical or spiritual, within this realm; and therefore I do utterly renounce and forsake all foreign jurisdictions, powers, superiorities, and authorities, and do promise that from henceforth I shall bear faith and true allegiance to the queen's highness, her heirs and lawful successors, and to my power shall assist and defend all jurisdictions, pre-eminences, privileges, and authorities granted or belonging to the queen's highness, her heirs and successors, or united and annexed to the imperial crown of this realm. So help me God, and by the contents of this book.' *Form of the oath.*

And that it may be also enacted, that if any such archbishop, bishop, or other ecclesiastical officer or minister, or any of the said temporal judges, justiciaries, or other lay officer or minister, shall peremptorily or obstinately refuse to take or receive the said oath, that then he so refusing shall forfeit and lose, only during his life, all and every ecclesiastical and spiritual promotion, benefice, and office, and every temporal and lay promotion and office, which he has solely at the time of such refusal made; and that the whole title, interest, and incumbency, in every such promotion, benefice, and other office, as against such person only so refusing, during his life, shall clearly cease and be void, as though the party so refusing were dead. *Penalty for those in office who refuse the oath.*

And that also all and every such person and persons so refusing to take the said oath, shall immediately after such refusal be from thenceforth, during his life, disabled to retain or exercise any office or other promotion which he, at the time of such refusal, has jointly, or in common, with any other person or persons. *Those refusing, incapable of holding office conjointly.*

And that all and every person and persons, that at any time hereafter shall be preferred, promoted, or collated to any archbishopric or bishopric, or to any other spiritual or ecclesiastical benefice, promotion, dignity, office, or ministry, or that shall be by your highness, your heirs or successors, preferred or promoted to any temporal or lay office, ministry, or service within this realm, or *The oath to be taken before entering on office.*

CHAP. I   in any your highness's dominions, before he or they shall take upon him or them to receive, use, exercise, supply, or occupy any such archbishopric, bishopric, promotion, dignity, office, ministry, or service, shall likewise make, take, and receive the said corporal oath before mentioned upon the evangelist, before such persons as have or shall have authority to admit any such person to any such office, ministry, or service, or else before such person or persons as by your highness, your heirs or successors, by commission under the great seal of England, shall be named, assigned, or appointed to minister the said oath.

Any promoted, &c., and obstinately refusing, incapable of taking office.

And that it may likewise be further enacted by the authority aforesaid, that if any such person or persons, as at any time hereafter shall be promoted, preferred, or collated to any such promotion spiritual or ecclesiastical, benefice, office, or ministry, or that by your highness, your heirs or successors, shall be promoted or preferred to any temporal or lay office, ministry, or service, shall and do peremptorily and obstinately refuse to take the same oath so to him to be offered; that then he or they so refusing shall presently be judged disabled in the law to receive, take, or have the same promotion spiritual or ecclesiastical, the same temporal office, ministry, or service within this realm, or any other your highness's dominions, to all intents, constructions, and purposes.

Persons suing livery of lands, doing homage, or entering the queen's service, shall take the oath.

And that it may be further enacted by the authority aforesaid, that all and every person and persons temporal, suing livery or *ouster le main* out of the hands of your highness, your heirs or successors, before his or their livery or *ouster le main* sued forth and allowed, and every temporal person or persons doing any homage to your highness, your heirs or successors, or that shall be received into service with your highness, your heirs or successors, shall make, take, and receive the said corporal oath before mentioned, before the Lord Chancellor of England, or the lord keeper of the great seal for the time being, or before such person or persons as by your highness, your heirs or successors, shall be named and appointed to accept or receive the same.

Those taking Holy Orders or university

And that also all and every person and persons taking orders, and all and every other person and persons which shall be promoted or preferred to any degree of learning in any University within this your realm or dominions [1], before he shall receive or take any such

---

[1] Extended in 5 Eliz. cap. 1 to all graduates, teachers, lawyers. Cf. p. 204.

orders, or be preferred to any degree of learning, shall make, take, and receive the said oath by this Act set forth and declared as is aforesaid, before his or their ordinary, commissary, chancellor or vice-chancellor, or their sufficient deputies in the said university.

<small>CHAP. I

degrees shall take the oath.</small>

Provided always, and that it may be further enacted by the authority aforesaid, that if any person, having any estate of inheritance in any temporal office or offices, shall hereafter obstinately and peremptorily refuse to accept and take the said oath as is aforesaid, and after, at any time during his life, shall willingly require to take and receive the said oath, and so do take and accept the same oath before any person or persons that shall have lawful authority to minister the same; that then every such person, immediately after he has so received the same oath, shall be vested, deemed, and judged in like estate and possession of the said office, as he was before the said refusal, and shall and may use and exercise the said office in such manner and form as he should or might have done before such refusal, anything in this Act contained to the contrary in any wise notwithstanding.

<small>Those who at first refuse and then accept the oath.</small>

And for the more sure observation of this Act, and the utter extinguishment of all foreign and usurped power and authority, may it please your highness, that it may be further enacted by the authority aforesaid, that if any person or persons dwelling or inhabiting within this your realm, or in any other your highness's realms or dominions, of what estate, dignity, or degree soever he or they be, after the end of thirty days next after the determination of this session of this present Parliament, shall by writing, printing, teaching, preaching, express words, deed or act, advisedly, maliciously, and directly affirm, hold, stand with, set forth, maintain, or defend the authority, pre-eminence, power or jurisdiction, spiritual or ecclesiastical, of any foreign prince, prelate, person, state, or potentate whatsoever, heretofore claimed, used, or usurped within this realm, or any dominion or country being within or under the power, dominion, or obeisance of your highness, or shall advisedly, maliciously, and directly put in ure or execute anything for the extolling, advancement, setting forth, maintenance, or defence of any such pretended or usurped jurisdiction, power, pre-eminence, or authority, or any part thereof; that then every such person and persons so doing and offending, their abettors, aiders, procurers, and counsellors, being thereof lawfully convicted and attainted, according to the due order and course of the common laws of

<small>Penalty for maintaining foreign authority.</small>

this realm, for his or their first offence shall forfeit and lose unto your highness, your heirs and successors, all his and their goods and chattels, as well real as personal.

Persons not having goods to the value of the penalty, to be imprisoned.

And if any such person so convicted or attainted shall not have or be worth of his proper goods and chattels to the value of twenty pounds, at the time of his conviction or attainder, that then every such person so convicted and attainted, over and besides the forfeiture of all his said goods and chattels, shall have and suffer imprisonment by the space of one whole year, without bail or mainprize.

Ecclesiastical offices forfeited for offending under this Act.

And that also all and every the benefices, prebends, and other ecclesiastical promotions and dignities whatsoever, of every spiritual person so offending, and being attainted, shall immediately after such attainder be utterly void to all intents and purposes, as though the incumbent thereof were dead; and that the patron and donor of every such benefice, prebend, spiritual promotion and dignity, shall and may lawfully present unto the same, or give the same, in such manner and form as if the said incumbent were dead.

Penalty for a second offence.

And if any such offender or offenders, after such conviction or attainder, do eftsoons commit or do the said offences, or any of them, in manner and form aforesaid, and be thereof duly convicted and attainted, as is aforesaid; that then every such offender and offenders shall for the same second offence incur into the dangers, penalties, and forfeitures ordained and provided by the statute of Provision and *Præmunire*, made in the sixteenth year of the reign of King Richard II.

Penalty for a third offence— high treason.

And if any such offender or offenders, at any time after the said second conviction and attainder, do the third time commit and do the said offences, or any of them, in manner and form aforesaid, and be thereof duly convicted and attainted, as is aforesaid; that then every such offence or offences shall be deemed and adjudged high treason, and that the offender and offenders therein, being thereof lawfully convicted and attainted, according to the laws of this realm, shall suffer pains of death, and other penalties, forfeitures, and losses, as in cases of high treason by the laws of this realm.

Within what time an offender shall be impeached.

And also that it may likewise please your highness, that it may be enacted by the authority aforesaid, that no manner of person or persons shall be molested or impeached for any of the offences aforesaid committed or perpetrated only by preaching, teaching, or words, unless he or they be thereof lawfully indicted within the space of one half-year next after his or their offences so committed; and in case any person or persons shall fortune to be imprisoned for any of the said offences committed by preaching, teaching, or words only, and be not thereof indicted within the space of one half-year next after his or their such offence so committed and done, that then the said person so imprisoned shall be set at liberty, and be no longer detained in prison for any such cause or offence.

CHAP. I

Provided always, and be it enacted by the authority aforesaid, that this Act, or anything therein contained, shall not in any wise extend to repeal any clause, matter, or sentence contained or specified in the said Act of repeal made in the said first and second years of the reigns of the said late King Philip and Queen Mary, as does in any wise touch or concern any matter or case of *Præmunire*, or that does make or ordain any matter or cause to be within the case of *Præmunire*; but that the same, for so much only as touches or concerns any case or matter of *Præmunire*, shall stand and remain in such force and effect as the same was before the making of this Act, anything in this Act contained to the contrary in any wise notwithstanding.

All things touching *præmunire*, in 1 & 2 Philip and Mary, c. 8, to continue in force.

Provided also, and be it enacted by the authority aforesaid, that this Act, or anything therein contained, shall not in any wise extend or be prejudicial to any person or persons for any offence or offences committed or done, or hereafter to be committed or done, contrary to the tenor and effect of any Act or statute now revived by this Act, before the end of thirty days next after the end of the session of this present Parliament; anything in this Act contained or any other matter or cause to the contrary notwithstanding.

Proviso for those who, within a certain time, offend under statutes now revived.

And if it happen that any peer of this realm shall fortune to be indicted of and for any offence that is revived or made *Præmunire* or treason by this Act, that then he so being indicted shall have his trial by his peers, in such like manner and form as in other cases of treason has been used.

Peers to be tried by peers.

[1] Provided always, and be it enacted as is aforesaid, that no manner of order, Act, or determination, for any matter of religion or cause ecclesiastical, had or made by the authority of this present Parliament, shall be accepted, deemed, interpreted, or adjudged at any time

No order, on matters of religion, made by this Parliament to be adjudged heresy.

[1] This and the following provisoes are annexed to the Parliament Roll in four separate schedules.

hereafter, to be any error, heresy, schism, or schismatical opinion; any order, decree, sentence, constitution, or law, whatsoever the same be, to the contrary notwithstanding.

Commissioners may adjudge such things heresy as are so declared by the Scripture, the first four general Councils, or by Parliament, with assent of Convocation.

Provided always, and be it enacted by the authority aforesaid, that such person or persons to whom your highness, your heirs or successors, shall hereafter, by letters patent, under the great seal of England, give authority to have or execute any jurisdiction, power, or authority spiritual, or to visit, reform, order, or correct any errors, heresies, schisms, abuses, or enormities by virtue of this Act, shall not in any wise have authority or power to order, determine, or adjudge any matter or cause to be heresy, but only such as heretofore have been determined, ordered, or adjudged to be heresy, by the authority of the canonical Scriptures, or by the first four general Councils, or any of them, or by any other general Council wherein the same was declared heresy by the express and plain words of the said canonical Scriptures, or such as hereafter shall be ordered, judged, or determined to be heresy by the High Court of Parliament of this realm, with the assent of the clergy in their Convocation; anything in this Act contained to the contrary notwithstanding.

How persons shall be indicted for offences under this Act.

And be it further enacted by the authority aforesaid, that no person or persons shall be hereafter indicted or arraigned for any the offences made, ordained, revived, or adjudged by this Act, unless there be two sufficient witnesses, or more, to testify and declare the said offences whereof he shall be indicted or arraigned; and that the said witnesses, or so many of them as shall be living and within this realm at the time of the arraignment of such person so indicted, shall be brought forth in person, face to face, before the party so arraigned, and there shall testify and declare what they can say against the party so arraigned, if he require the same.

Those aiding offenders shall be judged guilty.

Provided also, and be it further enacted by the authority aforesaid, that if any person or persons shall hereafter happen to give any relief, aid, or comfort, or in any wise be aiding, helping, or comforting to the person or persons of any that shall hereafter happen to be an offender in any matter or case of *Præmunire* or treason, revived or made by this Act, that then such relief, aid, or comfort given shall not be judged or taken to be any offence, unless there be two sufficient witnesses at the least, that can and will openly testify and declare that the person or persons that so gave such relief, aid, or comfort had notice and knowledge of such offence committed and done by the said offender, at the time of such relief, aid, or comfort so to him given or ministered; anything in this Act contained, or any other matter or cause to the contrary in any wise notwithstanding.

And where one pretended sentence has heretofore been given in the Consistory in Paul's before certain judges delegate, by the authority legatine of the late Cardinal Pole, by reason of a foreign usurped power and authority, against Richard Chetwood, Esq., and Agnes his wife, by the name of Agnes Woodhall, at the suit of Charles Tyrril, gentleman, in a cause of matrimony solemnized between the said Richard and Agnes, as by the same pretended sentence more plainly doth appear, from which sentence the said Richard and Agnes have appealed to the Court of Rome, which appeal does there remain, and yet is not determined: may it therefore please your highness, that it may be enacted by the authority aforesaid, that if sentence in the said appeal shall happen to be given at the said Court of Rome for and in the behalf of the said Richard and Agnes, for the reversing of the said pretensed sentence, before the end of threescore days next after the end of this session of this present Parliament, that then the same shall be judged and taken to be good and effectual in the law, and shall and may be used, pleaded, and allowed in any court or place within this realm; anything in this Act or any other Act or statute contained to the contrary notwithstanding.

And if no sentence shall be given at the Court of Rome in the said appeal for the reversing of the said pretended sentence before the end of the said threescore days, that then it shall and may be lawful for the said Richard and Agnes, and either of them, at any time hereafter, to commence, take, sue, and prosecute their said appeal from the said pretended sentence, and for the reversing of the said pretended sentence, within this realm, in such like manner and form as was used to be pursued, or might have been pursued, within this realm, at any time since the twenty-fourth year of the reign of the said late King Henry VIII, upon any sentences given in the court or courts of any archbishop within this realm.

And that such appeal as so hereafter shall be taken or pursued by the said Richard Chetwood and Agnes, or either of them, and the sentence that herein or thereupon shall hereafter be given, shall be judged to be good and effectual in the law to all intents and purposes; any law, custom, usage, canon, constitution, or any other matter or cause to the contrary notwithstanding.

CHAP. I

The case of Chetwood and wife: if the Court of Rome upholds their appeal, that upholding shall stand.

If no sentence be given by Rome, then their appeal shall be prosecuted in England.

The sentence given shall be held good.

<small>CHAP. I</small>

<small>Like proviso in another case of appeal.</small>

Provided also, and be it enacted by the authority aforesaid, that where there is the like appeal now depending in the said Court of Rome between one Robert Harcourt, merchant of the staple, and Elizabeth Harcourt, otherwise called Elizabeth Robins, of the one part, and Anthony Fydell, merchant-stranger, on the other part, that the said Robert, Elizabeth, and Anthony, and every of them, shall and may, for the prosecuting and trying of their said appeal, have and enjoy the like remedy, benefit, and advantage, in like manner and form as the said Richard and Agnes, or any of them, has, may, or ought to have and enjoy; this Act or anything therein contained to the contrary in any wise notwithstanding.

II.

An Act for the Uniformity of Common Prayer and Service in the Church and Administration of the Sacraments.

(1 Elizabeth, cap. 2.)

[Transcr. *Statutes of the Realm*, iv. pt. i. p. 355.]

<small>Edward VI's Act of Uniformity repealed by Mary.</small>

Where at the death of our late sovereign lord King Edward VI there remained one uniform order of common service and prayer, and of the administration of sacraments, rites, and ceremonies in the Church of England, which was set forth in one book, intituled: The Book of Common Prayer, and Administration of Sacraments, and other rites and ceremonies in the Church of England; authorized by Act of Parliament holden in the fifth and sixth years of our said late sovereign lord King Edward VI, intituled: An Act for the uniformity of common prayer, and administration of the sacraments; the which was repealed and taken away by Act of Parliament in the first year of the reign of our late sovereign lady Queen Mary, to the great decay of the due honour of God, and discomfort to the professors of the truth of Christ's religion:

<small>Repeal of Mary's Act of repeal.</small>

Be it therefore enacted by the authority of this present Parliament, that the said statute of repeal, and everything therein contained, only concerning the said book, and the service, administration of sacraments, rites, and ceremonies contained or appointed in or by the said book, shall be void and of none effect, from and after the feast of the Nativity of St. John Baptist next coming; and that the said book, with the order of service, and of the administration of sacraments, rites, and ceremonies, with the alterations and additions therein added and appointed by this statute, shall stand and be, from and after the said feast of the Nativity of St. John Baptist, in full force and effect, according to the tenor and effect of this statute; anything in the aforesaid statute of repeal to the contrary notwithstanding. {*Edward VI's Book of Common Prayer, with certain alterations and additions, re-established.*}

And further be it enacted by the queen's highness, with the assent of the Lords (*sic*) and Commons in this present Parliament assembled, and by authority of the same, that all and singular ministers in any cathedral or parish church, or other place within this realm of England, Wales, and the marches of the same, or other the queen's dominions, shall from and after the feast of the Nativity of St. John Baptist next coming be bounden to say and use the Matins, Evensong, celebration of the Lord's Supper and administration of each of the sacraments, and all their common and open prayer, in such order and form as is mentioned in the said book, so authorized by Parliament in the said fifth and sixth years of the reign of King Edward VI, with one alteration or addition of certain lessons to be used on every Sunday in the year, and the form of the Litany altered and corrected, and two sentences only added in the delivery of the sacrament to the communicants, and none other or otherwise. {*The alterations and additions enjoined.*}

And that if any manner of parson, vicar, or other whatsoever minister, that ought or should sing or say common prayer mentioned in the said book, or minister the sacraments, from and after the feast of the Nativity of St. John Baptist next coming, refuse to use the said common prayers, or to minister the sacraments in such cathedral or parish church, or other places as he should use to minister the same, in such order and form as they be mentioned and set forth in the said book, or shall wilfully or obstinately standing in the same, use any other rite, ceremony, order, form, or manner of celebrating of the Lord's Supper, openly or privily, or Matins, Evensong, administration of the sacraments, or other open prayers, than is mentioned and set forth in the said book (open prayer in and throughout this Act, is meant that prayer which is for other to come unto, or hear, either in common churches or private chapels or oratories, commonly called the service of the Church), or shall preach, declare, or speak anything in the derogation or depraving of the said book, or anything {*Penalty for using any other form of prayer or administration of the sacraments, or for speaking against the Book of Common Prayer.*} {*Definition of 'open prayer.'*}

therein contained, or of any part thereof, and shall be thereof lawfully convicted, according to the laws of this realm, by verdict of twelve men, or by his own confession, or by the notorious evidence of the fact, shall lose and forfeit to the queen's highness, her heirs and successors, for his first offence, the profit of all his spiritual benefices or promotions coming or arising in one whole year next after his conviction; and also that the person so convicted shall for the same offence suffer imprisonment by the space of six months, without bail or mainprize.

The penalty for a second offence. And if any such person once convicted of any offence concerning the premises, shall after his first conviction eftsoons offend, and be thereof, in form aforesaid, lawfully convicted, that then the same person shall for his second offence suffer imprisonment by the space of one whole year, and also shall therefor be deprived, *ipso facto*, of all his spiritual promotions; and that it shall be lawful to all patrons or donors of all and singular the same spiritual promotions, or of any of them, to present or collate to the same, as though the person and persons so offending were dead.

The penalty for a third offence. And that if any such person or persons, after he shall be twice convicted in form aforesaid, shall offend against any of the premises the third time, and shall be thereof, in form aforesaid, lawfully convicted, that then the person so offending and convicted the third time, shall be deprived, *ipso facto*, of all his spiritual promotions, and also shall suffer imprisonment during his life.

The penalty of an offender having no spiritual promotion. And if the person that shall offend, and be convicted in form aforesaid, concerning any of the premises, shall not be beneficed, nor have any spiritual promotion, that then the same person so offending and convicted shall for the first offence suffer imprisonment during one whole year next after his said conviction, without bail or mainprize. And if any such person, not having any spiritual promotion, after his first conviction shall eftsoons offend in anything concerning the premises, and shall be, in form aforesaid, thereof lawfully convicted, that then the same person shall for his second offence suffer imprisonment during his life.

Penalty for speaking against the said book on the stage or elsewhere, or And it is ordained and enacted by the authority aforesaid, that if any person or persons whatsoever, after the said feast of the Nativity of St. John Baptist next coming, shall in any interludes, plays, songs, rhymes, or by other open words, declare or speak anything in the derogation, depraving, or despising of the same book, or of anything therein contained, or any part thereof, or shall, by open fact, deed, or by open threatenings, compel or cause, or otherwise procure or maintain, any parson, vicar, or other minister in any cathedral or parish church, or in chapel, or in any other place, to sing or say any common or open prayer, or to minister any sacrament otherwise, or in any other manner and form, than is mentioned in the said book; or that by any of the said means shall unlawfully interrupt or let any parson, vicar, or other minister in any cathedral or parish church, chapel, or any other place, to sing or say common and open prayer, or to minister the sacraments or any of them, in such manner and form as is mentioned in the said book; that then every such person, being thereof lawfully convicted in form abovesaid, shall forfeit to the queen our sovereign lady, her heirs and successors, for the first offence a hundred marks. *for causing any other form of service to be used, or for interrupting the service.*

And if any person or persons, being once convicted of any such offence, eftsoons offend against any of the last recited offences, and shall, in form aforesaid, be thereof lawfully convicted, that then the same person so offending and convicted shall, for the second offence, forfeit to the queen our sovereign lady, her heirs and successors, four hundred marks. *Penalty for a second offence.*

And if any person, after he, in form aforesaid, shall have been twice convicted of any offence concerning any of the last recited offences, shall offend the third time, and be thereof, in form abovesaid, lawfully convicted, that then every person so offending and convicted shall for his third offence forfeit to our sovereign lady the queen all his goods and chattels, and shall suffer imprisonment during his life. *Penalty for a third offence.*

And if any person or persons, that for his first offence concerning the premises shall be convicted, in form aforesaid, do not pay the sum to be paid by virtue of his conviction, in such manner and form as the same ought to be paid, within six weeks next after his conviction; that then every person so convicted, and so not paying the same, shall for the same first offence, instead of the said sum, suffer imprisonment by the space of six months, without bail or mainprize. And if any person or persons, that for his second offence concerning the premises shall be convicted in form aforesaid, do not pay the said sum to be paid by virtue of his conviction and this statute, in such manner and form as the same ought to be paid, within six weeks next after his said second conviction; that then every person so convicted, and not so paying the same, shall, *Penalty of the convict not paying his forfeiture.*

CHAP. I   for the same second offence, in the stead of the said sum, suffer imprisonment during twelve months, without bail or mainprize.

Every person to attend church on Sundays and holy days under pain of censure of the Church and a fine to the poor.

And that from and after the said feast of the Nativity of St. John Baptist next coming, all and every person and persons inhabiting within this realm, or any other the queen's majesty's dominions, shall diligently and faithfully, having no lawful or reasonable excuse to be absent, endeavour themselves to resort to their parish church or chapel accustomed, or upon reasonable let thereof, to some usual place where common prayer and such service of God shall be used in such time of let, upon every Sunday and other days ordained and used to be kept as holy days, and then and there to abide orderly and soberly during the time of the common prayer, preachings, or other service of God there to be used and ministered; upon pain of punishment by the censures of the Church, and also upon pain that every person so offending shall forfeit for every such offence twelve pence, to be levied by the churchwardens of the parish where such offence shall be done, to the use of the poor of the same parish, of the goods, lands, and tenements of such offender, by way of distress.

The Church enjoined to execute this Act with diligence.

And for due execution hereof, the queen's most excellent majesty, the Lords temporal (*sic*), and all the Commons, in this present Parliament assembled, do in God's name earnestly require and charge all the archbishops, bishops, and other ordinaries, that they shall endeavour themselves to the uttermost of their knowledges, that the due and true execution hereof may be had throughout their dioceses and charges, as they will answer before God, for such evils and plagues wherewith Almighty God may justly punish His people for neglecting this good and wholesome law.

The ordinary may punish offenders by the censures of the Church.

And for their authority in this behalf, be it further enacted by the authority aforesaid, that all and singular the same archbishops, bishops, and all other their officers exercising ecclesiastical jurisdiction, as well in place exempt as not exempt, within their dioceses, shall have full power and authority by this Act to reform, correct, and punish by censures of the Church, all and singular persons which shall offend within any their jurisdictions or dioceses, after the said feast of the Nativity of St. John Baptist next coming, against this Act and statute; any other law, statute, privilege, liberty, or provision heretofore made, had, or suffered to the contrary notwithstanding.

Power of justices to

And it is ordained and enacted by the authority aforesaid, that all and every justices of *oyer* and *terminer*, or justices of assize, shall have full power and authority in every of their open and general sessions, to inquire, hear, and determine all and all manner of offences that shall be committed or done contrary to any article contained in this present Act, within the limits of the commission to them directed, and to make process for the execution of the same, as they may do against any person being indicted before them of trespass, or lawfully convicted thereof. Chap. I — punish offences.

Provided always, and be it enacted by the authority aforesaid, that all and every archbishop and bishop shall or may, at all time and times, at his liberty and pleasure, join and associate himself, by virtue of this Act, to the said justices of *oyer* and *terminer*, or to the said justices of assize, at every of the said open and general sessions to be holden in any place within his diocese, for and to the inquiry, hearing, and determining of the offences aforesaid. Bishops may join with justices to inquire of offences.

Provided also, and be it enacted by the authority aforesaid, that the books concerning the said services shall, at the cost and charges of the parishioners of every parish and cathedral church, be attained and gotten before the said feast of the Nativity of St. John Baptist next following; and that all such parishes and cathedral churches, or other places where the said books shall be attained and gotten before the said feast of the Nativity of St. John Baptist, shall, within three weeks next after the said books so attained and gotten, use the said service, and put the same in ure according to this Act. Books of Common Prayer to be provided at cost of parishioners, and the service used within three weeks after purchase.

And be it further enacted by the authority aforesaid, that no person or persons shall be at any time hereafter impeached or otherwise molested of or for any the offences above mentioned, hereafter to be committed or done contrary to this Act, unless he or they so offending be thereof indicted at the next general sessions to be holden before any such justices of *oyer* and *terminer* or justices of assize, next after any offence committed or done contrary to the tenor of this Act. Limit of time for prosecuting offenders.

Provided always, and be it ordained and enacted by the authority aforesaid, that all and singular lords of the Parliament, for the third offence above mentioned, shall be tried by their peers. Trial of peers.

Provided also, and be it ordained and enacted by the authority aforesaid, that the mayor of London, and all other mayors, bailiffs, and other head officers of all and singular cities, boroughs, and towns corporate within this realm, Wales, and the marches of the Chief officers of cities and boroughs, not usually

CHAP. I

Visited by justices, shall inquire of offenders.

same, to the which justices of assize do not commonly repair, shall have full power and authority by virtue of this Act to inquire, hear, and determine the offences abovesaid, and every of them, yearly within fifteen days after the feasts of Easter and St. Michael the Archangel, in like manner and form as justices of assize and *oyer* and *terminer* may do.

The ordinary's jurisdiction to remain as before.

Provided always, and be it ordained and enacted by the authority aforesaid, that all and singular archbishops and bishops, and every their chancellors, commissaries, archdeacons, and other ordinaries, having any peculiar ecclesiastical jurisdiction, shall have full power and authority by virtue of this Act, as well to inquire in their visitation, synods, and elsewhere within their jurisdiction at any other time and place, to take occasions (*sic*) and informations of all and every the things above mentioned, done, committed, or perpetrated within the limits of their jurisdictions and authority, and to punish the same by admonition, excommunication, sequestration, or deprivation, and other censures and processes, in like form as heretofore has been used in like cases by the queen's ecclesiastical laws.

But none to be punished more than once for one offence.

Provided always, and be it enacted, that whatsoever person offending in the premises shall, for the offence, first receive punishment of the ordinary, having a testimonial thereof under the said ordinary's seal, shall not for the same offence eftsoons be convicted before the justices: and likewise receiving, for the said offence, first punishment by the justices, he shall not for the same offence eftsoons receive punishment of the ordinary; anything contained in this Act to the contrary notwithstanding.

Ornaments of the church and ministers to continue as in 2 Edw. VI till further order.

Provided always, and be it enacted, that such ornaments of the church, and of the ministers thereof, shall be retained and be in use, as was in the Church of England, by authority of Parliament, in the second year of the reign of King Edward VI, until other order shall be therein taken by the authority of the queen's majesty, with the advice of her commissioners appointed and authorized, under the great seal of England, for causes ecclesiastical, or of the metropolitan of this realm.

On any contempt of ceremonies, or irreverence, further rites

And also, that if there shall happen any contempt or irreverence to be used in the ceremonies or rites of the Church, by the misusing of the orders appointed in this book, the queen's majesty may, by the like advice of the said commissioners or metropolitan, ordain and publish such further ceremonies or rites, as may be most for the advancement of God's glory, the edifying of His Church, and the due reverence of Christ's holy mysteries and sacraments.

And be it further enacted by the authority aforesaid, that all laws, statutes, and ordinances, wherein or whereby any other service, administration of sacraments or common prayer, is limited, established, or set forth to be used within this realm, or any other the queen's dominions or countries, shall from henceforth be utterly void and of none effect.

<small>CHAP. I

and ceremonies may be ordained.

Laws allowing the use of any other service made void.</small>

CHAPTER II

THE DEPRIVATION OF THE BISHOPS [1]

CHAP. II
Action before Parliament sat.

THERE were, in the sixteenth century, twenty-six sees in England and Wales. When Queen Elizabeth came to the throne six of these sees were vacant through death—Oxford, Salisbury, Bangor, Gloucester, Hereford, Canterbury; and four more were void from the same cause before the end of 1558—Rochester, Norwich, Chichester, Bristol. We have thus sixteen bishops to account for, as there was no fresh consecration until December, 1559. Watson, Bishop of Lincoln, came under the Queen's displeasure within the first month after her accession because of his incautious sermon preached at the funeral of Mary on December 14, 1558. By order of the Privy Council he was confined to the house until the restriction was removed four weeks later, on January 19 [2]. The case of Watson was the first warning to the bishops, and the beginning of twenty-five years of trouble and imprisonment for him. All the bishops, save Oglethorpe of Carlisle, refused to act at the Queen's coronation, and for this he appears to have been treated with rather more consideration than his

---

[1] Most writers have depended on Bishop Andrewes' *Tortura Torti*, 146. He in turn depends on Godwin, whose facts appear to have been tradition rather than history so far as the bishops were concerned. We have thought it best to discard all modern authorities, and have made use of the State Papers, the Spanish ambassador, and Machyn's *Diary*. We had put our notes together before seeing Messrs. Bridgett and Knox' *True Story of the Catholic Hierarchy*. We have acknowledged in the notes what we have further learned from their book.

[2] *Privy Council Acts*, Jan. 19, 1559.

brethren in the subsequent events of the year. Heath, Archbishop of York, resigned his Chancellorship before the end of 1558, and Bourne, of Bath and Wells, was deprived of the Presidency of Wales in the following February, soon after Parliament began to sit [1]. This loss of office in Bourne's case was the second warning of what was to come.

During the Parliament of 1559, the Bishops of Durham, Peterborough, Bath and Wells, and St. David's were absent from one cause and another, and Heath was appointed their proxy. Watson was absent through ill-health. Goldwell of St. Asaph was absent, and Thirlby of Ely was abroad as ambassador until April, when he attended the House of Lords at every sitting. In this way nine bishops only were actually present throughout the session, and these, as we might expect from what we have seen of Convocation, were continuous and consistent in their opposition to the course of ecclesiastical legislation. It is impossible to withhold our admiration of their pertinacity. The speech of the Archbishop of York against the Supremacy Bill and the utterances of the Bishop of Chester against this and the Uniformity Bill have been preserved [2].

Meanwhile, during the slow progress of these bills through both Houses, a diversion took place at the end of March in the shape of a public disputation between representatives of the Old Learning and the New. This discussion may have been intended as an answer to the protest of Convocation, or it may have been suggested by the famous Oxford disputation which led to the condemnation of Cranmer and his fellows in Queen Mary's reign. It proved somewhat of a fiasco, and is chiefly important as giving the Elizabethan divines an opportunity of justifying the principle of the first sentence in Article XX [3]. It is also important to us in this inquiry, because it was the means of bringing three of the bishops into trouble. The

The bishops in Parliament.

The Westminster Disputation involves some of the bishops in trouble.

---

[1] Bridgett and Knox, 19. [2] See Strype, *Ann.* i. 74 and Appendix.
[3] Collier, vi. 216; Strype, Appendix, No. xvi.

representatives of the Old Learning engaged in it were Bishops White of Winchester, Bayne of Lichfield and Coventry, Scott of Chester, Watson of Lincoln, Doctors Cole, J. Harpsfield, Chedsey, and Langdale. In the issue, Bishops White and Watson were committed to the Tower, and although it has often been said that they had threatened to excommunicate the Queen, we are not aware that any adequate proof of this assertion exists. It is, perhaps, scarcely conceivable that what was said in the debate was made the sole ground of their committal. Some words of the Spanish ambassador seem to give a clue; he says: 'In the afternoon' (i.e. after the debate was over) 'some of the bishops were summoned to the palace. ... I am told they will send the other six to the Tower[1].' The 'six,' from the context, means the two other bishops and four doctors who took part in the debate. Thus we conclude that in this further conference at 'the palace' fresh grounds of offence were given. A day or two later a special messenger was sent to the residences of the Bishops of Winchester and Lincoln 'to peruse their studies and writings[2].' Does not this give a hint of the expectation of finding some treasonable compromise which might justify the high-handed act of sending two bishops to the Tower when as yet there was neither Supremacy nor Uniformity Act? On the day after this messenger was dispatched, recognizances were taken of the Bishops of Lichfield, Chester, and Carlisle, and, with these, of three out of the four doctors. Now Oglethorpe of Carlisle had taken no part in the debate, and, as we have seen, was more in favour than the other bishops. It may therefore well seem to be the case that when the bishops were sent for 'to the palace' Oglethorpe also committed himself for some reason unspecified. The condition of the recognizance was that Bayne, Scott, and Oglethorpe should appear before the Lords of the Council every day, and not depart from

[1] *Spanish Calendar,* April 4, 1559. Yet see 'Il Schiffanoya,' *Venetian Calendar,* April 11. [2] *Privy Council Acts,* April 3.

London, Westminster, or the suburbs without licence. Moreover they were all 'to pay such fine as should be assessed upon them for the contempt of them of late committed against the Queen's Majesty's order[1].' We take 'order' here to mean the proposed settlement of religion as explained to them 'at the palace,' and not the transgression of any rule of debate or other enactment then existing; or is it the proclamation of December 27? A few days later it was decided that the three bishops should during Parliament record their daily appearance before 'Lord Great Seal.' On May 11 Bayne was fined £333 6s. 8d., Oglethorpe £250, Scott 200 marks. They had all been assiduous at the same time in their attendance in the House of Lords, opposing the Church bills at every stage.

When Parliament rose, the conformity of the bishops was one of the first things to be considered. Within two days the Spanish ambassador says[2]: 'The bishops are ordered not to leave London without the Queen's consent. They say the oath will at once be proffered to them, which they will not take, and that they will thereupon be deprived at one blow.' A few days later Grindal says: 'It is therefore commonly supposed that almost all the bishops ... will renounce their bishoprics[3].' Strype has a story that they were all called before the Queen, that they were found guilty of previous treasonable correspondence, and, although this seemed to be cleared by the general pardon at the accession, it was determined to administer the oath and so to deprive them if they refused[4]. The date for this summons to the Queen's presence is given by Strype as May 15, but his authority, *The Hunting of the Roman Fox*, is, to say the least of it, suspicious[5]. That book is too late a production for us to accept in the absence of all contemporary evidence; but at the same time it must be pointed out that the Spanish ambassador

First proceeding against the bishops after May 8, 1559.

---

[1] *Privy Council Acts*, April 4.
[2] *Calendar*, May 10. See too *Venetian Calendar*, same date.
[3] *Zurich Letters*, May 23.
[4] Strype, i. 139.
[5] Bridgett and Knox, 49, with references there given.

CHAP. II does, as we have seen, appear to hint at an audience with the Queen on April 3. But, be this as it may, the next step seems to be fairly clear. A commission for administering the oath was required by the Supremacy Act[1], and although it has been the fashion to say that such a commission does not exist, there can be no reasonable doubt that we possess it in the shape of the document which follows this chapter. It is well known that the early proceedings under the Supremacy Act are very hard to trace, and Sir Edward Coke half a century later complained of the way in which the records had perished or had never been engrossed[2]. Rymer, however, has printed the commission which we have copied[3], and a few moments' study of the names proves that it consisted of all the members of the Privy Council. Rymer gives 'ex autographo' as his authority, and states that the great seal was attached to the parchment. It is possible that the document itself or a contemporary copy may yet be found. It is a curious thing that it has never been enrolled on the Patent Roll.

Action under the commission of May 23. Taking this commission as authentic, we find it to have been issued on May 23. The deprivation of the bishops extended over some months, and the proceedings prove, what we shall find to have been the case with the clergy, that opportunity was given again and again to reconsider a refusal. Bonner was deprived on May 30, as appears by an entry in his own handwriting[4], which is confirmed by the fact that the temporalities were seized on June 2, and that the Spanish ambassador on June 19 notes that he had been deprived already. The ambassador says: 'They have just begun to carry out the law against the bishops, and have in fact deprived the Bishop and Dean of London, casting them out of their Church.' He goes on to say: 'It appears now that they find a difficulty in giving legal form to the deprivation, as the doctors here say the bishops cannot be deprived for disobeying the law whose adoption and promulgation they have

[1] See p. 14.   [2] Strype, i. 138.   [4] Strype, i. 138, corroborated by
[3] Rymer, xv. 518, 519.   *Venetian Calendar*, p. 94.

always opposed and resisted, alleging that it cannot be enforced according to the custom of the realm, as it is made in opposition to the whole ecclesiastical body[1].'

The oath tendered to justices and judges in June.

After the deprivation of Bonner a pause took place before a similar fate overtook the rest of the bishops. Whether the oath was pressed upon them in the meantime we do not know, but during the next three weeks, it seems, the justices and other crown officers were called upon to swear allegiance in accordance with the terms of the commission of May 23. Strype, in his *Life of Sir T. Smith*[2], shows that, at all events in Essex, the justices were being tendered the oath as early as June 16. In the letter just quoted the Spanish ambassador says: 'The judges of England ... who have come here for the terms have refused to swear, and have gone to their homes, as they have not dared to press them about it.' We do not know any independent proof of such refusal, but the entry shows that the oath was being administered to laymen in high position during June.

The bishops again examined.

The bishops were again taken in hand on June 21. There is some confusion in the names. Machyn's *Diary* has been the usual authority, and he is clearly in error, as he speaks of the Bishop of Llandaff (Kitchen) as deprived; but Llandaff was never deprived, for he was the only one of the sixteen who took the oath, though when he consented to do so does not appear. Machyn also says that the Bishops of Carlisle, Chester, Lichfield, and another were likewise deprived. The three bishops mentioned may stand, as their names are separately attested, and Worcester (Pates) is almost certainly 'another,' as the temporalities were seized on June 30[3]. The Bishop of St. Asaph is as certainly, we believe, the one misnamed Llandaff by Machyn. The Spanish ambassador has preserved an interesting account in a letter dated June 27: 'Last week they summoned five bishops to the Council, and proffered them the oath with great promises and threats as well, but

[1] *Calendars*, June 19.
[2] Strype's *Sir T. Smith*, 59.
[3] A list of such dates is given in Collier, vi. 252, from the Register.

CHAP. II none of them would swear, and they were ordered yesterday to return to the house of the Sheriff of London, whither they brought also the bishops from the Tower, and again tried to persuade them to swear, but they would not. They were greatly insulted and mocked at, and at last were ordered not to leave London until after September, and to go no further away than Westminster under pain of £500 each, and they had to find bail for this amount. The two were taken back to prison, and both they and the others deprived of their preferments *de facto*, since by law the doctors are still of opinion that they cannot be deprived for refusing to swear to the laws of the country. They summoned the Bishop of Ely with the other five, and afterwards sent to say that he need not come until they sent for him again.' The ambassador's account supplements Machyn very usefully. The only discrepancy is that Machyn makes the five to have been deprived on the 21st and the two from the Tower on the 26th, whilst the ambassador assigns the deprivation of all seven to the later date, but his detailed account inclines one to defer to his authority [1]. Watson, Bishop of Lincoln, was liberated on account of illness on July 1, and White, Bishop of Winchester, on the 7th. There were two more as yet undeprived, Heath and Thirlby. These were finally examined and deprived on July 5 [2].

Deprivations after July 7.

We have now accounted for eleven of the sixteen, bringing the story up to July 7, when one had taken the oath and ten had been deprived, but as yet there was no one of them in prison for refusing the oath. It is probable that the treatment of the bishops had caused some little commotion. On June 25 the Spanish ambassador wrote:

[1] The Venetian Dispatch of June 27 (*Cal.* 104) says that the bishops were 'bound not to depart from England, and *not to preach or exhort whatever* in public or private, and still less to write anything against the order and statutes of this Parliament, nor to [give occasion to] insurrection or any other scandalous act, *under pain of perpetual imprison-ment*, demanding security and promise to be given by one for the other.' It also says that on June 26 they received orders where to dwell. Attention is drawn to the words in italics, as throwing a light on what happened after. See below, pp. 144, 192.

[2] Machyn's *Diary*.

'I see the Queen and her councillors will be turned out and treated as they deserve, and that God will strike for His own cause.' As for the bishops, it is very likely that they turned their eyes on the King of Spain, and on July 12 the ambassador says: 'The bishops hope more than ever in your Majesty.' How far they entertained such hopes is not clear, but it seems certain that neither Philip nor the ambassador did very much to encourage them. We have not traced any direct intervention on the King's part until five years later [1], though some hint of his desire to influence the Queen in their favour is noted in March, 1561. Meanwhile the five remaining prelates were deprived in the course of the next few months. Writing on August 13, 1559, the ambassador notes that 'they have deprived the Bishops of St. David's and Exeter.' By an entry in a letter of Bishop Young of St. David's the actual day is proved to have been August 10 [2]. Tunstall, the aged Bishop of Durham, who had been a prelate for wellnigh forty years, had not been in London during the session of Parliament nor since the dissolution, but he was, as it seems, summoned in July, and entered the metropolis with sixty attendants on the 20th, proceeding, not to Durham House, but to a private residence in Southwark [3]. The other absentees, Morgan, Poole, and Turberville, were probably summoned at the same time. Turberville, as we have seen, was deprived on August 10; but Tunstall, apparently, was remanded in the hope of his consent to take the oath. On August 19 he writes to Cecil praying for an interview with the Queen, and in his letter deplores the present state of things which he sees in London, and expresses the hope that his own diocese may be spared a similar visitation [4]. On September 9 Tunstall was joined in commission with other bishops whose names are not given, for the consecration of the new primate, but no action was taken, perhaps owing to his refusal, or it may be owing to fresh delays in regard to the temporalities of the see of Canterbury. It is highly

[1] *Spanish Calendar*, Nov. 27, 1564.
[2] S. P. Dom. Eliz. xi. 38.
[3] Machyn's *Diary*.
[4] S. P. Dom. Eliz. vi. 22.

CHAP. II probable that the design was to associate with Tunstall the Bishops of Bath and Wells, Peterborough, and Llandaff. Of this there is no record, the commission having a blank after Tunstall's name [1]. He was finally deprived, says Machyn, on September 28. Bourne seems to have been allowed to go back to his see after Michaelmas, which date had been the limit of the restriction to town in the case of the other bishops. On October 18 letters patent were issued to four Somersetshire justices to tender the oath to him [2], but evidently he refused again, and was deprived soon after. It is by no means improbable that his case was reserved for the meeting of the ecclesiastical commissioners at London in the first week of November [3], and we shall not be far wrong in assigning the deprivation of the Bishop of Peterborough to the same period [4]. It is uncertain why Bourne's case was reserved so long, but we are inclined to think that there were hopes of his conformity, and also of Poole's: the latter was an old man.

Death of four of the bishops.   We have thus accounted for the sixteen diocesan bishops. Before the year ran out four of them were dead. Tunstall died on November 18, very probably at the same house to which he came in July. There is no evidence to prove that he was with Parker at the time, an assertion which has often been made, but the archbishop-elect seems to have sealed up 'two small caskets' which belonged to the bishop, acting thus, we may conjecture, in his capacity of ecclesiastical commissioner [5]. On the very same day Bayne died at Islington; Morgan on December 23; Oglethorpe in Chancery Lane on the last day of the year. Bayne and Oglethorpe were buried at St. Dunstan's in the West [6]. Bishop White died on January 12, 1560. We shall see elsewhere what became of the eleven survivors [7].

[1] S. P. Dom. Eliz. vi. 41.
[2] Pat. 1 Eliz. Part 2, m. 3, dors.; Rymer, xv. 545.
[3] See p. 140.
[4] The temporalities were seized Nov. 11, but the date is not conclusive as to the deprivation, for the Exeter temporalities were seized Nov. 16.
[5] S. P. Dom. vii. 39.
[6] These dates we get from Godwin's *De Praesulibus Angliae*.
[7] See pp. 144, 192.

Commission to the Privy Council to administer the Oath.

[De Recipiendo Sacramentum Suprematus et de Intendendo.]

Rymer's *Foedera*, vol. 15.

Elizabetha Dei gratia Angliae Franciae et Hiberniae Regina Fidei Defensor, &c.; praedilecto et fideli Consiliario nostro Nicholao Bacon, Militi, Magni Sigilli nostri Angliae Custodi; praedilectis et perquam fidelibus Consanguineis et Consiliariis nostris, Willielmo Marchioni Winton, Thesaurario nostro Angliae; Willielmo Marchioni Northampton; Henrico Comiti Arundellae, Domino Senescallo Hospitii nostri; Francisco Comiti Salopiae, Domino Praesidenti Concilii nostri in partibus borealibus; Edwardo Derby, Francisco Bedford, et Willielmo Pembroke, Comitibus; ac praedilectis et fidelibus Consiliariis nostris Edwardo Domino Clynton, Magno Admirallo nostro Angliae; Willielmo Domino Howarde de Effingham Hospitii nostri Camerario; Thomae Parry Militi Hospitii nostri Thesaurario; Edwardo Rogers Militi, Contrarotulatori; et Francisco Knolles, Militi, Vicecamerario dicti Hospitii nostri; Willielmo Cecill, Militi, Primario Secretario nostro; Ambrosio Cave, Militi, Cancellario Ducatus nostri Lancastriae; Willielmo Petre, Richardo Sakvile, et Johanni Mason, Militibus—salutem.

The queen greets the commissioners.

Sciatis quod dedimus vobis octodecim, septemdecim, sexdecim, quindecim, quatuordecim, tresdecim, duodecim, undecim, decem, novem, octo, septem, vel sex vestrum (quorum vos praedictos Custodem Magni Sigilli nostri, Marchionem Winton, Comitem Arundellae, Thomam Parry, Edwardum Rogers, Franciscum Knolles, et Willielmum Cecill, semper unum esse volumus), plenam potestatem et auctoritatem recipiendi de omnibus et singulis Archiepiscopis, Episcopis, et aliis Personis Ecclesiasticis, ac aliis Officiariis, et Ministris Ecclesiasticis, cujuscumque status, dignitatis, praeeminentiae, seu Gradus fuerint, seu eorum aliquis fuerit, ac de omnibus et singulis judicibus temporalibus, Justiciariis,

She appoints six at least to administer the Supremacy Oath to all ecclesiastical persons,

Chap. II
and to all lay office-holders holding the queen's commission.

Majoribus, ac aliis Laicis seu temporalibus Officiariis et Ministris, ac aliis quibuscumque personis habentibus feoda seu vadia nostra infra Regnum nostrum Angliae, aut aliqua dominia nostra, quoddam sacramentum corporale super sacrosancta Evangelia, coram vobis octodecim, septemdecim, sexdecim, quindecim, quatuordecim, tresdecim, duodecim, undecim, decem, novem, octo, septem, vel sex vestrum (quorum vos praedictos Custodem Magni Sigilli nostri, Marchionem Winton, Comitem Arundel, Thomam Parry, Edwardum Rogers, Franciscum Knolles, et Willielmum Cecill unum esse volumus), corporaliter per ipsos et eorum quemlibet praestandum, declaratum, et specificatum, in quodam Actu in Parliamento nostro apud Westmonasterium vicesimo quinto Die Januarii Anno Regni nostri primo tento, edito, juxta vim formam et effectum ejusdem actus.

Et ideo vobis octodecim, septemdecim, sexdecim, quindecim, quatuordecim, tresdecim, duodecim, undecim, decem, novem, octo, septem, vel sex vestrum (quorum vos praedictos Custodem Magni Sigilli nostri, Marchionem Winton, Comitem Arundell, Thomam Parry, Edwardum Rogers, Franciscum Knolles, et Willielmum

The taking of the oath is to be certified into Chancery.

Cecill, unum esse volumus), mandantes quod Sacramentum praedictum de omnibus et singulis Archiepiscopis, Episcopis, Personis, Officiariis, Ministris, ac aliis quibuscumque superius specificatis, ac de eorum quolibet, recipiatis; Et cum ea sic receperitis, nos inde in Cancellariam nostram, sub Sigillis vestris, octodecim, septemdecim, sexdecim, quindecim, quatuordecim, tresdecim, duodecim, undecim, decem, novem, octo, septem, vel sex vestrum (quorum vos praedictos Custodem Magni Sigilli nostri Marchionem Winton, Comitem Arundell, Thomam Parry, Edwardum Rogers, Franciscum Knolles, et Willielmum Cecill unum esse volumus), sine dilatione certificetis.

All the queen's subjects to aid in the discharge of this commission.

Mandantes autem universis et singulis Archiepiscopis, Ducibus, Marchionibus, Comitibus, Vicecomitibus, Episcopis, Baronibus, Militibus, Justiciariis, Majoribus, Vicecomitibus, Ballivis, et omnibus aliis Officiariis, Ministris, et Subditis nostris quibuscumque, quod vobis in Executione praemissorum intendentes sint, pariter et obedientes in omnibus, prout decet.

Dated May 23, 1559.

In cujus rei Testimonium has Litteras nostras fieri fecimus Patentes, Teste meipsa apud Westmonasterium vicesimo tertio Die Maii, Anno Regni nostri primo.

Sub Magno Sigillo Angliae pendente a cauda pergamenae.

CHAPTER III

ARRANGEMENTS FOR A ROYAL VISITATION

Having now traced out the deprivation of the bishops who refused the Oath of Supremacy as administered by the privy councillors named in the writ of May 23, 1559, we must go back to that date, and see what action was arranged to ensure the loyalty and religious uniformity of the clergy at large. Several weeks had to elapse before Midsummer Day, when the Prayer Book was to come into general use, and recusants would become liable to the penalties of the Uniformity Act. After the dissolution in May, the general body of the clergy, influenced doubtless by the attitude of the bishops, seem to have preserved a stubborn silence, awaiting the development of events. Thus on May 20, Cox, writing to Weidner, says of the clergy: 'The whole body remain unmoved.' Three days later, Grindal tells Hubert that 'it is commonly supposed that almost all the bishops and also many other beneficed persons will renounce their bishoprics and functions.' So too, on May 10, the Spanish ambassador, writing to his king, declares that 'not a single ecclesiastic has agreed to what the Queen has done,' referring to the proceedings of the Parliament just described[1]. Three weeks later Bishop Aquila informs the King that 'the number and constancy of the Catholics frighten them [the Queen and Council], because they see that they have not been able to gain over a single man of them.'

[1] So too the Venetian Dispatch.

CHAP. III

Deliberation of Cecil and his advisers.

In view of so much sullen reluctance, the deliberations of Cecil and his advisers must have been constant and anxious. From a reference in the letter of Grindal already quoted, it is just possible that some kind of proclamation or declaration of policy was made during May, for he says: 'During the prorogation of Parliament there has been published a proclamation (*edictum*) to banish the pope and his jurisdiction altogether, and to restore religion to that form which we had under Edward VI.' As the letter goes on to mention the Supremacy Oath and the use of the Prayer Book, it is more probable that the writer refers to the publication of the recent Acts: certainly no proclamation of the kind exists on the Patent Roll. The Acts of the Privy Council at this time have been lost. But, at all events, by May 28 it had been determined to undertake a general visitation of all the dioceses, and as well to establish a permanent ecclesiastical commission. In this action, of course, the authorities were employing the powers given them under the Supremacy Act. Under the date mentioned, Allen, writing to Abel[1], announces that the visitation will shortly take place. He mentions the names of Coke, Goodrich, May, Cox, Haddon, Wroth, the Earl of Bedford, Lord Mountjoy, and Weston, who are 'to be visitors, and also the Queen's commissioners for all ecclesiastical matters, with others added to them, so that they shall be in all fourteen.' This letter is important as drawing a clear distinction between the royal visitation of 1559 and the permanent commission which lasted until 1562, when it was renewed with some alteration of names and duties[2].

Scheme for a royal visitation.

In planning the royal visitation, Cecil was consciously copying the precedent set in the first year of Edward VI, when visitors went through the country, holding inquiries, and distributing the First Book of Homilies together with the Paraphrases of Erasmus, and, last but not least, the

---

[1] *For. Cal.*, May 28; cf. Churton's *Nowell*, 392.
[2] See below, p. 174.

Injunctions. Accordingly a set of Articles of Inquiry[1] were drawn up, which will be found at the end of this chapter, and the Edwardine Injunctions were revised and considerably enlarged. Both documents were complete by June 13, on which day Cecil says: 'The Queen, on the advice of the Council, is determined to have a great visitation; whereupon the Injunctions and Articles of Inquisition are already formed.' A collation of the Injunctions with those of 1547 is appended, from which it will be seen that the first twenty-eight correspond very closely with the older series. The second half is either new, or incorporates enactments and regulations which had appeared since 1547. It will be observed that several minor insertions deal with the conduct of divine service, and give a hint of expected difficulty in this respect. Most noticeable is the Appendix on the Supremacy. We find from a draft of this last which exists in Cecil's writing[2] that considerable care was taken with the wording, and the title of it is altered more than once. This Appendix proves that the oath was being much debated through the country, and the explanation given shows that it was thought politic to interpret the Supremacy Act as liberally as possible. Certainly the terms of the Act sound far more stringent than this authoritative exposition. The Injunctions conclude with a ratification which contains these words: 'All which and singular Injunctions the Queen's Majesty ministers unto her clergy and to all other her loving subjects, straitly charging and commanding them to observe and keep the same upon pain of deprivation, sequestration of fruits and benefices, suspension, excommunication, and such other coercion, as to ordinaries . . . shall be seen convenient.' These Injunctions are a very important document in the Elizabethan settlement, and form the invariable standard of discipline in the various matters

---

[1] Many of these Articles of Inquiry are new, but the substance and, in some cases, the wording of others are taken from the similar articles of 1547. Cardwell, *Documentary Annals*, i. 41.

[2] S. P. Dom. Eliz. xv. 27.

The writ of visitation. of which they treat for a long time to come. They were supplemented later by 'Interpretations and further Considerations,' which appeared in 1560[1].

Articles of Inquiry and Injunctions being now ready, it remained to issue the writ of visitation under letters patent in accordance with the Supremacy Act. Cecil had given notice on May 29 to the Vice-Chancellor at Cambridge of the intended visitation of the University and Eton[2]. The Universities were to have visitors distinct from the diocesan visitors, and indeed (as the Cambridge and Eton writ, preserved at Lambeth, proves) the character of the University visitation was somewhat different from that of the dioceses. The Cambridge letters patent were dated June 20. On Midsummer Day, the very day that the Prayer Book was to come into use, letters patent were issued for the visitation of the Northern Province[3]. A long search for the writs which were, without doubt, issued for the Southern Province has so far proved unsuccessful; there is nothing to be found amongst signed bills or on the Patent Roll. We may feel pretty safe in concluding that the date of all the letters patent was on or about June 24. On this point Strype has fallen into error, for in his *Annals*[4] he gives various dates for the different writs of visitation, but reference to his authority, viz. the Register of the Dean and Chapter of Canterbury (i.e. Sede Vacante Register for 1559 at Lambeth), shows that he confuses writs of inhibition to deans and chapters and similar documents which date to July and August, when the visitors were about to begin their work.

Probable discussion as to the method of visitation. We take it, then, that letters patent were issued before July, nominating visitors for the various groups of dioceses into which England and Wales were divided for the purposes of visitation, which groups were six in all—one for the Northern, five for the Southern Province. Representative visitors must have met together after their nomination in order to settle some *modus operandi*. One

---

[1] Strype, i. 213, where the text is given.
[2] S. P. Dom. Eliz. iv. 33.
[3] See below, p. 89.
[4] *Ann.* i. 167.

of the chief matters discussed would be the manner of tendering the oath to the clergy, and here an important piece of information is given us in a paper written somewhat later by Dr. Parker. He there speaks of 'the form of a subscription which we devised to be used in the order of visitation[1].' This form we possess in records of the visitation for North and South, in which it appears in substantially the same words, so that it is clear that the phrasing was settled by common conference before the visitation began. We reserve the document until it comes before us in the course of the visitation, but at this point it is material to notice that it was determined not to administer the Supremacy Oath pure and simple, but *a summary form of subscription to the settlement of religion as set out in the Supremacy Act, the Uniformity Act, and the Injunctions.* Supremacy, Prayer Book, Injunctions, therefore, were to be the three acknowledged bases of the settlement, and they continued to be so regarded until the final form of the Thirty-nine Articles took the place of the Injunctions in the form of subscription introduced by Whitgift in 1583, and adopted in the Canons of 1604[2].

Departure of the cloistered clergy.

The cloistered clergy had already commenced their exodus. On June 19 Aquila writes : ' The cloistered clergy here have already begun to depart. They are being given alms for the purpose in your Majesty's name[3].' Referring to these, perhaps, and to others of the clergy and laity, he had already said on May 10 : 'An infinite number of people would leave the country, if they would let them, which they

---

[1] Strype's *Parker*, i. 95.

[2] The Interpretations, Advertisements, &c., seem only to explain or expand the Injunctions. The very document in which Whitgift sets forth the terms of subscription in 1583 still refers to the Injunctions as binding (Reg. 1 Whitgift, fo. 97 a). In 1560 a set of articles were drawn up (Hardwick, *Articles*, cap. vi and Appendix iv) to be read by the clergy after institution, and on other occasions. Appended to these was a protestation to be subscribed by the clergy. At York the signatures are preserved in the Institution Book, and it is most likely that such subscription was demanded until the Subscription Act of 1571.

[3] *Spanish Calendar*, p. 77.

will not[1]. This previous prohibition cannot be traced, owing to the unfortunate lacuna in the Privy Council Acts as already mentioned. The same writer says on July 1 of the secular clergy: 'I know for certain that in the diocese of Winchester they have not received and will not take the oath, and that all is in confusion[2].' We shall see, however, that in this diocese and elsewhere, with whatever reluctance, yet the oath was largely taken before the autumn passed, whilst even before the visitation began, the same Spanish ambassador had to confess: 'Heresy is recovering furiously all the credit it had lost for years past[3].' The progress of the visitation will be traced in the next two chapters.

I.

THE ROYAL INJUNCTIONS OF 1559 COLLATED WITH THOSE OF EDWARD VI[4].

[Transcr. from a contemporary print at the British Museum, 5155. a. 14 (1).]

These Injunctions are to be observed under penalty by the queen's subjects.

The queen's most royal majesty, by the advice of her most honourable council, intending the advancement of the true honour of Almighty God, the suppression of superstition throughout all her highness's realms and dominions, and to plant true religion to the extirpation of all hypocrisy, enormities, and abuses (as to her duty appertaineth), doth minister unto her loving subjects these godly Injunctions hereafter following. All which Injunctions her highness willeth and commandeth her loving subjects obediently to receive, and truly to observe and keep, every man in their offices, degrees, and states, as they will avoid her highness's displeasure, and pains of the same hereafter expressed.

---

[1] *Spanish Calendar*, p. 68.
[2] Ibid. 92. [3] Ibid. 85.
[4] See above, p. 43. The marginal analysis is ours. The parts in brackets are additions to the series of 1547. The numbers in the inner margin refer to that series. The omissions and substitutions are indicated in footnotes.

ARRANGEMENTS FOR A ROYAL VISITATION 47

1 I. The first is, that all deans, archdeacons, parsons, vicars, and all other ecclesiastical persons shall faithfully keep and observe, and as far as in them may lie, shall cause to be observed and kept of other, all and singular laws and statutes made [for the restoring to the crown, the ancient jurisdiction over the state ecclesiastical, and abolishing of all foreign power repugnant to the same [1]]. And furthermore, all ecclesiastical persons having cure of souls shall to the uttermost of their wit, knowledge, and learning, purely [and [2]] sincerely, and without any colour or dissimulation, declare, manifest, and open four times every year at the least, in their sermons and other collations, that [all usurped and foreign power [3]] having no establishment nor ground by the law of God, [is, for [4]] most just causes, taken away and abolished; and that therefore no manner of obedience [and [5]] subjection within [her [6]] highness's realms and dominions is due unto [any such foreign power [7]]. And that the [queen's [8]] power within [her [6]] realms and dominions is the highest power under God, to whom all men, within the same realms and dominions, by God's law, owe most loyalty and obedience, afore and above all other powers and potentates in earth.

CHAP. III

1. All ecclesiastical persons to observe the royal supremacy, and to preach against the papal usurpation.

2 II. Besides this, to the intent that all superstition and hypocrisy crept into divers men's hearts may vanish away, they shall not set forth or extol [the dignity of [2]] any images, relics, or miracles; [but, declaring the abuse of the same [9],] they shall teach that all goodness, health, and grace ought to be both asked and looked for only of God, as of the very Author and Giver of the same, and of none other.

2. Images, relics, &c., not to be extolled.

3 III. Item, that they, the persons above rehearsed, shall [preach [10]] in their churches, and every other cure they have, one sermon every [month [11]] of the year at the least, wherein they shall purely and sincerely declare the word of God, and in the same

3. Monthly sermons to be preached. which shall de-

---

[1] as well for the abolishing and extirpation of the Bishop of Rome, his pretensed and usurped power and jurisdiction, as for the establishment and confirmation of the king's authority, jurisdiction, and supremacy of the Church of England and Ireland.
[2] Om.
[3] the Bishop of Rome's usurped power and jurisdiction.
[4] was of. [5] or. [6] his.
[7] him. [8] king's.
[9] for any superstition or lucre; nor allure the people by any enticements to the pilgrimage of any saint or image; but, reproving the same.
[10] make or cause to be made.
[11] quarter.

CHAP. III
nounce superstition.

4. Each parson to preach, or read a homily, once a quarter.

5. When there is no sermon the Lord's Prayer, &c., to be recited.

6. The Bible and Paraphrases to be set up, and Bible-reading to be encouraged.

exhort their hearers to the works of faith, [as [1]] mercy and charity especially prescribed and commanded in Scripture; and that [the [1]] works devised by man's fantasies, besides Scripture (as wandering [of [2]] pilgrimages, [setting up of candles [3],] praying upon beads, or such like superstition), have not only no promise of reward in Scripture for doing of them, but contrariwise great threatenings and maledictions of God, for that they [being [4]] things tending to idolatry and superstition, which of all other offences God Almighty doth most detest and abhor, for that the same most diminish His honour and glory.

IV. Item, that they, the persons above rehearsed, shall preach in their own persons, once in every quarter of the year at least, one sermon, being licensed especially thereunto, as is specified hereafter; or else shall read some homily prescribed to be used by the queen's authority every Sunday at the least, unless some other preacher sufficiently licensed, as hereafter, chance to come to the parish for the same purpose of preaching [5].

V. Item, that every holy-day through the year, when they have no sermon, they shall immediately after the Gospel openly and plainly recite to their parishioners in the pulpit the Pater noster, the Creed, and the Ten Commandments, in English, to the intent that the people may learn the same by heart; exhorting all parents and householders to teach their children and servants the same, as they are bound by the law of God and conscience to do [6].

VI. Also, that they shall provide within three months next after this visitation [at the charges of the parish [1]], one book of the whole Bible of the largest volume in English; and within one twelve months next after the said visitation, the Paraphrases of Erasmus also in English upon the Gospel, and the same set up in some convenient place within the said church that they have

---

[1] Om.
[2] to.
[3] offering of money, candles or tapers, to relics, or images, or kissing and licking of the same.
[4] be.
[5] This Injunction is new, and in the place of one which required the removal of all images, and the tapers or candles usually set before them, but expressly allowed 'two lights upon the high altar before the sacrament, which, for the signification that Christ is the very true light of the world, they shall suffer to remain still.' It appears however from the Injunctions of 1549 (No. 3), and the subsequent Injunctions of Bishop Ridley, 1550 (No. 2), that the permission had in the meantime been withdrawn.
[6] Verbatim.

cure of, whereas [the¹] parishioners may most commodiously resort unto the same, and read the same, [out of the time of common service²]. The charges of [the Paraphrases³] shall be [by the parson or proprietary and parishioners borne by equal portions⁴]; and they shall discourage no man⁵ from the reading of any part of the Bible, either in Latin or in English, but shall rather⁶ exhort every person to read the same with great humility and reverence, as the very lively word of God, and the especial food of man's soul, which all Christian persons are bound to embrace, believe, and follow, if they look to be saved; whereby they may the better know their duties to God, to their sovereign [lady the queen⁷,] and their neighbour; ever gently and charitably exhorting them, and in [her⁸] majesty's name straitly charging and commanding them, that in the reading thereof, no man to reason or contend, but quietly to hear the reader.

9   VII. Also, the said ecclesiastical persons shall in no wise at any unlawful time, nor for any other cause, than for their honest necessities, haunt or resort to any taverns or alehouses. And after their [meats⁹,] they shall not give themselves to drinking or riot, spending their time idly by day [and¹⁰] by night at dice, cards, or tables playing, or any other unlawful game; but at all times, as they shall have leisure, they shall hear or read somewhat of Holy Scripture, or shall occupy themselves with some other honest [study, or²] exercise; and that they always do the things which appertain to honesty, and endeavour to profit the commonwealth; having always in mind that they ought to excel all other in purity of life, and should be [examples¹¹] to the people to live well and Christianly.

7. All persons to lead exemplary lives.

11   VIII. Also, that they shall admit no man to preach within any of their cures, but such as shall appear unto them to be sufficiently licensed thereunto by the [queen's majesty, or¹²] the Archbishop of Canterbury or York, in [either of their provinces¹³,] or by the bishop of the diocese, [or by the queen's majesty's visitors²]. And such as shall be so licensed, they shall gladly receive to declare

8. All preachers to be duly licensed.

---

¹ their.   ² Om.   ³ which books.   ⁵ authorized and licensed thereto.
⁴ rateably borne between the parson and appropriatary and parishioners aforesaid, that is to say the one half by the parson or proprietary, and the other half by the parishioners.
⁶ comfort and.   ⁷ lord the king.
⁸ his.   ⁹ dinner or supper.
¹⁰ or.   ¹¹ an example.
¹² king's majesty.   ¹³ his province.

E

CHAP. III

9. Recusants to be denounced.

10. Register books to be kept in a parish chest.

11. Incumbents to give to the poor in proportion to their benefice.

the word of God at convenient times, without[1] resistance or contradiction. [And that no other be suffered to preach out of his own cure or parish, than such as shall be licensed, as is above expressed[2].]

IX. Also, if they do or shall know any man within their parish 13 or elsewhere, that is a letter of the word of God to be read in English, or sincerely preached, or of the execution of these the [queen's[3]] majesty's Injunctions, or a fautor of [any usurped and foreign[4]] power, now by the laws of this realm justly rejected and taken away, they shall detect and present the same to the [queen's majesty, or to her[5]] council, [or to the ordinary[2],] or to the justice of peace next adjoining.

X. Also, that the parson, vicar, or curate, and parishioners of 14 every parish within this realm, shall in their churches and chapels keep one book [of[6]] register, wherein they shall write the day and year of every wedding, christening, and burial made within their parish for their time, and so every man succeeding them likewise; and also therein shall write every person's name that shall be so wedded, christened, and buried. And for the safe keeping of the same book, the parish shall be bound to provide of their common charges one sure coffer, with two locks and keys, whereof the one to remain with the parson, vicar, or curate, and the other with the wardens of every parish church or chapel, wherein the said book shall be laid up. Which book they shall every Sunday take forth, and in the presence of the said wardens, or one of them, write and record in the same all the weddings, christenings, and burials, made the whole week before; and that done, to lay up the book in the said coffer as before: and for every time that the same shall be omitted, the party that shall be in the fault thereof shall forfeit to the said church 3s. 4d., to be employed [the one half[2]] to the poor men's box of that parish, [the other half towards the repairing of the church[2]].

XI. Furthermore, because the goods of the Church are called 15 the goods of the poor, and at these days nothing is less seen, than the poor to be sustained with the same; all parsons, vicars, pensionaries, prebendaries, and other beneficed men within this deanery, not being resident upon their benefices, which may dispend yearly 20l. or above, either within this deanery, or else-

[1] any.
[2] Om.
[3] king's.
[4] the Bishop of Rome's pretensed.
[5] king or.
[6] or.

where, shall distribute hereafter among their poor parishioners, or other inhabitants there, in the presence of the churchwardens, or some other honest man of the parish, the fortieth part of the fruits and revenues of [the said benefice [1];] lest they be worthily noted of ingratitude, which reserving so many parts to themselves, cannot vouchsafe to impart the fortieth portion thereof among the poor people of that parish, that is so fruitful and profitable unto them.

16 XII. And, to the intent that learned men may hereafter spring the more, for the execution of the premises, every parson, vicar, clerk, or beneficed man within this deanery, having yearly to dispend in benefices and other promotions of the Church 100*l.*, shall give [3*l.* 6*s.* 8*d.* in [2]] exhibition to one scholar [in any of the universities [3];] and for as many hundred pounds more as he may dispend, to so many scholars more shall give like exhibition in the University of Oxford or Cambridge, or some grammar school, which, after they have profited in good learning, may be partners of their patron's cure and charge, as well in preaching, as otherwise in executing of their offices, or may, when [time [4]] shall be, otherwise profit the commonweal with their counsel and wisdom.

12. Incumbents are to support exhibitioners.

17 XIII. Also, that [all [5]] proprietaries, parsons, vicars, and clerks, having churches, chapels, or mansions within this deanery, shall bestow yearly hereafter upon the same mansions or chancels of their churches, being in decay, the fifth part of that their benefices, till they be fully repaired, and [6] shall always keep and maintain in good estate.

13. Chancel and houses to be repaired by the incumbent.

18 XIV. Also, that the said parsons, vicars, and clerks shall once every quarter of the year read these Injunctions given unto them, openly and deliberately before all their parishioners at one time, or at two several times in one day; to the intent that both they may be the better admonished of their duty, and their said parishioners the more moved to follow the same for their part.

14. The Injunctions to be read regularly.

19 XV. Also, forasmuch as by [laws [7]] established, every man is bound to pay his tithes, no man shall by colour of duty omitted by their curates, detain their tithes and so [8] requite one wrong with another, or be his own judge; but shall truly pay the same, as [9]

15. Tithes to be paid duly.

---

[1] their said benefices.
[2] competent.   [3] Om.
[4] need.   [5] the.
[6] the same so repaired.
[7] a law.
[8] redub and.   [9] he.

hath been accustomed, to their parsons, vicars, and curates, without any restraint or diminution; and such lack and default as they can justly find in their parsons and curates, to call for reformation thereof at their ordinaries and other superiors [1], who, upon complaint and due proof thereof, shall reform the same accordingly.

16. All clergy under M.A. to provide Latin and English New Testament and Paraphrases.

XVI. Also, that every parson, vicar, curate, [and stipendiary priest [2],] being under the degree of a [master of art [3],] shall provide and have of his own, within three months after this visitation, the New Testament both in Latin and in English, with [paraphrases upon the same [4],] conferring the one with the other. And the bishops and other ordinaries by themselves or their officers, in their synods and visitations, shall examine the said ecclesiastical persons, how they have profited in the study of Holy Scripture.

17. The clergy to learn suitable Scripture for pastoral visitation.

XVII. Also, that the vice of damnable despair may be clearly taken away, and that firm belief and steadfast hope may be surely conceived of all their parishioners, being in any danger, they shall learn and have always in a readiness such comfortable places and sentences of Scripture, as do set forth the mercy, benefits, and goodness of Almighty God towards all penitent and believing persons; that they may at all times when necessity shall require, promptly comfort their flock with the lively word of God, which is the only stay of man's conscience [5].

18. The Litany substituted for all processions save at beating the bounds.

XVIII. Also, to avoid all contention and strife, which heretofore hath risen among the queen's majesty's subjects in sundry places of her realms and dominions, by reason of fond courtesy, and challenging of places in [the [6]] procession; and also that they may the more quietly hear that which is said or sung to their edifying, they shall not from henceforth in any parish church at any time use any procession about the church or churchyard, or other place; but immediately before [the time of communion of the Sacrament [7],] the priests with other of the quire shall kneel in the midst of the church, and sing or say plainly and distinctly the Litany, which is set forth in English, with all the suffrages following, to the intent the people may hear and answer; and none other procession or litany to be had or used, but the said Litany in

---

[1] hands.
[2] chantry priest and stipendiary.
[3] Bachelor of Divinity.
[4] the Paraphrase upon the same of Erasmus.
[5] Condensed from 23 Ed. VI.
[6] Om.
[7] high Mass.

ARRANGEMENTS FOR A ROYAL VISITATION

English, adding nothing thereto, but as [it is now appointed¹]. And in cathedral or collegiate churches the same shall be done in such places, and in such sort, as our commissioners in our visitation shall appoint. And in the time of the Litany, of the [common prayer²,] of the sermon, and when the priest readeth the Scripture to the parishioners, no manner of persons, without a just and urgent cause, shall [use any walking in the church, nor shall³] depart out of the church; and all ringing and knolling of bells shall be utterly forborne at that time, except one bell at convenient time to be rung or knolled before the sermon. [But yet for retaining of the perambulation of the circuits of parishes, they shall once in the year at the time accustomed, with the curate and substantial men of the parish, walk about the parishes, as they were accustomed, and at their return to the church, make their common prayers⁵.]

XIX. Provided, that the curate in their said common perambulations, used heretofore in the days of rogations, at certain convenient places shall admonish the people to give thanks to God, in the beholding of God's benefits, for the increase and abundance of His fruits upon the face of the earth, with the saying of the 103rd Psalm, '*Benedic anima mea*,' &c. At which time also the same minister shall inculcate these or such sentences: 'Cursed be he, which translateth the bounds and doles of his neighbour.' Or such other order of prayers, as shall be hereafter appointed⁴.

19. Rogations to be observed.

XX. Item⁵, all the [queen's⁶] faithful and loving subjects shall from henceforth celebrate and keep their holy day according to God's⁷ will and pleasure; that is, in hearing the word of God read and taught, in private and public prayers, in knowledging their offences unto God, and amendment of the same, in reconciling themselves charitably to their neighbours, where displeasure hath been, in oftentimes receiving the communion of the very Body and

20. Sunday to be suitably observed.

---

¹ our commissaries in our visitation shall appoint.
² Mass. ³ Om.
⁴ New.
⁵ Ed. VI adds, 'Like as the people be commonly occupied the work-day, with bodily labour, for their bodily sustenance, so was the holy day at the first beginning godly instituted and ordained, that the people should that day give themselves wholly to God. And whereas in our time, God is more offended than pleased, more dishonoured than honoured upon the holy day, because of idleness, pride, drunkenness, quarrelling and brawling, which are most used in such days, people nevertheless persuading themselves sufficiently to honour God on that day, if they hear Mass and service, though they understand nothing to their edifying: therefore.'
⁶ king's. ⁷ holy.

Blood of Christ, in visiting of the poor and sick, using all soberness and godly conversation. Yet notwithstanding, all parsons, vicars, and curates shall teach and declare unto their parishioners, that they may with a safe and quiet conscience, after their common prayer in the time of harvest, labour upon the holy and festival days, and save that thing which God hath sent; and if for any scrupulosity or grudge of conscience, men should superstitiously abstain from working upon those days, that then they should grievously offend and displease God.

21. Notorious sinners, &c., not to be admitted to Holy Communion.

XXI. Also, forasmuch as variance and contention is a thing that most displeases God, and is most contrary to the blessed communion of the Body and Blood of our Saviour Christ, curates shall in no wise admit to the receiving thereof any of their cure and flock, [which be openly known to live in sin notorious without repentance, or [1]] who hath maliciously and openly contended with his neighbour, unless the same do first charitably and openly reconcile himself again, remitting all rancour and malice, whatsoever controversy hath been between them. And nevertheless, their just titles and rights they may charitably prosecute before such as have authority to hear the same.

22. Church ceremonies to be taught as obligatory.

XXII. Also, that they shall instruct and teach in their cures, that no man ought obstinately and maliciously to break and violate the laudable ceremonies of the Church, [commanded by public authority to be observed [2]].

23. Shrines, &c., to be removed.

XXIII. Also, that they shall take away, utterly extinct, and destroy all shrines, coverings of shrines, all tables, candlesticks, trindals, and rolls of wax, pictures, paintings, and all other monu-

---

[1] Om.

[2] Ed. VI adds, 'by the king commanded to be observed, and as yet not abrogated. And on the other side, that whosoever doth superstitiously abuse them, doth the same to the great peril and danger of his soul's health: as in casting holy water upon his bed, upon images, and other dead things, or bearing about him holy bread, or St. John's Gospel, or making of crosses of wood upon Palm Sunday, in time of reading of the Passion, or keeping of private holy days, as bakers, brewers, smiths, shoemakers, and such other do; or ringing of holy bells; or blessing with the holy candle, to the intent thereby to be discharged of the burden of sin, or to drive away devils, or to put away dreams and phantasies, or in putting trust and confidence of health and salvation in the same ceremonies, when they be only ordained, instituted, and made, to put us in remembrance of the benefits which we have received by Christ. And if he use them for any other purpose, he grievously offendeth God.'

ARRANGEMENTS FOR A ROYAL VISITATION 55

ments of feigned miracles, pilgrimages, idolatry, and superstition, so that there remain no memory of the same in walls, glass windows, or elsewhere within their churches and houses; [preserving nevertheless, or repairing both the walls and glass windows[1];] and they shall exhort all their parishioners to do the like within their several houses.

29   XXIV. And that the churchwardens, at the common charge of the parishioners, in every church shall provide a comely and honest pulpit, to be set in a convenient place within the same, [and to be there seemly kept[2]] for the preaching of God's word.

24. A pulpit to be provided.

30   XXV. Also, they shall provide and have within three months after this visitation, a strong chest with a hole in the upper part thereof, to be provided at the cost and charge of the parish, having three keys, whereof one shall remain [with[3]] the parson, vicar, or curate, and the other two in the custody of the churchwardens, or any other two honest men, to be appointed by the parish from year to year; which chest you shall set and fasten [in a most convenient place[4],] to the intent the parishioners should put into it their oblations and alms for their poor neighbours. And the parson, vicar, and curate shall diligently from time to time, and especially when men make their testaments, call upon, exhort, and move their neighbours to confer and give, as they may well spare, to the said chest: declaring unto them, whereas heretofore they have been diligent to bestow much substance, otherwise than God commanded, upon pardons, pilgrimages, trentals, decking of images, offering of candles, giving to friars, and upon other like blind devotions, they ought at this time to be much more ready to help the poor and needy; knowing that to relieve the poor is a true worshipping of God, required earnestly upon pain of everlasting damnation; and that also whatsoever is given for their comfort, is given to Christ Himself, and so is accepted of Him, that He will mercifully reward the same with everlasting life. The which alms and devotions of the people the keepers of the keys shall at [all[1]] times convenient take out of the chest, and distribute the same in the presence of the whole parish, or six of them, to be truly and faithfully delivered to their most needy neighbours; and if they be provided for, then to the reparation of highways next adjoining, [or to the poor people of

25. An alms-chest to be supplied, and alms to be distributed. Guild moneys to be so applied.

CHAP. III

---

[1] Om.
[2] to be set in a convenient place within the same.
[3] in the custody of.
[4] near unto the high altar.

such parishes near, as shall be thought best to the said keepers of the keys ¹]. And also the moneys which rise of fraternities, guilds, and other stocks of the Church (except by the [queen's ²] majesty's authority it be otherwise appointed) shall be put in the said chest, and converted to the said use; and also the rents of lands, the profit of cattle, and money given or bequeathed [to obits and dirges, and ¹] to the finding of torches, lights, tapers, and lamps, shall be converted to the said use; saving that it shall be lawful for them to bestow part of the said profits upon the reparation of the said church, if great need require, and whereas the parish is very poor, and not able otherwise to repair the same.

26. Concerning simony.

XXVI. Also, to avoid the detestable sin of simony, because buying and selling of benefices is execrable before God, therefore all such persons, as buy any benefices, or come to them by fraud or deceit, shall be deprived of such benefices, and be made unable at any time after to receive any other spiritual promotion; and such as do sell them, or by any colour do bestow them for their own gain and profit, shall [use ³] their right and title of patronage and presentment for that time, and the gift thereof for that vacation shall appertain to the [queen's ²] majesty..

27. Homilies to be read.

XXVII. Also, because through lack of preachers in many places of the [queen's ²] realms and dominions the people continue in ignorance and blindness, all parsons, vicars, and curates shall read in their churches every Sunday one of the Homilies, which are and shall be set forth for the same purpose by the [queen's ²] authority, in such sort, as they shall be appointed to do in the preface of the same.

28. Concerning due respect for the clergy.

XXVIII. Item, whereas many indiscreet persons do at this day uncharitably contemn and abuse priests and ministers of the Church, because some of them (having small learning) have of long time favoured fond phantasies, rather than God's truth; yet forasmuch as their office and function is appointed of God, the [queen's ²] majesty willeth and chargeth all [her ⁴] loving subjects, that from henceforth they shall use them charitably and reverently for their office and ministration sake, and especially such as labour in the setting forth of God's holy word.

29. Regulations

XXIX ⁵. Item, although there be no prohibition by the word of

32

33

34

---

¹ Om.   ² king's.   are either new, or re-enactments of
³ lose.   ⁴ his.   customs and regulations later than
⁵ From this point the Injunctions   1547.

God, nor any example of the primitive Church, but that the priests and ministers of the Church may lawfully, for the avoiding of fornication, have an honest and sober wife, and that for the same purpose the same was by Act of Parliament in the time of our dear brother King Edward VI made lawful, whereupon a great number of the clergy of this realm were then married, and so yet continue; yet because there hath grown offence, and some slander to the Church by lack of discreet and sober behaviour in many ministers of the Church, both in choosing of their wives and indiscreet living with them, the remedy whereof is necessary to be sought: it is thought, therefore, very necessary that no manner of priest or deacon shall hereafter take to his wife any manner of woman without the advice and allowance first had upon good examination by the bishop of the same diocese, and two justices of the peace of the same shire, dwelling next to the place where the same woman hath made her most abode before her marriage; nor without the good will of the parents of the said woman, if she have any living, or two of the next of her kinsfolks, or, for lack of knowledge of such, of her master or mistress, where she serveth. And before he shall be contracted in any place, he shall make a good and certain proof thereof to the minister, or to the congregation assembled for that purpose, which shall be upon some holy day, where divers may be present. And if any shall do otherwise, that then they shall not be permitted to minister either the word or the sacraments of the Church, nor shall be capable of any ecclesiastical benefice. And for the manner of marriages of any bishops, the same shall be allowed and approved by the metropolitan of the province, and also by such commissioners as the queen's majesty shall thereunto appoint. And if any master or dean, or any head of any college, shall purpose to marry, the same shall not be allowed, but by such to whom the visitation of the same doth properly belong, who shall in any wise provide that the same tend not to the hindrance of their house.

XXX. Item, her majesty being desirous to have the prelacy and clergy of this realm to be had as well in outward reverence, as otherwise regarded for the worthiness of their ministries, and thinking it necessary to have them known to the people in all places and assemblies, both in the church and without, and thereby to receive the honour and estimation due to the special messengers and ministers of Almighty God, wills and commands that all archbishops and bishops, and all other that be called or admitted to preaching or ministry of the sacraments, or that be admitted into any vocation ecclesiastical, or into any society of learning in either of the universities, or elsewhere, shall use and wear such seemly habits, garments, and such square caps, as were most commonly and orderly received in the latter year of the reign of King Edward VI; not thereby meaning to attribute any holiness or special worthiness to the said garments, but as St. Paul writeth: *Omnia decenter et secundum ordinem fiant.* 1 Cor. 14 cap.

31. Heresy and error not to be maintained.
XXXI. Item, that no man shall wilfully and obstinately defend or maintain any heresies, errors, or false doctrine, contrary to the faith of Christ and His Holy Spirit.

32. Charms, &c., forbidden.
XXXII. Item, that no persons shall use charms, sorceries, enchantments, witchcraft, soothsaying, or any suchlike devilish device, nor shall resort at any time to the same for counsel or help.

33. Parishioners to attend their parish church.
XXXIII. Item, that no persons shall, neglecting their own parish church, resort to any other church in time of common prayer or preaching, except it be by the occasion of some extraordinary sermon in some parish of the same town.

34. No inns to sell in time of public worship.
XXXIV. Item, that no innholders or alehouse-keepers shall use to sell meat or drink in the time of common prayer, preaching, reading of the Homilies or Scriptures.

35. Images, &c., not to be kept privately.
XXXV. Item, that no persons keep in their houses any abused images, tables, pictures, paintings, and other monuments of feigned miracles, pilgrimages, idolatry, and superstition.

36. Preachers not to be disturbed.
XXXVI. Item, that no man shall willingly let or disturb the preacher in time of his sermon, or let or discourage any curate or minister to sing or say the divine service now set forth; nor mock or jest at the ministers of such service.

37. Rash use of Scripture forbidden.
XXXVII. Item, that no man shall talk or reason of the Holy Scriptures rashly or contentiously, nor maintain any false doctrine or error, but shall commune of the same, when occasion is given, reverently, humbly, and in the fear of God, for his comfort and better understanding.

38. Orderly behaviour in church.
XXXVIII. Item, that no man, woman, or child shall be otherwise occupied in the time of the service, than in quiet attendance to hear, mark, and understand that is read, preached, and ministered.

39. Of the use of the Primer.
XXXIX. Item, that every schoolmaster and teacher shall teach the Grammar set forth by King Henry VIII of noble memory, and continued in the time of King Edward VI, and none other.

ARRANGEMENTS FOR A ROYAL VISITATION

XL. Item, that no man shall take upon him to teach, but such as shall be allowed by the ordinary, and found meet as well for his learning and dexterity in teaching, as for sober and honest conversation, and also for right understanding of God's true religion. *40. Teachers to be properly qualified.*

XLI. Item, that all teachers of children shall stir and move them to the love and due reverence of God's true religion now truly set forth by public authority. *41. Teaching of children.*

XLII. Item, that they shall accustom their scholars reverently to learn such sentences of Scriptures as shall be most expedient to induce them to all godliness. *42. Scripture to be learnt by them.*

XLIII. Item, forasmuch as in these latter days many have been made priests, being children, and otherwise utterly unlearned, so that they could read to say Matins or Mass, the ordinaries shall not admit any such to any cure or spiritual function. *43. Irregular priests not to be admitted.*

XLIV. Every parson, vicar, and curate shall upon every holy day, and every second Sunday in the year, hear and instruct all the youth of the parish for half an hour at the least before evening prayer, in the Ten Commandments, the Articles of the Belief, and in the Lord's Prayer, and diligently examine them, and teach the Catechism set forth in the book of public prayer. *44. Of catechisms in church.*

XLV. Item, that the ordinary do exhibit unto our visitors their books, or a true copy of the same, containing the causes why any person was imprisoned, famished, or put to death for religion. *45. The cause of religious suffering to be certified.*

XLVI. Item, that in every parish three or four discreet men, which tender God's glory, and His true religion, shall be appointed by the ordinaries diligently to see that all the parishioners duly resort to their church upon all Sundays and holy days, and there to continue the whole time of the godly service; and all such as shall be found slack or negligent in resorting to the church, having no great nor urgent cause of absence, they shall straitly call upon them, and after due admonition if they amend not, they shall denounce them to the ordinary. *46. Overseers for church attendance to be appointed.*

XLVII. Item, that the churchwardens of every parish shall deliver unto our visitors the inventories of vestments, copes, and other ornaments, plate, books, and specially of grails, couchers, legends, processionals, manuals, hymnals, portasses, and such like appertaining to their church. *47. Inventories of church furniture to be delivered.*

XLVIII. Item, that weekly upon Wednesdays and Fridays, not *48. Services for*

CHAP. III | being holy days, the curate at the accustomed hours of service
Wednes- | shall resort to church, and cause warning to be given to the
day and | people by knolling of a bell, and say the Litany and prayers.
Friday.

49. Choral foundations to be kept. The service to be daily sung. A hymn to be allowed.

XLIX. Item, because in divers collegiate and also some parish churches heretofore there have been livings appointed for the maintenance of men and children to use singing in the church, by means whereof the laudable science of music has been had in estimation, and preserved in knowledge; the queen's majesty neither meaning in any wise the decay of anything that might conveniently tend to the use and continuance of the said science, neither to have the same in any part so abused in the church, that thereby the common prayer should be the worse understanded of the hearers, wills and commands, that first no alterations be made of such assignments of living, as heretofore has been appointed to the use of singing or music in the church, but that the same so remain. And that there be a modest and distinct song so used in all parts of the common prayers in the church, that the same may be as plainly understanded, as if it were read without singing; and yet nevertheless for the comforting of such that delight in music, it may be permitted, that in the beginning, or in the end of common prayers, either at morning or evening, there may be sung an hymn, or suchlike song to the praise of Almighty God, in the best sort of melody and music that may be conveniently devised, having respect that the sentence of the hymn may be understanded and perceived.

50. Religious disputation is forbidden.

L. Item, because in all alterations, and specially in rites and ceremonies, there happen discords amongst the people, and thereupon slanderous words and railings, whereby charity, the knot of all Christian society, is loosed; the queen's majesty being most desirous of all other earthly things, that her people should live in charity both towards God and man, and therein abound in good works, wills and straitly commands all manner her subjects to forbear all vain and contentious disputations in matters of religion, and not to use in despite or rebuke of any person these convicious words, papist or papistical heretic, schismatic or sacramentary, or any suchlike words of reproach. But if any manner of person shall deserve the accusation of any such, that first he be charitably admonished thereof; and if that shall not amend him, then to denounce the offender to the ordinary, or to some higher power having authority to correct the same.

LI. Item, because there is a great abuse in the printers of books, which for covetousness chiefly regard not what they print, so they may have gain, whereby ariseth great disorder by publication of unfruitful, vain, and infamous books and papers; the queen's majesty straitly charges and commands, that no manner of person shall print any manner of book or paper, of what sort, nature, or in what language soever it be, except the same be first licensed by her majesty by express words in writing, or by six of her privy council; or be perused and licensed by the archbishops of Canterbury and York, the Bishop of London, the chancellors of both universities, the bishop being ordinary, and the archdeacon also of the place, where any such shall be printed, or by two of them, whereof the ordinary of the place to be always one. And that the names of such as shall allow the same to be added in the end of every such work, for a testimony of the allowance thereof. And because many pamphlets, plays, and ballads be oftentimes printed, wherein regard would be had that nothing therein should be either heretical, seditious, or unseemly for Christian ears; her majesty likewise commands that no manner of person shall enterprise to print any such, except the same be to him licensed by such her majesty's commissioners, or three of them, as be appointed in the city of London to hear and determine divers causes ecclesiastical, tending to the execution of certain statutes made the last Parliament for uniformity of order in religion. And if any shall sell or utter any manner of books or papers, being not licensed as is abovesaid, that the same party shall be punished by order of the said commissioners, as to the quality of the fault shall be thought meet. And touching all other books of matters of religion, or policy, or governance that have been printed, either on this side the seas or on the other side, because the diversity of them is great, and that there needs good consideration to be had of the particularities thereof, her majesty refers the prohibition or permission thereof to the order which her said commissioners within the city of London shall take and notify. According to the which her majesty straitly commands all manner her subjects, and especially the wardens and company of Stationers, to be obedient.

Provided that these orders do not extend to any profane authors and works in any language, that have been heretofore commonly received or allowed in any the universities or schools, but the

CHAP. III

51. Printing to be licensed under penalty.

CHAP. III

52. Of reverence in worship and bowing at the Holy Name.

same may be printed and used as by good order they were accustomed.

LII. Item, although Almighty God is at all times to be honoured with all manner of reverence that may be devised; yet of all other times, in time of common prayer the same is most to be regarded; therefore it is to be necessarily received, that in time of the Litany, and all other collects and common supplications to Almighty God, all manner of people shall devoutly and humbly kneel upon their knees and give ear thereunto; and that whensoever the name of Jesus shall be in any lesson, sermon, or otherwise in the church pronounced, that due reverence be made of all persons young and old, with lowliness of courtesy and uncovering of heads of the menkind, as thereunto does necessarily belong, and heretofore has been accustomed.

53. All readers to read distinctly.

LIII. Item, that all ministers and readers of public prayers, chapters, and homilies shall be charged to read leisurely, plainly, and distinctly; and also such as are but mean readers shall peruse over before, once or twice, the chapters and homilies, to the intent they may read to the better understanding of the people, and the more encouragement to godliness.

An admonition to simple men deceived by malicious.

The Oath of Supremacy explained

The queen's majesty being informed that in certain places of this realm, sundry of her native subjects, being called to ecclesiastical ministry of the Church, be by sinister persuasion and perverse construction induced to find some scruple in the form of an oath, which by an Act of the last Parliament is prescribed to be required of divers persons for their recognition of their allegiance to her majesty, which certainly never was ever meant, nor by any equity of words or good sense can be thereof gathered; would that all her loving subjects should understand that nothing was, is, or shall be meant or intended by the same oath to have any other duty, allegiance, or bond required by the same oath, than was acknowledged to be due to the most noble kings of famous memory, King Henry VIII, her majesty's father, or King Edward VI, her majesty's brother.

as involving nothing new,

whilst sinister reports are not to

And further, her majesty forbids all manner her subjects to give ear or credit to such perverse and malicious persons, which most sinisterly and maliciously labour to notify to her loving subjects, how by the words of the said oath it may be collected, that the kings or queens of this realm, possessors of the crown, may challenge authority and power of ministry of divine offices in the church; wherein her said subjects be much abused by such evil-disposed persons. For certainly her majesty neither does nor ever will challenge any other authority than that was challenged and lately used by the said noble kings of famous memory, King Henry VIII and King Edward VI, which is and was of ancient time due to the imperial crown of this realm; that is, under God to the sovereignty and rule over all manner persons born within these her realms, dominions, and countries, of what estate, either ecclesiastical or temporal, soever they be, so as no other foreign power shall or ought to have any superiority over them. And if any person that has conceived any other sense of the form of the said oath shall accept the same oath with this interpretation, sense, or meaning, her majesty is well pleased to accept every such in that behalf, as her good and obedient subjects, and shall acquit them of all manner penalties contained in the said Act against such as shall peremptorily or obstinately refuse to take the same oath.

Chap. III — *be heard as to the queen's intentions.*

For tables in the church.

Whereas her majesty understands that in many and sundry parts of the realm the altars of the churches be removed, and tables placed for administration of the Holy Sacrament, according to the form of the law therefor provided; and in some other places the altars be not yet removed, upon opinion conceived of some order therein to be taken by her majesty's visitors; in the order whereof, saving for an uniformity, there seems no matter of great moment, so that the Sacrament be duly and reverently ministered; yet for observation of one uniformity through the whole realm, and for the better imitation of the law in that behalf, it is ordered that no altar be taken down, but by oversight of the curate of the church, and the churchwardens, or one of them at the least, wherein no riotous or disordered manner to be used. And that the holy table in every church be decently made, and set in the place where the altar stood, and there commonly covered, as thereto belongs, and as shall be appointed by the visitors, and so to stand, saving when the communion of the Sacrament is to be distributed; at which time the same shall be so placed in good sort within the chancel, as

No altar is to be taken down without proper supervision.

The holy table to stand where the altar stood, saving at the celebration.

CHAP. III — whereby the minister may be more conveniently heard of the communicants in his prayer and ministration, and the communicants also more conveniently and in more number communicate with the said minister. And after the communion done, from time to time the same holy table to be placed where it stood before.

Regulations for the sacramental bread. — Item, where also it was in the time of King Edward VI used to have the sacramental bread of common fine bread, it is ordered for the more reverence to be given to these holy mysteries, being the sacraments of the Body and Blood of our Saviour Jesus Christ, that the same sacramental bread be made and formed plain, without any figure thereupon, of the same fineness and fashion round, though somewhat bigger in compass and thickness, as the usual bread and water, heretofore named singing cakes, which served for the use of the private Mass.

The form of bidding the prayers to be used generally in this uniform sort.

Ye shall pray for Christ's Holy Catholic Church, that is for the whole congregation of Christian people dispersed throughout the whole world, and especially for the Church of England and Ireland. And herein I require you most specially to pray for the queen's most excellent majesty, our sovereign lady Elizabeth, queen of England, France, and Ireland, defender of the faith, and supreme governor of this realm as well in causes ecclesiastical as temporal. You shall also pray for the ministers of God's holy word and sacraments, as well archbishops and bishops, as other pastors and curates. You shall also pray for the queen's most honourable council and for all the nobility of this realm, that all and every of these in their calling, may serve truly and painfully to the glory of God and edifying of His people, remembering the account that they must make. Also ye shall pray for the whole Commons of this realm, that they may live in true faith and fear of God, in humble obedience and brotherly charity one to another. Finally, let us praise God for all those that are departed out of this life in the faith of Christ, and pray unto God that we have grace for to direct our lives after their good example, that after this life we with them may be made partakers of the glorious resurrection in the life everlasting.

And this done, show the holy-days and fasting days.   CHAP. III

All which and singular Injunctions[1] the queen's majesty ministers unto her clergy and to all other her loving subjects, straitly charging and commanding them to observe and keep the same upon pain of deprivation, sequestration of fruits and benefices, suspension, excommunication, and such other coercion, as to ordinaries, or other having ecclesiastical jurisdiction, whom her majesty has appointed, or shall appoint for the due execution of the same, shall be seen convenient; charging and commanding them to see these Injunctions observed and kept of all persons being under their jurisdiction, as they will answer to her majesty for the contrary. And her highness's pleasure is, that every justice of peace being required, shall assist the ordinaries, and every of them, for the due execution of the said Injunctions.

The ratification of the Injunctions.

II.

ARTICLES OF INQUIRY, 1559[2].

[Transcr. from a contemporary print in the British Museum, 5155 a. 14 (1).]

INJUNCTIONS GIVEN BY THE QUEEN'S MAJESTY, 1559.

First, whether any parson, vicar, or curate be resident continually upon his benefice, doing his duty in preaching, reading, and duly ministering the holy Sacraments.

1. Residence.

Item, whether in their churches and chapels all images, shrines, all tables, candlesticks, trindals, or rolls of wax, pictures, paintings, and all other monuments of feigned and false miracles, pilgrimages, idolatry, and superstition be removed, abolished, and destroyed.

2. False miracles.

Item, whether they do not every holy-day when they have no sermon, immediately after the Gospel, openly, plainly, and distinctly

3. Lord's Prayer.

---

[1] The archbishops and bishops afterwards drew up 'Interpretations and further Considerations' of these Injunctions for the better direction of the clergy, which may be seen collated with the text of the Injunctions here given in Cardwell's *Documentary Annals,* i. 203–209.

[2] See above, p. 43.

Chap. III recite to their parishioners in the pulpit the Lord's Prayer, the Belief, and the Ten Commandments in English.

4. To bring up youth. Item, whether they do charge fathers and mothers, masters and governors of youth to bring them up in some virtuous study and occupation.

5. Curates. Item, whether such beneficed men as be lawfully absent from their benefices do leave their cures to a rude and unlearned parson, and not to an honest, well learned, and expert curate, which can and will teach you wholesome doctrine.

6. Reading the Scriptures. Item, whether they do discourage any person from reading of any part of the Bible, either in Latin or English, and do not rather comfort and exhort every person to read the same at convenient times, as the very lively word of God, and the special food of man's soul.

7. Taverns and games. Item, whether parsons, vicars, curates, and other ministers, be common haunters and resorters to taverns or alehouses, giving themselves to drinking, rioting, and playing at unlawful games, and do not occupy themselves in the reading or hearing of some part of Holy Scripture, or in some other godly exercise.

8. Preachers. Item, whether they have admitted any man to preach in their cures, not being lawfully licensed thereunto, or have been licensed accordingly.

9. Superstition. Item, whether they use to declare to their parishioners anything to the extolling or setting forth of vain and superstitious religion, pilgrimages, relics, or images, or lighting of candles, kissing, kneeling, or decking of the same images.

10. Registers. Item, whether they have one book or register kept, wherein they write the day of every wedding, christening, and burying.

11. Obedience. Item, whether they have exhorted the people to obedience to the queen's majesty and ministers, and to charity and love one to another.

12. The Sacrament. Item, whether they have admonished their parishioners that they ought not to presume to receive the Sacrament of the Body and Blood of Christ, before they can say perfectly the Lord's Prayer, the Articles of Faith, and the Ten Commandments in English.

13. Hospitality. Item, whether they be resident upon their benefices, and keep hospitality or no. And if they be absent and keep no hospitality, whether do they relieve their parishioners, and what they give them.

14. Reparations. Item, whether proprietaries, parsons, vicars, and clerks having churches, chapels, and mansions do keep their chancels, rectories, vicarages, and all other houses, appertaining to them in due reparations.

Item, whether they do counsel or move their parishioners rather to pray in a tongue not known, than in English, or put their trust in any certain number of prayers, as in saying over a number of beads or other like. *15. Prayer in English. Beads.*

Item, whether they have received any persons to the communion being openly known to be out of charity with their neighbours, or defamed with any notorious crime, and not reformed. *16. Defamed persons.*

Item, whether they have provided and have a strong chest for the poor men's box, and set and fastened the same in a place of the church most convenient. *17. Poor men's box.*

Item, whether they have diligently called upon, exhorted, and moved their parishioners, and especially when they make their testaments, to give to the said poor men's box, and to bestow that upon the poor which they were wont to bestow upon pilgrimages, pardons, trentals, and upon other like blind devotions. *18. Testaments.*

Item, whether they have denied to visit the sick, or bury the dead, being brought to the church. *19. Sick burial.*

Item, whether they have bought their benefices, or come to them by fraud, guile, deceit, or simony. *20. Simony.*

Item, whether they have given open monition to their parishioners, to detect and present to their ordinary all adulterers and fornicators, and such men as have two wives living within their parishes. *21. Adulterers.*

Item, whether they have monished their parishioners openly that they should not sell, give, nor otherwise alienate any of their church goods. *22. Church goods.*

Item, whether they or any of them do keep more benefices and other ecclesiastical promotions than they ought to do, not having sufficient licences and dispensations thereunto, and how many there be, and their names. *23. Many benefices.*

Item, whether they minister the Holy Communion any other wise than only after such form and manner as it is set forth by the common authority of the queen's majesty and the Parliament. *24. Communion.*

Item, whether you know any person, within your parish or elsewhere, that is a letter of the word of God to be read in English, or sincerely preached in place and times convenient. *25. Letters of the word or preaching.*

Item, whether in the time of the Litany or any other common prayer in the time of the sermon or homily, and when the priest *26. Goers out of the church.*

CHAP. III readeth the Scriptures to the parishioners, any person have departed out of the church, without just and necessary cause, or disturb the minister otherwise.

27. Church money.
Item, whether the money coming or rising of any cattle or other movable stocks of the church, and money given and bequeathed to the finding of torches, lights, tapers, or lamps, not paid out of any lands, have not been employed to the poor men's chest.

28. Keepers of the church money.
Item, who hath the said stocks and money in their hands, and what be their names.

29. Contempt of priests.
Item, whether any indiscreet person do uncharitably contemn and abuse priests and ministers of the church.

30. The king's grammar.
Item, whether there be any other grammar taught in any school within this diocese than that which is set forth by the authority of King Henry the Eighth.

31. The time of service.
Item, whether the service of the church be done at due and convenient hours.

32. Talkers in church.
Item, whether any have used to commune, jangle, and talk in the church in the time of the prayer, reading of the homily, preaching, reading, or declaring of the Scripture.

33. Heresies.
Item, whether any have wilfully maintained and defended any heresies, errors, or false opinions, contrary to the faith of Christ and Holy Scripture.

34. Drunkards.
Item, whether any be common drunkards, swearers, or blasphemers of the name of God.

35. Adulterers.
Item, whether any have committed adultery, fornication, or incest, or be common bawds, or receivers of such evil persons, or vehemently suspected of any of the premises.

36. Brawlers.
Item, whether any be brawlers, slanderers, chiders, scolders, and sowers of discord between one person and another.

37. Sorcerers.
Item, whether you know any that do use charms, sorcery, enchantments, invocations, circles, witchcrafts, soothsaying, or any like crafts or imaginations invented by the devil, and specially in the time of women's travail.

38. Pulpits.
Item, whether the churches, pulpits, and other necessaries appertaining to the same be sufficiently repaired, and if they be not, in whose default the same is.

39. Resorters to other churches.
Item, whether you know any that in contempt of their parish church do resort to any other church.

40. Innholders.
Item, whether any innholders or alehouse-keepers do use com-

monly to sell meat and drink in the time of common prayer, preaching, reading of the homilies or Scripture.

Item, whether you know any to be married within the degrees prohibited by the laws of God, or that be separated or divorced without the degrees prohibited by the law of God, and whether any such have married again.

Item, whether do you know any to have made privy contracts of matrimony, not calling two or more witnesses thereunto, nor having thereto the consent of their parents.

Item, whether they have married solemnly, the banns not first lawfully asked.

Item, whether you know any executors or administrators of dead men's goods which do not duly bestow such of the said goods as were given and bequeathed or appointed to be distributed among the poor people, repairing of highways, finding of poor scholars, or marrying of poor maidens, or such other like charitable deeds.

Item, whether you know any that keep in their houses undefaced, any images, tables, pictures, paintings, or other monuments of feigned or false miracles, pilgrimages, idolatry, and superstition, and do adore them, and specially such as have been set up in churches, chapels, or oratories.

Item, what books of God's Scripture you have delivered to be burnt, or otherwise destroyed, and to whom you have delivered the same.

Item, what bribes the accusers, promoters, persecutors, ecclesiastical judges, and other the commissioners appointed within the several dioceses of this realm have received by themselves, or other of those persons which were in trouble, apprehended, or imprisoned for religion.

Item, what goods movable, lands, fees, offices, or promotions hath been wrongfully taken away in the time of Queen Mary's reign from any person which favoured the religion now set forth.

Item, how many persons for religion have died by fire, famine, or otherwise, and have been imprisoned for the same.

Item, that you make a true presentment of the number of all the persons which died within your parishes since the feast of St. John the Baptist, which was in the year of our Lord God 1558, unto the same feast last past; making therein a plain distinct declaration how many men, women, and men children the same were, and the names of the men.

Chap. III

51. Secret Masses. Item, whether you know any man in your parish secretly or in unlawful conventicles say or hear Mass, or any other service prohibited by the law.

52. False rumours. Unlawful books. Item, whether you know any person in your parish to be a slanderer of his neighbours, or a sower of discord between party and party, man and wife, parents and their children, or that hath invented, bruited, or set forth any rumours, false and seditious tales, slanders; or makers, bringers, buyers, sellers, keepers, or conveyors of any unlawful books, which might stir or provoke sedition, or maintain superstitious service within this realm; or any aiders, counsellors, procurers, or maintainers thereunto.

53. Patron. Tithes. Vacation. Item, whether the church of your parish be now vacant or no, who is the patron thereof, how long it hath been vacant, who doth receive the tithes, oblations, and other commodities during the time of the vacation, and by what authority, and in what estate the said church is at this time, and how long the parson or vicar hath had that benefice.

54. Minstrels. Item, whether any minstrels or any other persons do use to sing or say any songs or ditties that be vile or unclean, and especially in derision of any godly order now set forth and established.

55. Litany in English. Item, whether the Litany in English, with the Epistle and Gospel which was by the queen's highness's proclamation willed to be read to the people, were put in use in your churches; and if not, who were the letters thereof.

56. Distinct reading. Item, whether the curates and ministers do leisurely, plainly, and distinctly read the public prayers, chapters, and homilies as they ought to do.

GOD SAVE THE QUEEN.

CHAPTER IV

THE ROYAL VISITATION OF THE NORTHERN PROVINCE, 1559

WE have seen the preparations for the royal visitation which was to ensure the settlement of religion through the country. It is presumed that everything was ready at some time in the month of July, when in all probability notices were sent round to the various archdeacons, &c., announcing the fact and date of the approaching visitation. The royal visitors, together with the permanent Ecclesiastical Commission (which will be considered in a separate chapter for the sake of clearness[1]), were now the possessors of all ecclesiastical jurisdiction until fresh bishops were appointed in December to take the place of those who had been deprived. The country had been mapped out into six districts for the purposes of the visitation, and the whole of the Northern Province was assigned to one set of visitors. It will be convenient to take this first, as we have an excellent report of what was done.

The visitors for the north were Francis, Earl of Shrewsbury, President of the Council of the North; Edward, Earl of Derby; Thomas, Earl of Northumberland, Lord Warden of the East and Middle Marches; William, Lord Evers; Henry Percy, Thomas Gargrave, James Croftes, Henry Gates, knights; Edwin Sandys, D.D.; Henry Harvey, LL.D.; Richard Bowes, Christopher Estofte, George Browne,

Chap. IV — Arrangements complete in July, 1559.

Names of the visitors for the north.

---

[1] See below, Chap. VII.

Chap. IV

Richard Kingsmill, esquires. From the returns in the State Papers which give the names of those appointed lords lieutenant in the various counties[1] it appears that the noblemen on this and the other visitations held that or some similar office. They were not always in favour of the policy of the day, and, whether favourable or not, seldom took part in the work, their names being probably added in case of any disturbance, a contingency that did not occur in any known case. Of the rest, some were members of prominent county families: some were lawyers of position; on every commission there were one or more divines known to be favourable to the settlement. In the northern visitation Shrewsbury was not only President of the Council of the North, but Lord Lieutenant of Yorkshire; Derby was Lord Lieutenant of Chester and Lancaster; Northumberland, Warden of the East and Middle Marches, was Lord Lieutenant of Northumberland and the bishopric of Durham. Lord Evers and Henry Percy were captains respectively of Berwick and Norham Castle. Gargrave held the office of Vice-President of the Council of the North. The Lords Lieutenant of Cumberland and Westmoreland are significant omissions from the list as being disaffected. The former was Henry, Earl of Cumberland; the latter, Lord Dacres of Gilsland, about whom Bishop Best has bitter complaints to make[2].

Part taken by the visitors named.

The minimum number of visitors who could act was two; but, as we find from the proceedings, those present at each place were usually three, and sometimes four. The noblemen do not appear to have sat in the north, with the single exception of Lord Evers, who was present at the session held in Durham Chapter House on September 23. This was due probably to the large amount of business referred from other parts of the diocese. The burden of the work fell upon the shoulders of Sandys, Harvey, Gargrave, and Gates, who seem to have been present in all parts of the province. A special letter[3] was sent to Browne and

---

[1] S. P. Dom. Eliz. iv. 29, 30.   [2] Ibid. xviii. 21.   [3] Ibid. vi. 12.

Estofte on August 14. requiring their presence 'in the circuit northward,' 'at such time as the rest of the commissioners shall make their repair into the counties or diocese where you reside, and shall signify to you the time and place of their coming thither.' Accordingly we find that Estofte sat at Beverley on September 12, and Browne was with the visitors in the dioceses of Chester and Carlisle during October. They are spoken of as chosen for their 'knowledge of the common law of this realm.'

The original commission of visitation was dated June 24. We find from records in the Southern Province that after the visitors were appointed, an inhibition[1] was directed to the dean and chapter of each diocese. After reciting the terms of the commission with the names of the commissioners, the document inhibits the deans and chapters of the cathedrals, and all their registrars, officials, and ministers, from exercising any jurisdiction under penalty of contempt. It is natural to suppose that a similar notice was sent to the authorities of the four northern cathedrals. At all events the report, presently to be considered, shows that a special summons was addressed to the dean and chapter, or to the archdeacon, as the case might be, in which the clergy and people were summoned to be present on a particular day at a specified place. This was called the mandatory certificate, and at each new session evidence of its reception and promulgation was the first thing demanded by the visitors.

Issue of writs of inhibition.

Before tracing the progress of the visitors, it may be well to recall briefly the duties which they had to perform. Reference to the text of the letters patent will show the manifold details of these duties. Roughly, they may be comprised under two heads: (1) The visitors were to act as spiritual judges taking cognizance of all moral offences, and granting probate of wills, &c. (2) They were to enforce the settlement of religion, the 'suscepta religio' as it was called, and as it was set out in the Injunctions, and the Prayer Book of 1559, and established by the Act of Supremacy. With this in view they had power to deprive

Summary of the duties of the visitors.

[1] Regist. Dean and Chapt. Cant. at Lambeth, p. 4.

CHAP. IV

Narrative of the visitation.

and otherwise punish all recusant clergy; to institute to vacant benefices; to restore all who had been unjustly deprived. Such large and ample powers merit, perhaps, the criticism of Collier[1].

We are fortunate in possessing a fairly full account of all that the visitors did in the Northern Province. The letters patent had directed[2] that Thomas Percy and John Hodges should act as registrars for the due record of all the proceedings. This duty was faithfully carried out, and the result can be seen in a volume at the Public Records Office[3]. The narrative, prefaced with the full commission, is chiefly in Latin, and is excellently written. It was used by Burnet[4] for the terms of the commission which Cardwell[5] also copied. Strype[6] says: 'This commission I saw in the Queen's Paper House bound up in a volume in folio, containing all the Inquisitions and matters done and found in this large Northern Visitation.'

Nottingham.

The first place visited was St. Mary's, Nottingham, which was at that time in the diocese of York. The proceedings here are more or less typical of what went on at other places in the visitation. The account when translated is as follows: 'In the parish church of St. Mary in the town of Nottingham[7] in the diocese of York, Tuesday, August 22, in the year of our Lord 1559, and the first of the reign.

---

[1] vi. 262.

[2] See below, p. 92.

[3] The reference is S. P. Dom. Eliz. vol. x. This contains 400 pages. Bound up with it at the end is a book of the recognizances of clergy and others, with notes of their discharge. The contents of the report are as follows:—After the terms of commission an account is given of the visitation of the four dioceses, pp. 1-108. Then come 'acta et processus habiti et facti coram commissariis antedicto tempore visitationis regiae in et per totam provinciam Eboracensem in causis beneficiatorum et restitutionis beneficii,' &c., pp. 121-205. In this section there occurs, on pp. 183 sqq., a list of institutions made by the visitors. At p. 219 begins a summary of *Detectiones* and *Comperta*. At p. 371 occur the names of absentees from the visitation (infra, p. 83).

[4] See Burnet, *Hist. Ref.*, vol. ii. Coll. Book 3, Num. 7.

[5] See Cardwell, *Documentary Annals*, i. 247.

[6] Strype, *Ann.* i. 166.

[7] One or more (sometimes several) deaneries were represented at each place of visitation. The place was apparently determined by its relation to the archdeaconry, and by considerations of communication, and also by the size of the church.

On which date and place, prayers being ended, and the sacred word of God having been expounded to the people by the excellent man Master Edwin Sandys, D.D[1]., the aforesaid Edwin, together with Thomas Gargrave, Henry Gates, knights, and Henry Harvey, LL.D., repaired to a place duly made ready (*decenter ornatum*) in the chancel of the same church, and they, taking their seats there, received with all humility and proper reverence and obedience the letters commissional of our aforementioned most illustrious lady the Queen confirmed with the great seal, and they caused the same to be read publicly by Thomas Percy, the abovesaid notary public, scribe and registrar. They then straightway undertook the task of executing the same out of reverence and honour for so great a princess, and judicially determined to proceed, in accordance with the force, form, and effect of the same, to give all effect to the law, and so far as their jurisdiction appertained. Thereupon one Master Robert Cressye, official of the Archdeacon of Nottingham, appearing in person, brought in a citatory mandate addressed to him on the part of the aforesaid lady the Queen for summoning and citing the clergy and peoples of the deaneries of Nottingham to undergo the royal visitation at that time, along with a certificate of its execution, &c., and names and titles of all and singular summoned in that behalf, and further requisitions under lawful oath. The aforesaid commissioners caused all who were cited to be publicly preconized by name, and pronounced contumacious all who were summoned, preconized, and who did not appear.

---

[1] Sandys seems to have preached at Nottingham, Southwell, York, Hull, Durham, Newcastle, Carlisle, Richmond, Kendal, Manchester. Pilkington preached at Halifax, All Saints' York, and Wigan. Scambler preached (for there was power to appoint deputies) at St. Michael's York, Beverley, and Chester. These three men became bishops. At smaller places less eminent men were the preachers, e.g. R. Blunston at Blyth, R. Sewell at Auckland, J. Best at Northwich. The famous Bernard Gilpin (see p. 80) gave the sermon at Alnwick, doubtless because of his personal popularity in the Durham diocese. In Sandys' *Remains* there occurs a sermon very probably preached on this occasion at York, p. 235.

CHAP. IV

Returns furnished by churchwardens, &c.

'Thereafter, a learned exhortation having been addressed and held to the people by the aforementioned Master Edwin Sandys, they directed all the lay people, viz. the parishioners and churchwardens of any parish, after first touching the most holy Gospels of God, that after dinner at two o'clock they should furnish in writing their detections and answers on the Articles of Inquiry, along with the royal Injunctions, then read and given to them. The aforesaid lord commissioners likewise directed with firm injunction the rectors, vicars, chaplains, curates, and men without cure, being present, all and singular, that they personally appear at the said hour and place, to exhibit letters of orders, dispensations, and all other instruments as concerns each, and to do further what justice and equitable reason shall persuade. When the hour arrived, the aforesaid churchwardens and parishioners exhibited their bills of detections, along with the inventories of their church goods. Next they made careful examination of the condition, learning (*doctrina*), and conversation of the clergy and ecclesiastical persons, examining each one by himself, letters of orders and other documents having been exhibited by them.'

The order followed at Nottingham seems to have been copied at all other places in the visitation. The mass of business must have been enormous, and it is very difficult to understand how the commissioners dispatched the work that they had to do in the time that they allowed themselves. It will appear a little farther on that in one diocese, at all events, they had to appoint deputies to conclude what they had only begun.

Southwell.

The next session was held, August 24, at Southwell Minster for the deanery of Newark, and then in the Chapter House for the collegiate church on August 25. At the latter place five prebendaries put in no appearance, viz. W. Mowse, G. Dudley, G. Lambe, R. Snell, W. Saxye. On August 26 and 28 Blyth and Pontefract were visited for the deaneries of Retford and Laneham, of Doncaster and Pontefract respectively. At Halifax, on August 31,

Halifax.

another part of the deanery of Pontefract was visited. The commissioners were at Otley September 4, when Boies, Vicar of Gresley, Wood, Vicar of Otley, Wrigley, Vicar of Kildwick, and Jennynges, Vicar of Bingley, denied the royal supremacy. This brings us to an interesting point. Denial of the royal supremacy was regarded as a most serious offence. The recognizance was always less (e.g. £200, Marley of Durham) when that was allowed. Here Boies is eventually bound in a recognizance of £500 to appear before the Queen's commissioners residing in London. Most of these cases were decided at York, to which place they were referred. This postponement and reconsideration was usually allowed each recusant, and some of them gave in during the interval. Of the Southwell recusants, the other three were to come up whenever called upon, the living in each case being sequestered.

York was naturally a great centre, not only for the surrounding deaneries, but for the decision of cases referred during the previous fortnight from the various places of session. Accordingly we find that the visitation was held at the Chapter House September 6-9, at All Saints' September 7, at St. Michael's September 8, and at the Consistory Court on the 8th and 9th, the work being divided between Gargrave, Gates, Sandys, and Harvey. The cathedral chapter were summoned, and before those present Percy, the notary, read out 'distinctly' the form of subscription. Mr. John Rokesby, a member of the Council of the North, acted as spokesman for the chapter, and, says the record, 'ipse bono spiritu ductus, ut pauci arbitrantur, voluntarie subscripsit.' The form of oath taken by him and the rest of the conformist prebendaries is given in these words, which agree in general with the form used in the south : ' We, the clergy of the Cathedral and Metropolitical Church of York, whose names are subscribed, do humbly confess and acknowledge the restoring again of the ancient jurisdiction over the state ecclesiastical and spiritual to the crown of the realm, and the abolishing of all foreign power repugnant to the same, according to an oath thereof made in the late Parliament begun at Westminster the 23rd day of January, in the first year of the reign of our sovereign lady Queen Elizabeth, and there continued and kept until the 8th day of May next after ensuing. We confess also and acknowledge the administration of the Sacraments, the use and order of divine service in manner and form as it is set forth in the book commonly called the Book of Common Prayer, &c., established also by the same Act, and the orders and rules contained in the Injunctions given by the Queen's Majesty, and exhibited unto us in the present visitation, to be according to the true word of God, and agreeable to the doctrine of the primitive Church. In witness whereof, and that the premises be true, we have unfeignedly hereunto subscribed our names.' It will be seen, as pointed out in the last chapter, that this comprehensive form of subscription includes assent to the three crucial points, viz. the Supremacy Act, the Uniformity Act, and the Injunctions. The Uniformity Act was to be found at the beginning of the new Prayer Book as published in the preceding June, and so would be known to some extent. The Injunctions, however, had been presumably heard for the first time in their revised shape when Percy read them out in the morning of the day on which they were subscribed. The terms of the Supremacy Act had been in the mouths of all men.

Deprivations at York. Several of the York prebendaries put in no appearance at all, viz. J. Warren, Archdeacon of Cleveland, Alban Langdale, Arthur Lowe, J. Seaton, Peter Vannes, T. Arden, Geoffrey Morlaye, T. Clement, T. Cheston, G. Blithe. Four only of these, we shall find, were eventually deprived. Of those present two were deprived after repeated examination—G. Palmes and Roger Marshall; two had their benefices and promotions sequestered—Geoffrey Downes and Robert Pursglove, Bishop Suffragan of Hull; two were given a week to reconsider the matter, and were then ready to sign—Robert Bapthorp and G. Williamson. Reference to the list of those ultimately deprived shows which prebendaries persisted in refusal and were extruded. At the Consistory Court on September 9, H. More, Rector of St. Martin's Micklegate, York, and T. Jeffrison, Vicar of Ledesham, had their livings sequestered and were bound over to appear when called upon. The remaining places and dates from the diocese of York were these : Hull, September 11 ; Beverley, 12th; Malton, 14th; Northallerton, 17th. At the last of these, R. Salvyn, Rector of Hinderwell, refused subscription, and was referred to Durham on September 23.

The visitation of the diocese of Durham occupied what was left of September. The first session was held at Auckland on September 21. All the recusants were remanded to meet the commissioners at Durham, in the Chapter House. A special case was that of Dr. Robert Dalton, Canon of Durham, Vicar of Billingham and of Norton, the holder of valuable preferment. He is reported to have said 'That he believeth that he who sitteth in the seat of Rome hath and ought to have the jurisdiction ecclesiastical over all Christian realms.' Dalton was examined three times over, and was eventually deprived, together with Dr. Siggiswick, Vicar of Gainford. Dr. W. Bennet, Vicar of Aycliffe, and W. Whitehead, Vicar of Heighington, seem to have been deprived, but are not so traced in the Register. The Durham chapter were perhaps the most sturdy of all the cathedral chapters in resistance to the visitors. Dr. T. Robertson, the dean, was bound over in recognizances of £500 to appear in London. The following prebendaries were sequestered and bound over to appear either in the north or in London :— J. Cranforth, Stephen Marley, J. Tuttyn, Nich. Marley, G. Bullock, Ant. Salvyn, G. Clife. The final list will show that seven were deprived. Six minor canons were likewise bound over, as was the master of the Grammar School, W. Thewles. At St. Nicholas', Durham, on the following day, Dr. Carter, Archdeacon of Northumberland, was deprived. On the 27th the visitors sat at St. Nicholas', Newcastle. The place of session on the last day of

September was Alnwick. Here, in accordance with the liberty granted by the letters patent, the visitatorial powers were delegated to deputies 'for sufficient reasons.' Those who acted were Sir J. Foster, Bernard Gilpin, B.D., and W. Harrison, clk. The Northumbrian clergy seem to have been conformable, and there can be little doubt that in this attitude they were somewhat influenced by the example of Gilpin[1], who would be known to have subscribed himself, and whose position in the north would have great weight with the rest of the clergy.

Diocese of Carlisle.

The visitors began work in the diocese of Carlisle on October 3, after a week's rest from visiting, though not from travelling. The three places of meeting were the Chapter House, Carlisle, for the cathedral, on the 3rd; the cathedral, for the deaneries of Carlisle and Allerdale, on the 4th; Penrith parish church, for the deaneries of Cumberland and Westmoreland, on the 6th. There was very little opposition. In the Chapter House Dean Salkeld signed, 'voluntarie et bono animo,' with four canons and seven minor canons. The only apparent difficulty[2] was with Owen Hodgson, who was also Provost of Queen's College, Oxford. The visitation record does not mention him, but the earliest extant record in the Carlisle Register is the deed of his deprivation.

Appointment of assessors.

Reference to the terms of the commission shows that the

[1] It appears from the life of Bernard Gilpin, quoted by Strype, *Ann.* i. 166, that on the second day of the Durham visitation Gilpin had preached by special desire of the visitors, and that the subject assigned was the primacy of the Pope. The third and last day was that appointed for subscription. No one in the diocese was so well known or so highly respected as Gilpin : he was therefore first called upon to subscribe. There were, however, certain points which he scrupled, but 'he considered further that if he should refuse he should be a means to make many others refuse, and so consequently hinder the course of the word of God' (Strype, l. c.). Doubtless the subscription of this well-known Northumbrian carried with it the acquiescence of a very large number of the clergy in Durham diocese.

[2] Subscription in the diocese of Carlisle was almost universal, but the assent was somewhat feigned, as a letter from the bishop shows (S. P. Dom. July 19, 1561 (18, No. 21)). Lord Dacres shielded those who secretly sympathized with the old *régime*.

visitors had power to appoint assessors to help them in their work during the actual visitation, and also, if need were, to complete it after their departure. One such appointment we have been able to trace. In a document extant in Tunstall's Register at Durham, Roger Watson, D.D., and Bernard Gilpin, D.D., receive commission from Sandys, Harvey, and Browne to undertake all visitatorial power throughout the diocese of Durham as deputies of the said visitors. The commission includes summarily all the duties comprised in the original letters patent, and may be revoked at pleasure. One Christopher Clayton is named as registrar, and a full report is to be made when asked for. The document was sealed with the visitors' seal, and bore date October 8.

Gilpin, however, could not have begun his duties at once, for we find him with the visitors when they began operations for the diocese of Chester at Kendal on October 9, and at Lancaster on the 12th. A large part of the diocese as then constituted had already been visited three weeks earlier, viz. the deaneries of Richmond, Catterick, and Boroughbridge. The centre then selected had been Richmond, to which Sandys, Gates, and Harvey betook themselves from Northallerton, holding their session on September 18. Nothing of importance occurred there, or at any other place in the Chester diocese, until the commissioners came to Manchester on October 18 and 19. On the latter day they experienced slight opposition, when Richard Hart, a fellow of the Collegiate Church, refused to sign, and was cited to appear in London. Another, John Copage [1], absented himself. Next day another session was held at Northwich, and this proved to be the last, so far as the visitors proper were concerned. It appears from the returns of musters for 1559 that there was a great deal of sickness in England. The autumn weather had probably aggravated it, and so, 'because of the plague raging both in the city of Chester and the surrounding districts,' surrogates were appointed, viz. Sir E. Fytton, E. Scambler, B.D., and W. Morton, Esquire.

[1] Perhaps the Cubbage of Sanders' list, p. 228.

They sat at Tarvin on the 24th, and at Chester Cathedral on the 26th. They found a deplorable condition of things at the Cathedral. The see had been long vacant, and for two years there had been no dean. Of the prebendaries only two were resident. The church itself was so poor that even the servants of the cathedral could not be paid the wages due to them. It may be presumed that some of the non-resident canons appeared to answer their names: at all events no case of absence or refusal is noted.

Conclusion of the northern visitation. Our review of the northern visitation is now as complete as the materials allow. We shall consider in a later chapter its formal conclusion, but as that expressly permitted causes actually in progress to be completed, and as there were perhaps delegates appointed for the purpose in every diocese, we may suppose that a good deal of arrears had to be dispatched by these delegates after the visitation proper was over. The visitors had detected a certain amount of recalcitrance [1], which is noted in the report, but on the whole there is nothing to show any general disaffection of the people to the settlement of religion. Traces of local discontent and individual opposition will be considered later [2].

---

[1] Thus in the *Detectiones et Comperta* (f. 219), which are answers to the *Articles of Inquiry*, we find a few instances of reluctance to use the new prayer book. It must be remembered that these instances are given on the oath of churchwardens and parishioners. At St. Peter's, Nottingham, the curate had not used the Lord's Prayer, Belief, or Ten Commandments. This refers to the minimum of English prayer allowed by the proclamation of December, 1558. At Stoke the vicar had said no service since Midsummer. At Fishlake disturbance at prayers is noted. In York Cathedral 'the Gospel and Epistle are so read that no man can well understand.' At Radcliffe the clergyman 'does not read the Epistle and Gospel with the Litany according to the proclamation.' The same presentment is made elsewhere. In one or two places it is said that the Bible and prayer books belonging to the church in Edward's time had been burned. It might seem from one or two of the notes given above that the new prayer book had not found its way into some churches by the time the visitation began. Scarcity of prayer books on the borders of Wales had been noted on June 25, by Sir Hugh Poulet to Cecil, but two months had intervened since then.

[2] It is material to notice that a good many livings are returned as vacant. In the Diocese of York: Winthorpe, Edinge, Drayton, Fledborough, Thorne, Campsall, Maltby, Darfield, Huddersfield, Drypool, Keyingham, Ellerker, Raskelf, Folkton, Lythe, Annesley, Bonyne, Aponborough, Hoveringham, Lenton,

VISITATION OF THE NORTHERN PROVINCE

It remains now to add a list of the clergy who absented themselves from the visitation in the northern province. At this stage they were merely absentees, and were pronounced contumacious: we shall see what proportion of them eventually acquiesced in the changes.

I.

NAMES OF ABSENTEES FROM THE VISITATION[1].

[An asterisk denotes subsequent deprivation.]

Diocese of York[2].

Name of Person.	Name of Cure.	Name of Person.	Name of Cure.
Apeleye, Robt.	Beckingham.	Burgyn, J.	Mytton.
Arsleye, W.	South Scarle.	*Bury, W.	Kirkby in Cleveland.
Askam, Anth.	Methley.		
		Byas, Robt.	Wighill.
Barnbye, T.	Elmley.		
Barne, T.	Sessay.		
Barton, Jas.	Gringley.	Calverd, W.	Etton.
Bagley, Robt.	Attenborough.	Cayle, T.	Thormanby.
Bell, W.	Kirkburn.	Cleving, Robt.	Goodmanham.
Besakell, J.	Mappleton.	Cockeson, T.	Tankersley.
Borrow, T.	Holy Trinity, York, cur.	Coseleye, W.	South Collingham.
Brodebente, Jas.	Crofton.	Cowper, W.	Saxton, cur.
Brogden, W.	Wormsley and Birkin.	Creton, Jas.	Bugthorpe.
		Crofte, Vincent.	Hemsworth.

Stapleford, Scarrington, Edingley, Northcleston, Tuxford, Bawtry, East Retford, Stockwith, Sturton, Kirk Sandall, Wolley, Hickleton, St. Olave's York, Bilborough, East Ralsey—35 in all. In the Diocese of Durham: Ashe, Whitburn, Heighington. In the Diocese of Carlisle: Skelton and Kirk Andrews. In the Diocese of Chester: Sandbach, Macclesfield (unserved for four years), Clitheroe. Thus, besides livings sequestered, at least forty-three are returned as vacant, or as the phrase is, 'destituta curato.' There is some reason for believing that these lists for Carlisle and Chester are imperfect.

[1] We take it that the following list, which we have rearranged alphabetically from the report, f. 371, &c., represents all clerical absentees, whatever the cause of their absence, from the visitation.

[2] There were more than 600 clergy in the Diocese of York. A list of 1592 gives 634 (Lambeth, *Cart. Misc.* xii. 9. Thus perhaps a quarter of the total number were absent.

84   THE ELIZABETHAN CLERGY

CHAP. IV

Name of Person.	Name of Cure.	Name of Person.	Name of Cure.
Dacye, J.	Fockton.	Jackson, Brian.	Sandal Magna.
Dalisson, Roger.	Clayworth.	Jake, J.	Topcliffe.
Dene, Reg.	North Cave, cur.	Jakeson, J.	Acklam.
Diconson, Laur.	Brotherton.	*Jakeson, J.	Bulmer.
Donnaye, Vincent.	Sutton, cur.	Johnson, Jas.	St. Laurence, York.
Durham, J.	Foston, cur.		
		Keye, H.	Scawby.
Ellys, Stephen (Ludimr.)	Skipton.	Lane, G.	South Wheatley.
		Lecetor, Oliver.	Bingham.
*Ellys, W.	Hutton Cranswick.	Leither, T.	All Saints, York.
		Lodge, Geoff.	Normanton.
Ellys, W.	Adlingfleet.	Luddington, T.	Rolleston.
		Lyster, J.	Holme.
Fishborn, R.	North Muskham.	Machell, Philip.	Strensall.
Fishe, J.	Broughton.	Malberye, J.	Halton, near Newark.
Fisher, G.	Harworth.		
Fisher, J.	Welwicke.	Malevery, H.	Thurnscoe.
Fugall, T.	Lowthorpe.	Mallet, Fras.	Swillington.
		Markindale, T.	Willerbye.
Garnett, W.	Crayke.	Maxwell, Anth.	Ainsby.
Gledle, Hugh.	Huddersfield.	Mershall, J.	Misterton.
Gowland, J.	Ingleby Green[how], cur.	Mershall, J.	Kilnwick.
		Mershe, W.	Mattersey.
Gowle, W.	Roos, cur.	More, W.	Colston Bassett.
Green, J.	Badsworth.	Mores, W.	Bishops Hull.
Greyne, T.	Barwick, cur.	Myddelton, Robt.	Crambe, cur.
Hagger, J.	Rothwell.		
Hall, T.	Long Preston.	Newsome, J.	Hutton-Buscel.
Harde, R.	Garton, cur.	Norfolk, J.	Monk-Frystone, cur.
Harrison, J.	Halifax.		
Harrison, J.	Snaith, cur.	Normavell, J.	Alston and Broughton.
Harte, W.	Thornton.		
Hayward, R.	Sheffield.	Nutte, W.	Rawmarsh.
Herling, E.	East Drayton.		
Heworthe, J.	Huntington.	Otbye, E.	Terrington.
Holmes, W.	Escrick.	Otford, Robt.	Otterington.
Hopkinson, T.	Owthorne.	Oton, J.	Egmanton.
Houghton, W.	Appleton.	Owen, David.	Stangrave.
Huainson, Laur.	Rothwell.	Peerson, J.	Warsop.
Huntington, T.	Aldwark.	Percy, Alan.	Spofforth.
Huyson, J.	Swine.	Perpoincte, W.	Cotgrave.

Name of Person.	Name of Cure.	Name of Person.	Name of Cure.
Pickard, W.	Rampton.	Taylor, G.	Methley, cur.
Poisegate, J.	Salton.	Taylor, W.	Birdsall.
Preston, T.	—— cur.	Teesdale, Marmaduke.	Thormanby, cur.
Prise, H.	North Leverton.		
Purkin, W.	Goxhill, cur.	Thompson, R.	
		Thornley, J.	Worksop.
Raignold, J.	Aubourn, cur.	Thurland, E.	Clifton.
Rayner, Ch.	Kilburn, cur.	Thurland, T.	Cromwell and Gamston.
Richardson, J.	Finningley.		
Ringrose, Robt.	South-Dalton.	Thwaits, J.	Kirkby.
Robinson, Abraham.	Huggate.	Turner, Robt.	Brayton.
		Twenge, Robt.	Welton.
Rokebye, W.	Marske.	Tyndall, Edmund.	Gillingly.
Rowlinge, Arth.	Haworth, cur.		
Rudde, J.	Riston.		
		Vavizer, T.	Garforth.
Sandforthe, Ch.	Hawksworth.		
Shaw, H.	Nidd.	Ustler, Ch.	Elvington.
Shipman, T.	Thorpe in the Glebe.		
		Walker, R.	Great Leake.
Silles, Peter.	Sprotborough.	Walker, Roger.	Elland.
Skelton, W.	Hovingham, cur.	*Washington, T.	Fledborough.
		Watson, T.	Sherburn.
Smythson, W.	Upper Helmsley.	Waynehouse, J.	Kirksmeaton.
		Westcrope, Ralph.	Salton.
Snytall, R.	Normanton.		
Sowthill, H.	Kirkburton.	Wetherall, W.	Epperstone and Lancham.
Stafford, Leonard.	Carlton.		
Stalinge, Robt.	Langtoft.	Wheatley, Jas.	Barton.
Stampe, E.	Wressle.	Wiclife, Anth.	Kirkby in Ashfield.
Staneley, T.	Dunnington.		
Stapleton, R.	Ormesby.	*Wilson, T.	Arncliffe.
Stevenson, Martin.	Speeton.	Wood, R.	Sandby.
		Wormmall, E.	Burnholme.
Stubbes, Edmund.	Widmerpool.	Wright, T.	Walkington.
		Wyngrene, Edmund.	Bole.
Suell, Robt.	Westlow.		
Swane, T.	Tadcaster.		
Symson, J.	Hawnby.	Yarrowe, Miles.	Riccall.

Diocese of Durham[1].

Name of Person.	Name of Cure.	Name of Person.	Name of Cure.
Barrowe, Anth.	Warden, cur.	Mawen, N.	Warden, stip.
*Baynes, Brian.	Eaglescliff.	Mershall, R.	Corbridge.
Bell, W.	Middleton-in-Teesdale.		
		Ogle, T.	Sheepwash.
Collinwood, W.	Ford.	*Passe, R.	Bothal.
Crawforth, R.	Billingham, cur.	Peterson, Robt.	Sockburn, cur.
Daker, J.	Morpeth.	Ranys, J.	West Spittle (warden).
Ellison, Cuthbert.	Masindewe.	Rayne, G.	Cockfield, cur.
Eltringham, Ralph.	Corbridge, cur.	Robinson, G.	Newburn.
Foster, J.	Edmundbyers.	Sare, J.	Elton, cur.
Foster, N.	Brancepeth.	Selbye, Oliver.	Tynemouth.
		Semer, J.	Stranton.
Halman, T.	Masindewe.	Sheppard, W.	Darlington, cur.
Halman, T.	Ponteland.	Sparke, T.	Wolsingham.
*Hartburn, R.	Longnewton.	Stevenson, W.	Eaglescliff, cur.
Hymners, G.	Alnham.	Tesedale, Robt.	Knaresdale.
Lakynby, Jas.	Stranton.	Thomson, T.	Houghton.
Lewen, Gilbert.	Masindewe. (Master of St. Mary's Hospital.)	Trowtbecke, E.	Morpeth, cur.
		Watson, J.	Muggleswick, cur.
Lewes, Ch.	Chollerton, cur.	Watson, W.	Bedlington.

Diocese of Carlisle[2].

Name of Person.	Name of Cure.	Name of Person.	Name of Cure.
Barton, G.	Cliburn, cur.	Bowman, Stephen.	Renwick, cur.
Barton, Hugh.	Barton, cur.		
Bell, E.	Denton.	Brandlinge, Ralph.	Thursby.
Benson, J.	Dufton, cur.		

---

[1] This list gives 35 absentees. There were some 180 clergymen in the diocese (Harl. MS. 594, f. 186).

[2] The total number is 35 out of more than 100 clergy. Cf. Harl. MS. 595, f. 85. Bishop Best speaks somewhat later (S. P. Dom. xviii. 21, July 19, 1561) of the outward conformity of the clergy, but says 'only fear maketh them obedient.'

Name of Person.	Name of Cure.	Name of Person.	Name of Cure.
Burye, W.	Marton.	Nevill, G.	Bolton.
Crakinthorpe, Mighell.	Kirkby-Thore.	Nicolson, Jas.	Ireby, cur.
		Nutthide, Robt.	Kirkby-Thoro, cur.
Dane, J.	Greystoke.	Place, R.	Orton.
Dawson, Adam.	Barton, stip.	Porter, W.	Plumbland.
Gargate, W.	Warcop, cur.	Ratclif, J.	Crosthwaite.
Harrison, J.	Bampton, cur.	Riverney, T.	Kirk Andrews.
*Hodgeson, Hugh.	Skelton.	Robinson, J.	Bowness.
		Scales, J.	Kirkoswald.
Hogeson, R.	Thursby, cur.	Shaltild, Robt.	Shap, cur.
Kirkebecke, J.	Musgrave.	Smythe, T.	Barton.
Knyppe, E.	Cliburn.	*Thompson, Robt.	Beaumont.
Levagies, Launcelot.	Crosthwaite, stip.	Threlket, Roland.	Dufton.
		Towson, R.	Hutton.
		Twentyman, T.	Orton, cur.
Murrey, J.	Burgh, cur.	Vanes, Peter.	Kirkby-Stephen.
Murrey, Launcelot.	Crosthwaite, stip.		

Diocese of Chester [1].

Name of Person.	Name of Cure.	Name of Person.	Name of Cure.
Ambros, Elizeus.	Ormskirk.	Brocke, Robt.	Aldingham.
		Broke, Jas.	Wilmslow, cur.
Apowell, Hugh.	Astbury.	Buckleye, T.	Cheadle.
Backehouse, J.	Aysgarth.	Charleton, Alan.	Tarporley.
Ballarde, Robt.	Sephton.	Charleton, W.	Bangor.
Barker, W.	Arlesdon, cur.	Clarke, T.	Mobberley, cur.
Baven, R.	Whitegate.	Collingwood, W.	Christleton.
Beckewith, Ch.	Barneston.	Copeland, Nic.	Haile.
Bell, Dd.	Moor Monkton, cur.	Davison, Jas.	Mobberley.
		Davye, T.	Backford.
Braithwayte, Mich.	Whitbecke, cur.	Dickenson, E.	Little Ouseburn.
		Dickenson, T.	Aldingham, stip.

---

[1] The return gives 90 names of absentees, and as there were perhaps 250 clergy in the diocese, cf. Harl. MS. 594, f. 146, the proportion is higher than in Carlisle and Durham.

Name of Person.	Name of Cure.	Name of Person.	Name of Cure.
Dickeson, J.	Wathe, cur.	*Parcevall, Robt.	Ripley.
Dickson, T.	Wybunbury, stip.	Parr, R.	Brigham.
		Philipe, Ralph.	Hanmer.
Dowson, W.	Grinton.	Pirrey, E.	Aldingham, stip.
Ducks, Chas.	St. Mary, Chester.	Plante, Robt.	Swettenham.
		Pockeson, J.	Farnham.
Dudley, Arthur.	Malpas (rector of a moiety).	Prestland, P.	Soulby.
		Redshawe, Robt.	Gt. Ouseburn.
Ellerkar, J.	Cundall.	Robinson, J.	Ashton.
Gardener, Robt.	Aldingham, cur.	Roper, H.	Ince, cur.
Gascoyne, W.	Stanley.	Sell, Leon.	Aldingham, stip.
Graye, W.	Kirkby on the Moor.	Seller, Jas.	Wathe.
		Sheppard, Simon.	Davenham.
Grindall, J.	St. Bees, cur.		
Halsall, H.	Halsall, cur.	Smyth, T.	Brearton.
Halsall, R.	Halsall.	Sodor, Bishop of,	Wigan.
Harris, R.	Hawkshead, cur.	Stanley, T.	Winwick.
Hawson, J.	Rochdale, cur.	Stringer, W.	Gosforthe.
Helme, J.	Patrick Brompton.	Sudall, H.	Barrow.
		Swayne, R.	Goostree, cur.
Hill, W.	Malpas (rector of a moiety).	Sympson, Ch.	Kirkby-Fleetham.
Hindmere, Reg.	Wensley.	Syngilton, T.	Hawkshead, stip.
Jagger, Fras.		Tassye, T.	Wallasey.
		Thomlinson, Roger.	Askrigg.
Kellett, Hugh.	Hawkshead, stip.	Tobman, W.	Muncaster, cur.
Kynsey, Robt.	Barthomley.	Towreson, W.	Whicham.
Ladd, Robt.	Harrington.	Tunstall, J.	[W.] Tanfield.
Lambe, G.	Copgrove.	Wadforthe, J.	Kirklington.
Langfellowe, R.	Arkendale.	Wainwrighte, Chas.	Leyland.
Lee, W.	Gawsworth.		
Lemyng, T.	Croston,	Walker, J.	Plemstall.
Longleye, W.	Prestwich.	Walker, R.	Kirby.
Lowe, Arth.	Stockport.	Warde, R.	Hawkshead, stip.
Mershall, Robt.	Aldburgh.	Woddye, J.	Eccleston.
Mollyneux, Anth.	Walton.	Wooddall, H.	Brigham, [? cur.]
		Woode, Math.	Wybunbury.
Morecrofte, E.	Aikton.	Wybram, W.	Aldford.
		Wyneslowe, Ralph.	Tattenhall.
Nelson, Robt.	Prescott, cur.		
Olyver, J.	Baddiley.	Ylkins, —	Bedale.

Restitutions of those previously deprived[1] in the Northern Province.

Restored.	Benefice.	Removed.
Ant. Blake.	Whiston.	J. Atkinson.
W. Soorye.	Sedbergh.	T. Atkinson.
W. Denman.	Ordsall.	Rob. Blunston.
J. Rudd.	Preb. Durham.	G. Bullock.
W. Latimer.	Kirby in Cleveland.	W. Bury.
R. Baldwyn.	S. Nich. Hosp., Richmond.	W. Bury.
T. Atkinson.	Elwick.	G. Clife.
W. Soorye.	Urswick.	T. Dobson.
T. Whytbee.	Hutton.	W. Ellys.
Percival Wharton.	Bridekirk.	W. Gray.
J. Horleston.	Archdn. Richmond.	J. Hanson.
J. Adams.	Hocherton.	T. Huddleston.
Ant. Blake.	Doncaster.	J. Hudson.
G. Taylor.	Bulmer.	J. Jackson.
W. Harrison.	Bothal.	Rob. Pates.
Marm. Pulleyn.	Ripley.	Rob. Percival.
Edw. Sandys.	Eversham.	J. Redman.
Ant. Holgate.	Burnsall.	R. Summerscale.
Chris. Sugden.	Newark.	J. Taversham.
Rob. Wisdom.	Setterington.	J. Thornton.
Ol. Columben.	Stainford.	Eliz. Umfrye.
T. Atkinson.	Ormside.	J. Yates.

II.

LETTERS PATENT DIRECTING THE NORTHERN VISITATION OF 1559[2].

[Transcr. from S. P. Dom. Eliz. x. p. 1.]

Elizabetha Dei gratia Angliae, Franciae, et Hiberniae Regina, Fidei Defensor, charissimis consanguineis et consiliariis nostris, Francisco Comiti de Salope Domino Presidenti Consilii nostri in

The Queen greets the Commissioners herein named.

---

[1] This list is taken from the Report, f. 121, and the names are chiefly those of clergymen who had been deprived under Queen Mary, on the ground of their marriage. See the provision in the Commission, p. 92.

[2] This document is given in the Report, but is not to be traced in the Patent Rolls.

CHAP. IV — partibus borealibus, et Edwardo Comiti de Darbia, ac charissimo consanguineo nostro Thomae comiti Northumbriae Domino Guardiano sive custodi marchiarum nostrarum de le Estmarche et Mydlemarche versus Scotiam, ac praedilecto et fideli nostro Willelmo Domino Evers; ac etiam dilectis et fidelibus nostris Henrico Percy, Thomae Gargrave, Jacobo Croftes, et Henrico Gates militibus : necnon dilectis Edwino Sandys, S.T.D., Henrico Harvy, LL.D., Ricardo Bowes, Christophoro Estofte, Georgio Browne, et Ricardo Kingsmyll Armigeris—salutem.

It being the Queen's office to spread true religion and pure worship, she determines to visit the realm;

Quoniam Deus populum suum Anglicanum imperio nostro subjecit, hujus regalis suscepti muneris rationem perfecte reddere non possumus nisi veram religionem et sincerum numinis Divini cultum in omnibus regni nostri partibus propagaverimus: nos igitur, regalis et absolutae pietatis nostrae nobis in hoc regno nostro commissae respectu, quoniam utrumque regni nostri statum, tam ecclesiasticum quam laicum, visitare et certas pietatis et virtutis regulas illis praescribere constituimus, praefatos [here follow the names as above given] ad infrascripta, vice nomine et auctoritate nostris, exequendum, vos quattuor, tres, aut duo vestrum ad minimum,

and deputes the aforesaid: (1) to visit all churches in the Northern Province both clergy and people;

deputamus et substituimus ad visitandum igitur tam in capite quam in membris Ecclesias Cathedrales Civitates et Dioceses Eboracen. Dunelmen. Carliolen. et Cestren., necnon quascunque alias collegiatas, parochiales, et prebendales ecclesias, ac loca alia ecclesiastica quaecunque, tam exempta quam non exempta, in et per easdem civitates et dioceses ubilibet constituta; clerumque et populum

(2) to inquire into the state of churches and places, and the lives of the clergy;

earundem in eisdem degentem sive residentem; deque statu ecclesiarum et locorum hujusmodi, necnon vita, moribus, et conversatione, ac etiam qualitatibus personarum in ecclesiis et locis praedictis, degentium sive ministrantium, modis omnibus quibus id melius aut efficacius poteritis, inquirendum et investigandum;

(3) to deprive criminous and recusant clerks, or to punish them by sequestration, &c., in order to correct them;

criminosos ac susceptae religioni subscribere obstinate et peremptorie recusantes, vel quocunque alio modo delinquentes atque culpabiles condignis poenis etiam usque ad beneficiorum, dignitatum, sive officiorum suorum privationem, fructuumve, reddituum, et proventuum ecclesiarum et locorum quibus praesunt sequestrationem—vel quamcunque aliam congruam et competentem coercitionem, inclusive puniendum, et corrigendum, atque ad probatiores vivendi mores, modis omnibus quibus id melius et efficacius poteritis, reducendum;

(4) to grant probate of

Testamenta quoruncunque defunctorum infra loca praedicta decedentium probandum, approbandum, et insummandum; administrationesque bonorum eorundem executoribus in eisdem testamentis nominatim committendum; administrationesque insuper ac sequestrationes bonorum abintestato decedentium, in debita juris forma expediendum, concedendum, et committendum; comperta quoque, tam executorum quam administratorum, et sequestratorum quoruncunque, recipiendum, examinandum, et admittendum, ac insuper, eosdem executores, administratores, et sequestratores, omnes et singulos, acquietandum, relaxandum, et finaliter dimittendum; causasque instantiarum quascunque examinandum et finaliter terminandum; contumaces autem et rebelles, cujuscunque conditionis sive status fuerint, si quos inveneritis, tam per censuras ecclesiasticas quam personarum apprehensionem ac incarcerationem ac recognitionum acceptionem, ac quaecunque alia juris regni nostri remedia compescendum; necnon Injunctiones praesentibus annexas personis in eisdem nominatis nomine nostro tradendum, aliasque injunctiones congruas et opportunas, vice et auctoritate nostris eis indicendum, et assignandum, poenasque convenientes in earum violatores infligendum et irrogandum; Ecclesias etiam et alia loca dimissas vacare et pro vacantibus habendas fore decernendum et declarandum, pensionesque legitimas congruas et competentes cedentibus vel resignantibus hujusmodi assignandum et limitandum; Praesentationes quoque ad beneficia ecclesiastica quaecunque infra civitates ecclesias aut dioceses praedictas constituta, durante visitatione nostra hujusmodi, si habiles fuerint et idonei, ad eadem admittendum, ac in et de eisdem instituendum et investiendum cum suis juribus et pertinentiis universis, eosque in realem actualem et corporalem possessionem eorundem inducendum, et induci faciendum, atque mandandum; necnon clericorum et beneficiatorum quoruncunque, tam pro ordinibus quam beneficiis per eos adeptis, literas et instrumenta exigendum et recipiendum, eaque diligenter examinandum et discutiendum, et quos non sufficienter munitos in ea parte comperitis ab officio dimittendum, et pro sic non munitis declarandum et pronunciandum; synodos quoque et capitula, tam generalia quam specialia cleri et populi hujusmodi, pro executione praemissorum aut reformatione quacunque, faciendum et convocandum; procurationes et synodalia ratione hujus nostrae visitationis debitas petendum exigendum et levandum, ac etiam non solventes aut solide recusantes per censuras ecclesiasticas compellendum, coercendum, et cogendum; necnon contionandi potestatem hujusmodi personis concedendum quas ad hoc divinum munus sus-

CHAP. IV

wills and administration of goods, and letters of administration for intestates;

(5) to restrain the contumacious and recalcitrant by censure, imprisonment, or recognizance;

(6) to deliver the injunctions annexed and others if necessary, with suitable penalty;

(7) to declare all vacancies and to assign pensions to the deprived;

(8) to receive presentations, to institute, and to induct during the visitation;

(9) to examine letters of orders and certificates of institution, removing doubtful cases;

(10) to summon synods and chapters of clergy and people;

(11) to exact fees for this visitation, to censure and commit recusants.

CHAP. IV

(12) to commission fit preachers.
(13) to examine and restore in cases of unlawful imprisonment.
(14) to examine and restore in cases of unlawful deprivation;
(15) to have full power of action in all matters as necessity requires.

Power too is given to appoint assessors who shall execute all orders and articles, even when the visitation is over, summoning those who contravene them, and determining all complaints, remitting them to the permanent commissioners in London.
All local authorities are bidden to assist in carrying out the premises.
For due record of all that shall be done, two notaries public are appointed,

cipiendum aptas esse judicaveritis; incarceratos et vinculis commissos ob religionis tam antea licet nulliter condempnatos, causis incarcerationis et condempnationis hujusmodi prius examinatis et plenarie discussis, examinandum discutiendum ac in integrum, justicia id suadente, restituendum, deliberandum et extra prisonam dimittendum; necnon causas deprivationum examinandum et contra statuta et ordinationes hujus regni nostri Angliae vel juris ecclesiastici ordinem deprivatos restituendum; ac omnia et singula alia quae circa hujusmodi visitationis seu reformationis vigorem necessaria fuerint seu quomodolibet opportuna, etiam si verba magis specialia de se exigunt et requirunt, faciendum et expediendum—vobis tribus aut duobus vestrum, ut praefertur, de quorum eminenti doctrina, morumque et consilii gravitate, ac in verbis gerendis fide et industria plurimum confidimus, vices nostras committimus, ac plenam in Domino, tenore praesentium, concedimus facultatem, cum cujuslibet congruae et legitimae coercitionis potestate, et praeterea certos viros prudentes ac pios assignandi et nominandi, per quos de statu rerum instruemini et quorum opera praesentes utemini in omnibus causis ad hanc visitationem nostram spectantibus, quantum vobis convenire videbitur. Idem viri a vobis commissariis assignati et nominati plenam potestatem habebunt, etiam post commissionis decessum et post finitum visitationis tempus, de omnibus articulis, ordinibus, et institutis ejusdem visitationis inquirendi, et violatores eorum cujuscunque conditionis fuerint conveniendi et examinandi, et omnes querelas, quatenus ullum impedimentum aut offensionem nostrae visitationis continebunt, accipiendi et audiendi, et hujusmodi personas, offensiones, et querelas, commissariis nostris Londini residentibus, et ad ecclesiasticarum rerum reformationem designatis, praesentabunt et exhibebunt, illis viis et modis quibus hoc convenientissime videbunt fieri posse: Mandantes omnibus et singulis majoribus, vicecomitibus, justiciariis, et quibuscunque aliis officiariis, ministris, et subditis nostris, quatenus vobis in et circa praemissorum executionem effectualiter assistant, auxilientur, et suffragentur. Ut insuper sagacitatis, diligentiae, factorumque vestrorum omnium evidens et perpetuum specimen nobis posterisque nostris remaneat, inventaque et invenienda pro recordatorum defectu debitam reformationem correctionemve non subterfugiant, aut e memoria prolabantur, nos suprema ac regali auctoritate nostra praedicta dilectos et fideles subditos nostros Thomam Percy et Johannem

Hoges, et eorum deputatos, per commissarios nostros approbandos notarios publicos preantea legitime existentium actorum, instrumentorum, decretorum, sententiarum, judiciorum, censurarum, ceterorumque omnium et singulorum quae per vos vestrumve aliquem in visitatione hac nostra regia peragentur, judicabuntur, decernentur, fient, ferentur, et pronunciabuntur, scribas et registrarios nostros publicos et principales conjunctim et divisim ordinamus, nominamus, et constituimus, eisque officium et officia registrari et scribae nostri publici, cum omnibus officia praedicta tangentibus, eorumque deputatis per dictos commissarios approbandis conjunctim et divisim damus, deputamus, assignamus, et decernimus per praesentes.

In cujus rei testimonium has literas nostras fieri fecimus patentes. Teste me ipsa apud Westmonasterium vicesimo quarto die Junii anno regni nostri primo.

Chap. IV with assistants, who shall be approved by the commissioners. Dated at Westminster, June 24, 1559.

CHAPTER V

THE SOUTHERN VISITATION, 1559

CHAP. V
Our materials for the Southern Visitation.

IN the absence of the official report, which has not survived for the visitation of the Southern Province, the presumption is that the proceedings correspond very closely with those which we have traced in the four northern dioceses. Some few particulars and allusions have been collected, and we are able to supply a list, not here of absentees, but of those who signed the form of acceptance in several dioceses. From these lists we shall be able in some cases to get an approximate estimate of those who at this stage embraced the new *régime*, though we shall not feel absolutely certain of the result, as it is highly probable that many benefices were vacant at the time of the visitation[1].

1. London, Norwich, and Ely.

London, Norwich, and Ely were combined for the purposes of visitation. The letters patent may be understood to have been issued with those for the Northern Province, on or about June 24. Strype gives August 21 as the date, but he has confused a writ[2] of the visitors bearing that date and directed to the Court of Audience of Canterbury. The visitors appointed were Sir Nicholas Bacon, Thomas Duke of Norfolk, John Earl of Oxford, Francis Earl of Bedford, Thomas Lord Wentworth, Edward Lord North, Lord John Gray; Thomas Parry, Ralph Sadler, Anthony Cook, Thomas Wroth, Thomas Smith, Edmund Wyndham, Christopher Heydon, William Woodhouse, Knights;

---

[1] See above, p. 82, note 2. [2] From Parker's Register.

Richard Gooderick and Avinus Hopton, Esquires; Robert Horne, D.D., Thomas Huyck, LL.D., John Salvyn, Lawyer. The same principle of choice is observable here as in the former commission. Sir Nicholas Bacon was Lord Keeper of the Great Seal; the Duke of Norfolk, Earl Marshal, Lord Lieutenant of Norfolk, Suffolk, and the city of Norwich; the Earl of Oxford was Lord Lieutenant of Essex, which was at that time in the diocese of London; Lord North held the same office for Cambridgeshire. The Earl of Bedford was apparently added for political reasons, as being one of the most trusted of the Queen's counsellors. He was a great favourer of the Swiss reformers, and in the Zurich letters some of his correspondence is preserved. It must however be emphasized that the visitors do not as a rule appear to have been chosen on account of their religious opinions. The only exception is in the case of the divines who accompanied the visitors as preachers: they were in every instance in sympathy with the principles of the settlement. It was the business of the others to administer that settlement and to do nothing else.

The places of session we can follow from the list of signatories to which reference has been made, and Strype has preserved some record of what was done in London. The proceedings began in the Chapter House of St. Paul's on August 11, and the report follows very closely the procedure in the north. The cathedral clergy largely absented themselves when the Articles of Inquiry and the Injunctions were delivered. Next day, when subscription was demanded, John and Nicholas Harpsfeld, Willerton and others, refused to sign, and, their benefices being sequestered, they were remanded until the conclusion of the visitation. What then took place in regard to these and the absentees we shall see later.

Proceeding from St. Paul's, the visitors sat at other churches in London as centres for the various deaneries. Thus we find them at the Hospital of the Savoy, where one or two of the Prebendaries of St. Paul's seem to have changed their mind, and to have subscribed, a proceeding

Chap. V which finds a parallel in other dioceses. Indeed it seems certain that every opportunity for signing was given to those who at first refused or hesitated. At the parish church of Clerkenwell the signatures were received of the clergy of Islington, Enfield, Edmonton, and other villages in North Middlesex. St. Margaret's Westminster, St. Bride's, St. Lawrence Jewry, St. Michael's Cornhill, were the other places of session for Middlesex. The visitors reached the last-named church on St. Bartholomew's Eve, and there received the Inventory of the goods of St. Paul's Cathedral. For that part of the diocese of London which lay in Essex and Hertfordshire, sessions were held at Weald, Chelmsford, Stortford, Dunmow, Colchester. In this way the whole of the diocese of London was completed by about the end of August. The rapidity of the movements of the visitors suggests that they were very probably obliged to appoint assessors, or to reserve very largely for the Permanent Commissioners in November: they could not have done the work with any thoroughness in so short a time. The list of signatures gives rather over 400 names for the diocese of London. It has been calculated on a careful research [1] that there were some 800 clergymen in that diocese; so that, speaking roughly, one half of the clergy subscribed when the visitors went round. It would seem that many of those who now refused or withheld subscription saw fit to change their minds in November.

c. Norwich. The diocese of Norwich came next. Dr. Jessopp [2] computes that there were some six hundred clergymen of all kinds here resident. There were eighteen different sessions at Ipswich, Blythburgh, Beccles, Norwich Cathedral, St. Peter Mancroft Norwich, North Walsham, Walsingham, Lynn, Swaffham, Thetford, Bury. These occupied the greater part of September, for as one signatory has appended the date September 29 to his name in the first session at Bury, we are able to reckon backwards and forwards from

---

[1] By the Rev. George Hennessy.
[2] In a letter to the writer. A return of parishes in 1593 gives 1,162 parishes and chapelries. Many were held in combination.

that day. There are rather over 500 signatures for the whole diocese, which seems to indicate a more ready acceptance of the settlement. _{CHAP. V}

The small diocese of Ely occupied the attention of the visitors during some part of October. Here the centres were Ely Cathedral, two sessions; Cambridge, two sessions; and another place not identified. There are ninety-eight signatures; and as Bishop Cox gives, in a return made within the next year[1], 152 cures, of which many were vacant, this seems to be a high percentage. *d. Ely.*

The next group of dioceses comprised Oxford, Lincoln, Peterborough, Coventry, and Lichfield. The visitors were first, the following Lords Lieutenant, William Marquis of Northampton for Northamptonshire, Henry Earl of Rutland for Rutland, Francis Earl of Huntingdon for Leicestershire, Oliver Lord St. John of Bletsoe for Bedfordshire, William Lord Willoughby, Sir Robert Tyrwhitt the younger, Sir E. Dymock, and Sir Francis Askew for Lincolnshire, Sir Ambrose Cave for Warwickshire (Lord Robert Dudley being omitted). Of other men of position were George Lord Zouche, Henry Lord Hastings eldest son of the Earl of Huntingdon, Sir Francis Knollys, Sir William Cecil, Sir Richard Blount, Sir R. Thimelby, Sir Walter Mildmay, Sir Thomas Nevill of Holt, Sir Thomas Cockyn, Sir Robert Lane, Sir John Gascoigne. Besides these there were Jas. Harrington, Thos. Lucy, Thos. Marrow, E. Mountain, Edm. Brudenell, Robert Wingfield, Laurence Gresley, Esquires. Finally, Alexander Nowell, afterwards Dean of St. Paul's, and T. Bentham, afterwards Bishop of Coventry and Lichfield, were the only clerical representatives; whilst the lawyers were William Fleetwood and Dr. Stephen Nevinson. *2. Oxford, Lincoln, Peterborough, Coventry and Lichfield.*

The visitors issued their writ of inhibition to the Deans and Chapters of the Cathedrals as guardians of the spiritualties, and to their registrars, officials, and ministers, forbidding them to exercise any jurisdiction from the time of receiving the document. This writ, preserved in the

[1] Add. MS. 5813, f. 78.

Register of the Dean and Chapter of Canterbury at Lambeth, is dated July 22, and Strype has again confused this with the issue of the letters patent. A good many of the signatures for this visitation are preserved at Lambeth[1]. There is a possible loss of a portion of those belonging to the diocese of Lincoln, but the rest seem to be complete, for London, Oxford, Coventry and Lichfield[2]. The Peterborough subscriptions are not known to be extant.

From a later diocesan return in the British Museum[3] there seem to have been about 500 parishes in the diocese of Coventry and Lichfield, represented by 351 signatures. In Oxford there were 195 parishes and 104 signatures. In Lincoln, about 1,160 parishes, for which we have imperfect returns containing 343 names.

3. Salisbury, Bristol, Exeter, Bath and Wells, Gloucester.

For the rest of the dioceses of the Southern Province we have very few details; something may possibly be gathered for the Cathedrals in the Chapter Act and other books, but those we have been able to consult do not, with one important exception presently to be mentioned, contain much information. The western group of dioceses, viz. Salisbury, Bristol, Exeter, Bath and Wells, and Gloucester, were to be visited by the following:—William Earl of Pembroke, Lord Lieutenant of Somerset and Wilts; Thomas Viscount Howard of Bindon, son of the Duke of Norfolk, recently ennobled, and a man of position in Dorset; John Lord St. John; George Lord Zouche; James Lord Moutrye, Lord Lieutenant of Dorset; Edmund Lord Chandos, Lord Lieutenant of Gloucestershire; Sir William Fitzwilliams, and Sir H. Nevill, Lords Lieutenant of Berkshire. The Lord Lieutenant of Devonshire and Cornwall was the Earl of Bedford, but his name occurs on two other commissions, and in his place are Sir John St. Leger, Sir Peter Carewe, Sir Richard Edgecombe, Sir Maurice Berkeley. Besides these there were Sir John Chichester, Sir

---

[1] *Cartae Miscell.* xiii. pt. 2. See below, p. 118.

[2] The completeness is suggested by the centres named and the appearance of the subscription sheets.

[3] For the year 1563, in Harl. MS. 595.

William Wroughton, Sir John Thynne, Sir George Norton, Sir Thomas Dyer, Sir John Pollard, and Sir Arthur Champion. Then there were Reginald Mohunt, John Mallet, and Humphry Coles, Esquires; John Jewell, D.D., afterwards bishop of Salisbury; and the lawyers Henry Parry and William Lovelace. No signatures have been discovered for this visitation. At Salisbury, Wells, Gloucester, and Bristol, there are no records in the Chapter Acts, so far as we can ascertain, save a mention here and there of the fact of visitation. In the Zurich letters, Jewel writing on August 1, says: 'I am on the point of setting out upon a long and troublesome commission for the establishment of religion. . . . The extent of my journey will be about 700 miles, so that I imagine we shall hardly be able to return in less than four months.' In another letter written in November, and frequently quoted, Jewel shows that he reached London on October 31. He says: 'We found everywhere the people sufficiently well disposed towards religion, and even in those quarters where we expected most difficulty. It is however hardly credible what a harvest, or rather what a wilderness of superstition had sprung up in the darkness of the Marian times. We found in all places votive relics of saints, nails with which the infatuated people dreamed that Christ had been pierced, and I know not what small fragments of the sacred cross. The number of witches and sorceresses had everywhere become enormous. The cathedral churches were nothing else but dens of thieves, or worse, if anything worse or more foul can be mentioned. If inveterate obstinacy was found anywhere, it was altogether among the priests, those especially who had once been on our side. They are now throwing all things into confusion, in order, I suppose, that they may not seem to have changed their opinions without due consideration. But let them make what disturbance they please: we have in the meantime disturbed them from their rank and office (illos de gradu et de sacerdotiis exturbavimus).'

Besides the view here given of the state of popular religion in the West of England, this letter is important as showing that some of the clergy, at all events, were ejected by the visitors; and we see that the deprived took pleasure in causing all possible trouble and confusion, as we shall find it to have been the case elsewhere[1].

Route of the western visitors.

The route taken by the western visitors cannot be clearly traced. Jewel gives the names of the places in the following order:—Gloucester, Bristol, Bath, Wells, Exeter, Cornwall, Dorset, Salisbury. But as it has been recorded in his life that he was at Salisbury on Aug. 10, the itinerary is probably not given in its proper order. We find from a later entry in the Lambeth Register that the visitors were at Wells on September 8. From the Exeter Chapter Acts we discover that they reached Exeter Cathedral late in September. In this book the record of proceedings is unusually full for that class of document. It says that the visitors, Sir Peter Carewe, Sir John St. Leger, Sir John Chichester, Sir Arthur Champernowne, with John Jewel, Henry Parry, and William Lovelace, began the visitation in the Chapter House. They then proceeded to other churches in the city, and afterwards left for Barnstaple. They returned to Exeter on October 8, and the following day (Monday) proceeded with the visitation until Friday. After leaving on that day they sent back certain injunctions for the Cathedral, signed by Jewel and Parry only. These injunctions were a set of explicit instructions, thirty-three in number, for the due discharge of the duties of the various officials connected with the cathedral. Some such injunctions appear to have been given at every cathedral during the visitation of this year; and in the metropolitan visitation of 1560, a further set was delivered by the archbishop.

4. Canterbury, Rochester, Winchester, Chichester.

Strype has made no mention of the visitation which dealt with the south-east of England, and comprised the dioceses of Canterbury, Rochester, Winchester, and Chichester. We have recovered the names of the visitors from a contemporary list preserved in Parker's *Antiquities* at Lambeth in manuscript[2]. They were:—William Marquis of Winchester, Lord Treasurer, and Lord Lieutenant

---

[1] See below, p. 161.   [2] Lambeth MS. 959, f. 424.

of Hampshire and the Isle of Wight; Henry Earl of Arundel, Lord Steward, and Lord Lieutenant of Sussex and Surrey; Henry Earl of Hertford; Lord Cobham, Warden of the Cinque Ports and Lord Lieutenant of Kent. The Knights were Sir R. Sackville, Sir T. Cawerden, Sir H. Seymour, Sir W. Callaway, Sir T. Finch. The Esquires were T. Wotton, J. Carell, R. Kingsmill, E. Isack, Humphrey Hales, E. Boyse, R. Worsley. The rest were T. Beacon, Robert Weston, Robert Nowell, and Alexander Nowell. The last is described as Contionator, but as he occupied apparently the same office in the visitation of the Midlands, there must be a mistake in one or other place. The number of divines in this visitation is noticeable.

For the visitation of Wales and the dioceses of Hereford and Worcester, we have recovered nothing more than the names of the visitors. Welsh diocesan documents have been badly kept, and in proof of this we may mention that St. David's alone has an episcopal register for the period we are considering. Some of the bishops' certificates, however, still exist, but they are incomplete. The visitors for this group of dioceses were John Lord Williams, President of the Council for Wales, Sir Hugh Palles, Sir Nicholas Arundel, Sir John Pott, Sir James Baskerville, Sir T. Russell; also John Throgmorton, William Sheldon, Thomas Hobbey, and William Gerrard; Dr. Davies and T. Yonge, divines; Dr. Roland Meyrick and Richard Pates (lawyers). Of these Dr. Davies became Bishop of St. Asaph, and Yonge of St. David's, whence he was translated to the Archbishopric of York.

5. Welsh dioceses, with Hereford and Worcester.

For the visitations of the Southern Province, as has been said, we have no official list of absentees like that given above for the northern dioceses[1]. Strype[2], however, makes mention of a list of signatures which he saw at Lambeth, but he did not make any use of it. We have found the documents

Signatories in the Southern Visitations.

---

[1] See above, p. 83.
[2] Strype, *Ann.* i. 72. In his life of Parker Strype was inclined to assign these signatures to the metropolitical visitation of 1560, but they belong to the visitation of 1559, as is proved by the institution books, and by the fact that the date is given in one place.

CHAP. V referred to, and note that they comprise at least the bulk of subscriptions made in two of the visitations for 1559, and represent the dioceses of London, Norwich, Ely, Coventry and Lichfield, Lincoln. From the appearance of the manuscript we are inclined to think that the signatures are nearly complete [1]. It is at once apparent that a large proportion of the clergy did not sign during the visitation, and it will be our business in subsequent chapters to see what was done with the recusants.

ALPHABETICAL LIST OF EXTANT SUBSCRIPTIONS, 1559 [2].

1. *Diocese of London.*

[*The signatures have been here rearranged in alphabetical order. A few signatories belong to other dioceses. Doubtful identifications are marked with a query. An asterisk denotes that the person was ultimately deprived.*]

Name of Person.	Name of Cure.	Name of Person.	Name of Cure.
Alexander, Robt.	Hatfield Regis.	Appryce, E.	
*Alford, J.		Apryse, Philip.	
Allaman, H.	Chaplain, Lincoln's Inn.	Armour, J.	St. Dion Backchurch.
Allen, J.	Bromley, cur.	Ashebury, Ch.	St. Michael, CrookedLane.
Allen, Robt.	Chickney.		
Alrad, J. (B.D.)		Asheton, Robert.	Stondon.
Anderton, J.	St. Michael, Bassishaw.	Atkynson, H.	St. Sepulchre.
		*Atkynson, W.	Shalford.
Andrew, J.	Barkway.	Awdley, N.	

[1] Lincoln is an exception.
[2] The subscriptions are usually autograph signatures. Sometimes a proxy signs. The cure is not by any means always inserted. Remarks are sometimes annexed to the name. Thus *articulis praedictis subscripsi,* or *omnibus et singulis praemissis subscripsi,* is fairly frequent. *Volens subscripsi* or some such phrase is varyingly added. The addition appears to be a matter of fashion, as it occurs regularly at some centres, seldom or else not at all in others. The first sheet or so in the Norwich diocese, for instance, exhibits no occurrence of the words, whilst at St. Peter Mancroft and other places it is constant. In Ely it is found five times. In the group Lincoln, Oxford, Coventry, and Lichfield it is almost continuous. Other remarks are annexed very sparingly. The two most interesting may be quoted. Thus Edward Walker at Woodstock has recorded *hic nomen meum volens et non coactus subscribo, veram in sacra religione a superis reformationem implorans.* The date of Walker's institution has not been ascertained. James Bibney at Chelmsford says *ore non tantum sed ab intimo corde.*

Name of Person.	Name of Cure.	Name of Person.	Name of Cure.	Chap. V
Awgest, T.	St. Giles, cur.	Bordman, E.	Althorne.	
Ayre, J.	North Fambridge.	Borough, R.	(Formerly of) Ardleigh.	London subscriptions.
Ayshton, J.	Great Leighs.	Bownell, J.	St. James, cur.	
Bacon, Robt.	Stanford-le-Hope.	Braban, J.		
		Braker, H.	Stanstead Abbots.	
Bactar, J.	St. Botolph's, Aldgate.	Bratchard, Robt. (B.D.)	Aveley.	
Baker, J.		Bredkerke, H.	Abbot's Roding.	
Baker, J.	Little Canfield.	Brett, Robt.	St. Giles, cur.	
Baker, J.	Broomfield.	Bretton, W.	Hordon on the Hill, cur.	
Baker, R.	St. Olave's, Old Jewry.	Brian, T.	Preb. of St. Elizeus.	
Balgaye, J.				
Banks, E.	St. John's, Walbrook.	Brown, J.	St. Mildred, Bread Street.	
Barker, E.	Great Braxted.			
Barker, W.	Langdon Hills.	Brown, J.	Walden.	
*Barslowe, Robt.	Braintree.	Brown, T.	St. Mary, Colchester.	
*Bartleton, T.	Bishop Stortford.	Browne, Robt.	Fobbing.	
Baydyll, G.	Widdington, cur.	Bryggs, T.	Gt. Bromly.	
Baynbryg, Geoff.	Bursted.	*Burton, Robt.	Corringham.	
Beccham, T.	Theydon Garnon.	Bury, R.	Stapleford Abbots.	
Bendall, J.	Ware.	Bushby, Hum. (LL.D.)	Fulbourn, dioc. Ely.	
Bennet, J.	Netteswell.			
Bentley, Ralph.	St. Olave's.	Busshe, N.	Copford End, cur.	
Besfeld, J.	Colne-Earls.			
Best, R.		Bycardyke, Marmaduke.	Horley, cur.	
Beulay, Gregory.	West Hanningfield, cur.			
		Byeryll, R.	Newport.	
Bewley, T.	Wanstead.	Bynonson, F.	Little Thurrock.	
Bibney, Jas.		Byrch, Ralph.	? Dottilham, cur.	
Bingay, W.		Byrch, T.[1]	Witley.	
Bishop, W.		Byrchley, Roger.	Little Parndon.	
Blackborne, Edmund.	Boreham.	Calley, J.	West Bardfield, cur.	
Blakburn, J.				
Blakhede, R.	High Roding.	Campyon, Sylvester.	Gt. and Little Henny.	
Bland, Ch.	Littlebury.			
Bond, W.	Little Allhallows, cur.	*Caston, Stephen.	St. Mary's ? cur.	

[1] See above, p. 3.

Name of Person.	Name of Cure.	Name of Person.	Name of Cure.
Caterall, Stephen.	Inworth.	Danver, W.	Barking.
		Darby, G.	Gt. Holland.
Calson, R.	St. Dion, cur.	Davye, Robt.	Esse aīs Ashen.
Cawseon, Anth.	Roydon.	Davys, Robt.	Shenfield.
Chadfounte, Ch.	Upminster, cur.	Davyson, R.	? Oldayer.
Chamber, T.	Holy Trinity.	Dean, J.	Great St. Bartholomew, cur.
Channey, Edmund.	Verley.		
		Desham, Baldwin.	Bradwell, cur.
Chapman, G.			
Chyld, J.	Writtle.	Dobson, W.	Gt. Wigborough.
Chyld, Roger.	Maching.	Dodpont, V.	
Clapham, R.	Enfield.	Donell, T.	
Clarke, J.	——, cur.	Dyer, J.	Ickenham.
Clarke, J.	Woodford.	Dyer, W.	Clavering, cur.
Clarke, Robt.	Walden, cur.	Edmonds, Robt.	
Clayton, Laur.	Aythorp Roding.	Eland, E.	Steeple, cur.
Clayton, Oliver.	Stock Harward.	Enssken, Stephen.	
Clayton, Roger.	White Roding.		
Clypsham, Martin.	St. Vedast.	Estobye, W.	Lindsell.
		Eton, Ch.	Wickford.
Coalles, Robt.	Bow.	Evans, Hugh.	Preb. of Hopton.
Coker, Roger.	Mundon.		
Cokerell, G.	Portio Richardi.	Farthing, J.	St. Margaret's, Lothbury.
Colborne, G.			
Coll, Leonard.	? Halsted.	Feld, Laur.	St. John the Evangelist ? cur.
Colliar, N.	Hallingbury.		
Columbell, R.			
Compton, N.	Much Hadham, cur.	Fennymore, J.	
		Fisher, J.	St. Catherine Cree, cur.
Copland, J.	Fingringho.		
Copman, Albert.	cur. St. Botolph, Bishopsgate.	Fleett, W.	Rickling.
		Forester, T.	Ramsden-Bellhouse.
Copschef, J.	Latchingdon, cur.		
		Forster, T.	Easthorpe.
Cordall, Walter.	Cranford.	Frampton, J.	
Cormoth, J.		Franklyn, T.	St. Mary Steynings.
Cornwayll, T.			
Cowke, W.	Writtle, cur.	Frauncis, J.	Coggeshall, or Chishall.
Coxall, J.			
Croft, Brian.		Frauncis, T.	Markshall.
		Gardner, J.	
Daniel, E.	Peldon.	Garrard, Giles.	St. Mary Woolnoth.
Dannel, Robt.	Christ Church, cur.		
		Gaudyn, T.	

London subscriptions.

Name of Person.	Name of Cure.	Name of Person.	Name of Cure.
Gayll, Ch.	St. Mary, Whitechapel.	Hodson, H.	London subscriptions.
		Hollonde, T.	Little Burstead.
Giles, T.	St. W——?	Holte, J.	
Glascoikn, W.	Barnston, cur.	Hontington, J.	
Glascok, T.	Doddinghurst.	Hopkinson, E.	
Glyn, J.[1]	St. Christopher le Stocks.	*Hopper, J.	Reed.
		Horsnayle, J.	
Goodman, J.	Clavering.	Hoskyn, T.	Laver Magdalen.
Gravener, W.	St. Martin, Outwich.		
		Houseman, J.	Master of the Temple.
Gray, W.	St. Peter, cur.		
Gregill, J.[1]	Barking.	How, W.	Harlow.
Grening, Ch.	Colne-Engain.	Hughes, J.	
Gruffyth, J.	Gt. Maplestead.	Hurst, Jas.	St. Michael le Querne, cur.
Gryffith, J.	Wicken-Bonhunt.		
		Hycks, Jas.	Wyddial.
Gyl, R.	Layer-Marney.	Hyll, J.	St. Olave's, Silver Street.
Gyppes, W.	Arkesden.		
		Hyll, R.	Chingford, cur.
Hale, J.	Danbury.	Hyll, W.	East Horndon.
Hale, W.	St. Mary Swinfoy.	Ingham, see Yngham.	
Halewell, R.		Jackson, Ralph.	
Hall, J.		Jackson, R.	Mashbury.
Hamet, J.		Jaclyn, Robt.	Stanwell.
Hapwode, R.	Woodham-Mortimer, cur.	James, Robt.	
		Jenings, T.	St. Michael, Wood Street.
Hardyn, W.			
Hardynge, W.	East Hanningfield.	Jenyns, T.	
		Jenkenson, W.	
Harmann, J.	Tollesbury.	Jerves, W.	All Saints, Maldon.
Harward, W.	St. Anne's, Aldgate.		
		Johns, Geoff.	St. Mary Woolchurch.
Harwood, W.			
Hatton, R.		Johnson, H.	Mistley.
Hatton, Robt.	St. Swithin.	Joly, W.	Pentlow.
Hawkar, H.	Theydon Bois.	Jones, Walter.	Islington.
Hawks, Robt.	North Shobury.	Jonson, E.	Stevenage.
Henshaw, W. (twice).		Jonson, J.	St. Clement Danes.
Hensworth, T.			
Henton, W.	West Mersea.	Katty, J.	
Herwood, W.		Kemp, D.	Wood Street.

[1] See above, p. 3.

CHAP. V
London subscriptions.

Name of Person.	Name of Cure.	Name of Person.	Name of Cure.
Ketill, R.	St. Stephen, Coleman Street.	Marshall, W.	Hawkwell.
		Martyn, T.	Easterbury.
		Martyn, W.	Wendon parva.
Kichin, Ch.	Anstey.	Mason, G.	Bradwell juxta mare.
Kyng, J.	Bocking.		
		Mason, J.	S. Fambridge.
Lacy, J.	Elsenham.	Mason, W.	
Lambe, Jas.		Maxon, H.	———, cur.
Langhorn, W.	Wrabness.	Merriman, Ralph.	St. Peter le Poer.
Lawrence, Edmund.			
		Miller, W.	Little Baddow.
Laveroke, R.	Rettendon.	Moke, T.	
Law, Owen.	Lambourne.	More, Giles.	St. Catherine-Coleman.
Lawe, J.	St. Whittington College, cur.		
		More, Miles.	Hockley, cur.
Lawson, W.	St. Martin's, cur.	Morpeth, J.	
Le Marynel, T.	West Tilbury.	Mortlake, Robt.	Foxearth.
Ledem, G.		Mountague, T.	St. Pancras, cur.
Leder, J.	? Torche.	Mundye, W.	
Leder, R.	Upminster.	Murffett, W.	Bulphan.
Leghtoman, E.			
		Nele, W.	
Leke, J.	Frinton.	Neto, Hugh.	St. Mary Magdalene, Milk Street.
Lench, W.	Beauchamp-Roding.		
Lloyd, E.	Little Bentley.		
Lolly, R.	St. Edmund's, cur.	Nettelt, T.	
		Nevard, W.	(Clerk in) Colchester.
Love, Philip.	St. Martin's, Ludgate.		
		Nevell, Edmund.	St. Helen's, London.
Lynch, W.	Willingale.		
Lyving, W.	St. Bride's.	Neytol, J.	Edmonton.
		Norryson, Jas.	St. Michael's, Cornhill.
Mackbraye, J.	Shoreditch.		
*Madoc, Hugh.		Nowglass, J.	
Madoc, Lewis.		Nuthal, T.	Beardon.
Mady, J.			
Mainwaring, R.	South Ockendon.	Osome, Robt.	St. Leonard's.
		Otwell, W.	Widford.
Malan, Pat.		Par, Robt.	Gt. Bardfield.
Malet, H.	St. Martin.	Parkars, Chas.	Parndon.
Mann, G.	St. Michael's.	Parker, J.	
Markyk, J.	St. Dunstan's, cur.	Parker, Robt.	Little Bardfield.
		Parker, T.	Benfleet.
Marsden, J.	———, cur.	Parys, T.	

Name of Person.	Name of Cure.	Name of Person.	Name of Cure.	CHAP. V
Pechen, Lambert.	Helmingham.	Rotliff, T.		London subscriptions.
		Rowe, Robt.		
Pennel, W.	Kirby.	Rughsyche, Hum.	Heybridge.	
Peyrson, E.	St. Bartholomew the Less.	Rust, W.	Rayleigh.	
Pheron, Robt.	St. Ethelburga.	Rust, W.	Felstead.	
Pinner, Jas.	Rawreth.	Ryche, W.	Stebbing.	
Pokyse, J.	St. Benet, Paul's Wharf, cur.	Ryddysdall, J.	St. Austin's.	
		Rylay, T.	St. Andrew's, Holborn.	
Polson, J.	Cranford.			
Ponder, Roger.	Gt. Yeldham.	Ryley, E.	St. Andrew Undershaft.	
Portar, J.	All Saints, Steynings.			
		Rysshbroke, W.	Walton-le-Soken.	
Poxleye, E.	Gt. Wigborough.			
Preston, R.	Layston.	Sadler, J.	Dunton-Wayllet.	
Purzaunt, J.	Thaxted.			
Pynder, Edmund.		Saunderson, T.		
		Say, Robt.		
		Semer, J. (Preb.)		
Rawdon, J.	Little Waltham.	Shepherd, W.	Heydon.	
Rawlins, W. (Petty Canon.)		Sherburn, J.	Gt. Warley.	
		Shew, R.		
		Shirm, J.	Bulmer.	
Rawlyn, J.	Farnham.	Silvester, T.	———, cur.	
Reaz, Laur.	St. James, Colchester, cur.	Simonds, Jas. (see below, Symond).		
Redfern, Anth.	Chesterford parva.			
		Smith, R.	Wargrave.	
Richardson, Adam.	Panfield.	Smith, R.	St. Peter's, West-Cheap.	
Richardson, Adam.	Gt. Oakley.	Smyth, N.		
		Smyth, Robt.	Thundridge.	
Richardson, J.	St. George, Eastcheap.	Smyth, Robt.	Amwell.	
		Smythe, Alex.		
Richardson, Robt.		Smythe, J.	St. Osyth, Colchester.	
Robson, J.	St. Clement, Eastcheap.	Sowdley, J.		
		Sprotte, Robt.		
Robson, R.	Frating.	Squyer, J.		
Robson, T.	———, cur.	Squyer, R.	Gt. Barlyng.	
Robynson, G.	Tottenham.	Stanbancke, J.	High Laver.	
Roger, R.	Cole Abbey.	Staworthe, J.	Gt. Stambridge.	
Rogerson, T.		Stayns, E.		
Rothewell, Jas.	Langenhoe.	Stene, W.		

	Name of Person.	Name of Cure.	Name of Person.	Name of Cure.
Chap. V London subscriptions.	Stokes, Robt.	Hackney.	Tomson, E.	Allhallows, London Wall.
	Stoks, Alex.	Langley, cur.		
	Stokton, Robt.	Coggeshall.	Thystylthwayte, Cyprian.	
	Stone, L.			
	Store, W.	Thundersley, cur.	Tofte, W.	St. John Zachary, cur.
	Stretham, Edmund.	Kelvedon.	Toppom, Anth.	Elmdon.
			Trowell, Robt.	? Ashdon.
	*Swadell, Tristram.	Preb. of Rugmere.	Tull, J.	Alresford.
			Turner, E.	
	*Swadell, Tristram.		Tylney, J.	
	*Swadell, Tristram.	Stepney (r.).	Underward, J.	Ingatestone.
	Swane, W.	St. Magnus.		
	Syddall, H.	Walthamstow.	Valle, P.	Boxted.
	Symond, T. (see above, Simonds).	(Late of) Rettendon, cur.	Waklyn, J.	
			*Walker, P.	
	Sympson, J.	Gt. Stanmore, cur.	Walker, P.	St. Leonard's, ? Witham.
	Sympson, M.		Walker, R.	Stansted-Montfishet.
	Sympson, T.	St. Mary's, Honey Lane.	Warbar, T. (Ludimagister).	
	Symson, Marband.	Vange.	Watson, J.	
	Symson, T.	Little Hadham.	Watson, Ralph.	Heston.
	*Symnell, R.	Boxted.	Weale, J.	St. Mildred, ? Poultry.
	Talbot, W.	Manningtree and Rainham.	Wells, J.	Streathall.
			Welltham, P.	
	Tatem, Ch.		Whitbroch, W.	
	Taw, Edmund.		*White, T.	Sturmer.
	Taylor, Hugh.	Woodham-Ferrers.	White, W.	Sheering.
			Whiting, J.	Wrington (co. Som.).
	Taylor, R.	St. Mary Botolph.	Whytlyn, Ralph.	St. Andrew's, Holborn.
	Teyrre, Ralph.	Little Leighs.		
	Thomas, J.	Stepney (v.).	Widdowson, W.	Chap. to Drapers of London.
	Thomas, J.	Prittlewell.		
	Thomas, Walter.	Sible-Hedingham.	Wilson, T.	(Formerly of) Langford.
	Thompson, R.	St. Leonard's.	Wilson, T.	Little Gaddesden.
	Thomson, Robt.			

Name of Person.	Name of Cure.	Name of Person.	Name of Cure.
Wodthorpe, J.		Wyley, P.	
Wood, Marmaduke.	Stoke Newington, cur.	Wynsehent, Alex.	St. Mary, Aldermary.
Woodley, W.	St. Laurence Pountney, cur.	Yate, Alex.	Bosvile Porcion.
Woollen, R.	——, cur.	Yngham, Robt.	Pelham Furneaux.
Worthynton, E.	Ramsden-Crays.	Yonge, Hugh.	Little Mundon, cur.
Wright, Arthur.	Hornchurch.		
Wryght, W.	Little Ongar.	The Vicar of St. Giles, Cripplegate [1].	
Wyldman, Geoff.			

London subscriptions.

2. *Diocese of Norwich.*

Name of Person.	Name of Cure.	Name of Person.	Name of Cure.
Abadam, J.	Kilverstone.	Bakelar, T.	St. Nicholas (? S. Elmham), cur.
Abŕtt, W.			
Adamson, Philip.		Balard, W.	Ormesby.
Adran, J.		Banyard, T.	
Akers, J.		Banystre, T. (plebanus).	
Albon, J.	Brooke.		
Alem, Robt.		Barker, Adam.	Canon of Norwich.
Alen, J.			
Amgar, R.	Aldeburgh, cur.	Barker, T.	Knoddishall.
Andrew, Robt.		Barnage, Robt.	Sternfield.
*Appultoft, R.	Offton.	Barne, J.	
Armitage, T.		Barrett, J.	Preb. Norwich.
Asche, W.	Heigham.	Barrett, W.	
Assheworth, Laur.		Battye, Ch.	St. Margaret's.
		Baxter, W.	
Athowe, T. (twice).		Bayforth, W.	Worlingham.
		Baymine, J.	West Rudham.
Atkynson, J.	Hollesley.	Baynbrigge, W. (Hypodidasculus).	
Augier, T.			
Awdley, Robt.			
Aynesworth, G.		Baynbriggs, T.	
		Beare, J.	Newton Flotman.
Bacheler, E.	Garveston.		
Backhows, Raphael.		Beccet, J.	
		Bellowes, T.	Saxlingham-Nethergate.
Badcok, H.			

[1] *Sic.* He was W. Granger.

110   THE ELIZABETHAN CLERGY

Chap. V

Norwich subscriptions.

Name of Person.	Name of Cure.	Name of Person.	Name of Cure.
Bendrysche, H.		Byncks, Robt.	
Bennett, R.	Cretingham, cur.	Byrd, H.	
Benson, T.	Holton.	Bysshop, Gregory (twice).	
Best, Robt.			
Beverley, Robt.	St. Mary's, Bungay, cur.	Bywell, J.	
Beverley, Robt.	Spixworth.	Cachard, J.	
Blackburn, R.		Calwer, N.	
Blamefield, Stephen.	Debenham.	Carewe, Matthew.	Arch. Norf.
Boneham, R.		Carter, H.	
Borrow, Edmund.		Carton, T.	
		Cawse, J.	
Bossall, Robt.	Ringshall.	Chadwyck, J.	
Boste, W.		Chane, J. (twice).	
Botswayne, W.	Horham.		
Bowman, Robt.		Chapman, Ch.	Lavenham.
Bownes, Edmund.	Somerleyton.	Chapman, W.	Freston.
		Churche, Nich.	
Bowrowe, R.		Claibourne, T.	
*Bradley, Thurstan.	Westfield.	Clapton, Martin.	
		Clay, J.	Whatfield.
Brancker, W.		Clegg, R.	
Bretland, T.		Cobham, J.	
Brewerton, R.	Wells.	Codling, Robt.	
Brightyre, J.		Cokke, Jas.	
Broughton, J.	Stradbroke.	*Cole, And.	
Browne, J.	Wreningham.	Colisman, W.	
Browne, J.	Risby.	Collyn, W.	
Brownsmyth, W.	Styvekey.	Collys, W.	
Bryggs, T.		Company, R.	
Bukkes, J. (Ludimagister).		Coningford, J.	
		Conyers, T.	Weybread, cur.
Bulhey, J.	Bentley.	Cooke, J.	
Bull, J.		Cooke, R.	
Burnam, Robt.		Cooper, T.	
Burnett, R.	Denver.	Coote, W.	Mendham.
Burton, W.		Corker, N.	
Burwyk, Jas.		Corker, T.	
Burywey, W.	Gorleston.	Cornwall, H.	
Busshe, J.	Filby.	Cosyn, J.	
Busshe, J.		Cotton, J.	
Bycher, W.	Acton.	Cowper, Walter.	? Southacre.
Byckerdyck, J.	Shipdham.	Crample, Oliver	Stonham-Aspal.

Name of Person.	Name of Cure.	Name of Person.	Name of Cure.
Crosier, J.	Barrow.	Farmer, als Oxford, Matthew.	Norwich subscriptions.
Crosley, T.	Mautby.		
Crosse, W.	Canon, Norwich.	Farquharson, see Pharkson.	
Crowes, Laur.	Fordley.		
Cundall, Ralph.		Farrold, Bernard.	
Curtes, Robt.		Fascet, Alex.	
		Fawcet, W. (see below, Forset).	
Daddesburye, Hugh.	Howe.		
		Fawpeet, Reynold.	
Dale, E.			
Darlaye, J.		Fayrhayre, J.	
Davys, R.	Henstead.	Feltham, J.	
Dawson, W.	Felixstowe.	Fenne, G.	Belstead.
Denny, Edmund.	Watlington.	Ferne, Stephen.	East Dereham.
Denston, W.	Bedfield.	Ferrer, J.	
Deyer, P.	Lowestoft, cur.	Fisscher, J.	
Donatson, R.	Bage cum Buly.	Fletcher, R.	Mutford.
Donatson, R.	Hasketon.	Flynt, R.	
Downabi, W.	Reepham.	Ford, Ralph.	Woodbridge.
Downes, T.	Hethersett.	Forset, Alex. (see above, Fawcet).	Brockley.
Dowson, R.			
Dukker, Ralph.			
Dumont, P.		Fox, J.	Reydon.
Dunche, And.	? Benchfield.	Franch, T.	
Dye, Edmund.		Frecke, T.	Downham.
Dyxon, Ch.		Frettwell, T.	
Dyxon, R. (B.A.)		Fykays, W.	Ufford.
Dyxon, Robt.			
		Gaisley, R.	
Ebbs, T.		Galte, P.	? Marlney.
Eckersall, W.		Garett, R.	
Edderych, T.	Pettistree, cur.	Garnett, R.	
Edriche, als James, W.	Wilby.	Gartfolde, R.	
		Gaytes, als Yatts, T.	
Edwards, W.			
Ellys, W.		Gerne, Ch.	
Elmyn, J.		Gerrard, W.	? Cheadon.
Elsley, E.	Flixton.	Glasyer, Robt.	Stoke.
Emerson, Geoff.		Glowgate, Edmund.	Wetherden.
Ems, Alex.	Glemsford, cur.		
Eudus, Hugh.	Acle.	Goldbure, T.	
		Goodfellay, W.	Brandeston.
Famma, Edmund.		Goodwyn, T.	
Farewell, W.		Goshawk, W.	

Chap. V
Norwich subscriptions.

Name of Person.	Name of Cure.	Name of Person.	Name of Cure.
Gosselynge, J.	Nacton.	Heyly, Hugh.	
Gouttrell, W.	Burnham-Norton.	Heyton, Ralph.	
		Hochynson, P.	Battisford, cur.
Gowgh, J.	Benhall.	Hogeson, T.	Lound.
Graunge, Gregory.		Hollwey, J.	
		Holt, Arlot.	
Greet, W.	Holbrook.	Holtby, W.	
Grene, Jas.	Yelverton and Surlingham.	Hongon, Anth.	
		Hornse, N. (Ludimagister).	Southwold.
Grewe, E.			
Gryffynson, Chas.	Sweffling.	Hossert, W.	? Daccrosse.
		Houldam, W.	
Grymsby, W.		Hovell, J.	
Gybbons, W.	——, cur.	Howorthe, J.	Swilland.
Gybson, G.		Howse, Robt.	
Gybson, J.	Tatterset.	Hubbard, P.	Dennington.
Gybson, R.		Hudson, R.	
Gyppes, W.		Hudson, W. (twice).	
Hall, T.		Hughson, T.	
Halstyd, G.		Hull, T.	Thurston.
Handcok, Jas.	? Pentney, cur.	Hunt, T.	
Handcok, J.		Huwett, Robt.	Linstead, cur
Harcoks, Edmund.		Hycss, Edmund.	Rushmere.
Hardy, J.		Hyll, H.	
Harlam, J.		Hyll, T.	
Hartley, Bernard.	Roydon.	Hylton, J.	
		Hyndmershe, Cuthbert.	
Hartley, Bernard.	(Without name of cure.)	Ide, W.	? Debredford.
Haryson, G.	Saxmundham.	Inglott, Edmund.	
Haryson, J.		Inman, see Ynman.	
Haryson, J.	Colveston.		
Haryson, R.		Irby, Ambrose.	
Haryson, W.			
Hay, J.		Jackson, E.	West Harling.
Hayle, T.	Micklefield.	Jackson, J.	
Hayton, W.		James, W. (see also Edriche).	Framlingham, cur.
Hede, J.			
Hellyer, J.	Moulton, cur.	Jekler, Robt.	Ashill.
Henyter, T.		Jellow, Simon.	
*Heyber, Oliver.	Hethel.	Joye, Ch.	Colney with Earlham.

Name of Person.	Name of Cure.	Name of Person.	Name of Cure.	CHAP. V
Kempe, J.		Marshall, W.		Norwich subscriptions.
Knolles, T.		Martin, Gregory.		
Kylbury, P.	Hepworth.	Mason, T.		
Kyrklye, Robt.		Mathe, W.	Marlingford, cur.	
Kyrkman, G.	Tattington.	Matheus, Oliver.		
*Lache, R.		Maund, T.	Hockering.	
Lakers, W.	Welborne.	Maydwell, J.		
Lambe, T.		Melton, Alan.	Tittleshall.	
Lamson, Jas.	Leiston, cur.	Merman, J.	Theberton.	
Langley, J.	Chevington.	Merre, E.	Tredisborth?	
Langton, P.		Merycoke, —.	St. Margaret's.	
Lanman, J.		Mody, W.	Cockfield.	
Laws, Geoff.		Moley, R.		
Laynning, T.	Stow-Bardolph.	More, R.	Rendham.	
Legewyn, W.	Sotterley.	Morley, Robt.	Bradwell.	
Leman, T.	Canon, Norwich.	Morton, Robt.		
Linchon, N.	Brampton.	Murake, Robt.	Cratfield.	
Locke, N.	Uggeshall and Sutton.	Myller, N.		
Lofthowse, Adam.		Neham, Robt.		
		Newton, Ralph.	Beccles.	
Lokett, J.		Nicholas, H.		
Long, Stephen.		Nicolls, Simon.	Sprenton?	
Longworth, J.		Norton, J.		
Love, Robt.		Nowelly, J.		
Lovett, T.		Nudde, Robt.	Pakefield.	
Lupton, T.		Nuttall, Ch.		
Lyne, Barth.		Nyells, Robt.		
Lynne, T.				
Lyster, Robt.	Bildeston and Alpheton.	Ocley, Roger.	North Pickenham.	
Lytton, G.		Okam, see Raky.		
		Oxford, see Farmer.		
Mably, R.	Timworth, cur.			
Maddock, W.				
Madis, Gregory.		Pacher, R.	Bradenham.	
Makyn, R.		Pachet, Robt.		
Mannell, H.	Preb., Norwich.	Page, J.	Stratford St. Andrew.	
Manus, R.	Marlesford.			
Manus, Robt.				
Marcall, T.		Page, J.		
Marke, R.		Palmer, Ambrose.	Frettenham.	
Marser, T.	Ampton.			

I

	Name of Person.	Name of Cure.	Name of Person.	Name of Cure.
Norwich subscriptions.	Palmer, T. (twice).		Renerl, J.	
			Ricters, G.	
	Parke, H.	Buckenham.	Rix, W.	
	Parker, N.		Robinson, Jas.	Carbrooke, in Thetford Deanery, cur.
	Passefont, T.	Buxhall.		
	Paternoster, Robt.	Rattlesden.		
			Robinson, J.	
	Patteson, J.		Robinson, Lancelot.	
	Pecke, J.	Canon, Norwich.		
			Rochester, E.	
	Pecoke, T.	——, cur.	Rod, W.	
	Pedder, Meleus.		Rogerson, T.	
	Peell, Robt.		Rogges, Fras.	Athelington, cur.
	Pepper, Roger.		Rok, T.	Ash-Bocking.
	Percye, Alan.	Earsham, Mulbarton, and Cressingham.	Rowghton, W.	Walingworth.
			Ruckwode, T.	Fakenham Parva.
	Person, Robt.		Rudde, J.	
	Peyntour, Robt.		Runce, R.	
	Peyntour, W.		Russell, Laur.	
	Pharkson, T.		Russell, R.	
	Picto, Robt.		Rust, E.	
	Pott, J.		Ruston, Robt.	
	Powle, Roger.		Rycherdson, J.	Needham.
	Powle, T.		Rydyngs, T.	Henley, cur.
	Pratte, R.		Rynger, H.	All Saints —— ?
	Prester, T.		Ryshetan, G.	
	Proctour, J.			
	Prowett, Stephen.		Sadler, T.	
			Salebanke, W.	
	Punder, T.		Salter, W.	
	Pye, T.	Flempton.	Saltunstall, Gilbert.	
	Pyks, T.		Sankey, J.	
			Sclayter, Jas. (twice).	
	Raben, Matthew.	Romington ?		
			Scorbrugg, J.	
	Raby, Radaud.		Scot, J.	
	Raky, a's Okam, Miles.		Scott, J.	
			Seanton, Robt.	Canon, Norwich.
	Randal, John.	Peasenhall.	Searle, T.	
	Randolf, Robt.		Selvin, J.	
	Redwycke, J.	St. James —— ?	Seman, Robt.	Twyford.
	Reed, J.		Seman, T.	Wickham-Market.
	Reed, T.			

Name of Person.	Name of Cure.	Name of Person.	Name of Cure.	CHAP. V
Sergeant, T.		Steuardson, P.		Norwich subscriptions.
*Sewell, J.		Stevyns, Robt.		
Scyton, W.		Stokys, J.		
Shakylton, T.	Kenton.	Stokys, J.	Downham.	
Sharpe, Robt.		Storer, Anth.		
Shaw, Robt.	Hopton.	(Ludima-		
Shepherd, Jas.	Hoxne and Denham.	gister).		
		Susanne, W.		
Sherbroke, Cuthbert.		Swycar, J.		
		Symonds, H.		
Sherman, J.	Wangford.	Symsone, J.	Fressingfield.	
Sifton, W.	Harkstead, cur.	Symsune, J.	Winston.	
Singleton, T.	Samston?			
Skarlett, J.		Tailer, J.	Ranworth, cur.	
Skelton, J.		Tailer, N.		
Skoyle, J.		(Parvorum		
Skypp, R.		Moderator).		
Smethe, R.		*Tailer, R.		
Smithe, H.	Canon, Norwich.	(twice).		
Smyth, J.	Glemham.	Tailer, T.		
Smyth, J.	Withersdale.	Talybut, H.		
Smythe, Ch.		Tassell, Geoff.		
Smythe, N.		Thaxster, Robt.		
Smythe, Robt.		Thembylthorp, Edmund.		
Sotheran, H.	Wymondham, cur.	Thomson, Robt.	Westleton.	
Southwell, T.	Hemingstone and Akenham.	Thorneton, H.		
		Thorp, W.		
		Throder, Ch.		
Spells,—.		Thurlow, J.		
Spensor, Milo.	Preb., Norwich.	Thurston, G.		
Spurgyn, Robt.		Thurston, W.		
Spynk, J.		Thyrketyll, Robt.		
Stacy, J.	Lackford.			
Stanclyff, P.	Burnham-Thorpe.	Thyrlyng, N.	Huntingfield, cur.	
Stanley, H.		Toller, J.	Canon, Norwich.	
*Stanley, Jas.	Washbrook.			
Stapleton, R.		Tryket, Stephen.		
Stapleton, Robt.		Tuddenham, J.	Canon, Norwich.	
Starker, Emericus.		Tudman, H.		
Sterne, Edmund.		Tugnye, W.	Saxlingham-Thorpe.	

Chap. V
Norwich subscriptions.

Name of Person.	Name of Cure.	Name of Person.	Name of Cure.
Tugnye, W.		Webster, R.	Blaxall and Tunstall.
Turner, Geoff.			
Twaytes, E.	Higham and Hardingham.	Webster, Robt.	Burnham.
		Whitby, T.	
Tylney, Hugh.	Capel.	Whyte, J.	
		Whyttyngton, J.	
Underwood, J.	Burgh-Castle.	Whytwell, J.	Hitcham.
Underwood, R. (twice).	Arch., Norwich.	Wilkinson, Anth.	Bramfield.
Urlkar, Roger.	Stradsett.	Wilkinson, Robt.	
Urtaye, Robt.			
Uttley, W.			
Uxton, Robt.	Wereham and Stoke-Ferry.	Willens, T.	
		Williams, Roger.	
		Williamson, E.	
Vicarary, J.		Willughby, J.	Skeyton.
Vollkyll, W.	Great Livermere.	Woode, Matthew.	
		Woodyard, W.	
Vyncent, T.		Wyckham, T.	
		Wyllett, Walter.	Rendlesham.
Walker, J.	Dallinghoe.	Wyllson, H.	Great Barton.
Walldon, T.	Martlesham.	Wyllson, J.	
Wallett, J.		Wyllys, J.	
Wallrond, Robt.	Wolferton.	Wylson, Ch.	Stratford.
Walsingham, J.	Metfield, cur.	Wylson, Hum.	
Walton, Robt.	Woolverstone.	Wylson, J.	
Wamoke, Jas.	Whinbergh cum Westfield.	Wylson, T.	
		Wyncopp, Robt.	Great Melton.
Waoter, Edmund.		Wynder, Jas.	
		Wyngseans, R.	
Ward, W.	Aldringham.	Yatts, *see* Gaytes.	
Warde, W.			
Wardman, H.	Hemley, cur.		
Waren, Gilbert.		Ynman, J.	
Watling, J.		Yonger, Hum.	
Watson, J.		Yonger, J.	
Watson, T.	Bitchamwell, als Bysham All Saints.	Yoyle, Fras.	Oulton.
		The Rector of Titteshall (by proxy).	
Watts, Peter.	Sterston?		

3. Diocese of Ely.

Name of Person.	Name of Cure.	Name of Person.	Name of Cure.
Atkins, Walter.	Lidlington.	Gale, J.	
Aynsworthe, Fras.		Gawber, G.	
		Gegewycke, N.	
Ayscheby, Robt.	Tadlow.	Goodwyn, H.	
Barton, R.	*Gospeller*.	Hargrave, Robt.	
Bland, R.		Harryson, Robt.	Linton.
Blande, E.	Gransden.	Hawes, H.	
Boninton, Edmund.	Kingston.	Hill, Ralph.	Chelerley?
		Hill, W.	Subcanon, Ely.
Boynton, T.	St. Andrew's, Cambridge.	Holand, Robt.	Great Shelford.
		Howell, W.	Conington.
Bretton, W.	Dullingham.	Hynd, T.	Guisdon parva?
Brodley, W.	Abington.		
Brond, Simon.	Hilgay.		
Burnett, R.		Jhonsone, Jonas.	Thriplow.
		Jyer . . ., John.	
Chapman, Robt.	Registrar, Ely Dioc.	Kent, Robt.	Carlton cum Willingham.
Chekeryng, Robt.			
Cherch, J.		Latham, Ch.	
Christyan, J.		Leder, J.	Isleham.
Clerke, J.	Croydon.	Leeds, E.	
Clough, T.	Caldecot.	Legh, Edmund.	
Cooke, R.		Long, G.	Elm with Emneth.
Crany, W.			
Crawforthe, W.	Hauxton.	Lorde, W.	Hatley.
		Lyddington, J.	
Damer, Emericus.	Hockington.	Mare, H.	
Deane, And.		Margeson, Hugh.	
Dobyson, T.	Bassingbourne.	Marshall, W.	Thetford.
Etwold, J.	Chesterton.	Marshall, Randall.	
Folberin, J. (Hypodidasculus).		Mason, Anth.	
		Meij, J.	
		Middleton, J.	
Froste, W.	Doddington.	Mores, W.	Papworth, St. Agnes.
Fynche, J.			
Fynkel, H.			

THE ELIZABETHAN CLERGY

Chap. V
Ely subscriptions.

Name of Person.	Name of Cure.	Name of Person.	Name of Cure.
Nappe, Simon.	Sutton.	Stanley, J.	Haddenham, cur.
Neve, Marmaduke.		Stenett, N.	Hardwicke.
		Stethe, E.	
Parkynson, T.	Willingham.		
Parson, Robt.	Sawston, cur.	Tayler, W.	
Parye, J.	Landbeach.	Taskworth, J.	
Pernby, T.	Long Stow.	Thurguy, Robt.	Abington.
Pernby, T.	Hinxton.	Trygarny, Griffin.	Heslyne?
Perne, And.	Dean of Ely.		
Plandon, And.	Fulbourn All Saints, cur.	Turner, W.	
		Tye, Ch.	
Proctor, Robt.		Tyleard, J.	Bottisham.
		Tylney, J.	Harlton.
Redford, Aemerus.	Easthallan?	Umfrey, Edmund.	Melbourne.
Relff, J.	Orwell.		
Robynson, J.			
		Ward, W.	Clapton.
Scargyll, Fras.	Knapwell.	Webster, R.	Wendy.
Scargyll, Fras.	Shepreth.	Wetwot, Othivell.	
Sheffelde, T.			
Smyth, G.	Witchford.	Whyte, T.	Horseheath.
Smyth, W.		Wrightson, J.	(Ludimagister, St. Albans).
Speght, Jas. (Ludimagister).		Wylkynson, T.	Redbourn.

4. Diocese of Oxford.

Name of Person.	Name of Cure.	Name of Person.	Name of Cure.
Abbot, Robert.		Browne, Robt.	
Allmark, R.	Salford.	Browne, T.	Waterstock.
Annullyng, J.		Brownyng, W.	
Asplen, T.		Buknal, W.	
Bass, J.		Burne, W.	
Bede, Robt.		Chapman, J.	Woolston.
Bennett, R.		Clerke, Alexr.	
Bower, Hum.		Clerke, W.	
Bridger, R.	Drayton.	Coheney, T.	B—— and Haseley.
Briggs, R.			
Brivyll, T.		Colman, H.	

Name of Person.	Name of Cure.	Name of Person.	Name of Cure.	CHAP. V
Conal, W.		Kyng, R.		Oxford subscriptions.
Cory, Robt.		Kyrkley, Robt.		
Danyell, J.		Lancaster, Ambrose.		
Davis, W.				
Davy, E.	Chinnor.	Lay, T.		
Debank, Robt.				
Donnekley, W.	Nuneham, cur.	Malbon, Hamlet.		
Dosyn, H.				
Dycheffelde, Roger.		Mastroder, Edm.		
		Mendons, Ph.		
Edlyngsun, W.		Meykoc, T.		
Evett, Jas.		Michell, Ch.	Chastleton.	
		Mitchell, J.	Somerton.	
Fell, Jas.		More, W.		
Foster, Robt.		Moreson, T.		
Fyssher, W.		Morleys, David.		
		Morys, —.		
Gardiner, E.	Swerford.			
Glave, Matt.		Norwood, Robt.		
Goch, Griffith.				
Goch, Hugh.		Obell, T.		
Griffin, Ralph.		Osborn, W.		
Gybbun, W.		Owsley, W.		
Gyles, Laur.				
		Pope, W.		
Hale, T.		Powell, W.	Halton?	
Harley, T.	Broughton.	Pryce, Lewis.		
Hatton, Augustine.		Pytts, J.		
Hawardyn, J.		Richard, P.		
Henshaw, Hugh.		Rodlay, J.		
		Rothwell, W.	Stoke Talmage.	
Hodson, J.		Sadleyer, H.		
Horne, W.	Cornwell.	Scott, Alan.	Charlton.	
Horwood, J.		Sharpe, Edm.		
Hubank, J.		Shawe, J.		
		Shevyn, Ralph.		
Ifel, J.		Slynger, Geoff.		
		Spencer, R.		
Jevans, David.		Standesche, Thurstan.		
Johnson, Ralph.				
Jolybrande, Nich.		Sthone, T.		

CHAP. V
Oxford subscriptions.

Name of Person.	Name of Cure.	Name of Person.	Name of Cure.
Touneys, T.		Webbe, T.	
Towneley, W.	Halton, cur.	Wolff, Edm.	Brightwell.
Tylar, Hugh.		Wydder, W.	
		Wyllat, Ralph.	
Wade, J.			
Walker, E.			
Warner, J.		Yate, J.	
Watson, J.	Heyford.	Yate, Laur.	
Watson, R.		Yonge, T.	Bampton.

5. Diocese of Coventry and Lichfield.

Name of Person.	Name of Cure.	Name of Person.	Name of Cure.
Abell, J.		Barley, W.	
Adde, J.		Barnes, T.	
Alcocke, T.		Barnes, W.	
Aleyn, Gervase.		Barthylmew, Roger.	
Allen, Jas.			
Alpden, Robt.		Bate, Hugh.	
Alsop, J.		Baxter, H.	
Alsop, Robt.		Baxter, Ralph.	
Alsop, W.		Beche, W.	
Ap Richart, Hugh.		Bees, W.	
		Bennett, Edm.	
Ashelake, T.		Bennett, E.	
*Asheley, W.		Bennett, W.	Holy Trinity, Coventry.
Astley, W.			
Aston, Robt.		Bernereape, T.	
Astyn, T.		Bettreton, J.	
Atkyns, T.		Blakemeyre, H.	
Averell, H.		Blythe, W.	
Awdley, J.		Bolt, T.	Preb. of Stotfold.
Babyngton, W.		Borthe, H.	
Bache, J.		Bower, Ralph.	
Bacon, W.	Standon.	Bowmne, R.	
Badnall, T.		Bowyer, And.	Ashton.
Bagaley, Nich.		Bradocke, T.	
Bakewell, T.		Bradshawe, J.	
Baldwin, R.		Brett, Ralph.	
Banaster, W.		Brock, Ralph.	
Banrenson, J.		Broke, Adam.	
Barbar, Edm.		Browyne, Sylvester.	
Barlowe, Alex.			

Name of Person.	Name of Cure.	Name of Person.	Name of Cure.	Chap. V
Brune, Stephen.		Downam, T.		Coventry and Lichfield subscriptions.
Bryan, W.		Downe, Anth.	Kinnersley.	
Brymley, W.		Drakcoferd, T.		
Bulter, J.		Drury, Robt.		
Burton, T.		Dudley, Arthur.		
Burtonton, Edm.		Dudley, Dion.		
		Dycher, Jas.	Little Ercall, cur.	
Butler, T.		Dycher, J.		
Butterton, R.		Dyckenson, J.	Pubis Derbiensis moderator.	
Byrd, T.				
		Dylke, T.		
Carlelley, Robt.				
Cartelle, W.		Edwards, R.		
Carter, W.		Eiton, T.		
Cartwright, J.				
Caryngton, Roger.		Fell, R.		
		Fenton, J.		
Caterbanke, W.		Fermer, T.		
Cawappe, E.		Fildhows, R.		
Cowappe, Ralph.		Fletchur, E.		
		Fliming, H.		
Chapleyn, Thurstan.		Foster, W.		
		Fox, Jas.		
Chelton, Nich.		Fox, T.		
Churcheley, W.		Frere, J.		
Clement, T.		Fyldisend, W.		
Clerke, Ralph.				
Clerke, W.		Gainson, Robt.		
Cleyton, Nich.		Ganull, G.		
Cleyton, Ralph.		*Gardiner, T.		
Cliffe, R.		Garlec, J.		
Coke, Robt.		Garret, W.		
Cole, J.		Gilbert, T.	Longford.	
Cooke, Robt.		Godwyn, J.		
Copysette, Roger.		Goldsmith, Randolf.		
Coton, T.		Golstun, T.		
Cowper, R.		Goosnell, T.		
Crane, G.		Gosling, Geoff.		
Crane, J.		Green, Ch.		
Crow, W.		Green, Edm.		
Cruse, J.		Gyttyns, R.		
Dauson, Ralph.		Haih, W.		
Daygle, T.		Halen, Robt.		

THE ELIZABETHAN CLERGY

Chap. V
Coventry and Lichfield subscriptions.

Name of Person.	Name of Cure.	Name of Person.	Name of Cure.
Hancoks, J.		Kymberleyns, Fras.	
Harall, W.		Kyrkbie, Barth.	
Harbarbard, R.		Lancashire, Robt.	
Hardinge, T.		Lancashire, W.	
Harrys, T.		Lancastell, als Hewster, Roger.	
Hatton, R.			
Hawes, E.			
Haystings, Bernard.			
Hensham, H.		Lane, J.	
Henson, Roger.		Lane, J.	
Herod, G.		Lane, Martin.	
Hether, W.		Laneham, G.	
Heydock, T.		Langton, Fras.	
Heylyn, Robt.	Petton.	Larch, T.	
Heyton, J.	Ludimagister (Shrewsbury School).	Lee, G.	
		Leson, Anth.	
		Leveson, J.	
Heyward, J.		Leyke, T.	
Hilton, G.		Like, T.	
Hodson, Roger.		Lloyd, J.	
Hoggyns, R.		Longford, J.	
Hollynshed, R.		Lord, Griffith.	
Holone, Edm.		Luter, Roger.	
Holone, R.		Lydyatt, T.	
Holwey, J.		Lye, T.	Wroxeter.
Horton, Hum.		Lyghtfoot, Hum.	
Houghton, Roger.		Lyngard, J.	
Howbyn, Laur.			
Howys, J.		Madford, E.	
Hulley, T.		Mainwaring, J.	
Hulme, Robt.		Marler, T.	
Hunt, T.		Marris, T.	
Hussey, H.		Marshall, J.	
Hygdon, Robt.		Massy, Bernard.	
Hyggyns, J.		Massy, W.	Chaplain.
Hyll, R.		Mateson, Ralph.	
		Mericke, Edm.	
Jamys, E.		Merton, W.	
Jobber, W.		Meyre, Nich.	
Jurden, E.		Miller, J.	
		More, Robt.	
*Key, R.		More, W.	
Knyston, R.		Morehall, J.	

THE SOUTHERN VISITATION

Name of Person.	Name of Cure.	Name of Person.	Name of Cure.	CHAP. V
Moreton, J.		Rydavure, W.	Swinnerton.	Coventry and Lichfield subscriptions.
Morys, Robt.		Ryder, T.		
Mower, T.				
Mowre, Robt.		Sadler, J.		
		Sale, W.		
Nedham, J.		Sandford, Brian.		
Nicson, T.		Satten. Robt.	Preb. of Bubbenhall.	
Norman, W.				
Nycholls, R.	Milwich.	Schepey, Hugh.		
Nycools, J.		Scherar, R.		
		Sclater, W.		
Okeley, R.		Seele, W.		
Olde, W.		Shaw, Ralph.		
Ollerton, W.		Shelden, J.		
Orpe, T.		Sheldon, Hugh.		
Otley, Roger.		Shelton, Geoff.		
Otuwey, Robt.		Sheppard, T.		
		Sherard, A.		
P...., R. (*sic*)		Sherard, T.		
Palmer, R.		Sherman, T.		
Parker, Ralph.		Sherwyn, Robt.		
Pendelton, W.		Shrygley, W.		
Pendlebury, P.		Silvester, Nich.		
Penn, W.		Slany, R.		
Perkyn, W.		Smyth, R.		
Perseval, Jas.		Smyth, T.		
Perstell, T.		Smyth, W.		
Pese, W.		Smyth, W.		
Port, R.		Snape, R.		
Porter, W.		Snowdon, W.		
Powes, W.		Snowe, Nich.		
Preston, T.		Stanbanke, W.		
Prod, W.	Berrington.	Stanley, J.		
		Stele, T.		
Radoss, Ralph.		Stetten, H.		
Ravis, W.		Stevensone, Jas.		
Richardson, W.				
Robyns, Hum.				
Roderaon, R.		Stynton, Reuben.	Preb. of ——?	
Roger, Laur.				
Rood, H.	Sheldon.	Sutton, Robt.		
Rouley, W.		Swetnam, T.		
Rowbe, J.	——, cur.	Swettonham, Randolf.		
Rusheton, R.				
Russell, J.		Symon, W.		

124 THE ELIZABETHAN CLERGY

CHAP. V
Coventry and Lichfield subscriptions.

Name of Person.	Name of Cure.	Name of Person.	Name of Cure.
Tailfurth, J.		Walkys, R.	
Tailyer, W.		Watson, Robt.	Walsall, cur.
Tarrleton, Robt.		Webb, G.	
Tempol, Ralph.		Webb, Nich.	
Todd, Nich.		Weddysburghe, Robt.	
Torleton, W.			
Tott, J.		Welshaw, H.	
Trylenter, H.		Wendlocke, R.	
Tukyson, Hugh.		Wering, Hum.	
Turner, Edm.		Werynton, J.	
Turner, G.		West, Leon.	
Turner, J.		Wever, R.	
Twysse, T.		Whorwood, R.	
		Wielde, R.	
Underhill, J.		Wightman, J.	
Underwood, T.		Wild, Edm.	
		Wilkinson, Ch.	
Waikefyld, Stephen.		Woddroff, Thurstan.	
Waite, R.	Ulveton?	Wollaston, H.	
Waker, Edm.		Wrexhay, W.	
Walkeden, W.		Wright, J.	
Walker, Jas.		Wrygley, Ralph.	
Walker, R.	Preb. of Pipe Minor.	Wyclyn, W.	
		Wydd, J.	
Walker, T.		Wyldblod, J.	
Walker, W.		Wyldy, Rory.	
Walter, R.		Wylson, G.	
Walton, J.		Wylson, R.	
Walton, W.		Wylson, T.	
Ward, J.		Wynne, J.	
Ward, R.		Wytwyll, J.	
Warton, R.			
Washington, W.		Yoppe, Nich.	

6. *Diocese of Lincoln* (*imperfect*).

Name of Person.	Name of Place, &c.	Name of Person.	Name of Place, &c.
Acton, T.		Arnolds, J.	
Addams, T.		Ashwyn, J.	
Alcocke, R.	Morcott.	Aspinall, Nich.	
Allen, J.		Assheby, W.	
Alford, W.		Atkynson, T.	
Andro, J.		Ayslabye, J.	

Name of Person.	Name of Cure.	Name of Person.	Name of Cure.	CHAP. V
Baitsoms, Robt.		Cantrell, W.		Lincoln subscriptions.
Baikar, Robt.	Chalvey.	Capperson, J.		
Ban, Roger.		Cartwryght, T.	Vicar of Lincoln.	
Bancroft, Jas.		Carvar, R.		
Bankes, H.		Caslyn, T.		
Bapster, J.		Catton, H.		
Barbar, R.	Arch. Bedford and Preb. of Liddington.	Chester, T.		
		Cheyney, J.		
		Chomley, E.		
Barker, Ph.		Choyse, J.		
Barlawe, Geoff.		Chyese, W.		
Bartram, Robt.		Clerke, J.		
Battye, J.		Clerke, T.		
Bayly, Matt.		Clerke, W.		
Bayns, R.		Clypsham, E.		
Bays, W.		Cocket, G.		
Becke, Barth.		Cocks, R.		
Bedall, J.		Cocks, W.		
Bell, T.		Collynwood, T.		
Beller, P.		Corker, W.		
Bennett, Nich.		Coshey, Ralph.		
Bentey, W.		Coton, Nich.		
Bentley, J.		Cotyer, Ralph.		
Bery, W.		Cowper, T.		
Berydge, W.		Crakell, W.	Leadenham, cur.	
Blands, Gibisert.		Crofts, Robt.		
Bolton, W.		Cruke, T.		
Bowlton, J.		Cudbart, Ch.		
Bovell, H.		Cursson, G.		
Bowoirs, W.				
Boylston, Roger.		Dakyn, Ralph.		
Braye, J.		Davyson, Roger.	Precentor of Lincoln Cathedral.	
Brettyn, Hum.	Choral vicar of Lincoln Cathedral.			
		Debank, J.		
Briskowe, R.		Dend, W.		
Browne, J.		Denham, R.		
Browne, Robt.		Dent, Robt.		
Browne, Walter.		Dewsnap, W.		
Bull, W.		Deyre, J.		
Buson, E.		Digbie, Leon.		
Butterworthe, E.		Dorman, Edm.	Chalfont St. Peter and St. Giles.	
Bylcliffe, Thurstan.				
Byngley, Robt.				

126   THE ELIZABETHAN CLERGY

Chap. V

Lincoln subscriptions.

Name of Person.	Name of Cure.	Name of Person.	Name of Cure.
Dryng, T.		Hadcocke, R.	
Dyer, Ralph.		Halme, T.	
		Halyday, Ch.	
Eglate, R.		Hammersley, T.	
Ellis, Percival.		Hancocke, T.	
Eston, J.	Stoughton.	Harpham, T.	Flixborough.
Evinggam, Jas.		Harrys, W.	
Eyr, T.		Harwar, Nich.	
		Hawys, W.	
Farent, J.		Haycón, R.	
Farmar, J.		Hayle, T.	
Farmery, J.		Helds, J.	
Feyrust, R.		Herde, J.	Preb. of Sleaford.
Fishborn, Brian.		Hethcott, W.	
Fishborn, Gervase.		Hewet, T.	
		Heyton, J.	
Flivet, Ch.		Hill, J.	
Forman, Robt.		Hill, R.	
Forster, Giles.	Preb. of Biggleswade.	Hill, T.	
Fothergill, Roger.		Hobson, G.	
Foward, H.		Hocston, R.	Norton.
Fowne, Leon.		Hopkyn, R.	Preb. Sanctae Crucis [als Spaldwick].
Foxcroft, W.			
Freman, Oliver.		Horwarms, W.	
Freman, Robt.		Howson, Fras.	
Fyssher, W.		Huddylston, W.	
Fytto, J.		Hudson, E.	
		Hudson, H., junr.	
Gamble, J.			
Gavyn, J.	Skeffington.	Hulme, Richard.	
Goddall, J.	Ludensis pedagogus (Louth).	Humfrey, Elisha.	
		Hutchyn, H.	
Grace, Robt.		Hyckman, Nich.	
Gray, R.		Hyllins, W.	Queen's Proctor.
Gray, T.		Hylon, Hum.	
Great, Robt.		Hynman, Jas.	
Great, W.		Hynthton, H.	
Green, Nich.	Vicar of Lincoln.	Jareake, W.	
Green, R.		Jenkynson, W.	
Grenes, W.		Johnson, G.	
Grove, J.		Johnson, T.	
Gudwin, Ch.		Johnson, W.	

Name of Person.	Name of Cure.	Name of Person.	Name of Cure.	CHAP. V
Kennes, Miles.	Melton.	Obrey, J.		Lincoln subscriptions.
Knolles, Edm.		Ofspryng, G.		
Knyght, Robt.		Oldman, J.		
Kyashe, T.		Olverley, J.		
Kyng, Greg.		Orrell, W.		
Kyngston, W.		Overton, Jas.		
Lambert, J.		Pagett, T.		
Langton, Robt.		Papenry, Hugh.		
Lanmett, J.		Parke, J.		
Laxe, Jas.		Parker, T.		
Laynge, Dychard.		Pell, W.		
Leasbie, T.		Penyngton, G.		
Letherland, H.		Perseval, J.		
Leyke, W.		Peychyll, J.		
Lovett, T.		Peyrson, H.		
Lygh, J.	Blaby.	Pollard, W.		
		Pott, Ph.		
Mansfield, J.		Powtrell, T.		
Marshall, J.		Presberi, H.		
Marson, Ch.		Preston, J.		
Marston, T.		Preston, Roger.		
Martin, W.		Pullay, H.		
Mathew, J.				
Matys, Robt.		Ratcliffe, Geoff.		
Maynman, J.		Ratlyns, Ch.	Preb. of Brampton.	
Mericke, W.				
Metcalff, G.		Ravyn, G.		
Midleton, J.		Remyngton, W.		
Middleton, T.		Richardson, R.		
Monnson, G.	Preb. of [Welton] Paynshall.	Robinson, E.		
		Robinsonnes, R.		
		Rod, W.		
Moreton, J.		Rods, T.		
Morys, R.		Rypham, Robt.		
Motte, Robt.				
Mownforth, T.	Leicester.	Salisbury, J.	Chancellor of Lincoln Cathedral.	
Myle, Hamlet.				
Mynteyng, R.				
		Sapcote, W.	Preb. Sexaginta Solidorum.	
Newby, Anth.				
Norreys, Robt.		Saunderson, W.		
Northends, R.		Savage, G.		
Nott..., Robt.				

Chap. V.	Name of Person.	Name of Cure.	Name of Person.	Name of Cure.
Lincoln subscriptions.	Savage, J.		Thirkylby, Simon.	
	Sawar, R.		Thomson, E.	
	Sawdill, J.		Thorneys, T.	
	Schepey, R.		Thorpe, T.	
	Sewell, W.		Thurman, Robt.	
	Seyllank, Hugh.		Todd, W.	
	Seynt, Nich.		Tomson, T.	
	Shaw, H.		Tomson, T.	Preb. of St. Botolph's.
	Simmerley, G.			
	Skypwith, Roger.		Townrawe, W.	
	Smeythman, T.		Toyler, J.	
	Smyth, E.		Tyndale, Hum.	
	Smyth, Fras.		Tyrer, Edm.	
	Smyth, H.		Tyson, J.	
	Smyth, J.			
	Smyth, R.		Ufton, T.	
	Smyth, T.			
	Smytheson, W.		Waikefyld, Ralph.	
	Smytheth, Edm.		Walkwyd, J.	Ludensis Hypodidasculus
	Sowre, Ellis.			
	Spencer, R.			
	Spenser, R.		Ward, R.	
	Standesche, J.		Ward, W.	
	Stevynsone, J.		Washington, T.	
	Stocker, W.	Preb. of Milton.	Watmough, E. (*and see* Whatmo).	
	Stocks, Nich.			
	Storye, T.			
	Sturge, Gilbert.		Watson, J.	
	Sugden, Ch.		Watson, Robt.	
	Swetlad, T.		Webster, E.	
	Sympson, T.		Webster, Robt.	
	Symson, J.		Webster, T.	
	Symson, Pat.		Wellche, J.	
			Wells, W.	
	Tailyer, G.		West, Edm.	
	Taylor, H.		Westmills, J.	
	Tayler, J.		Wethestall, Gilbert.	
	Tayler, R.			
	Tayler, R.	Preb. of Carlton cum Thurlby.	Whatmo, Hugh (*and see* Watmough).	Prestwold
	Tenand, R.			
	Thœpe, W.		Whelpdarnell, J.	
	Thirkell, R.		Whitlock, R.	

Name of Person.	Name of Cure.	Name of Person.	Name of Cure.	CHAP. V
Whytlyn, Ralph.		Wright, T.		Lincoln subscriptions.
Wilcocks, R.		Wylliams, J.		
Witte, Roger.		Wylson, Jas.		
Wodhouse, J.		Wylson, W.		
Wollverston, Edm.		Wythin, Cuthbert.		
Wond, T.				
Wright, J.		Ylston, T.		
Wright, J.	Burton Overy.	Yonge, J.		
Wright, R.		Yonge, Robt.		

CHAPTER VI

VISITATION OF THE UNIVERSITIES, 1559

CHAP. VI

The Oxford Visitation, as described by Wood.

WRITS of Visitation for the two Universities were issued in June, 1559. The Oxford Commission does not appear to have survived. The visitors were Sir T. Parry, Sir J. Mason, Sir T. Smith, Sir T. Benger, Mr. R. Gooderick, Mr. D. Master, Alex. Nowell, and David Whitehead. So the names stand in a contemporary MS. list which belonged to Parker[1], but as Alex. Nowell was engaged upon the South-Eastern Visitation, according to the same list, it is scarcely probable that he acted at Oxford as well, though the dates of the respective visitations might have allowed him to serve on both. Wood in his Annals gives the name of Cox, and the correction is probable, as Cox had served in a similar capacity at Oxford before, under Edward VI. With regard to what the visitors actually did, we have gathered no information beyond that given in Wood's Annals. If we may judge from the Cambridge writ which has survived, the purpose of the visitors was not wholly to press the oath, but as much to see to the general well-being of the University. We must remember that when Elizabeth came to the throne Oxford theology was thoroughly in sympathy with the Marian reaction. Thus in one of his letters Jewell tells us in May, 1559, just before the visitation: 'at Oxford there are scarcely two individuals who think with us. . . . That despicable friar Soto and another Spanish monk, I know not who, have so torn up by the roots all that Peter Martyr had so prosperously planted that they have reduced the vineyard

---
[1] Lambeth MS. 959, f. 424.

of the Lord into a wilderness¹.' The Spanish monk would seem to be John de Villa Garcia, Regius Professor of Divinity. To press the oath of supremacy very rigorously would have meant to turn out practically all the Heads of Colleges and the majority of the Fellows. Accordingly it was determined, as we gather from the result, to proceed gently, and to give those in authority every opportunity of conforming, or as Wood puts it, 'to make a mild and gentle, not rigorous, reformation.' The visitors, according to the same authority, began work at the end of June. They restored those who had been unjustly ejected under Mary, but of whom we have found no list, and in turn deprived a certain number of those who scrupled the oath of supremacy. Their action does not appear to have been rigorous, for the University thanked the Queen for the moderation shown by the visitors.

But who were actually deprived? Wood needs careful reading, which he has not always received, for Tierney and others have drawn up lists of the ejected, not noticing that they are placing together the names of those whose deprivation occurred in subsequent visitations. We shall recur to Tierney's names when we look at his list for the whole country, but as it regards Oxford a few criticisms may be made here. He does not notice that Wood² speaks of the deprived as ejected 'about these times,' and so includes such names as Bristowe, who was a pervert to Rome in 1566, and Neale, who was ejected in 1570. He speaks of twenty-three Fellows of New College who 'refused to subscribe to Queen Elizabeth's Injunctions.' This is inaccurate: some of them were ejected by Horne a year or two later, and some later still for refusing to attend the College service. Several were ordained abroad; another was ejected for refusing to take orders; another became a Doctor of Medicine in 1565. Of course from its Winchester connexion New College at that time was devoted to the old *régime* represented by Gardiner, and opposition to change was natural, but, as we read Wood,

Number of the deprived at Oxford.

¹ Zurich Letters, i. 14.   ² See Gutch's *Wood*, ii. 145.

we doubt very much whether more than five or six of the twenty-three were deprived by the visitors of 1559. The same line of argument applies to others said to have been ejected at this time. Thus Coveney, President of Magdalen, was turned out because he was not in Orders; Tresham was forced to resign his Canonry at Christ Church, but was allowed to retain the rectory of Bugbrook, Northants; Smith held the Provostship of Oriel, but was bidden to vacate the Margaret Professorship of Divinity. We have not had access to the College records in order to make up a complete list of deprived Fellows, but until this is done we do not think it possible to prove that many were turned out in 1559. At the same time we do not imagine that those who assented to change did so willingly, for as Wood says: 'many conformed for a certain time, till they saw how matters would be determined.' The deprivations by the visitors, which may be regarded as practically certain, will be found at the end of this chapter, and the reader is referred for further annotation of Wood's list to a later chapter [1].

The Cambridge Visitation.

The Cambridge Visitation appears to have set to work rather later than the Oxford visitors, if Wood is not mixing up the date of the writ and the date of session. At Cambridge the visitors sat during some parts, at all events, of August and September, and the place of inquiry was King's College Chapel. Our authorities are C. H. Cooper's *Annals of Cambridge*, and Mr. Mullinger's *University of Cambridge*. We have been able to glean nothing more, save the writ directing the commission, which exists in copy at Lambeth, and is appended to this chapter. It will be seen that it is mainly educational. For the purposes of visitation, Cambridge was joined with Eton, and the visitors were Sir W. Cecil, Sir Anthony Coke, Mr. Walter Haddon, Dr. Parker, Dr. Bill, Dr. May, Mr. Wendy, Mr. James Pilkington, Mr. Robert Horne. Parker, Bill, May, Pilkington, and Horne were, of course, ecclesiastics; three of them became bishops, and May

[1] See below, p. 223.

was elected to York in 1560. The tone of the University was very different to that at Oxford[1], and it is probable that no great amount of opposition was manifested. This will account for the brevity of the list of Cambridge *deprivati*, though we do not feel quite certain of its completeness. At the same time, almost as many heads of houses were deprived as at Oxford, and, though no special details have been traced of ejected Fellows, it is probable that a few were dispossessed by the visitors[2]. At Cambridge there are not as yet the same opportunities for verifying the Fellows of Colleges as at Oxford.

CHAP. VI

I.

THE WRIT OF VISITATION FOR CAMBRIDGE AND ETON, JUNE 20, 1559.

[Transcr. Lambeth MS. 1166, No. 3.]

Elizabetha Dei gratia etc. dilecto ac fideli consiliario nostro Willelmo Cicello militi, Academiae nostrae Cantabrigiensis summo Cancellario; ac dilectis nobis Antonio Coko militi, Matthaeo Parkero Sacrae Theologiae Doctori; Willelmo Billo Sacrae Theologiae Doctori, ac magno nostro eleemosynario; Gualtero Haddono Armigero, Legum Doctori ac supplicum libellorum Magistro; Willelmo Majo Legum Doctori ac Ecclesiae Cathedralis Divi Pauli Decano; Thomae Wendeo armigero, Medicinae Doctori, ac uni e Medicis nostris; Roberto Horno Sacrae Theologiae Professori; Jacobo Pilkintono Sacrae Theologiae Professori—salutem. *The Queen greets her visitors hereby appointed.*

Cum a Deo Patre in lucem editi omnes et suscepti sumus ut Deum auctorem omnium gloria afficiamus, prima omnium cura debet esse ut quae sit Dei vera gloria intelligamus, atque eam omnibus officiis et studiis persequamur; e cognitione enim debet efflorescere actio, quae, nisi certa scientia et vera in Deum fide nitatur, complacita esse Deo nullo modo potest. Academiae autem nostrae non modo seminaria, et fontes virtutum scientiarumque, sed quasi metropolis quaedam sunt studiorum, quae si non recte excolantur, in graves et perniciosos errores omnes regni nostri *Regarding God's glory, the true end of knowledge, and the objects of a University,*

---

[1] See Mullinger's *University of Cambridge,* 167.
[2] Cooper's *Annals of Cambridge,* ii. 154; Mullinger, 177.

CHAP. VI *partes misere adducentur. Itaque ut ratio aliqua ineatur qua
fontes literarum purgentur, vitia corrigantur, pietasque augeatur de
judicio Consiliariorum nostrorum, assignavimus gravissimos viros
praedictos [names given] vos novem, octo, septem, sex, quinque,
quatuor, tres vestrum ad minimum, delegatos nostros commissarios,
ad ea quae infra scribuntur exequenda : ad visitandum igitur in
capite et in membris tam Collegium nostrum de Eton, quam
Universitatem nostram Cantabrigiae, ac omnia et singula Collegia,
Aulas, Hospitia, et loca alia quaecunque exercitio Ecclesiastico
deputata, tam exempta quam non exempta, ibidem constituta,
eorum Praepositos, Magistros sive Custodes, ac socios, scholares,
studentes, ministros et personas alias quascunque in eisdem
commorantes, deque statu locorum hujusmodi, necnon studio, vita,
moribus, conversatione, ac etiam qualitatibus personarum in
eisdem degentium sive ministrantium, modis omnibus quibus id
melius et efficacius poteritis inquirendum, et investigandum ;
criminosos ac delinquentes, socordes, ignavos, culpabiles, et eos,
qui susceptae jam emendatae religioni subscribere obstinate ac
peremptorie recusent, condignis paenis usque ad dignitatum,
societatum, ac officiorum suorum privationem, aut stipendiorum
proventuum, vel emolumentorum suorum quoruncunque, sequestrationem, vel quamcunque aliam congruam et competentem
correctionem puniendum et corrigendum, atque probatiores vivendi
mores, modis omnibus quibus id melius et efficacius poteritis
reducendum ; contumaces, aut recusantes et rebelles, cujuscunque
status et conditionis fuerint, siquos inveneritis, tam per censuras
ecclesiasticas, quam etiam incarcerationem ac recognitionum
receptationem, et quaecunque alia juris regni nostri remedia
compescendum ; pecunias impendendas quotannis in exequias et
convivia, aut in lectiones publicas vel privatas, aut in alios usus
magis convenientes convertendum; pecunias item in aliquo
collegio impendendas, ex fundatione ejusdem collegii, in choristas,
cantores, et alias impensas, ratione quotidiani servitii (ut vocant)
ecclesiastici, si ita vobis commodum visum fuerit, ad alimentum
sociorum vel scholasticorum ad philosophiam, vel alias literas
discendas, in eodem vel alio collegio constituendorum, committendum ; Magistros, Praepositos, Praesidentes, Socios, Lectores,
tam publicos quam privatos, vel scholares quoscunque, illis officiis
indignos, non proficientes, statutis collegii vel commodo republicae
et bonarum literarum id exigentibus, expellendum, aut amovendum,

(Side notes:)
she appoints her visitors to carry out this commission for the visitation of Cambridge and Eton in head and members.

Their duties are:
(1) to inquire into the life and learning of all therein, and to correct errors;
(2) to enforce subscription under pain of deprivation or other punishment;
(3) to repress and divert lavish expenditure;
(4) to transfer, if need be, choral foundations to a better use;
(5) to remove all useless members of colleges;

et alium vel alios in amotorum loco praeficiendum et substituendum; cessiones praeterea quoruncunque, praepositurus, magisteria, praesidentias, gardianas, societates, seu officia, in locis praedictis, habentium, coram vobis factas et exhibitas auctoritate vestra admittendum, eaque vacare et pro vacantibus decernere, et in loca per cessionem aut alio quovis modo vacantia, personas habiles et idoneas substituendum; cantarias, nominaque cantariarum, item stipendiarios presbyteros, qui ad missas solummodo celebrandas praeficiuntur, in quocunque collegio fundatae fuerunt, et earum fundationes mutandum, aliasque appellationes illis imponendum, et fructus, redditus, et proventus dictarum cantariarum et stipendiorum, ad scholarium exhibitionem assignandum; et dictae universitatis nostrae, et collegiorum ac aularum incorporationes, fundationes, statuta, ordinationes, privilegia, compositiones, compotus, et alia munimenta quaecunque exigendum et recipiendum, eaque diligenter examinandum, et discutiendum; formas officiorum divinorum, et disputationum, et publicarum Lectionum, collationes quoque graduum et honorum, qui eruditionis ergo in studiosos conferuntur immutandum, et in commodiorem rationem instituendum; necnon injunctiones, statuta, quae vobis pro commodiore ordine videbuntur idonea, personis in eisdem degentibus nomine nostro tradendum, et vice ac auctoritate nostris eis indicendum, et assignandum, poenasque convenientes in eorum violatores infligendum, et irrogandum, statutaque, ordinationes, consuetudines, et compositiones, si quas compereritis eisdem contrarias, sive repugnantes, tollendum, et penitus annihilandum; Item concionandi potestatem hujusmodi personis concedendum, quas ad hoc divinum munus suscipiendum aptas esse judicaveritis.

(Chap. VI — and to supply their places; (6) to reform and change all chantry foundations; (7) to examine all university and college records; (8) to settle college services, and public exercises and lectures; (9) to prescribe injunctions and statutes; (10) to license preachers; (11) to impose the supremacy oath, calling all necessary meetings for the purpose; (12) to restore all unjustly deprived, determining all causes herein.)

Juramentum insuper obedientiae et fidelitatis nobis et heredibus debitae, deque renuntianda, renuenda, ac penitus abneganda, extranea potestate quacunque, et quaecunque alia juramenta ex statutis hujus regni praedicti requisita ab omnibus intra loca praedicta constitutis exigendum et recipiendum; congregationes et convocationes praepositorum, gardianorum, audientium, et ministrorum, hujusmodi, pro executione praemissorum, aut reformatione quacunque faciendum, conciendum et convocandum; magistros autem collegiorum et socios, qui propter religionem, aut aliam causam quamcunque minus legitimam, magisterio et societate sua injuste privati fuerint, restituendum in integrum; causas etiam instantiarum examinandum, et jure debito terminandum, ac omnia

CHAP. VI — Power to execute all these duties is confirmed.

et singula alia quae circa hujusmodi visitationis, seu reformationis totius academiae negotia, sive hic expressa fuerint, sive non expressa, quae necessaria fuerint, seu quomodolibet opportuna, faciendum et exequendum. Vobis et singulis vestrum, quorum doctrina, et morum consilii gravitate, ac in rebus gerendis fide, et industria, plurimum confidimus, vices nostras committimus ac plenam tenore praesentium concedimus potestatem etiam si ejusmodi sint quae magis specialia verba et expressa requirunt, cum cujuslibet congruae ac legitimae coercitionis potestate. Mandantes omnibus et singulis vicecomitibus etc. In cujus rei testimonium has literas nostras fieri fecimus patentes. Teste me ipsa apud Westmonasterium vicesimo die Junii anno regni nostri primo.

II.
OXFORD UNIVERSITY DEPRIVATIONS, 1559[1].

Heads of Houses.	Fellows of Colleges.
Alex. Belsire, St. John's.	Ant. Atkins, Merton.
W. Chedsey, C. C. C.	J. Catagre, New.
Hugh Hodgson, Queen's.	Rob. Dawkes, Merton.
R. Marshall, Ch. Ch.	T. Dolman, All Souls.
T. Palmer, Gloucester Hall.	T. Dorman, All Souls.
T. Reynolds, Ch. Ch.	W. Knott, New.
T. Slithurst, Trinity.	J. Marshall, New.
W. Wright, Balliol.	R. Smith, Canon of Ch. Ch.
	W. Tresham, Canon of Ch. Ch.
	T. Stapleton, New.

Professors.
J. de Villa Garcia, Reg. Prof. Div.
J. Smith, Marg. Prof. Div.

III.
CAMBRIDGE UNIVERSITY DEPRIVATIONS, 1559.

Heads of Houses.	Fellows of Colleges[2].
G. Bullock, St. John's.	
N. Carre, Magdalene.	
E. Cosyn, St. Catharine's.	
W. Mosse, Trinity Hall.	
T. Peacock, Queen's.	
T. Redman, Jesus.	
W. Taylor, Christ's.	
J. Young, Pembroke.	

[1] For some other Oxford deprivations, see pp. 224 and 232.
[2] No list has been preserved, but see Mullinger, 177.

CHAPTER VII

THE FIRST ECCLESIASTICAL COMMISSION, 1559–1562

HAVING traced the visitations of 1559 to their general conclusion at the end of October, we must now go back in order to seek for the origin of the permanent Ecclesiastical Commission which dates to the same year. It was a thing entirely distinct from the temporary visitations, and its relation to these has frequently been obscured by historians. It will be worth while to investigate the point, not only for the sake of our present purpose, but in order to throw what light we may upon the history of an important piece of ecclesiastical machinery.

As we have already seen, powers were given under the Supremacy Act 'by letters patent under the great seal of England, to assign, name, and authorize when and as often as your highness, your heirs or successors shall think meet and convenient, and for such and so long time as shall please your highness, your heirs or successors, such person or persons being natural born subjects to your highness, your heirs and successors, as your majesty, your heirs and successors shall think meet to exercise, use, occupy and execute under your highness, your heirs and successors, all manner of jurisdictions, privileges and pre-eminences in any wise touching or concerning any spiritual or ecclesiastical jurisdiction within these your realms of England and Ireland, or any other your highness' dominions or countries; and to visit, reform,

CHAP. VII

Distinction between the Visitation and the Commission.

The Supremacy Act contemplates such a commission.

CHAP. VII

First hint of the commission.

redress, order, correct, and amend all such errors, heresies, schisms, abuses, offences, contempts, and enormities whatsoever, which by any manner spiritual or ecclesiastical power, authority, or jurisdiction, can or may lawfully be reformed, ordered, redressed, corrected, restrained, or amended, to the pleasure of Almighty God, the increase of virtue, and the conservation of the peace and unity of this realm, and that such person or persons so to be named, assigned, authorized, and appointed by your highness, your heirs or successors, after the said letters patent to him or them made and delivered, as is aforesaid, shall have full power and authority, by virtue of this Act, and of the said letters patent, under your highness, your heirs and successors, to exercise, use and execute all the premises, according to the tenor and effect of the said letters patent; any matter or cause to the contrary in any wise notwithstanding.'

This section of the Act, then, gave full power to constitute either visitations for temporary purposes, or more permanent commissions, at the pleasure of the sovereign. A letter previously quoted from the State Papers, dated May 28, 1559, or within a month of the passing of the Supremacy Act, shows that Cecil already contemplated the series of temporary visitations which we have traced, and also a permanent ecclesiastical commission. The letter is written by Edward Allen to Abel, and says that Coke, Gooderick, May, Cox, Haddon, Wroth, Weston, and Lords Bedford and Mountjoy 'are to be visitors and also the Queen's commissioners for all ecclesiastical matters, with others added to them, so that they shall be in all fourteen[1].'

If we may consider the writer well informed, it is obvious from the sequel that changes took place both in the number and the names of those who actually served. But be that as it may, we find that on July 19 letters patent were issued under the great seal to nineteen persons who should act as the Queen's commissioners for the purpose of seeing the Supremacy and Uniformity Acts duly executed. It is clear

---

[1] For. Cal. May 28; cf. Churton's *Nowell*, 392. See above, p. 42.

from the terms of the commission that it was intended to be more permanent. Thus the commissioners are to serve 'from time to time, and at all times during our pleasure'; and mention is made not only of offences actually committed, but of such as 'hereafter' shall arise.

A general glance at the duties of the commissioners gives the same impression of the permanent character of the Ecclesiastical Court thus erected. Briefly the duties are these. The commissioners are to inquire into the working of the Acts of Supremacy and Uniformity; to examine all seditious and heretical opinions and reports ; to investigate all cases of disturbance of church services, and irregularities of ministers therein ; to investigate and punish cases of wilful absence from church; to have full and universal ecclesiastical jurisdiction ; to restore all clergy unjustly deprived ; to determine all other moral or ecclesiastical offences. Most of these duties had been discharged by the temporary visitors, but it is set down more than once in the document appointing them that the powers of the *visitors* were to last *durante visitatione nostra*, and their suspension is clearly contemplated where the writ speaks of delegating causes begun to other commissioners *post finitum visitationis tempus*.

Another point comes out on comparing the writ of visitation with that of the commission. The commissioners are referred to prospectively in the former as 'commissarii nostri Londini residentes et ad ecclesiasticarum rerum reformationem designati[1];' and they are there regarded as a kind of final court for the reference of causes and complaints which have not been determined by the visitation. The names of the nineteen commissioners show that they were more or less by office or by residence connected with London. In this connexion, too, we notice that they had a special authority 'to inquire of and search out all ruleless men, quarrellers, vagrants and suspect persons within our city of London, and ten miles' compass about the same

---

[1] See p. 92, and the Injunctions, p. 67.

CHAP. VII city, and of all assaults and frays done and committed within the same city and the compass aforesaid.'

Loss of records of the commission.

Such, then, was the permanent commission issued on July 19, 1559. It had been contemplated ever since parliament rose, and its duties were general ecclesiastical jurisdiction over 'any county, city, borough, or other place or places within this our realm of England,' whilst it had a particular jurisdiction within ten miles of London, and also formed a convenient final tribunal for cases referred by the visitors. How far can we trace its action? It ought to be possible to follow its proceedings in detail, for explicit direction was given to appoint one John Skinner to register all 'acts, decrees, and proceedings,' whilst an account of all fines and expenses was to be certified into the Exchequer. Unfortunately these records no longer exist. They must have been carelessly kept, but as Sir Edward Coke observed, half a century later, there was considerable neglect in the matter of recording[1]. After a protracted search in the Public Records, the British Museum, and the Lambeth Library we have failed to trace any official record drawn up by the Registrar, or to find the returns certified into the Exchequer.

It was to sit in November, 1559.

But although a detailed account of the early work of the commission exists no longer, a few allusions to it have been collected. In the book of recognizances mentioned above[2], a form of entry appears more than once to the effect that $A.B.$ is to appear 'before the Queen's Majesty's commissioners at London appointed for ecclesiastical matters, either in the Consistory of Paul's at London, or at such other place and places as the said commissioners shall fortune to sit and be in or about the said city of London between November 1st and 7th.' It seems clear, then, that the ecclesiastical commissioners had arranged to sit in London at the Consistory Court of St. Paul's or elsewhere at the beginning of November, in order to try the cases referred to them. This procedure must have been settled at some meeting held soon after their appointment in July or

[1] See Strype, *Ann.* i. 138. [2] See p. 74, note 3.

August, and before the visitation of the dioceses actually began. After the commencement of these visitations the commissioners cannot have met together, as they were dispersed over England, for most of them were serving that summer as visitors in one or other of the temporary visitations.

But before we trace out these allusions to the commissioners' work in November, we must go back to the conclusion of the visitations. They all finished, it is probable, about the end of October. Accordingly a writ was issued for the formal suspension of the powers of the visitors. Here again we have no trace of this document on the Patent Rolls, where we should naturally look for it, but there exists in the state papers a contemporary draft of it. This runs as follows: 'Whereas upon divers urgent considerations us thereto moving, we directed our commission unto you, among others, this last summer, authorizing you thereby to visit, and publish certain our injunctions in the diocese of ——, which as we be informed ye have done accordingly: we now have thought it convenient to will and require you to surcease from any further intermeddling therein, by force of our said commission, and that ye deliver your acts registered, together with the seal of jurisdiction in that behalf used, to our principal secretary, to be further ordered as we shall see cause, reserving nevertheless unto you power and authority to examine and determine all such matters only, *and no others* as have been in your progress exhibited for redress of such disorders *determinable by your commissioners*, as be unto you detected, in as ample and large manner as if our said commission had not been revoked.' The form here given is the preliminary draft of the actual writ of suspension, as seems evident from the fact that the sentences in italics have been added in Cecil's own handwriting. No date is found in the document. It is proved to refer to the visitation in question by the addition overleaf of the names of the chief commissioners in each group of dioceses. We may probably assign the writ of suspension to the latter end of

Suspensions of the visitations in October.

October. The conclusion of cases actually in progress, which is here allowed, had been contemplated before the visitation began, and, as we have seen in the case of Durham, assessors had been appointed there on October 8 for the determination of such cases.

A new writ issued to the commission.   We have already stated that the commissioners were to try in November any cases referred to them. It had been the chief business of the visitors during the summer to get the subscription of the clergy to the settlement of religion. They had treated with special severity those who had refused assent to the Royal Supremacy, and the bulk of the cases referred to the commissioners seem to have been those in which the parties had scrupled the supremacy. In the writ of July 19, which established the commission, nothing had been said specifically of administering the supremacy oath. Accordingly in view of the necessity of administering it, which now confronted the commissioners, fresh letters patent were issued on October 20, empowering them to take the oath of all archbishops, bishops, and other ecclesiastical persons, and other officers and ministers ecclesiastical [1]. The commissioners are those of July 19, with the addition of Cox, afterwards Bishop of Ely, and they seem under these letters patent to receive additional powers, not only to administer the oath in the cases of recusancy now referred to them, but as occasion may arise in the future. Certainly there was no idea of instituting a fresh taking of the oath from all sorts and conditions of clerics throughout the country, which might seem to be the natural meaning of the words employed. A very large number of the clergy had already taken the oath in the summary form provided by the visitors during the previous months, and it was quite unnecessary to refer them to the commissioners residing at London. We conclude therefore that provision was now made for the administration of the oath, first to those referred by the visitors, and then in any cases which might arise.

Proceedings in   This being the state of the case, the commissioners met at London during the first week of November. Strype has,

[1] See p. 152.

THE FIRST ECCLESIASTICAL COMMISSION   143

as it appears to us, mixed up the final session of the London
visitors and the November sessions of the commissioners.
He refers us to Grindal's Register as his authority for the
account given of the clergy examined and deprived in
November, but after searching the register we have found
no mention of the proceedings which Strype has described,
nor is there any such account in the archives of St. Paul's
Cathedral. We reconstruct Strype's narrative as follows.
The London *visitors*, as empowered by the writ [1], met at
St. Paul's on November 3, to consider certain cases which
they had postponed. They settled some of these, depriving
Prebendaries Marshal, Murmere [2], Stopes, and Minor Canons
Stubbs, Hawkes, and Wynyer, all of whom did not appear.
Darbishire they referred to the commissioners. On the
same day the commissioners sat in the Consistory Court of
St. Paul's, and began to consider the cases referred to them
from the whole country. They appear also to have preconized all the clergy who had been absent in the London
visitation. Appended to the visitation subscriptions are
two lists of those who now signed. These include forty-six
names, and amongst them are one or two recently appointed
to livings, who perhaps had no earlier opportunity of
signing.

According to Strype's authority the referred cases were
still given time to repent, and after a fortnight sentence was
pronounced, when those who refused the oath tendered by
the commissioners were finally deprived. There is no note
given of the number. The Crown Presentations, however,
for November, 1559, appear to give evidence of considerable
movement amongst the clergy at that time. Two contemporary lists of these exist [3]. In that of the Lord Keeper
there are no presentations between November 1st and 7th,
and from that date to the 24th there are seventeen, which
is a large proportion when compared with a similar space
of time elsewhere in the same list. The other list is that of

---

[1] See above, p. 92.
[2] Probably misread for Murren.
[3] Lansdowne MS. 443 ; *cf.* p. 238 below.

Chap. VII *Lord Privy Seal*. It records the appointment to two prebends after deprivation on the 2nd and 5th, from which date to the end of the month there are thirty-five presentations, the largest number for twenty-six days that we have noticed in that document. Of course it may be purely accidental that the numbers should be so high just in that month, but the fact deserves recording.

Proceedings with the deprived bishops.

It is very likely that some of the bishops were re-examined at this time, and that hopes were entertained at first of their giving in, for no appointment had been made to some of the vacancies, though nominations had taken place to others in the summer. Probably Bourne and Poole were deprived by the commissioners in November. There is no satisfactory evidence that any of the deprived bishops were under special surveillance during the winter of 1559 and the earlier months of 1560. In custody or restraint they certainly were not. At the same time the ecclesiastical commissioners must have had their eye upon them from time to time. One clause in the commission directed that the commissioners were 'to inquire, search out, and to order, correct, and reform all such persons as hereafter shall or will obstinately absent themselves from church, and such divine service as by the statutes and laws of this realm is appointed to be had and used.' The punishment for offences herein was fine or imprisonment. It is not surprising therefore that Bonner found his way 'by order of the commissioners' into the Marshalsea within a week of Easter Sunday, 1560. This is the beginning of the long story of imprisonment, which ends only with the death of the last survivor, Bishop Watson, in 1585. Just after Ascension Day Watson and Pates were sent to the Tower, where they were joined on Whit Monday by Heath and Thirlby, and on June 18 by Turberville and Bourne. Bishop Scott was imprisoned in the Fleet on May 13. A list of state prisoners, which was drawn up in 1561, gives the dates of their committal[1]. In the case of Scott and Bonner, it says that they were imprisoned by the commissioners.

[1] S. P. Dom. Eliz. xviii. 1–5.

A letter of Jewel, dated May 22, 1560, says: 'Bonner, ... Pate, ... and Watson are sent to prison for having obstinately refused attendance on public worship, and everywhere declaiming and railing against that religion which we now profess[1].' Elsewhere the Zurich letters show that it had scarcely been safe for Bonner, and perhaps some of the others, to venture out into the streets, so great was the reprobation of their persecuting conduct in the previous reign. We have thus seen eight of the surviving ten Marian bishops placed in prison. Of the other two, Goldwell had gone into exile immediately after his deprivation in June, 1559, leaving the disposition of his affairs to his brother[2]. Bishop Poole too was never in prison, but was presently restricted within a circuit of three miles from London[3]. His easier treatment was due probably to his age, for he is not without suspicion of having caused trouble. The eight imprisoned bishops continued under restraint until 1563. Those in the Tower were 'close and severally kept,' and that they were not let out in the meantime is evident from the fact that their names appear at intervals on the list of prisoners with the original date of committal appended to each one. There is however some slight proof of treasonable correspondence on the part of Heath, Thirlby, and Bonner in 1562. This is found in the anonymous letter of a writer who had picked up some hints from one John Payne, the servant of Sir Francis Englefield, a gentleman who was under strong suspicion of secret and treasonable practices. The mysterious writer speaks as if Sir Francis were plotting abroad: 'He told me that the old laws should up again, and that divers good well-learned men do know it very well, as Dr. Heath, late Bishop of York, Dr. Thirlby, Dr. Bonner, Dr. Feckenham, late Abbot of Westminster, and that they all should take place again and that shortly[4].'

To the bishops we will return again later. They were not alone in their imprisonment. There is an extant list of prisoners in the Fleet, written in 1562. The names are given

Other prisoners at this time.

---

[1] Zurich Letters under date. See above too, p. 36, note.
[2] S. P. Dom. iv. 71.   [3] See below, p. 179.   [4] S. P. Dom. xxiii. 60.

CHAP. VII of fourteen 'prisoners for religion since the first year of the reign of Queen Elizabeth,' besides Bishop Scott. The most important were Nicholas and John Harpsfield, Drs. Cole and Darbishire, and Mr. Thos. Wood, who in 1558 had been elected bishop of some see unnamed[1]. Wood had previously been placed in the Marshalsea by the commissioners. In the Tower were Deans Ramridge and Boxall, and Abbot Feckenham. There were among the fourteen a few clergymen of inferior degree in prison, besides the bishops and doctors already mentioned. It is specified that some are there for 'disobeying the Queen's Majesty's Injunctions,' others for ' transgressing the Queen's Majesty's proceedings concerning religion,' one ' upon the Bishop of London's commandment,' others ' for saying Mass.' Setting side by side the lists of prisoners in King's Bench, Marshalsea, Tower, and Fleet[2], we find that there were some thirty in prison in July, 1561, all apparently for opposing the settlement of religion, but a few only are specified ' by authority of the commissioners.' Now inasmuch as one of the lists just mentioned gives ten prisoners at that time in the Fleet, and another of 1562[3] assigns only fifteen to that prison for religious offences since the Queen's accession, it seems fair to conclude that those who were imprisoned in London for opposition to the new *régime* were so far not very numerous, and that choice was usually made of the more distinguished clergy, that their sufferings might warn others.

Conclusion. We have thus traced the early history of the Ecclesiastical Commission as far as our scanty materials enable us to do so. We shall come to a fresh stage in its history in a later chapter[4], when a new writ was issued, with somewhat enlarged scope, and a different procedure was adopted with regard to recusants. So far the commission cannot be accused of any very rigorous treatment on a large scale.

---

[1] Harl. MS. 360, f. 7.   [2] S. P. Dom. xviii. 1-5.
[3] S. P. Dom. xviii. 5 and Harl. MS. 360, f. 7.
[4] See below, Chap. X.

I.

WRIT FOR THE ISSUE OF THE PERMANENT COMMISSION, JULY 19, 1559.

[Transcr. from Patent Roll 1 Eliz. pt. 9, m. 23 d.]

Elizabeth, by the grace of God, &c., to the Reverend Father in God Matthew Parker nominated Bishop (*sic*) of Canterbury, and Edmond Grindall nominated Bishop of London; and to our right trusty and right well-beloved Councillor Francis Knowles, our Vice-chamberlain, and Ambrose Cave, Knights; and to our trusty and well-beloved Anthony Cook, and Thomas Smith, Knights; William Bill our Almoner, Walter Haddon and Thomas Sackforde, Masters of our Requests; Rowland Hill and William Chester, Knights; Randall Cholmely and John Southcote, Sergeants at the Law; William Maie, Doctor of Lawe; Francis Cave, Richard Gooderick, and Gilbert Gerrard, Esqrs.; Robert Weston and   Huick, Doctors of Law, greeting. Where at our parliament holden at Westminster the five and twentieth day of January, and there continued and kept until the   of May then next following, amongst other things there was two Acts and Statutes made and established, the one entitled 'An Act for the uniformity of Common Prayer and Service in the Church and administration of the Sacraments,' and the other entitled 'An Act restoring to the Crown the Ancient Jurisdiction of the state ecclesiastical and spiritual, and abolishing all foreign power repugnant to the same,' as by the same several Acts more at large doth appear; and where divers seditious and slanderous persons do not cease daily to invent and set forth false rumours, tales, and seditious slanders, not only against us and the said good laws and statutes, but also have set forth divers seditious books within this our realm of England, meaning thereby to move and procure strife, division, and dissension amongst our loving and obedient subjects, much to the disquieting of us and our people:

Wherefore we earnestly minding to have the same Acts before mentioned to be duly put in execution, and such persons as shall hereafter offend in anything contrary to the tenor and effect of the said several Statutes to be condignly punished, and having especial trust and confidence in your wisdoms and discretions,

Marginalia:
I. Reasons of the commission.
The Queen greets the commissioners.
Despite the recent Uniformity and Supremacy Acts,
seditious slanders have been uttered and seditious books published.
Accordingly this commission is appointed to give effect to

CHAP. VII
the said acts during the Queen's pleasure.

II. Matters to be investigated by them.

(1) To inquire into the working of the Acts;

(2) to examine all seditions, heretical opinions, reports, &c.;

have authorized, assigned, and appointed you to be our Commissioners, and by these presents do give our full power and authority to you or six of you, whereof you the said Matthew Parker, Edmond Grindall, Thomas Smith, Walter Haddon, Thomas Sackforde, Richard Gooderick, and Gilbert Gerrard to be one from time to time hereafter during our pleasure, to inquire as well by the oaths of twelve good and lawful men, as also by witnesses and all other ways and means you can devise for all offences, misdoers, and misdemeanours done and committed, and hereafter to be committed or done contrary to the tenor and effect of the said several Acts and Statutes, and either of them; and also of all and singular heretical opinions, seditious books, contempts, conspiracies, false rumours, tales, seditious misbehaviours, slanderous words or showings published, invented or set forth or hereafter to be published, invented or set forth by any person or persons against us or contrary or against any the laws or statutes of this our realm, or against the quiet governance and rule of our people and subjects in any county, city, borough or other place or places within this our realm of England, and of all and every the coadjutors, counsellors, comforters, procurers and abettors of every such offender; and further we do give power and authority to you or six of you, whereof the said Matthew Parker, Edmond Grindall, Thomas Smith, Walter Haddon, Thomas Sackforde, Richard Gooderick, or Gilbert Gerrard to be one from time to time hereafter during our pleasure, as well to hear and determine all the premises,

(3) to investigate all cases of disturbance of church services, and irregularities of ministers therein;

(4) to investigate wilful absence from church;

(5) to have full ecclesiastical jurisdiction;

as also to inquire, hear, and determine all and singular enormities, disturbance, and misbehaviour done and committed or hereafter to be done and committed in any church or chapel, or against any divine service or the minister or ministers of the same, contrary to the laws and statutes of this realm. And also to inquire of, search out, and to order, correct, and reform all such persons as hereafter shall or will obstinately absent themselves from church and such divine service as by the laws and statutes of this realm is appointed to be had and used; and also we do give and grant full power and authority unto you and six of you, whereof you the said Matthew Parker, Edmond Grindall, Thomas Smith, Walter Haddon, Thomas Sackford, Richard Gooderick, or Gilbert Gerrard to be one from time to time and at all times during our pleasure, to visit, reform, redress, order, correct and amend in all places within this our realm of England all such errors, heresies, crimes, abuses, offences,

THE FIRST ECCLESIASTICAL COMMISSION 149

contempts, and enormities spiritual and ecclesiastical wheresoever, which by any spiritual or ecclesiastical power, authority, or jurisdiction can or may lawfully be reformed, ordered, redressed, corrected, restrained or amended to the pleasure of Almighty God, the increase of virtue and the conservation of the peace and unity of this our realm, and according to the authority and power limited, given and appointed by any laws or statutes of this realm. And also that you and six of you, whereof the said Matthew Parker, Edmond Grindall, Thomas Smith, Walter Haddon, Thomas Sackforde, Richard Gooderick or Gilbert Gerrard to be one, shall likewise have full power and authority from time to time, to inquire of and search out all ruleless men, quarrellers, vagrants and suspect persons within our city of London and ten miles' compass about the same city, and of all assaults and frays done and committed within the same city and the compass aforesaid.

CHAP. VII
———

(6) to investigate all disorders in and near London;

And also we give full power and authority unto you and six of you as before, summarily to hear and finally determine according to your discretions and by the laws of this realm all causes and complaints of all them which in respect of religion or for lawful matrimony contracted and allowed by the same were injuriously deprived, defrauded or spoiled of their lands, goods, possessions, rights, dignities, livings, offices spiritual or temporal; and them so deprived as before, to restore into their said livings and put them into possession, amoving the usurpers in convenient speed, as it shall seem to your discretions good by your letters missive or otherwise, all frustratory appellations clearly rejected. And further we do give power and authority unto you and six of you, whereof you the said Matthew Parker, Edmond Grindall, Thomas Smith, Walter Haddon, Thomas Sackforde, Richard Gooderick or Gilbert Gerrard to be one, by virtue hereof full power and authority, not only to hear and determine the same and all other offences and matters before mentioned and rehearsed, but also all other notorious and manifest advoutries, fornications, and ecclesiastical crimes and offences within this our realm, according to your wisdoms, consciences, and discretions; willing and commanding you or six of you, whereof you the said Matthew Parker, Edmond Grindall, Thomas Smith, Walter Haddon, Thomas Sackforde, Richard Gooderick or Gilbert Gerrard to be one from time to time hereafter, to use and devise all such politic ways and means for the trial and searching out of all the premises as by you or six of you as

(7) to restore all unjustly deprived;

(8) to determine all other moral or ecclesiastical offences;

III. Methods to be employed:

CHAP. VII

(1 To use all necessary means;

(2 to award such punishment as may be expedient;

(3 to summon all offenders and suspects with requisite witnesses;

(4) to imprison all who refuse to come;

(5) to receive recognizances for appearance.

aforesaid shall be thought most expedient and necessary. And upon due proof had and the offence or offences before specified, or any of them sufficiently proved against any person or persons as by you or six of you by confession of the party, or by lawful witnesses, or by any other due means before you or six of you, whereof the said Matthew, Edmond, Thomas Smith, Walter Haddon, Thomas Sackforde, Richard Gooderick or Gilbert Gerrard to be one, that then you or six of you as aforesaid shall have full power and authority to award such punishment to every offender by fine, imprisonment, or otherwise by all or any of the ways aforesaid, and to take such order for the redress of the same as to your wisdoms and discretions or six of you, whereof the said Matthew Parker, Edmond Grindall, Thomas Smith, Walter Haddon, Thomas Sackforde, Richard Gooderick or Gilbert Gerrard to be one, to call before you or six of you as aforesaid, from time to time all and every offender or offenders, and such as by you or six of you as aforesaid, shall seem to be suspect persons in any of the premises. And also all such witnesses as you or six of you as aforesaid shall think to be called before you or six of you as aforesaid; and you and every of you to examine upon their corporal oaths for the better trial and opening of the premises or any part thereof; and if you or six of you as aforesaid shall find any person or persons obstinate or disobedient, either in their apparel before you or six of you as aforesaid at your calling and commandment, or else not accomplishing or not obeying your orders, decrees, and commandments in any thing touching the premises or any part thereof, that then you or six of you as aforesaid shall have full power and authority to commit the same person or persons so offending to ward, there to remain till he or they shall be by you or six of you as aforesaid enlarged and delivered.

And further we do give unto you and six of you, whereof the said Matthew Parker, Edmond Grindall, Thomas Smith, Walter Haddon, Thomas Sackforde, Richard Gooderick or Gilbert Gerrard to be one, full power and authority by these presents, to take and receive by your discretion of every offender or suspect person to be convicted and brought before you, a recognizance or recognizances, obligation or obligations to our use in such sum or sums of money as to you or six of you as aforesaid shall seem convenient, as well for their personal appearance before you or six of you as aforesaid, as also for the performance and accomplishment of your orders and decrees in case you or six of you as aforesaid shall see it so convenient. And further our will and pleasure is that you shall appoint our trusty and well-beloved John Skynner to be your Registrar of all your Acts, Decrees, and Proceedings by virtue of this commission, and in his default one other sufficient person; and that you or six of you as aforesaid shall give such allowance to the same Registrar for his pains and his clerks, to be levied of the fines and other profits that shall rise by force of this commission and your doings in the premises, as to your discretions shall be thought meet; and further our will and pleasure is, that you or six of you as aforesaid shall name and appoint one other sufficient person to gather up and receive all such sums of money as shall be assessed and taxed by you or six of you as aforesaid for any fine or fines, upon any person or persons for their offences, and that you or six or you as aforesaid by bill or bills signed with your hands shall and may assign and appoint, as well to the said person for his pains in receiving the said sums, as also to your messengers and attendants upon you for their travail, pains, and charges to be sustained for us about the premises or any part thereof, such sums of money for their rewards as by you or six of you as aforesaid shall be thought expedient. Willing and commanding you or six of you as aforesaid, after the time of this our commission expired, to certify into our Court of Exchequer as well the name of the said Receiver as also a note of such fines as shall be set or taxed before you. To the intent that upon the determination of account of the said Receiver, we be answered of that, that to us shall justly appertain; willing and commanding also our auditors and other officers upon the sight of the said bills signed with the hands of you or six of you as aforesaid, to make unto the said Receiver due allowances, according to the said bills upon his account; wherefore we will and command you our commissioners with diligence to execute the premises with effect, any of our laws, statutes, proclamations, or other grants, privileges or ordinances which be or may seem to be contrary to the premises notwithstanding. And more we will and command all and singular Justices of the Peace, Mayors, Sheriffs, Bailiffs, Constables, and other our officers, ministers and faithful subjects to be aiding, helping, and assisting you, and at your commandment in the due execution hereof as they tender our pleasure and will answer to

IV. Of officials, fees, &c.

(1) A registrar and substitute appointed with allowance.

(3) A receiver to be appointed with fees, and so for all service requisite.

(3) All expenses to be certified into the Exchequer and allowed by the auditors.

(4) All officials to help in the execution of the premises.

CHAP. VII the contrary at their utmost perils. And we will and grant that these our Letters Patents shall be a sufficient warrant and discharge for you and every of you against us, our heirs and successors, and all and every person or persons whatsoever they be of and for, or concerning the premises or any parcel thereof, of or for the execution of this our commission or any part thereof.

(5) These letters patent to be sufficient warrant.

Witness the Queen at Westminster, the nineteenth day of July. Per ipsam Reginam.

Dated July 19, 1559.

II.

WRIT OF OCTOBER 20, 1559, FOR ADMINISTERING THE OATH.

(De Commissione ad Sacramentum ab Ecclesiasticis Recipiendum.)

[Patent Roll 1 Eliz. Part 2, M. 32 d; cf. Rymer, *Foedera*, xv. p. 546.]

The Queen to her commissioners.

REGINA Reverendissimo in Christo Patri Matheo Cantuariensi, Archiepiscopo; ac, Reverendis in Christo Patribus Edmundo Londoniensi Episcopo, ac Ricardo Eliensi Episcopo; ac etiam dilectis et fidelibus Consiliariis suis Francisco Knolles, Militi, Vicecamerario suo, Ambrosio Cave, Militi, Cancellario Ducatus sui Lancastriae; necnon dilectis et fidelibus suis, Anthonio Cooke, Militi, Thomae Smythe, Militi, Willielmo Byll, Sacrae Theologiae Doctori, ac Eleemosinario suo, Waltero Haddon, et Thomae Sackeford, Armigeris, Magistris Requisitionum, Roulando Hill, Militi, Ranulpho Cholmeley, et Johanni Southcot, Servientibus ad Legem, Willielmo Maye, Legum Doctori, Francisco Cave, Ricardo Goodricke, Armigeris, Gilberto Gerrard, Attornato suo Generali, Thomae Huyk, et Roberto Weston, Legum Doctoribus, salutem:

Certain ecclesiastical persons refused the settlement of religion in the late visitation.

Quandoquidem nos fideliter accepimus, quod in postrema visitatione accepta per Commissionarios nostros per nos nuper in diversis regni nostri partibus assignatos, quaedam personae ecclesiasticae coram eis comparentes, qui ritus, ceremonia, ac divina servitia infra dictum regnum nostrum et alia dominia nostra, per leges, statuta, et injunctiones nostras ordinata et provisa, observare recusabunt:

Nos igitur in animo habentes eorum reformationem, ne divinus ac verus Dei cultus, per tales perversos homines, in aliquo impediatur vel molestetur, ac in approbata pietate, sapientia, prudentia, et circumspectione vestris plurimum confidentes, assignavimus vos Commissionarios nostros, ac per praesentes damus vobis decem et octo, decem et septem, sexdecim, quindecim, quatuordecim, tresdecim, duodecim, undecim, decem, novem, octo, septem, sex, quinque, et quatuor, vestrum (quorum vos praefatos Archiepiscopum Cantuariensem, Episcopum Londoniensem, et Episcopum Eliensem unum esse volumus) plenam potestatem et auctoritatem recipiendi de omnibus et singulis Archiepiscopis, Episcopis, et aliis personis ecclesiasticis, ac aliis officiariis et ministris ecclesiasticis, cujuscumque status, dignitatis, praeeminentiae, seu gradus fuerint, seu eorum aliquis fuerit, quoddam Sacramentum corporaliter super sacrosancta Dei Evangelia, coram vobis aut quatuor vestrum (quorum vos praefatos Archiepiscopum Cantuariensem, Episcopum Londoniensem, et Episcopum Eliensem unum esse volumus) corporaliter per ipsos et eorum quemlibet praestandum, declaratum et specificatum in quodam Actu Parliamenti nostri apud Westmonasterium vicesimo quinto die Januarii anno regni nostri primo, tenti, edito, juxta vim formam et effectum ejusdem Actus.

Et ideo vobis, et quatuor vestrum (quorum vos praefatos Archiepiscopum Cantuariensem, Episcopum Londoniensem, et Episcopum Eliensem unum esse volumus) mandamus quod Sacramentum praedictum, de omnibus et singulis Archiepiscopis, Episcopis, ac aliis personis, officiariis, et ministris ecclesiasticis quibuscumque superius specificatis, ac de eorum quolibet recipiatis, et cum ea sic receperitis, nos inde in Cancellariam nostram sub sigillis vestris vel quatuor vestrum (quorum vos praefatos Archiepiscopum Cantuariensem, Episcopum Londoniensem, et Episcopum Eliensem unum esse volumus), sine dilatione certificetis, et si contingat praedictos, Archiepiscopos, Episcopos, personas, officiarios, sive alios Ministros nostros quoscumque superius specificatos, aut eorum aliquem, Sacramentum praedictum peremptorie et obstinato animo accipere recusare, tum et eorum recusationem et recusationes et eorum cujuslibet, nos in Cancellariam nostram, sub sigillis vestris vel quatuor vestrum (ut praedictum est) sine dilatione certiores faciatis.

Mandamus autem universis et singulis Archiepiscopis, Ducibus, Marchionibus, Comitibus, Vicecomitibus, Episcopis, Baronibus,

CHAP. VII
execution
of the
premises.
Dated
October
20, 1559.

Militibus, Justiciariis, Majoribus, Vicecomitibus, Ballivis, et omnibus aliis Officiariis, Ministris, et subditis nostris quibuscumque, quod vobis in executione praemissorum intendentes sint pariter et obedientes in omnibus, prout decet. In cujus rei, &c. Teste Regina apud Westmonasterium vicesimo die Octobris.

Per ipsam Reginam.

III.

SUPPLEMENTARY LISTS OF SIGNATURES, NOVEMBER, 1559 [1].

(a)

Barkar, W.
Barley, Oliver.
Blakwyn, R.
Blennerhas-
set, E.
Bridgwater, J.
Brownhall, Roger. — Branston and Warboys; sub-dean of Lincoln; canon and preb. of Louth.
Cabt [...] Edm. — Mugginton.
Dowle, W.
Hand [...] H. — Appointed vicar of Caley.
Hare, Edm.
Hatkyns, W.
Marshall, R.
Mason, G.
Price, Lewis.
Rand, Robt.

Shut[e], Robt. — Professor of Theology: appointed vicar of Cubbington.
Stemple, T. — LL.D.; preb. of Marston St. Lawrence (Lincoln).
Swyft, Nich. — Bramshall.
Taylboys, W. — Scrivelsby, and preb. of Nassington (Lincoln).
Thirland, T. — Appointed rector of Fishtoft.
Tucfeld, Emery.
Vaughan, R.
Whyt, Gabriel. — Preb. of Leighton Buzzard (Lincoln).
Wood, W.

[1] From Cart. Miscell. Lambeth, xiii. pt. 2.

(b)

Benhere, Aug.	Lakin, T.	
Bernard, T.	Longland, J.	
Byckley, T.	Mainwar-	Drayton
Cottrell, J.	ingg, R.	(Salop).
Crosse, Aug. Dorney.	Malet, H.	
Dighton, Robt.	Proctor, Jas.	
	Samuell, W.	
Fyssher, J. Milton.	Suddall, H.	
Gardiner, T.	Thomson, J.	Rotherfield
Godwyn, T.		Peppard.
	Watson, Mich.	
Harrison, W.	West, R.	
Hilton, H.	Wryght, Walter.	

CHAPTER VIII

THE METROPOLITICAL VISITATION OF 1560-1

CHAP. VIII

Settlement of sees in the interval Dec. 1559-March, 1560.

AFTER the proceedings of the ecclesiastical commissioners in November, 1559, there seems to have been a breathing space allowed. At all events no special steps were taken to enforce conformity to the settlement of religion, until the Metropolitical Visitation, which began in the autumn of 1560. Parker, who had already played so important a part in Church matters, was consecrated Archbishop of Canterbury on December 17, 1559. Four days later, the first batch of bishops were consecrated to fill vacant sees, viz. Grindal for London, Cox for Ely, Sandys for Worcester, Meyrick for Bangor. Bishops Barlow and Scory were confirmed the day before, the former in the bishopric of Chichester, and the latter in that of Hereford. On the 27th an important letter was written by Cecil himself to the Queen, on behalf of the council, on the present state of affairs. Amongst other things the Council advise 'that the governance of the Church be better seen unto and established, and the state ecclesiastical duly placed, and the care of all things thereto belonging remitted to the clergy, as in all your progenitors' times have been, preferring the credit and reputation thereof, as in all commonwealths well ordered ought to be [1].' This utterance of the council plainly shows that the so-called 'parliamentary' character of the settlement of the Church was regarded by Cecil and his

[1] S. P. Dom. vii. 73.

supporters as a matter of necessity only, and in no sense as ideal. The letter was also a tacit rebuke of the Queen, who had kept the sees vacant so long, and, as we shall see, did not nominate to the northern dioceses and some others until long after it was written. This protest bore some fruit, for on January 21, 1560, five more bishops were consecrated—Young to St. Davids, Bullingham to Lincoln, Jewel to Salisbury, Davies to St. Asaph; on March 24, Guest to Rochester, Berkeley to Bath and Wells, Bentham to Lichfield and Coventry.

If the Supremacy Oath was at this time being tendered to any of the inferior clergy it must have been ministered by the ecclesiastical commissioners, who alone had the power so to do; but we have found no record of oath taking during the winter of 1559–60. It seems possible, however, that some of the new bishops did now and again associate themselves with the justices during the early months of 1560, in accordance with the provision to that effect in the Uniformity Act, and that cases came up under the Supremacy Act in which those who had scrupled the oath were willing to take it or were pressed to take it. Thus Dean Horne of Durham, on February 18, 1560, says: 'Three prebendaries of the Cathedral Church of Duresme, Robert Dalton, Nicholas Marley, and John Cutting, doth refuse the oath. and I think Antony Salvine will do the same.' As a matter of fact these prebendaries had refused subscription in the visitation of the previous year, and this entry looks as if pressure were again being brought to bear upon those who had then refused. A letter written three years later, in speaking of this time, appears to prove that Barlow was trying to influence some recusant prebendaries at Chichester[1]. In the Zurich letters, Cox, Bishop of Ely, in an undated letter, which the editors assign to the beginning of 1560, says: 'The popish priests among us are daily relinquishing their ministry, lest, as they say, they should be compelled to give their sanction to heresies.' It is not

The Supremacy Oath not strictly tendered during the interval before the metropolitical visitation.

---

[1] S. P. Dom. xi. 25, wrongly placed.

CHAP. VIII clear whether the reference is to those who had signed feignedly, or to those who had not taken the oath at all.

State of the North to April, 1560.
On the whole, therefore, no very stringent means can be traced in the interval before the Metropolitical Visitation now to be described. A note of 'Bishops' uniformity' in Cecil's memoranda of business, March 25[1], may suggest that the council had the question of uniformity, if not of the oath, before them. The state of the North was causing much anxious thought to those in authority. Dean Horne had complained in his letter of February 18 about the grievous irregularities which existed in the diocese of Durham. Cecil notes the vacancy of all the northern sees on April 6. On the 12th, under the head of 'Things necessary for the conservation of this realm in safety and good order,' he sets down 'that the realm may not be thus desolated for lack of bishops, but that some may be specially appointed to have charge thereof.' On May 1 he has another list of vacant bishoprics for consideration. For the present, however, the North was left to the care of the Council of the North, and the Deans and Chapters administered Church affairs as guardians of the spiritualities for the remainder of 1560, and well on into 1561, when severer measures had to be taken.

Parker inhibits the southern bishops from visiting, May, 1560.
In the Southern Province Bishop Scory of Hereford may be supposed to have contemplated a visitation of his diocese in the spring of 1560. His letters of the next year, to be considered in their place, make it evident that there was a good deal of nonconformity, open or secret, amongst his clergy. On May 17, 1560, the archbishop, who was now considering a metropolitical visitation of the Southern Province, issued his inhibition to the Bishop of Hereford to proceed in his diocesan visitation[2]. Ten days later, a similar prohibition was issued to the Bishop of London, and through him to the rest of the suffragan bishops of Canterbury[3].

His commissions
From this point until August no very definite information is forthcoming as regards Church affairs. The ecclesiastical

[1] S. P. Dom.   [2] Reg. 220 b.   [3] Ibid.

commissioners sat at Lambeth in June and July[1], but we have no record of their proceedings. The Marquis of Winchester wrote somewhere about this time, asking the Council 'to cause commission to be sent to Duresme for the execution of justice[2].' At last the archbishop's plans were ready for execution. On August 8 he issued five commissions, to Dr. Weston to visit the diocese of Coventry and Lichfield, and to the bishops of St. Davids, St. Asaph, Bangor, Bath and Wells to visit their respective dioceses as his commissaries[3]. The visitors seem to have begun work in September and October, as appears from one or two entries in the Registers, but we have not found any general return[4]. The commissions which are given in Parker's Register are drawn up on a very close resemblance to the Visitation Writ of June, 1559. The duties of the visitors are almost the same, but nothing is said specifically of administering the oath. Articles of Inquiry were drawn up and presented, and these too are to a large extent a reminiscence, though not a reproduction, of those of the previous year.

On September 8[5] a commission was directed by the Archbishop to Jewel for the visitation of the dioceses of Salisbury and Bristol, but by a further writ of November 9 Salisbury Cathedral was taken out of this commission and was intrusted for purposes of visitation to Dr. Cottrell, on the ground that visitation by the bishop would have interfered with the rights and liberties of the Cathedral Church. Commission was likewise given on December 3 to T. Powell for Gloucester, and on December 19 to T. Yale and another to visit the diocese of Peterborough. In this way provision was made for the visitation of nearly all the southern dioceses. In every case the visitation was undertaken by commission from Parker. We should have ex-

Chap. VIII
———
issued in August, 1560.

Further commissions, 1560.

---

[1] So Strype says.
[2] S. P. Dom. xiv. 37.
[3] Reg. 314.
[4] It seems clear that the Canterbury visitation was over in November, 1560, as in Parker's Register, 224, commission is given to Stephen Nevinson and Alex. Nowell to punish all crimes detected in the late visitation, dated Nov. 11.
[5] Reg. 315, 316.

pected the archbishop to have undertaken, at all events, Canterbury, and perhaps Rochester as being contiguous; but on September 11 he commissioned Yale, Leedes, Nevinson, and Alex. Nowell to act in his stead, on the ground that he was himself hindered by 'certain sufficient causes.' These may have been connected with a return of the ill-health which had troubled him in the early months of 1559. Other reasons may be suggested in the spread of anabaptism, the beginnings of treasonable correspondence with foreign Romanists, and the necessities of general supervision of the Church—matters which appear to have occupied the ecclesiastical commissioners at this time. We have proof otherwise that Parker was not idle, for in November, when the visitation was in progress, he sent round letters from Lambeth to all the bishops of the Southern Province, directing them to furnish full particulars about the numbers, condition, residence, &c., of all the clergy in their dioceses [1].

Object of this visitation.

We have now brought down this visitation to the end of the year 1560. It is clear that its object was to test the working of the Uniformity Act, to guage the obedience of the clergy to the Injunctions, and to bring to light and correct moral offences amongst the clergy and the laity too. It was no part of the duty of these visitors to administer the Supremacy Oath. Returns were probably made in full, as a registrar was appointed to each commission, but these have not survived. Strype has preserved a few details about Bath and Wells, from which we see that there was a good deal of nonconformity amongst the clergy, and a good deal of clerical absenteeism [2]. These cases were to be 'roundly dealt with,' and on the whole, as the Wells Register is witness to very few cases of deprivation, it cannot be supposed that the recalcitrance of these clergy lasted very long.

Revival of the visitation for

The metropolitical visitation was revived in 1561 for some other dioceses—Worcester, February 18, Oxford,

[1] Strype's *Parker*, p. 94. The returns are at C. C. C., Cambridge.
[2] Strype's *Parker*, p. 77.

April 24, Exeter, May 30, Hereford, July 14[1]; but here again we have no formal returns extant. At Hereford Scory had considerable trouble, owing to the strenuous opposition of the cathedral clergy, who were backed up by the mayor and other justices of the peace. As the cathedral body were exempt from episcopal jurisdiction, the difficulties of the bishop were considerably increased. Perhaps it was with a view to tighten the reins of government that Scory appears to have designed a visitation of the diocese the year before. Two of his letters to Cecil throw an interesting light upon the condition of the diocese. On June 21 he makes a request that some impartial persons should be nominated to survey the bishopric, and lamenting the condition of the cathedral, he calls it 'a very nursery of blasphemy, whoredom, pride, superstition, and ignorance[2].' The date of the commission before given, viz. July 14, shows that action was soon to be taken, but it is not clear why it was so long delayed. The second letter, dated August 17[3], and evidently before the commission got to work, gives some details of the proceedings of the 'popish justices,' who were reviving 'abrogate fasts.' The bishop says: 'I have brought the country to conformity of the laws herein by punishing of divers transgressors, yet the city being exempt from my jurisdiction remaineth as before. Mug, Blaxton, Arden, Gregory, Ely, Havard, that were driven out of Exeter, Worcester, and other places . . . have been so maintained, feasted, and magnified, with bringing them through the streets with torchlight in the winter, that they could not much more reverently have entertained Christ Himself. . . . I am in this country a mere stranger, abhorred of the most part for religion, living among them not without danger. Among the worshipful of this shire there be not many favourers of true religion. If it was not for fear of the honourable house and council of the

other dioceses, 1561. Scory's letters.

---

[1] Parker's Register, ff. 317-318.   [2] S. P. Dom. xvii. 32.
[3] Ibid. xix. 24.

CHAP. VIII

Importance of Scory's letters.

Visitation of Eton.

Proceedings of Horne, June, 1561.

marches the event should soon declare my writing herein to be true.'

This correspondence of Scory is important, because it shows the considerable amount of latent opposition which existed in that district, as in some other parts of England, an opposition which was ready, on opportunity given, to declare itself. The letter shows also that the bishops were acting with the justices of *oyer* and *terminer* in accordance with the provisions of the Act of Uniformity.

One more visitation was ordered on August 22, 1561, when Parker, Horne, and Cook were commissioned to visit Eton. This was in consequence of the reported nonconformity of some of the Fellows, in addition to other irregularities. As the report of the previous visitation in 1559 is not extant, we are in the dark as to whether these Fellows had submitted at that time. The record of 1561 still survives. Kirton, Ashbrook, Pratt, and Durston were deprived, as also was Legge, a conduct. The oath of supremacy was tendered in this case, two of the visitors being also ecclesiastical commissioners.

The archbishop had not at this time commissioned any visitation of the dioceses of Winchester and Chichester. We have already noticed that Barlow had been concerned with enforcing uniformity amongst the Canons of Chichester Cathedral[1]. Bishop Horne of Winchester has given us in his correspondence with Cecil some account of what was being done in his diocese. He was occupied with a visitation in May and June, 1561, the inhibition of 1560 having now, it is presumed, lapsed. Writing to Cecil on June 8, he says that he has visited Surrey and a good part of Hampshire, and is going on to Southampton and the Isle of Wight. He says also: 'I have not found any repugning to the ordinances of the realm concerning religion, neither the ministers dissenting from the same, but conforming themselves as it was required of them, and in testification thereof have subscribed to the declaration

---

[1] See above, p. 157.

for uniformity of doctrine. Nevertheless I have found many absent, and many churches destitute of incumbents and ministers. . . . The absence of many proceedeth partly through the wilfulness of some who have purposely withdrawn themselves, or otherwise under colour absenting them, and partly under pretence that they serve noblemen. Against all which I mean to proceed as may seem best to appertain, meaning to have them come to me, my visitation ended. For the rest that I have to do, my hope is to find the like conformity, and namely in the ministers, as by the mutual consent in profession of doctrine and agreement of judgement, quiet and unity may increase and be preserved amongst us [1].'

Another letter from Horne, dated August 29, 1561 [2], shows that he was proceeding under the Uniformity Act, not this time in the matter of the clergy, but to enforce the conformity of the laity. He has 'joined with H. Seymour and Mr. Foster in a certain course of conformity.' He speaks of letters from the council which had 'stricken no small terror into men's minds.' They specially concerned the breach of certain statutes, and so he explained these to the constables and tithing-men. As a result of the proceedings consequent on this action, he finds that people shift from one division to another where the dealing is less severe. The great noblemen of the county stir up disaffection against the bishop. The reference in this letter is very probably to church attendance as prescribed by the Act of Uniformity. During September, Horne was engaged upon the visitation of those colleges in Oxford in which he was, by virtue of his office, the visitor.

Further action of Horne.

At this point we leave the metropolitical visitation of 1560 and 1561. Its main objects had been to secure uniformity, and to improve the state of the clergy. It brought to light a varying condition of affairs which may be summed up in a sentence from a letter written by Horne at Oxford in September, 1561, in which he speaks

Summary.

---

[1] S. P. Dom. xvii. 23.   [2] Ibid. xix. 36.

Chap. VIII of the Supremacy, the Prayer Book, and the Injunctions as 'commonly and everywhere almost through the realm received of all sorts[1].' The exceptions to the rule were in such places as Hereford, where disaffection to the settlement was fostered by justices of the peace or the great noblemen of the district. This was the case, we shall find, in the Northern Province as well.

[1] S. P. Dom. xix. 56.

CHAPTER IX

NORTHERN COMMISSIONS DURING 1561 AND 1562

No single bishopric was filled up in the Northern Province until 1561, and meanwhile the revenues of the sees, as one of the Zurich letters notes, 'did gloriously replenish the Exchequer.' The returns of these sums have been preserved, entered under the 'Foreign' Accounts of Elizabeth[1]. The deans and chapters were, of course, guardians of the spiritualities. A few words must be said now of the state of conformity in the four dioceses of the north during the intervening period. The Duke of Norfolk, Lieutenant-General of the Forces of the North, writing to Cecil from Newcastle on January 10, 1560, speaks of 'the altars still standing in the churches, contrary to the Queen's Majesty's proceedings. It would be well that her Majesty's commission should be addressed to the Dean of Durham, and such others as shall be thought meet, authorizing them to see these matters reformed[2].' On February 16 he again urges the commission to the Dean of Durham, ' to try spiritual causes which in many things run out of order[3].' In the previous letter the writer speaks of the unavoidable delay of a commission of *oyer* and *terminer*, 'of which there is great need.' It appears that this latter commission was appointed on July 20, 1560[4], by the Council of the North, and it would, by the terms of the Uniformity Act, deal with any questions of nonconformity which might arise.

Chap. IX. State of conformity during the vacancy of the northern dioceses.

---

[1] I.e. accounts foreign to the jurisdiction of the sheriff.
[2] For. Cal. p. 572. [3] Ibid. p. 736. [4] Ibid. under date.

CHAP. IX

From a note of Cecil's on March 25, 1560, which stands: 'The two commissions, whereof one at Carlisle, the other at Newcastle: Dean of Durham in the commission[1],' it seems as if some special commission were actually issued, though it is not entered on the Patent Roll. The Dean in a letter, quoted already, speaks as if the whole diocese were in a deplorable condition: 'the face of the church in these parts is so blemished with ignorance and licentious living, through want of a godly instruction, and due correction, that if there be not some speedy remedy found to instruct the consciences with knowledge in the true fear of God, and correct the lives of these libertines (I may well so term them) with severe discipline, they shall fall to barbarous atheism.' He also speaks of the administering of the oath to certain prebendaries of Durham, which again suggests the work of a commission.

The sees at last filled up, 1561.

In June, 1560, Dr. May was nominated to the Archbishopric of York, but died before he was consecrated. After some months Parker wrote very strongly to Cecil about the vacant sees, and recommended Dr. Young, Bishop of St. Davids, for York, and the Bishop of Rochester (Guest) for Durham[2]. Nothing was done at the time, however, to supply the vacancies. Further evidence is given by the Marquis of Winchester on November 1 of the need of a special commission for Durham, and by Dean Horne on November 16 of the dearth of competent clergy in the north. At last the bishops were appointed and consecrated—Pilkington for Durham and Best for Carlisle on March 2, 1561, whilst Young was translated to York from St. Davids on February 20, and Downham was consecrated Bishop of Chester on May 4 of the same year.

Issue of a commission to administer the oath, May 5, 1561.

It was now determined to proceed against the clergy who had evaded subscription to the settlement of religion during the visitation of 1559, and had not yet signed. Great irregularities had prevailed during the vacancy of the sees, and at the beginning of 1561 a com-

[1] S. P. Dom. xi. 36.   [2] Ibid. xii. 42.

mission[1] had been issued to the Earl of Rutland, the new Lord President of the North, to inquire into certain illicit congregations and conventicles, in the counties of York, Northumberland, Cumberland, Westmorland, and Durham. In all probability these were maintained by what Strype calls the 'popish clergy.' Accordingly on May 5, 1561, fresh letters patent were issued to the chief civil and ecclesiastical authorities of the North to administer the oath of supremacy to the clergy[2]. Those on the commission were the Archbishop of York, the Earl of Rutland, the Bishops of Durham and Carlisle, Sir Henry Percy, Sir Thomas Gargrave, Sir Henry Gates, and certain others, including the Archdeacons of Brecon, Nottingham, and York. The preface recites the fact that in the last visitation 'quaedam personae ecclesiasticae coram commissionariis nostris comparuerunt, quaedam contumaces sese absentantes et animo obstinato latitantes, quae ritus, cerimonias, ac divinum servitium infra dictum regnum nostrum et alia dominia nostra, per leges, statuta et munitiones nostras ordinata et provisa observare recusabant in animarum suarum grave periculum, et subditorum nostrorum fidelium periculosum exemplum.' The writ then follows the wording of that issued for the ecclesiastical commissioners on October 20, 1559, save that it restricts the administering of the oath to 'ecclesiastical persons, and other ecclesiastical officers and ministers dwelling, staying, or journeying within the province of York.' Here again we presume that the idea was not to administer the oath afresh to all ecclesiastics, but only to those who had refused subscription before.

Two or three letters show how the terms of the commission were executed. From these it appears that the bishops undertook a visitation of their dioceses, and administered the oath[3]. As four commissioners were required to administer, some of the lay members must have accompanied the bishop in each case. On July 19,

Episcopal visitation and reports.

1. Best.

---

[1] Patent Roll, 3 Eliz. part ii.
[2] See below, p. 172.
[3] They could not do this on their own responsibility until the Act of 1563, infra, p. 205.

CHAP. IX

1561, Best tells Cecil of his proceedings in the diocese of Carlisle. He speaks of having preached three times in the cathedral, when large congregations met him. The common people affirmed they had been deceived, 'which also happened throughout all my visitation. The priests are wicked imps of antichrist, and for the most part very ignorant, and stubborn, past measure false and subtle: only fear maketh them obedient. Only three absented themselves in my visitation, and fled because they would not subscribe; of the which two belong to my Lord Dacres, and one to the Earl of Cumberland. I have assigned days to them under deprivation.' He also says that twelve or thirteen churches on Lord Dacres' land have not been represented in the visitation. 'I do not meddle until I have some aid from the Council of the North. I doubt not by policy to make them obedient[1].' Thus we see that the oath was administered, and was pretty generally taken, the recusants sheltering themselves under the protection of noblemen in that part who favoured the old *régime*. We also see that the bishops threatened the recalcitrant clergy with the Council of the North, a point to which we shall return.

2. Pilkington.

Pilkington writes to Cecil on October 13, 1561. The chief point in his letter is a complaint that he had been shorn of the powers of the palatinate, a fact which is otherwise attested. He did not regain the full powers for some time. He says: 'The more I try the more grief I find. . . . Here needs rather power and authority to be given than to be taken away. . . . The people be rude and heady, and by these occasions more bold[2].' He also alludes to the administration of the oath, but here in the case of a lay official, Sergeant Menel. A month later Pilkington writes again with the same complaint. He says: 'I do not see that they will be ruled without a great power. . . . I am grown into such displeasure with them (the people), part for religion, and part for ministering the oath of the Queen's superiority, that I know not whether they like

[1] S. P. Dom. xvii. 21. [2] Ibid. xx. 5.

me worse or I them.' He also says that the refusers' names have been returned to the Lord Keeper. The letter concludes: 'The last day of my visitation a young priest being called with his churchwardens to take his oath as the rest, to present such things as were amiss according to the Queen's Injunctions, refused "on the ground that the Injunctions hang on further authority than he cannot allow, for that only the Pope has spiritual authority." This boldness the people grow into, because they see that such as refuse to acknowledge their due allegiance escape not only punishment, but are had in authority and estimation.' From this letter we may perhaps gather that the bishop was administering the oath to the recusant clergy, and that in addition to this all clergy and churchwardens were sworn to make returns for their parishes to articles of visitation.

The episcopal visitations of 1561 in the north must have been very partially successful. As the returns of clerical recusancy which were to be made into Chancery do not survive, we cannot tell what proportion of those who refused in the royal visitation of 1559 signed in the episcopal visitation of 1561. Best, writing from Rose Castle on January 14, 1561, speaks of 'punishing and depriving ... evil men which neither would do their office according to the good laws of this realm, nor acknowledge the Queen's Majesty's supremacy, neither yet obey me as ordinary ... yet such men are put in authority[1].'

On January 25 we have a letter from the Archbishop of York, which seems to be written in his capacity as President of the Council of the North. It has no reference to the clergy, but is worth mentioning, as it shows that the laity in Yorkshire, at all events, had escaped the taking of the oath in very many instances. It will have been observed, perhaps, that the letters patent of May 5, 1561, say nothing of the *laity*, and there is no special commission directing the administration of the oath to

[1] S. P. Dom. xxi. 13.

CHAP. IX lay officials within the survey of the Council of the North, between the visitation of 1559 and the date of Archbishop Young's letter. For the palatinate of Chester there was such a commission issued on February 27, 1560[1]. It is, however, very likely that in some instructions for the Council of the North, which we have not seen, direction was given to tender the oath to the justices of the peace, mayors, and others. But at all events the archbishop in the letter above mentioned says that he finds 'the said oaths were a strange thing unto the justices of peace in Yorkshire, and as divers of worship being present affirmed there was no such thing required nor given before. . . . It seemed unto me there hath been some sinister practices touching that oath heretofore. . . . Wherefore for avoiding of division and factions, and the setting forth of uniformity (under your correction), I think it good that a commission were directed into these parts to minister and receive the oath, as well of all justices of peace as of other ministers and officers of the laity. I am assured it would do much good, and be with all obedience and quietness received.'

Instructions for the Council of the North, 1562.

No commission appears to have been issued for this purpose during the remainder of the year 1562, but in November lengthy instructions were issued to the Archbishop of York, as President of the Council of the North in succession to the Earl of Rutland. It is expressly stated that 'Her Majesty's pleasure is that the said Lord President, or Vice-President, and Council shall aid, help, and assist all the bishops, ordinaries, and commissioners for matters of religion within the limit and jurisdiction of the said council, as well for the due observation and execution of all things set forth in the book of Common Prayer and administration of the sacraments, and in the Injunctions, as also for the apprehension and punishment of all singular persons as shall contemn or disobey the said bishops, ordinaries, or commissioners[2].' Thus the

---

[1] Pat. Roll, 2 Eliz. pt. 7.   [2] Cotton MS. Titus F. xiii. f. 249.

bishops, with the assistance of the council, carried out the enforcement of the Uniformity Act, and the commissioners doubtless tendered the oath when occasion arose in the various dioceses. For the palatinate of Chester a special commission was issued on July 20, 1562, to try offences connected with religion. It was directed to Lord Derby and others. We possess, however, no information as to what was done in this commission, or by the Council of the North[1].

We have thus reached roughly the end of 1562. With the prospect of a parliament at the commencement of the new year the authorities seem to have taken little trouble in the closing months of 1562 in the matter of uniformity and the taking of the oath. At all events we trace no reference in the State Papers and correspondence of the time to any fresh or more vigorous action. There are no letters from the bishops, and no fresh commissions. Reviewing, then, the proceedings up to the point reached, it seems that after the visitation of 1559 little was done in the north to enforce conformity until the bishops' visitations of 1561. The bishops appear to have then acted with vigour so far as the clergy are concerned, in consequence of a new commission, and it seems probable that a good many of those who had refused conformity before, now gave in. Isolated instances of recusancy probably came before the Council of the North, whose powers were always at hand to back up the action of bishops and commissioners.

Summary of the position, December, 1562.

[1] No official reports of the Council are known.

Chap. IX

Commission to Administer the Oath in the North.

Commissio ad Capiendum Sacramentum ab Ecclesiasticis in Provincia Eborum.

[Patent Roll, 3 Eliz. part 10, m. 34 dors.; cf. Rymer's *Foedera*, xv. p. 611.]

The Queen greets her commissioners.

ELIZABETHA Dei Gratia, Angliae, Franciae, et Hiberniae Regina, Fidei Defensor, &c., Reverendissimo in Christo Patri Thomae Eboracensi Archiepiscopo, Angliae Primati, Metropolitano; ac praedilecto consanguineo et consiliario suo, Henrico Comiti Rutlandiae Praesidenti Concilii sui in partibus borealibus; ac reverendis in Christo Patribus Jacobo Dunelmensi Episcopo, et Johanni Carliolensi Episcopo; ac etiam dilectis et fidelibus subditis suis, Henrico Percy, Thomae Gargrave, et Henrico Gates, Militibus; necnon dilectis sibi Johanni Vaughan, Christofero Estofte, Thomae Haynes, Armigeris; Johanni Rokeby, Legum Doctori; Waltero Jones, Archidiacono Brechon, Willelmo Daye, Archidiacono Nottinghamiae, Johanni Stokes, Archidiacono Eboracensi; Thomae Layken, Artium Magistro; Roberto Pecock, et Willelmo Watson, Aldermannis civitatis nostrae Eboraci—salutem.

Certain ecclesiastical persons absented themselves from the last visitation.

Quandoquidem nos fideliter accepimus quod in postrema visitatione nostra, nuper in diversis regni nostri partibus assignata, quaedam personae ecclesiasticae coram commissionariis nostris comparuerunt, quaedam contumaces sese absentantes et animo obstinato latitantes, quae ritus, ceremonias ac divinum servitium, infra dictum regnum nostrum et alia dominia nostra, per leges, statuta, et munitiones nostras, ordinata et provisa, observare recusabant, in animarum suarum grave periculum, et subditorum nostrorum fidelium periculosum exemplum:

The aforesaid commissioners are therefore appointed.

Nos igitur in animo habentes eorum reformationem, ne divinus et verus Dei cultus per tales perversos homines in aliquo impediatur vel molestetur, ac in approbata pietate, sapientia, prudentia, et circumspectione vestra plurimum confidentes, assignavimus vos commissionarios nostros, ac per praesentes damus et concedimus vobis septemdecim, sexdecim, quindecim, quatuordecim, tresdecim, duodecim, undecim, decem, novem, octo, septem, sex, quinque, et quatuor vestrum (quorum vos praefatos Thomam Archiepiscopum Eboracensem, Henricum Comitem Rutlandiae, Jacobum Episcopum

Dunelmensem, Thomam Gargrave, Militem, vel Walterum Jones unum esse volumus) plenam potestatem et auctoritatem capiendi et recipiendi de omnibus et singulis archiepiscopis, episcopiis, et aliis personis ecclesiasticis, et aliis officiariis et ministris ecclesiasticis, infra provinciam Eboracensem commorantibus, degentibus, sive itinerantibus, cujuscunque status, dignitatis praeeminentiae, seu gradus fuerint, seu eorum aliquis fuerit, quoddam sacramentum corporale super sacrosancta Dei Evangelia coram vobis aut quatuor vestrum (quorum vos praefatos Thomam Archiepiscopum Eboracensem, Henricum Comitem Rutlandiae, Jacobum Episcopum Dunelmensem, Thomam Gargrave Militem, vel Walterum Jones, unum esse volumus) corporaliter per ipsos et eorum quemlibet praestandum, declaratum et specificatum in quodam Actu Parliamenti nostri apud Westmonasterium vicesimo quinto die Januarii anno regni nostri primo habito tento edito, juxta vim formam et effectum ejusdem Actus.

CHAP. IX — to administer the oath to all ecclesiastical persons in the Northern Province.

Et ideo vobis et quatuor vestrum (quorum vos praefatos Thomam Archiepiscopum Eboracensem, Henricum Comitem Rutlandiae, Jacobum Episcopum Dunelmensem, Thomam Gargrave Militem, vel Walterum Jones, unum esse volumus) mandamus insuper quod sacramenta praedicta de omnibus et singulis archiepiscopis, episcopis, et aliis personis, officiariis, et ministris ecclesiasticis quibuscunque superius specificatis, ac de eorum quolibet, recipiatis; et cum ea sic ceperitis, nos inde in Cancellariam nostram sub sigillis vestris vel quatuor vestrum (quorum vos praefatos Thomam Archiepiscopum Eboracensem, Henricum Comitem Rutlandiae, Jacobum Episcopum Dunelmensem, Thomam Gargrave Militem, vel Walterum Jones, unum esse volumus) sine dilatione certificetis; et si contingat praedictum archiepiscopum, episcopos, personas, officiarios, sive alios ministros quoscunque superius specificatos aut eorum aliquem, sacramentum praedictum peremptorie et obstinato animo accipere recusare, tum et eorum recusationem et recusationes, et eorum cujuslibet vos in Cancellariam nostram sub sigillis vestris vel quatuor vestrum (ut praedictum est) sine dilatione nos certiores faciatis. Mandamus quoque universis et singulis Archiepiscopis, Ducibus, Marchionibus, Comitibus, Vicecomitibus, Episcopis, Baronibus, Militibus, Justiciariis, Majoribus, Ballivis, et omnibus aliis officiariis, ministris, et subditis nostris quibuscunque, quod vobis in executione praemissorum intendentes sint pariter et obedientes prout decet.

The commissioners shall certify the reception and refusal of the oath into Chancery.

In cujus rei, etc. Teste Regina apud Westmonasterium quinto die Maii. Per ipsam Reginam.

CHAPTER X

THE SECOND ECCLESIASTICAL COMMISSION, 1562

Chap. X
A new commission in 1562.

RETURNING to the south a new point of departure comes before us in the issue of a second ecclesiastical commission in 1562. The writ is dated July 20, and is directed to the Archbishop of Canterbury and others, twenty-seven in all. The commission is evidently intended to take the place of that which we considered in an earlier chapter, and which had been in existence for exactly three years. There had been nineteen members on the first commission, supplemented on October 20, 1559, by the addition of the bishop-elect of Ely, Richard Cox. Many who had served before were included in the new list, whilst five had been removed by death, and with the addition of twelve new names the sum total was increased to twenty-seven. In 1559 six at least had constituted an effective number; in 1562 this was reduced to a necessary three. The reason of the new commission is probably not far to seek. A contemporary Zurich letter from Cox to Peter Martyr, written on August 5, says: 'There is everywhere an immense number of papists, though for the most part concealed; they have been quiet hitherto, except that they are cherishing their errors in their secret assemblies. . . . The papists are wonderfully raising their spirits since the disorders in France.' About the same time Jewel writes: 'The obstinacy of the papists is now greater than ever. They are depending, it seems, upon the result of events in France.' The reference is to the events which followed the massacre of Vassy on March 1, 1562. The massacre began the religious wars in France, and, when these broke out, the papal sympathisers in England expected to see England soon embroiled, and the religious policy of the last three years reversed. The fear of such a contingency seems to have led to the issue of the commission of July 20.

First proceedings under the new commission.

It is highly probable that some exhibition of severity was made at once by the commissioners, and on August 6 they committed Dr. Chedsey, late Archdeacon of Middlesex, to the Fleet, and with him Dr. Antony Draycot, formerly Archdeacon of Huntingdon, &c. The latter held preferment is so many dioceses, as the registers show, that he was widely known, whilst Chedsey was notorious as a member of the Westminster Disputation of 1559, for his attitude on which occasion he had already suffered. There was perhaps some talk at first of further proceeding against the imprisoned bishops, as Parkhurst tells Bullinger on August 20 that 'the pseudo-bishops who are in the Tower will very soon render an account of their breach of faith (reddent rationem suae perfidiae), so I hear.' *Perfidia* may perhaps denote the secret correspondence hinted at above [1], but there is no proof that anything was now done so far as the bishops are concerned. One of the first proceedings of the commission was to send letters to the diocesan bishops, bidding them set inquiries on foot as to the amount of recusancy in their dioceses. Thus Parkhurst writes in the same letter: 'I received a letter from my Lord of Canterbury four days ago: the substance of it is this, that I should diligently ascertain by every means in my power, though secretly, who and how many there are in my diocese who do not comply with the true religion. This is, I suspect, with the intention of punishing their breach of faith (*perfidiae* again) [2].'

Restraint and surveillance of recusants.

Action seems to have been taken in accordance with these returns. There exists amongst the State Papers an undated list [3] of clerical and lay recusants, which is assigned by Strype to the year 1561, but from internal

---

[1] See p. 145.   [2] *Zurich Letters*, Aug. 20, 1562.
[3] See below, p. 179.

evidence it cannot belong to a date earlier than August 6, 1562, for Dr. Chedsey is in this list the most recent prisoner in the Fleet, and the day of his committal as already stated is accurately known. The list too, cannot be put much later than August, 1562, and thus we here discover an entirely fresh procedure in restraining recusants within bounds. These are classed in four divisions: (1) recusants which are abroad and bound to certain places; (2) a list of certain evil-disposed persons of whom complaint hath been made, which lurk so secretly that processes cannot be served upon them; (3) others fled as was reported over the seas; (4) prisoners by order from the commissioners. A glance at the list shows that those restrained were usually people of some position, including Bishop Poole of Peterborough and several deans and other dignitaries. Their bounds set prove that the idea was to keep them from those districts in which their influence was likely to be felt. In all some sixty persons are so restrained, and the majority of these are certainly clergymen. Of the 'evil-disposed persons,' twelve appear to be clergymen. Seven clerics had fled 'over the seas,' and of sixteen prisoners in the Fleet, Marshalsea. &c., twelve were in Orders. It must however be noted that the list is only of those under surveillance of the commissioners; nothing is said of the bishops in the Tower, nor is mention made of the lesser clerical and lay recusants who had perhaps been dealt with by the magistrates, by the Council of the North, and that of the Marches. Instances of such dealing, however, are more easily imagined than proved, for no returns exist of imprisonment or fine as inflicted by justices or council during the early years of Elizabeth, so far as our knowledge extends. Later on in the reign we get ample material.

Other duties of the new commission. Another interesting instruction for the commission of 1562 may be mentioned, though it is beside our purpose to examine its execution here. We refer to the provision by which the commissioners were directed 'to examine the rules and statutes of all ecclesiastical incorporations founded by her Highness' father King Henry VIII, or since, and to certify her Highness of their enormities, together with such orders as they think meet to be appointed, and made for the same incorporations, to the end her Majesty may thereupon alter or change the same orders, or make new according to a statute made in the first year of her Majesty's reign.'

We have thus brought down the outline of the history of the ecclesiastical commission to the end of 1562, and almost to the eve of Elizabeth's second parliament, when fresh legislation was enacted which we may consider in a separate chapter. But before we leave the commissions which had now been at work for some three years, we may say of their proceedings that there is little proof at this stage, or indeed for the next year or two, of any very rigorous fining or imprisonment. Our conviction is that the commissioners may have imprisoned some twenty-five people altogether, before 1563, whilst in the Exchequer records there is no existing proof of the receipt of the fines which were to be paid into the Exchequer[1], although the Exchequer records seem to have been carefully kept at that time. In and after 1564 the cases brought before the commission were chiefly connected with the vestiarian controversy. Great changes were introduced in 1570 and 1571, after the excommunication of the Queen, when the whole constitution and working of the ecclesiastical commission were altered[2].

Summary of the work of the commissions, 1559-1562.

---

[1] See p. 179.
[2] The references to the Patent Rolls for other early Elizabethan commissions are 10 Eliz. pt. 2, to the Archbishop of York, &c.; 13 Eliz. pt. 7, for Lincoln and Peterborough; 14 Eliz. pt. 8, a fresh ecclesiastical commission issued to the Archbishop of Canterbury, &c. See too Watson's Patent Roll (so-called), for 15 Eliz. no. 29, an important series of commissions for various counties; ibid. 16 Eliz., for other parts; Patent Roll, 19 Eliz. pt. 12, for Province of York; also ibid., special commission for Norwich (see too Cotton MS. Titus B. III) and Durham, and 21 Eliz. pt. 7, for Wales. Lansdowne MS. 396, Cotton Vesp. F. ix., Cleop. F. ii. f. 139, may also be consulted for proceedings of the commissioners under Elizabeth. There are some returns at P. R. O. after about 1570.

CHAP. X

I.

OFFICIAL ABSTRACT OF THE WRIT OF JULY 20, 1562.

[Transcr. from S. P. Dom. Eliz. xxvi. 41.]

Abstract of Heads of the Ecclesiastical Commission.

First, authority is given unto them to put in execution two statutes made in the first year of the Queen's Majesty's reign, the one entitled An Act for the Uniformity of Common Prayer and Service of the Church and the Administration of the Sacraments; and the other entitled, An Act restoring to the Crown the ancient jurisdiction over the estate ecclesiastical and spiritual, and abolishing all foreign power repugnant to the same.

2. Also to inquire of all heresies and seditious books, and such other contrary to the laws of the realm, and the quiet government of the same, &c.

3. Also to inquire of all enormities and misbehaviours, &c., in any church or chapel, &c.

4. Also to inquire, search out, and correct all such as shall obstinately absent themselves from the divine service.

5. Also to redress, correct, and amend all contempts and enormities ecclesiastical, which by ecclesiastical power may be corrected by censures ecclesiastical, deprivation, or such like.

6. Also to inquire and search out all masterless men, quarrellers, and vagrant persons in London or within ten miles' compass.

7. Also to hear and finally determine according to the laws of the realm, the causes and complaints of all such which in respect of religion or for lawful matrimony were deprived or spoiled of their living or goods, and to restore them, &c.

8. Also to hear and determine all notorious adulteries, fornications, and ecclesiastical crimes.

9. And thereupon commanding them to execute due punishment upon every offender in any of the premises by imprisonment, fine, or otherwise.

10. And authority to take body bonds for appearance for observing these orders, &c.

11. And also to examine the rules and statutes of all ecclesiastical incorporations founded by her Highness' father King Henry VIII, or since, and to certify her Highness of their enormities, together with such orders as they think meet to be appointed and

made for the same incorporations, to the end her Majesty may thereupon alter or change the same orders, or make new according to a statute made in the first year of her Majesty's reign.

12. Also to tender and receive the oath appointed in the said Act, entitled, An Act for the restoring to the Crown the ancient jurisdiction, &c., of all ecclesiastical persons, and to certify the recusations into the Chancery, &c.

13. And to allow the register and other travellers herein of commodity rising hereof.

14. And to certify the fines into the Exchequer.

II.

RECUSANTS WHICH ARE ABROAD AND BOUND TO CERTAIN PLACES[1].

[Transcr. from S. P. Dom. Eliz., Addenda xi. 45.]

*Alexander Belsar, clerk, to remain in the town of Hanborough, in the county of Oxford, or within two miles' compass about the same. *(Old, wealthy, and stubborn.)*

*Doctor Poole, late bishop of Peterborough, to remain in the city of London and suburbs, or within three miles' compass about the same. *(A man known and reported to live quietly, and therefore hitherto tolerated.)*

*Thomas Wyllanton, late chaplain to Doctor Bonner, to remain in the counties of Middlesex or Buckingham, or the city of London, and bound to appear once every term. *(Stiff and not unlearned.)*

*Robert Purseglove, late suffragan of Hull, and before an abbot or a prior, to remain in the town of Ugthorpe in the county of York, or within twelve miles' compass about the same. *(Very wealthy and stiff in papistry, and of estimation in the country.)*

*Roger Marshall, once prior of Sempringham, to remain in the town of Newmarket or within six miles' compass about the same. *(Not unlearned and wealthy.)*

*Thomas Seagiswick, Doctor of Divinity, to remain in the town of Richmond, or within ten miles' compass about the same. *(Learned, but not very wise.)*

---

[1] An asterisk denotes ascertained deprivation. The spelling of proper names is retained. See the list, p. 252, and Strype, *Ann.* i. 241.

Not unlearned, but very stubborn and to be considered.	*William Carter, Doctor of Divinity, late archdeacon of Northumberland, to remain in the town of Thirsk in the county of York, or within ten miles' compass about the same.
Learned, in King Edward's time preached the truth earnestly, and now stiff in papistry, and thinketh very much good of himself.	*Thomas Harding, Doctor of Divinity, to remain in the town of Monkton Farleigh, in the county of Wiltshire, or sixteen miles' compass about the same, or within the town of Toller Whelme in the county of Dorset, or twenty miles' compass about the same.
An unlearned priest, but very stubborn.	*Richard Dominick, clerk, late parson of Stratford, in the diocese of Salisbury, to remain in the town of East Knoyle in the county of Wiltshire, or within sixteen miles' compass about the same.
Not unlearned, but very wilful and stubborn.	William Boys, clerk, late parson of Gresley in Yorkshire, to remain in the town of Southwell, in the county of Nottingham, or within twenty-four miles' compass about the same.
Very stubborn, and worthy to be looked unto.	*David de la Hide, an Irishman, late scholar of Oxford, at his liberty, saving that he is restrained to come within twenty miles of either of the universities.
Wilful scholars.	Edward Brunbrough, *Robert Dawkes, George Simpson } late scholars of Oxford, restrained as before.
An unlearned priest, very wilful.	*Anthony Atkyns, clerk, late of Oxford, to remain within the counties of Gloucester or Shropshire.
	William Thules, late schoolmaster of Durham, bound for his good behaviour in matters of religion, and restrained from the diocese of Durham.
Late a superstitious monk of Mont Grace, and unlearned.	*Roger Thompson, clerk, restrained from the diocese of York and Durham.
Wilful scholars, and not learned in divinity.	*John Rastall, Nicholas Fox, Robert Davies, William Giblett, John Durham } late scholars of Oxford, restrained from the universities, and bound for their quiet behaviour in matters of religion.
An unlearned priest.	*Richard Halse, late prebendary of Exeter, to remain in the counties of Devon or Cornwall, the city of Exeter and within three miles of either of his late benefices always excepted.

THE SECOND ECCLESIASTICAL COMMISSION 181

CHAP. X

Two stubborn persons; divers processes being sent for them, are so supported in Herefordshire that the same cannot be executed against them, and reported to be maintained by Mr. J. Skydmore, Mr. Pie, and one William Luson, a prebendary of Hereford.
*John Blaxton } late prebendaries of Exeter, to re-
*Walter Mugge } main in the county of Hereford.

Unlearned, wealthy, and stiff.
*Robert Dalton, clerk, late prebendary of Durham, to remain with the Lord Dakers of the north.

Unlearned.
*Nicholas Marley, late prebendary of Durham, to remain in the bishopric of Durham, so as he come not within eight miles of Durham.

Unlearned.
*Thomas Redman, late chaplain to the late bishop of Ely, to remain in the counties of York, Westmorland, and Lancaster.

Learned, but wilful and meet to be considered.
*Henry Comberforde, late of Lichfield, to remain in the county of Suffolk, with liberty to travel twice every year into Staffordshire, allowing six weeks at every time of his travel.

*John Ramridge, lately punished, bound to be quiet and to go to the service, and sureties bound for his appearance when he shall be called.

Learned, settled in papistry.
*John Ceaton, Doctor of Divinity, to remain in the city of London, or within twenty miles' compass about the same.

An unlearned priest.
John Erle, clerk, late of Winton, to remain in the county of Southampton, so that he always gives notice at Hyde in the said county, where always he shall make his abode, so as he come not to the Trinity Church or college in Winton.

These two are thought to behave themselves very seditiously and contrary to their recognizances, secretly lurk in Lancashire, and are thought to be maintained there by rulers and gentlemen of that country.
*Lawrence Vawce, late warden of Manchester, to remain in the county of Worcester.

Richard Hart, late one of the curates of Manchester aforesaid, to remain in the counties of Kent or Sussex.

*Anthony Salvyn, late prebendary of Durham, to remain in the town of Kirkby Moorside, in the county of York, or elsewhere within the said county, the city of York only excepted, so that he passeth not above five miles northward of Kirkby Moorside aforesaid.

*Robert Manners, late parson of Watton at Stone, to remain in the town of Baldock in the county of Hertford, or within twenty miles' compass about the same.

*Edmund Daniell, late dean of Hereford, to remain with the Lord Treasurer, or within twelve miles' compass of his house where he maketh his abode.

*Thomas Hide, late schoolmaster of Winton, with the Lord Treasurer.

*Robert Hill, late commissary at Calais, to remain in the town of Burton-upon-Trent, in the county of Staffordshire, or elsewhere within the said county.

Nicholas Banester, to remain in the county of Lancaster, the town of Preston in Amounderness always excepted. He was a schoolmaster at Preston.

William Winck, late of Cambridge, to remain in Norfolk.

*Clement Burdet, late of Bath, to remain in Crondall in Hampshire, or else in Sonning in Berkshire.

*Doctor Tresham, late of Oxford, to remain in Northamptonshire.

*Albone Langdall, Doctor of Divinity, to remain with the Lord Montacute, or where his lordship shall appoint, and to appear within twelve days after monition given to the said Lord Montacute or his officers before the commissioners.

*John Porter, late parson of Crondall in Kent, to remain in Maidstone in the county of Kent, or the city of London or suburbs, or in any place within the said county of Kent, the city of Canterbury excepted, so that always he give intimation to the sheriff of Kent of his present abode.

THE SECOND ECCLESIASTICAL COMMISSION 183

<small>Not altogether unlearned, but very perverse.</small>

John Dale, late of Cambridge, to remain in the town of Newmarket, or ten miles' compass about the same, saving towards London and Cambridge but four miles.

Alan Cope }
William Lewes }
late scholars of Oxford. The said Cope is bound to appear once within fourteen days, and the said Lewes restrained from the universities, otherwise at liberty.

Stephen Hopkyns, clerk, confessor (as he saith) to the bishop of Aquila, and a daily resorter unto him. He was delivered out of the Fleet by the Queen's Majesty's express commandment to the Lord of Canterbury.

<small>Altogether unlearned, but yet very subtle.</small>

*Tristram Swadell, late Dr. Bonner's servant, and yet thought to be a practitioner for him.

Thomas Dormer, late scholar of Oxford, restrained from the universities.

<small>Unlearned, stubborn priests, late of the diocese of Worcester.</small>

Henry Johnson, clerk, late parson of Broadwas in Worcestershire, to remain in the county of Hereford.
Robert Shawe, late prebendary of Worcester, to remain in the county of Shropshire.
Robert Shelmerden, clerk, to remain in the county of Northampton.
William Burton, clerk, to remain in Oxfordshire.
Henry Saunders, clerk, to remain in the county of Warwick.

<small>Wilful scholars.</small>

Edward Atislowe
Walter Russell
Robert Yonge
Robert Fenne
Raff Keat
} late scholars of Oxford, restrained from the universities.

Certain evil-disposed persons, of whom complaint hath been made, which lurk so secretly that process cannot be served upon them.

{ *Philip Morgan, late of Oxford.
*John Arden, late prebendary of Worcester.
Friar Gregory, alias Gregory Basset, a common Mass sayer; one *Ely, late Master of St. John's College in Oxford; one *Haverde, late chaplain to Mres. Claurenciaulx.

Are supported in Herefordshire, especially by the parties above named.

*William Norfolk, late prebendary of Worcester.

*Dr. Marshall, late Dean of Christ Church in Oxford, who hath had recourse to the Earl of Cumberland, and one Mr. Metcalf his brother-in-law, in Wensleydale in Yorkshire, as it is reported.

*Dr. Robinson, late Dean of Durham, is excused by his lameness, one thought to do much hurt in Yorkshire.

*One Morren, late chaplain to Dr. Bonner, wandereth in Cheshire, Staffordshire, and Lancashire very seditiously; it is he that did cast abroad the seditious libel in Chester.

Robert Grey, priest, who hath been much supported at Sir Thomas Fitzharbert's, and now it is said wandereth in like sort; a man meet to be looked unto.

*One Dr. Hoskyns, late of Salisbury, a subtle adversary.

*Baldwin Norton, late chaplain to the Archbishop of York.

Item, we are informed that through the example of Sir Thomas Fitzharbert, John Sacheverell, and John Draycot, Esquires, being by us committed to prison and so remaining, and through the bearing and supporting of their wives, friends, kinsfolk, allies, and servants, a great part of the shires of Stafford and Derby are generally evil inclined towards religion, and forbear coming to church and participating of the sacraments, using also very broad speeches in alehouses and elsewhere, and therefore it may please your honours to have special regard unto these parts.

Also certain others are fled, as is reported, over the seas.

*Dr. Bullock, late prebendary of Durham.
*Dr. Darbyshire, late chancellor to Dr. Bonner, and his kinsman.
*William Taylor, late chaplain to the Archbishop of York.
*John Hanson, late chaplain to Dr. Scott.
*John Parfewe, nephew to the late bishop of Hereford.

*Henry Henshawe, late rector of Lincoln College in Oxford.
*One Bovell, late prebendary of Southwell.
    (Signed) Edmund London,
            Richard Ely,
            Walter Haddon,
            T. Huycke.

    Prisoners in the Fleet, by order from us.

Sir Thomas Fitzharbert, Knight.
*Dr. Scott, late bishop of Chester.
*Dr. Harpisfelde, late archdeacon of London.
*Thomas Woode, late parson of High Ongar in Essex, and chaplain to Queen Mary.
*Dr. Coole, late dean of Powles.
Thomas Somerset, gent.
*Dr. Draycot.
*Dr. Chedsey.

    Prisoners in the Marshalsea, by order from us.

*Dr. Bonner, late bishop of London.
*John Symes, a priest of Somersetshire.

    Prisoner in the Counter in the Poultry, by us as aforesaid.

John Draycot, gentleman.

    Prisoners in the Counter in Wood Street, by order as aforesaid.

Dr. Yonge.
John Sacheverell, Esq.
Thomas Atkinson, clerk, late one of the Fellows of Lincoln College in Oxford.
*John Greete, a priest, late beneficed in Hampshire.

    In the King's Bench, by order as aforesaid.

John Baker, clerk, late parson of Standford Rivers in Essex.
    (Signed) Edmund London,
            Richard Ely,
            William Chester,
            Gabriell Goodmayn,
            T. Huycke.

Endorsed:—A list of Recusants.

CHAPTER XI

THE PENAL LAWS OF ELIZABETH'S SECOND PARLIAMENT, 1563

<small>Chap. XI
Fear of papal sympathy.</small>
A NEW parliament met on January 12, 1563. From the speech then made by the Lord Keeper Bacon, the reasons which determined the Queen to call it were declared to be partly the need of church discipline, partly the want of domestic legislation, and finally the fear of 'the enemy as well here bred amongst us as abroad.' Now it is quite clear that the famous convocation which began to sit coincidently, and the new ecclesiastical commission not yet a year old, were perfectly competent to undertake all questions of necessary discipline. At this time, however, the religious wars in France, and the proceedings of Mary Queen of Scots and the possibilities of a combination in which the King of Spain might join, made it imperative to stamp out any secret or open sympathy with the Romanists abroad. That the existing laws had not been sharply pressed is made evident by the Lord Keeper's words: 'As heretofore the discipline of the Church hath not been good, and again that the ministers thereof have been slothful, even so for want of the same hath sprung two enormities: the first is that for lack thereof every man liveth as he will without fear; and secondly many ceremonies agreed on, but the ornaments agreed thereon are either left undone or forgotten. As in one point, for want of discipline it is that so few come to service, and the Church so unreplenished, notwithstanding that at the last parliament a law was made for

good order to be observed in the same, but yet as appeareth not executed, therefore if it be too easy, let it be made sharper, and if already well, then see it executed.' The determination to introduce fresh penal laws was quickened by the discovery of a plot in favour of Mary Queen of Scots, wherein one item was treasonable correspondence with Bishop Goldwell at Rome 'to be mean to the pope for his aid in these conspiracies, with promise of restitution of religion within this realm of England for such his aid and help.' The general feeling of disquiet by reason of such action is illustrated by a petition of the Commons addressed to the Queen, in which it is said: 'We fear a faction of heretics in your realm, contentious and malicious papists, lest they most unnaturally against their country, most madly against their own safety, and most treacherously against your Highness, not only hope for the woeful day of your death, but also lie in wait to advance some title under which they may revive their late unspeakable cruelty.' In consequence of all this, in an age which knew no method of repression save penal statutes, the Commons concluded their petition in these terms: 'Your subjects on their behalfs, for your Majesty's further assurance whereupon their own preservation wholly dependeth, shall employ their whole endeavours and wits and power to renew, devise, and establish the most strong and beneficial acts and laws of preservation, and surety of your Majesty, and of your issue, in the imperial crown of this realm, and the most penal, sharp, and terrible statutes[1].'

Such being the temper of the Commons who delivered this petition on January 28, a bill seems to have been drawn within the next fortnight, being at first described as 'the bill against those that extol the Bishop of Rome and refuse the oath of allegiance.' The bill was read a second time on February 16, a third time on the 20th, when it was sent up to the Lords. As soon as it reaches the Lords, the bill receives the title which it afterwards

A new bill for the assurance of supremacy.

[1] See D'Ewes' *Journal* for the chief facts of the section.

CHAP. XI retains: 'the bill for the assurance of the Queen's Majesty's royal power over all estates and subjects within her dominions.' It was read a first time on February 25, a second on March 1, when a proviso was debated and read twice. The last reading took place two days later, when this proviso and others annexed were read as custom demanded, and the whole bill was passed, receiving the royal assent on April 10.

Comparison with 1 Eliz.cap.i. The 'Assurance of Supremacy Act' is not a reproduction of the previous Supremacy Act. Its purpose is narrower. The previous Act had repealed many Acts of Mary, reviving others of Henry VIII and Edward VI, and had annexed ecclesiastical jurisdiction to the Crown, and above all had given powers for ecclesiastical commissions. The present Act assumes all this, and as the first title of the bill in the Commons sets forth, is directed towards two special points which the first Act also contemplated: viz. (1) the repression of papal sympathy, (2) the tender and refusal of the oath of allegiance.

Two chief points: i. Papal sympathy. On the question of papal sympathy this Act is, of course, much more full and explicit than the first. All who manifest such sympathy are liable to the penalties of praemunire as before, but the duty of searching and trying the offending parties is laid down far more elaborately. All justices now have power to take up such cases, remitting them to the Court of King's Bench. Thus a new court is commissioned to have the ultimate decision of these cases, for hitherto the King's Bench has had no matters of nonconformity referred to it.

ii. Oath of allegiance. The oath of allegiance is to be tendered far more widely than in the first year. Then it was to be ministered to all ecclesiastical graduates on ordination, and 'every temporal judge, justice, mayor, and other lay or temporal officer and minister, and every other person having her Highness' fee or wages.' Now it is to be taken as well by all these, whether clerical or lay, as by all lay graduates, schoolmasters, teachers, barristers, lawyers. The penalties, moreover, are more severe than formerly, for then the refusal of the oath involved forfeiture of goods for life, but now praemunire, which in theory, at all events, meant imprisonment and total confiscation of property. A second refusal made the recusant liable to a traitor's death, whereas in the first Act the penalty was praemunire.

The special severity of the Act as regards the oath.

The real sting of the Act was in a proviso, added, it seems, by the Lords, which specified the persons to whom the oath should be tendered again the second time three months after a first refusal under this Act. There were five classes of such persons :—

1. Such as had, have, or shall have, in the time of one of the reigns of the Queen's Majesty's most noble father, brother, or sister, or in the time of the reign of the Queen's Majesty, her heirs or successors, charge, cure or office in the Church.

2. Such as had, have, or shall have any office or ministry in any ecclesiastical court, with the same specification of time.

3. Such as shall wilfully refuse to observe the orders and rites for divine service, after they shall be publicly admonished by the ordinary.

4. Such as shall openly and advisedly deprave the rites and ceremonies of the Church.

5. Such as shall say or hear any private mass.

Here too the recusants are to be certified into the Court of King's Bench as in the previous cases, but the penalty is that of treason. The tendering of the oath, moreover, is facilitated by permitting the bishop to tender it to all ecclesiastics in his diocese. In the case of the laity, commission may be issued by the Lord Chancellor to administer the oath. Thus a moment's reflexion will show the entirely new stage which is commenced in the 'Assurance of Supremacy Act.' It really erects new machinery to enforce conformity by giving the bishops power to tender the oath on their own responsibility to ecclesiastics, and by permitting the issue of local commissions in the case of the laity, so that, although the ecclesiastical commission in London still exists, it will be no longer necessary to

The new stage indicated by this Act.

CHAP. XI remit cases of nonconformity to it. In a word, a significant sentence of the Lord Keeper's speech is followed out, in which he says: 'in my opinion the device is good that in every diocese there be officers appointed and devised as hath been thought good, to sit for redress of these and such like errors, twice or thrice a year, till the faults be amended. In which well doing the head officers are to be borne withal and maintained, and laws to be made for the purpose.' The details of this proposed plan were not carried out now, but effect is given to the principle of local commissions and episcopal jurisdiction, which is the most important difference in this new Act.

Spiritual censures and the writ 'de excommunicato capiendo.'

The repressive policy of the parliament did not end with the 'Assurance of Supremacy Act.' Spiritual censures were not forgotten. It is often assumed that conformity under Elizabeth was only enforced by parliament. This is not strictly true, for from the first the operation of spiritual censures had been contemplated. Thus in the Uniformity Act of 1559 it had been provided that every person should attend church on Sundays and holy days, under pain of censure of the Church, and a fine of one shilling to the poor. We have only noticed a few cases of such excommunication before 1563: Bonner at Paul's Cross, July 28, 1560, Heath and Thirlby in February, 1561 [1]. Excommunication, however, had somewhat lost its ancient terrors, and was rarely inflicted at this time in any very severe form. According to the ancient law of the land, which dates back at least to the thirteenth century, it was customary, after sentence pronounced by the church authority, for the bishop to issue to the Court of Chancery a letter of request asking for a writ to be made out. In accordance with this notice the Court of Chancery then issued a writ *de excommunicato capiendo* or *capias* to the sheriff, who then arrested and imprisoned the excommunicate person. Such procedure, which was intended of course only for grave cases, was cumbersome and tedious, and moreover often failed to gain its end, owing to the un-

[1] A few are given in Parker's Register.

willingness of the sheriff to act upon the writs. The main defect in the old custom was that the writ to the sheriff was somewhat indeterminate, as it gave a direction to proceed without providing for any return to be made of the execution of the sentence, so that there was really no hold upon the sheriff at all. Such was the position, then, in 1563, and it is patent that, considering the backwardness of sheriffs and such officials in the matter of uniformity, these writs were very likely to remain inoperative. It was determined to remedy this, and accordingly a bill was introduced 'for the execution of the writ *De excommunicato capiendo*.' It was the outcome of debates in the upper house of convocation, which was then considering the question of discipline, and it appears to have been originally drafted by Archbishop Parker[1]. The bill was introduced in the House of Lords, and sent down by them to the House of Commons on March 29, where some changes were made, and the bill finally passed on April 9, receiving the royal assent next day.

The most noticeable points in the Act are these. After describing the reasons which called for the statute, direction is given that the writ be returnable into the King's Bench. Provision is then made for the issue of a *capias*, as many times as may be necessary, in case the excommunicate be returned as *non est inventus*. Then when the excommunicate surrenders, imprisonment is to follow as specified in the original writ. Power, however, is reserved to the bishop who pronounced the excommunication to receive the submission of the excommunicate. In every case it is a *sine qua non* that the original writ to the sheriff should precisely contain the crime with which the person is charged. This last point and the direction for the return of the writ into the King's Bench seem to be the only strictly novel methods of procedure which the Act contains[2]. Its importance for us lies in the fact that we have here an enactment which directs the record of all such cases of

[1] Strype, i. 308.
[2] See Makower, *Const. Hist. Ch. of England*, p. 452.

CHAP. XI excommunication, in a quarter where it should not be hard for us to discover the returns.

These two Acts were not pressed severely. We have thus traced in the two Acts under consideration a formidable addition to the penal legislation of the reign. Enough has been said to show that there was sufficient machinery to crush out all nonconformity, whether manifested by clergy or laity, but, as the sequel shows, these laws were designed to be rather *in terrorem* than actually carried out. In this Elizabeth was following the policy of her father and brother, for savage as the penal laws were in their reigns, the actual number of those who suffered under them is not great. It was Mary who revived the heresy Acts in 1554, and in the short space of four years put some 290 people to death. Suffering and death were to come in Elizabeth's reign, but death not yet, whilst even the cases of suffering cannot be proved to have been very numerous in the first years after the passing of the Acts. But whether the Acts were meant to be *in terrorem* or no, the possible death penalty under the Supremacy Act occasioned the archbishop 'some pensive thoughts,' as Strype quaintly puts it. He wrote to his episcopal brethren begging them to be exceedingly careful about enforcing the oath, and not to tender it a second time without consulting him.

The imprisoned bishops in relation to this legislation. In consequence of this, Bonner alone of the imprisoned bishops had the oath tendered to him. Some interval, however, elapsed before this was done, and it may be worth while to go back in order to pick up again the story of the bishops whom we left still in prison in the summer of 1562, committed to stricter custody, owing, it would seem, to some secret plotting or conference. Thus when the Act of 1563 became law in April of that year, the bishops had been in prison for about three years. *Scott escapes.* Scott had in the interval managed to elude the vigilance of the commissioners, and had fled the country. At some time in 1562 or 1563 he was released from the Fleet, and by the new plan of the commissioners was confined to a radius of twenty miles from Finchingfield in Essex[1]. He was bound by recogni-

---
[1] Above, p. 176.

zance, and this was read out before the commissioners when his surety appeared at their summons: 'The condition of this obligation is such that if Mr. Doctor Scott be forthcoming at all time and times, and do make his personal appearance before the Queen's Majesty's commissioners[1], &c.' His surety replied that he understood Scott to have died in London, May 6, 1563, and that the bishop had lived at Gosfield since the bond until April 22, 1563, when the Warden of the Fleet summoned him thither. May we suppose that Scott really was summoned to London at that time, and then made his escape? It is known that he made his way to Belgium at some time and died at Louvain in 1565. His flight did an injury to the other prisoners, who were kept all the more severely in consequence.

Another coincidence of date shows the probability of our theory concerning Bishop Scott and the oath. It is noted in the Spanish Calendar, May 9, 1563, that 'last week a commission was issued to summon for trial four of the Catholic prisoners, two bishops of London and Lincoln (Watson) and two doctors, Cole and Storey.' The word 'commission' is probably inexact, but the allusion is valuable as showing that the ecclesiastical commissioners were considering the bishops and the oath at this time (May, 1563), but we have no further particulars. It may be presumed that Bonner was offered the oath now for the first time under the new Act, and that he was left in the Marshalsea for another year, as he is still there when we next hear of him. Probably Watson was selected as a representative of the bishops in the Tower, and remitted thither until September, 1563.

Bonner and Watson.

At some time in the spring or summer of 1563 the Emperor Ferdinand interceded for the imprisoned bishops, but we do not possess his letter or the Queen's reply. In all probability the latter was favourable to a certain extent, and may have held out promises of some relief, but at all events an excuse for greater leniency now presented itself.

The Emperor intercedes for the bishops.

In July, 1563, the plague broke out, and raged with great

[1] S. P. Dom. xxxv. 38.

severity. In consequence of this it was determined to release the six bishops in the Tower, but Bonner, apparently, was not set free from the Marshalsea. Liberated on September 6, Heath and Turberville were restricted to certain localities, as Bishop Scott had been before his escape. Pate may have been similarly restricted, but there is no evidence to prove it. He went abroad in any case, was present at Trent, and died in 1565. The other three set free from the Tower were, according to Stow, billeted on the bishops: Thirlby went to Parker, Bourne to Bullingham of Lincoln, Watson to Grindal. With these prelates they remained for the present.

The release of the bishops took place on September 6, 1563. On the 24th, when, presumably, the Emperor had heard of it, he wrote again to Elizabeth, asking for the concession of one church in each city for the Romanists. The letter was answered on November 3. The reply is of sufficient importance to quote here, as it seems to show the real reasons which prompted the Government to continue the imprisonment, reasons which contemporary writers confirm [1]. After saying that she was glad to consider and allow all she could, the Queen continues: 'permagni enim res erat momenti tam benigne agere cum illis hominibus, qui tam insolenter palam contra leges nostras, contra quietem amantium et fidorum nostrorum subditorum, reluctantes sese intentaverant. Inter quos hi praecipui etiam sunt qui regnantibus patre et fratre nostro, nobilissimis principibus, mente et manu, publice et contionibus et scriptis, cum ipsi essent non privati homines sed publici magistratus, eandem ipsam doctrinam aliis ultro offerebant quam ipsi nunc tam obstinate rejiciunt. His tamen hominibus nos ad respectum postulati vestrae Majestatis nostra quidem gratia sed cum nostrorum non levi offensu pepercimus [2].'

After refusing the request about the churches, which is

---

[1] See Clerke's *Fidelis servi*, &c., O. 2. This appears to be ignored by Messrs. Bridgett and Knox, *True Story of the Catholic Hierarchy*.

[2] For this correspondence see Strype, *Ann.* ii. 572.

followed by a defence of the settlement as authorized by the primitive and Catholic Church, the letter thus concludes: 'Paucorum hominum privatam insolentiam nonnihil connivendo sanare concupivimus, ita eorundem hominum praefractas mentes et consimilium vel pares vel projectiores animos nimium indulgendo fovere atque alere nullo modo possumus [1].'

After some time it was determined to present the oath again to Bonner. The Marshalsea was in the diocese of Winchester, and there on April 26, 1564, Bishop Horne again administered the oath [2]. The possibility of a traitor's death was now before Bonner, but he did not quail, and, as the subsequent return says, 'recipere aut pronunciare recusavit.' The death penalty, however, which Henry VIII had exacted from the Carthusian monks was not inflicted. Bonner was committed again to the Marshalsea, where he died in 1569, after a further imprisonment of five years. Of that interval we have scarcely a detail. Bishop Andrewes has described the lenity of Bonner's lot during those years [3], but we have found no strictly contemporary evidence to prove this: rather the reverse, for in March, 1566 [4], he was more straitly imprisoned because of treasonable correspondence. This correspondence was very probably with the King of Spain, and perhaps through Englefield, that inveterate plotter, as the Spanish ambassador on January 28, 1566, speaks of the imprisoned bishops (i. e. Bonner and Watson) looking to the King for deliverance.

And here a few words may be said of the other bishops. Of those set at liberty in September, 1563, Heath retired to his own house at Chobham, where he died in 1579. Turberville is said to have died in 1570. Thirlby stayed with Parker at Bekesbourne or Lambeth, at the Council's expense, until he died in 1570. Three years before this event Cecil,

Bonner and the oath, 1564.

Sequel as regards the other Marian bishops.

---

[1] The Emperor's letter of September 24 is preserved in Cotton MS. Vesp. F. 3, f. 64. The Queen's answer is in S. P., Foreign, Eliz. Nov. 3, 1563 (Calendar, p. 581).

[2] For the circumstances of his refusal and the points raised, see Mr. G. F. Cobb's tract in the Church Historical Society's publications.

[3] *Tortura Torti*, 146, A.D. 1609.

[4] Spanish Calendar, January 28 and March, 1566.

CHAP. XI says the Spanish ambassador[1], scolded Parker for allowing Thirlby and Boxall too much liberty. Bourne remained with Bullingham till 1566, was then transferred to his friend Dean Carewe of Exeter, and died September 10, 1569. Watson's fate was the most tragic. He was transferred after a short time from Grindal to Cox, and in January, 1566, to the Tower, for attempted correspondence with Spain, it may be surmised. He was still there in April, 1570. In 1574 he was shifted to the Marshalsea, where Bonner had died five years before. Under a bond he was then liberated, and taken to his brother's house. Here he seems to have engaged himself in some correspondence with other Romanists, and so in the summer of 1577 he was placed under Horne's care by the Privy Council's order, who gave strict regulations as to how he should be kept[2]. From Horne he was transferred to the Bishop of Rochester in 1579. Then began a correspondence between Watson and the Douay College, in consequence of which he fell under suspicion, and was removed to Wisbeach Castle in the fen country, where he died on September 27, 1584[3].

Bishop Poole.

Thus we have traced all the Marian bishops to their death, save Poole. This bishop never had been in prison, but by the commissioners of 1562 he was restricted to London and a circuit of three miles. Some relaxation of this restriction must have taken place subsequently, for in 1564 the Bishop of Coventry and Lichfield says: 'the abiding of Dr. Poole, late Bishop of Peterborough, in that shire with Bryan Fowler, Esquire, a little from Stafford, causeth many people think worse of the regiment and religion than else they would do, because that divers lewd priests resort thither, but what conference they have I cannot learn[4].' He died in June, 1568.

In review the Assurance

None of the bishops, then, suffered the extreme penalties of the Assurance of Supremacy Act, and, as we have shown,

---

[1] Spanish Calendar, Nov. 1, 1567.
[2] P. C. Register, ii. 246.
[3] Watson's fate has been worked out by Bridgett and Knox, *op. cit.*
[4] Below, p. 201.

Bonner and Watson alone can be proved to have come at all under the direct operation of that Act. Their custody would have been probably less severe but for their correspondence with foreign Romanists. The treatment of the rest of the clergy was somewhat similar, a few only being picked out as examples, for a warning to the rest. Of dignitaries we have only traced the cases of Drs. Cole and Storey before mentioned, and Dr. Palmes, late of Southwell and York. The returns into the King's Bench give one or two names of clergymen, prior to our limit in November, 1564, who were certified for refusing the oath. Thus Dr. Palmes is certified by the Archbishop of York as having refused the oath when tendered in June, 1564 [1]. A schoolmaster of Macclesfield, named William Sutton, is also returned for a similar refusal in the previous year [2]. We have looked through the *Coram Rege* rolls for the time pretty carefully. They contain the refusal of Bonner and those mentioned (Palmes and Sutton), but we have not noticed any others before the end of 1564. It is certain that they cannot have been numerous.

Nor is the case different, so far as the clergy are concerned, when we search the *Coram Rege* rolls to see the operation of the Act 'de excommunicato capiendo.' We can only discover the case of a single clergyman returned under the Act between Trinity Term, 1563, and Hilary Term, 1565. This solitary instance was J. Lettock, clerk, of the diocese of Winchester. Within the same limits we have noticed about fifty cases of lay excommunicates so returned. The noticeable thing is that they are not so much from towns, but are dotted about over the country, very frequently in out of the way places; and this gives the idea that the same course was pursued of picking out people here and there to serve as examples to the rest. It is frequently returned by the sheriff that the person 'non est inventus.' Sometimes the sheriff is said not to have returned the writ as directed. In a very few cases imprisonment is spoken of. In most it does not

[1] Coram Rege, 1211.   [2] Ib. 1209.

CHAP. XI appear what was done. At all events our search seems to have proved that these severe acts were not pressed with drastic severity, as they certainly could have been if the evidence of reluctance given by the bishops to the Privy Council in November, 1564, is to be trusted [1].

A possible explanation for clerical acquiescence at this time.
The position then is this: there are practically no cases of clerical excommunication under the Act in that behalf, whilst there are very few returns indeed of refusing the oath. If the oath was at all widely tendered by the bishops in 1563 and 1564 it must have been pretty readily taken. A paper which professes to be contemporary may perhaps supply a reason for such acceptance. The document, written by one E. Dennum from Venice to Cecil in April, 1564, purports to disclose to him certain plots and practices of the Romanist party on the Continent in secret correspondence with their friends in England. One item runs thus: 'it was ordered for the better assurance of further intelligence to the see of Rome, to give licenses to any that shall swear to the supremacy due obedience, and allegiance to her, powers to dispense with the sacraments, baptism, marriage, and other ceremonies of our now established Church in England, that the parties so obliged may possess and enjoy any office, employment, either ecclesiastical, military, or civil, and to take such oaths as shall be imposed upon them, provided that the said oaths be taken with a reserve for to serve the mother church of Rome whenever opportunity serveth, and thereby in so doing the Act in Council was passed, it was no sin but meritorious until occasion served to the contrary, and that when it so served for Rome's advantage, the party was absolved from his oath [2].' It is clear that if such

---

[1] Below, p. 200.

[2] The document is headed 'A list of several consultations amongst the Cardinals, Bishops, and others of the several orders of Rome now a contriving and conspiring against her gracious Majesty and the established Church of England.' It then goes on: 'Pius having consulted with the clergy of Italy, and assembling them together, it was by general consent voted that the immunity of the Romish Church and her jurisdiction is required to be defended by all her princes as the principal Church of God. And to encourage the same, the council hath voted that Pius should bestow her grace's realm on

policy were adopted by those who objected to the Eliza- CHAP. XI
bethan *régime*, a large number of those compelled to take
the oath under the new Act would be emboldened to make
a feigned subscription.

But to proceed. It will be remembered that this same The Privy
'Assurance of Supremacy Act' had given a special pro- Council
minence to Justices of the Peace who were directed to to the
search out cases of papal sympathy and to certify them Justices,
into the King's Bench. Under the Uniformity Act they 1564.
were not so commissioned, and it therefore became necessary to inquire into the character of the Justices of the
Peace. Consequently in October, 1564, the Privy Council
wrote round to all the bishops, asking them to certify those
favourable and those unfavourable to the settlement, and
also to send the names of any who were fit to be added
to the commission of the peace. We are fortunate in
being able to follow the bishops' returns in an important
manuscript at Hatfield House[1]. The return gives a very
good general idea of the state of conformity throughout the
country, though three of the Welsh dioceses and two of
the English are wanting. 'The dioceses reported to be
most hostile to the government were those of the north
and west: Carlisle, Durham, York, Worcester, Hereford,
and Exeter were strong in opposition. . . . Where the towns
are mentioned, these are found to be in nearly every case

that prince who shall attempt to con-quer it. There was a council ordered by way of a committee, who contain three of the cardinals, two of the archbishops, six of the bishops, and as many of the late order of the Jesuits who daily increase and come into great favour with the Pope of late, these do present weekly methods, ways, and contrivances for the Church of Rome, which hold the great council for the week following in employment how to order all things for the advancement of the Roman faith, some of these con-trivances coming to my hands by the help of the silver key be as follow.' The chief articles are quoted by Strype, i. 412. He seems to have seen the form of the paper in Stowe MSS. 155, f. 2. It occurs also in MSS. Add. 4784, where the preamble is as quoted above. In both cases the MS. is stated to have been copied by King, dean and minister of Tuam, 1656, from certain papers of Cecil. In MS. Add. the date was 1565, but this has been altered to 1564 by a later hand.

[1] Lately edited for the Camden Society by Miss Bateson.

more hostile to the government than the counties[1].' The document of course does not profess to deal with the conformity of the clergy, but incidentally some information is given. Thus we find that some of the deprived clergy were still harboured in private houses, where they said Mass and confirmed the household and their friends in the old religion. So the Bishop of Worcester writes: 'popish and perverse priests which, misliking religion, have forsaken the ministry and yet live in corners, are kept in gentlemen's houses, and had in great estimation with the people, where they marvellously pervert the simple and blaspheme the truth.' The Bishop of Hereford complains that his diocese is still suffering from the extruded clergy whom we have already noted there: 'there be also in this diocese and county of Hereford divers fostered and maintained that be judged and esteemed some of them to be learned, which in Queen Mary's days had livings and offices in the Church, which be mortal and deadly enemies to this religion. Their names be Blaxton, Mugge, Arden, Ely, Friar Gregory, Howard, Rastall of Gloucester, Johnson, Menevar, Oswald, Hamerson, Ledbury, and certain others whose names I know not. These go from one gentleman's house to another, where they know to be welcome.' Scambler, Bishop of Peterborough, recommends that 'the learned adversaries being ecclesiastical persons to be either banished or sequestered from conference with such as be fautors of their religion, or else the oath to be tendered to them forthwith, considering they have so little passed of the Queen's Majesty's clemency to them showed these six years, whereby it doth appear that they be more stubborn, and more encouraged than they were before. Item that the straggling doctors and priests who have liberty to stay at their pleasure within this realm do much hurt secretly and in corners, therefore it were good they might be called before the high commissioners, and to show their conformity in religion by subscribing or open recantation,

[1] See Miss Bateson's preface.

or else to be restrained from their said liberty.' The Bishop of Coventry and Lichfield, as we have seen, writes that 'Doctor Poole, late bishop of Peterborough ... a little from Stafford causeth many people think worse of the regiment and religion than else they would do, because that divers lewd priests have resort thither, but what conference they have I cannot learn.'

The Bishop of Durham adds an interesting note: 'There be two things in my opinion which hinder religion here much. The Scottish priests that are fled out of Scotland for their wickedness, and here be hired in parishes on the border because they take less wages than the other, and do more harm than other could or would in dissuading the people[1]. The other thing is the great number of scholars born here about, now living at Louvain without license, and sending in books and letters which cause many times evil rumours to be spread and disquiet the people. They be maintained by the hospitals of the New Castle and the wealthiest of that town and this shire, as it is judged, and be their near cousins.'

One more point in the bishops' return may be noted. It proves that no commission had as yet (October, 1564) been issued by the Lord Chancellor to administer the oath to lay suspects. The Bishop of Peterborough asks for such a commission to be issued, and so does the Bishop of Coventry and Lichfield. In the passage already quoted from the Bishop of Worcester's report, it seems that the oath needed pressing there amongst the deprived clergy, and elsewhere he gives the idea that it had not been widely taken by the justices. *No commission yet issued under the Assurance Act.*

With the bishops' return in 1564 we have reached the limit that we had proposed to ourselves. In that year the question of conformity took a new turn with the vestiarian controversy, which we do not intend to follow out here. *Our limit reached, November 1564.*

In the two following chapters we shall attempt to estimate the number of clergy deprived within the period under review for their refusal to accept the settlement of religion. After that we shall briefly review the results of our inquiry.

[1] Names of these are given in Harl. MS. 594, f. 187.

CHAP. XI

I.

AN ACT FOR THE ASSURANCE OF THE QUEEN'S MAJESTY'S ROYAL POWER OVER ALL ESTATES AND SUBJECTS WITHIN HER HIGHNESS' DOMINIONS.

[Transcr. from Statutes of the Realm, iv. pt. 1, 402.]
(5 Eliz. cap. 1.)

For protection of the realm against papal usurpation recently asserting itself again,

1. For preservation of the Queen's most excellent Highness, her heirs and successors, and the dignity of the Imperial Crown of this realm of England, and for avoiding both of such hurts, perils, dishonours, and inconveniences as have before time befallen, as well to the Queen's Majesty's noble progenitors, Kings of this realm, as for the whole estate thereof, by means of the jurisdiction and power of the see of Rome, unjustly claimed and usurped within this realm and the dominions thereof, and also of the dangers by the fautors of the said usurped power at this time grown to marvellous outrage and licentious boldness, and now requiring more sharp restraint and correction of laws than hitherto in the time of the Queen's Majesty's most mild and merciful reign, have been had, used, or established: Be it therefore enacted, ordained, and established by the Queen our sovereign lady, and the Lords spiritual and temporal, and the Commons in this present Parliament assembled, and by the authority of the same, that if any person or persons dwelling, inhabiting, or resident within this realm or within any other the Queen's dominions, seigniories, or countries or the marches of the same, or elsewhere within or under her obedience and power, of what estate, dignity, pre-eminence, order, degree or condition soever he or they be, after the 1st day of April, which shall be in the year of our Lord God 1563, shall by writing, cyphering, printing, preaching, or teaching, deed, or act, advisedly and wittingly hold or stand with to extol, set forth, maintain, or defend the authority, jurisdiction, or power of the bishop of Rome, or of his see, heretofore claimed, used, or usurped, within this realm, or in any dominion or country being of, within, or under the Queen's power or obeisance, or by any speech, open deed, or act, advisedly and wittingly attribute any such manner of jurisdiction, authority, or pre-eminence to the said see of Rome, or to any bishop of the same see for the time being within this realm or in any of the Queen's dominions or countries; that then every such person or persons so doing or offending, their abettors, procurers, and counsellors, and also their

any attempt to aid and abet such power and jurisdiction after April 1, 1563,

aiders, assistants, and comforters upon purpose, and to the intent to set forth further and extol the said usurped power, authority, or jurisdiction of any of the said bishop or bishops of Rome, and every of them, being thereof lawfully indicted or presented, within one year next after any such offences by him or them committed, and being lawfully convicted or attainted at any time after, according to the laws of this realm, for every such default and offence shall incur into the dangers, penalties, pain, and forfeitures ordained and provided by the Statute of Provision and Praemunire made in the sixteenth year of the reign of King Richard the Second.

Chap. XI — from whomsoever proceeding shall involve penalties of praemunire.

2. And it is also enacted by the authority aforesaid, that as well Justices of Assize in their circuits, as Justices of Peace within the limits of their commission and authority, or two of every such Justices of Peace at the least, whereof one to be of the quorum, shall have full power and authority by virtue of this Act in their Quarter or open Session to inquire of all offences, contempts, and transgressions perpetrated, committed, or done contrary to the true meaning of the premises, in like manner and form as they may of other offences against the Queen's peace, and shall certify every presentment before them, or any of them, had or made concerning the same, or any part thereof, before the Queen, her heirs and successors, in her or their Court commonly called the King's Bench, within forty days next after any such presentment had or made, if the term be then open, and if not, at the first day of the full term next following the said forty-one days, upon pain that every of the Justices of Assize, or Justices of the Peace, before whom such presentment shall be made, making default of such certificate contrary to the statute, to lose and forfeit for every such default £100 to the Queen's Highness, her heirs and successors.

Hence all Justices in Quarter or open Sessions shall have power to inquire of such offences and certify the presentment into King's Bench under penalty.

3. And it is enacted by the authority aforesaid, that the Justices of the King's Bench, as well upon every such certificate, as by inquiry before themselves within the limits of their authorities, shall have full power and authority to hear, order, and determine every such offence, done or committed contrary to the true meaning of this present Act according to the laws of this realm, in such like manner and form, to all intents and purposes, as if the person or persons against whom any presentment shall be had upon this statute, had been presented upon any matter or offence expressed in the said statute made in the said sixteenth year of the reign of King Richard the Second.

Whereupon the King's Bench shall proceed as in offences under Statute of Praemunire.

CHAP. XI

Further, the Oath of Supremacy is to be taken as prescribed in 1 Eliz. cap. 1, and by all in Orders, or to be ordained in universities, and by all teachers, graduates, lawyers, and other legal officials, before admission to office.

4. And moreover be it enacted by the authority aforesaid, that as well all manner of persons expressed and appointed in and by the Act made in the first year of the Queen's Majesty's reign that now is, intituled 'An Act restoring to the Crown the ancient jurisdiction over the Estate Ecclesiastical and Spiritual, and abolishing all foreign powers repugnant to the same,' to take the oath expressed and set forth in the same, as all other persons which have taken or shall take Orders, commonly called Ordines Sacros or Ecclesiastical Orders, have been or shall be promoted, preferred or admitted to any degree of learning in any university within this realm or dominions to the same belonging, and all schoolmasters and public and private teachers of children, as also all manner of person and persons that have taken or hereafter shall take any degree of learning in or at Common Laws of this realm, as well outer barristers as benchers, readers, ancients in any house or houses of Court, and all principal treasurers, and such as be of the Grand Company in every Inn of Chancery, and all attorneys, prothonotaries, and philizers towards the laws of the realm, and all manner of sheriffs, escheators, and feodaries, and all other person and persons, which have taken or shall take upon him or them, or have been or shall be admitted to any ministry or office in, at, or belonging to the common or law, any other law or laws, or to or for the execution of them, or any of them, used or allowed, or at any time hereafter to be used or allowed within this realm, or any of the dominions or countries belonging, or which hereafter shall happen to belong to the Crown or dignity of the same, and all other officers or ministers of or towards any Court whatsoever, and every of them, shall take and pronounce a corporal oath upon the Evangelists before he or they shall be admitted, allowed, or suffered to take upon him or them, to use, exercise, supply or occupy any such vocation, office, degree, ministry, room, or service, as is aforesaid, and that in the open Court whereunto he doth or shall serve or belong, and if he or they do not or shall not serve or belong to any ordinary or open Court, then he or they shall take and pronounce the oath aforesaid in an open place before a convenient assembly to witness the same, and before such person or persons as have or shall have authority by common use or otherwise to admit or call any such person or persons as is aforesaid to any such vocation, office, ministry, room, or service, or else before such person or persons as by the Queen's Highness, her

heirs or successors, by commission under the Great Seal of England shall be named or assigned to accept and take the same according to the tenor, effect, and form of the same oath verbatim, which is and as it is already set forth to be taken in the aforesaid Act made in the first year of the Queen's Majesty's reign.

<small>CHAP. XI</small>

5. And also be it enacted by the authority of this present Parliament, that every archbishop and bishop within this realm and dominions of the same, shall have full power and authority by virtue of this Act to tender or minister the oath aforesaid to every or any spiritual or ecclesiastical person within their proper diocese, as well in places and jurisdictions exempt as elsewhere.

<small>Bishops shall minister the oath to ecclesiastics.</small>

6. And be it enacted by the authority aforesaid, that the Lord Chancellor or Keeper of the Great Seal of England for the time being, shall and may at all times hereafter by virtue of this Act, without further warrant, make and direct commission or commissions under the Great Seal of England to any person or persons, giving them or some of them thereby authority to tender and minister the oath aforesaid to such person or persons as by the aforesaid commission or commissions the said commissioners shall be authorized to tender the same oath unto.

<small>The Lord Chancellor may appoint commissions to administer the oath.</small>

7. And be it also further enacted by the authority of this present Parliament, that if any person or persons appointed or compellable by this Act, or by the said Act made in the said first year to take the said oath, or if any person or persons to whom the said oath by any such commission or commissions shall be limited and appointed to be tendered as is aforesaid, do or shall at the time of the said oath so tendered refuse to take or pronounce the said oath in manner and form aforesaid, that then the party so refusing and being thereof lawfully indicted or presented within one year next after any such refusal, and convicted or attainted at any time after, according to the laws of this realm, shall suffer and incur the dangers, penalties, pains and forfeitures ordained and provided by the Statute of Provision and Praemunire aforesaid made in the sixteenth year of the reign of King Richard the Second.

<small>A first refusal renders the recusant liable to praemunire.</small>

8. And furthermore be it enacted by the authority aforesaid, that all and every such person and persons having authority to tender the oath aforesaid, shall within forty days next after such refusal or refusals of the said oath, if the term be then open, and if not then at the first day of the full term next following the said forty days, make true certificate under his or their seal or seals of the names,

<small>Recusancy to be certified into King's Bench under penalty.</small>

CHAP. XI

The sheriff shall have power to empanel a jury to inquire of the refusals.

places, and degrees of the person or persons so refusing the same oath, before the Queen, her heirs or successors, in her or their Court commonly called the King's Bench, upon pain that every of the said persons having such authority to tender the said oath making default of such certificate, shall for every such default forfeit £100 to the Queen's Highness, her heirs or successors. And that the sheriff of the county where the said Court, commonly called the King's Bench, shall for the time be holden, shall or may by virtue of this Act empanel a jury of the same county, to enquire of and upon every such refusal and refusals, which jury shall or may, upon every such certificate and other evidence to them in that behalf to be given by virtue of this Act, proceed to indict the person and persons so offending in such sort and degree, to all intents and purposes, as the same jury may do of any offence or offences against the Queen's Majesty's peace, perpetrated, committed, or done within the same county, of and for the which the same jury is so empanelled.

For repetition of previous offences under this Act, or a second refusal of the oath, the penalty is as in high treason.

9. And for stronger defence and maintenance of this Act, it is further ordained, enacted, and established by the authority aforesaid, that if any such offender or offenders as is aforesaid, of the first part or branch of this statute, that is to say by writing, cyphering, printing, preaching or teaching, deed or act, advisedly and wittingly hold or stand with to extol, set forth, maintain or defend, the authority, jurisdiction, or power of the bishop of Rome, or of his see, heretofore claimed, used, or usurped within this realm, or in any dominion or country, being of, within, or under the Queen's power or obeisance, or by any speech, open deed, or act, advisedly and wittingly attribute any such manner of jurisdiction, authority, or pre-eminence to the said see of Rome, or to any bishop of the same see, for the time being, within this realm, or in any the Queen's dominions or countries, or be to any such offender or offenders abetting, procuring, or counselling or aiding, assisting, or comforting, upon purpose and to the intent to set forth further and extol the said usurped power, authority, or jurisdiction, after such conviction and attainder as is aforesaid, do eftsoons commit or do the said offences, or any of them, in manner and form aforesaid, and be thereof duly convicted and attainted, as is aforesaid; and also that if any the persons above named and appointed by this Act to take the oath aforesaid, do after the space of three months next after the first tender thereof, the second time refuse to take and pronounce, or do not take or pronounce the same in form

aforesaid to be tendered, that then every such offender or offenders for the same second offence and offences, shall forfeit, lose, and suffer such like and the same pains, forfeitures, judgements, and execution, as is used in cases of high treason.

10. Provided always, that this Act nor anything therein contained, nor any attainder to be had by force and virtue of this Act, shall not extend to make any corruption of blood, the disheriting of any heir, forfeiture of dower, nor to the prejudice of the right or title of any person or persons other than the right or title of the offender or offenders during his, her, or their natural lives only. And that it shall and may be lawful to every person and persons to whom the right or interest of any lands, tenements, or hereditaments, after the death of any such offender or offenders, should or might have appertained, if no such attainder had been, to enter into the same without any *ouster le main*, to be served in such sort as he or they might have done if this Act had never been had nor made.

The penalty is not to descend to heirs and successors.

11. Provided also, that the oath expressed in the said Act made in the said first year shall be taken and expounded in such form as is set forth in an admonition annexed to the Queen's Majesty's injunctions, published in the first year of Her Majesty's reign, that is to say, to confess and acknowledge in her Majesty, her heirs and successors, no other authority than that was challenged and lately used by the noble King Henry the Eighth and King Edward the Sixth, as in the said admonition more plainly may appear.

The oath to be interpreted as the injunctions explain.

12. And be it enacted by the authority aforesaid, that this Act shall be openly read and published at every Quarter Sessions by the Clerk of the Peace, and at every Leet and law day by the Steward of the Court, and once in every term in the open Hall of every house and houses of Court and Chancery at the times and by the persons thereunto to be limited and appointed by the Lord Chancellor or Keeper of the Great Seal for the time being.

This Act to be published at stated times and places.

13. And be it further enacted, that every person which hereafter shall be elected or appointed a Knight, Citizen, or Burgess or Baron of any of the Five Ports, for any Parliament or Parliaments hereafter to be holden, shall from henceforth before he shall enter into the Parliament House, or have any voice there, openly receive and pronounce the said oath before the Lord Steward for the time being or his deputy or deputies for that time to be appointed, and that he which shall enter into the Parliament House without taking the said oath shall be deemed no Knight, Citizen, Burgess, nor Baron for

All officers of Cinque Ports to take the oath before entering office.

CHAP. XI that Parliament, nor shall have any voice, but shall be to all intents, constructions, (and) purposes as if he had never been returned nor elected Knight, Citizen, Burgess or Baron for that Parliament, and shall suffer such pains and penalties as if he had presumed to sit in the same without election, return, or authority.

No temporal Lord need take the oath.

14. Provided always, that forasmuch as the Queen's Majesty is otherwise sufficiently assured of the faith and loyalty of the Temporal Lords of Her Highness' Court of Parliament, therefore this Act nor anything therein contained, shall not extend to compel any temporal person, of or above the degree of a Baron of this realm, to take or pronounce the oath above said nor to incur any penalty limited by this Act for not taking or refusing the same, anything in this Act to the contrary in anywise notwithstanding.

Alms to recusants is not malicious aid.

15. Provided and be it enacted by the authority aforesaid, that charitable giving of reasonable alms to any of the offender or offenders above specified, without fraud or covin, shall not be taken or interpreted to be any such abetment, procuring, counselling, aiding, assisting or comforting, as thereby the giver of such alms shall incur any pain, penalty, or forfeiture appointed in this Act.

Peers offending to be tried by peers.

16. Provided also and be it enacted by the authority of this present Parliament, that if any peer of this realm shall hereafter offend contrary to this Act, or any branch or article thereof, that in that and all such cases and case they shall be tried by their peers, in such manner and form as in other cases of treasons they have used to be tried, and by none other means.

Provision that second tendering of oath is only to ecclesiastics formerly or now in office; to those who refuse Prayer Book after admonition; to those that hear Mass.

17. Provided also further and be it enacted, that no person shall be compelled by virtue of this Act to take the oath above mentioned, at or upon the second time of offering the same, according to the form appointed by this Statute, except the same person hath been, is, or shall be an ecclesiastical person, that had, hath, or shall have in the time of one of the reigns of the Queen's Majesty's most noble father, brother, or sister, or in the time of the reign of the Queen's Majesty, her heirs or successors, charge, cure, or office in the Church, or such person or persons as had, hath, or hereafter shall have any office or ministry in any Ecclesiastical Court of this realm, under any archbishop or bishop in any the times or reigns aforesaid; or such person or persons as shall willingly refuse to observe the orders and rites for divine service, that be authorized to be used and observed in the Church of England, after that he or they shall be publicly by the ordinary or some of his officers

for ecclesiastical causes admonished to keep and observe the same, or such as shall openly and advisedly deprave, by words or writings or any other open fact, any of the rites and ceremonies at any time used and authorized to be used in the Church of England ; or that shall say or hear the private Mass prohibited by the laws of this realm, and that all such persons shall be compellable to take the oath upon the second tender or offer of the same, and incur the penalties for not taking of the said oath, and none other.

18. And forasmuch as it is doubtful whether, by the laws of this realm, there be any punishment for such as kill or slay any person or persons attainted in or upon a praemunire, be it therefore enacted by authority aforesaid, that it shall not be lawful to any person or persons to slay or kill any person or persons in any manner attainted, or hereafter to be attainted of, in, or upon any praemunire by pretence, reason, or authority of any judgement given, or hereafter to be given, in or upon the same, or by pretence, reason, or force of any word or words, thing or things contained or specified in any statute or law of provision and praemunire, or in any of them, any law or statute, or opinion or exposition of any law or statute to the contrary in anywise notwithstanding: saving always the due execution of all and every person and persons attainted or to be attainted for any offence whereupon judgement of death now is or ought to be, or hereafter may lawfully be given by reason of this statute or otherwise ; and saving always all and every such pains of death or other hurt or punishment as heretofore might without danger or law be done upon any person or persons that shall send or bring into this realm or any other the Queen's dominions, or within the same shall execute any summons, sentence, excommunication, or other process, against any person or persons from the bishop of Rome for the time being, or by or from the see of Rome or the authority or jurisdiction of the same see. *No attainted person to be executed, save in accordance with the provisions of this Act or other anti-papal legislation.*

19. Provided always and be it enacted by the authority aforesaid, that no person or persons shall hereafter be indicted for assisting, aiding, maintaining, comforting, or abetting of any person or persons for any of the said offences in extolling, setting forth, or defending of the usurped power and authority of the bishop of Rome, unless he or they be thereof lawfully accused, by such good and sufficient testimony or proof, as by the jury by whom he shall so be indicted shall be thought good, lawful, and sufficient to prove him or them guilty of the said offences. *Those only indicted for abetting who shall be convicted after due trial.*

II.

AN ACT FOR THE DUE EXECUTION OF THE WRIT DE EXCOMMUNICATO CAPIENDO.

[Transcr. from Statutes of the Realm, iv. pt. 1, p. 451.]
(5 Elizabeth, cap. 23.)

§ 1. Reason of the Act. The writ de Excommunicato capiendo has been much neglected by sheriffs, as being unreturnable into any court.

Forasmuch as divers persons offending in many great crimes and offences appertaining merely to the jurisdiction and determination of the ecclesiastical courts and judges of this realm, are many times unpunished for lack and want of the good and due execution of the writ *de Excommunicato capiendo* directed to the sheriff of any county for the taking and apprehending of such offenders, the great abuse whereof as it should seem hath grown for that the said writ is not returnable into any court that might have the judgement of the well executing and serving of the said writ according to the contents thereof, but hitherto have been left only to the discretion of the sheriffs and their deputies, by whose negligence and defaults for the most part the said writ is not executed upon the offenders as it ought to be, by reason whereof such offenders be greatly encouraged to continue their sinful and criminal life, much to the displeasure of Almighty God, and to the great contempt of the ecclesiastical laws of this realm:

§§ 2, 3. Return of the writ. Every writ shall now be returnable into the King's Bench after twenty days,

2. Wherefore for the redress thereof, be it enacted by the Queen's most excellent Majesty, with the assent of the Lords spiritual and temporal and the Commons in this present parliament assembled, and by the authority of the same, that from and after the first day of May next coming every writ of *Excommunicato capiendo* that shall be granted and awarded out of the high court of Chancery, against any person or persons within the realm of England, shall be made in the time of the term, and returnable before the Queen's Highness, her heirs and successors, in the Court commonly called the King's Bench in the term next after the *Teste* of the same writ, and that the same writ shall be made to contain at the least twenty days between the issuing and the return thereof. And after the same writ shall be so made and sealed, that then the said writ shall be forthwith brought into the said Court of the King's Bench, and there in the presence of the justices shall be opened and delivered of record to the sheriff or

other officer to whom the serving and execution thereof shall appertain, or to his or their deputy or deputies. And if afterwards it shall or may appear to the justices of the same court for the time being, that the same writ so delivered of record be not duly returned before them at the day of the return thereof, or that any other default or negligence hath been used or had in the not well serving and executing of the said writ, that then the justices of the said Court shall and may, by authority of this Act, assess such amerciament upon the said sheriff or other officer in whom such default shall appear, as to the discretion of the said justices shall be thought meet and convenient, which amerciament so assessed shall be estreated into the Court of Exchequer, as other amerciaments have been used.

CHAP. XI

and the sheriff shall be amerced for not returning the writ.

3. And be it further enacted by the authority aforesaid, that the sheriff or other officer to whom such writ of *Excommunicato capiendo* or other process by virtue of this Act shall be directed, shall not in anywise be compelled to bring the body of such person or persons as shall be named in the said writ or process into the said Court of the King's Bench at the day of the return thereof, but shall only return the same writ and process thither, with declaration briefly how and in what manner he hath served and executed the same, to the intent that thereupon the said justices may then further therein proceed, according to the tenor and effect of this present Act.

The writ shall be returned without the person of the excommunicate.

4. And if the said sheriff or other officer to whom the execution of the said writ shall so appertain, do or shall return that the party or parties named in the said writ cannot be found within his bailiwick, that then the said justices of the King's Bench for the time being, upon every such return, shall award one writ of capias against the said person or persons named in the said writ of *Excommunicato capiendo*, returnable in the same court in the term time, two months at least next after the *Teste* thereof, with a proclamation to be contained within the said writ of capias, that the sheriff or other officer to whom the same writ shall be directed, in the full County Court or else at the general Assizes and goal-delivery to be holden within the said county, or at a Quarter Sessions to be holden before the justices of peace within the same county, shall make open proclamation ten days at the least before the return, that the party or parties named in the said writ shall, within six days next after such proclamation, yield his or their body or bodies to the gaol and prison of the said sheriff or other

§§ 4-7. Of the capias. In case of non est inventus a first capias shall be issued by the King's Bench, with a proclamation to the local justice to direct the surrender of the excommunicate, who shall then remain in prison as the first writ

CHAP. XI
directed, the sheriff making return.

such officer, there to remain as a prisoner according to the tenor and effect of the first writ of *Excommunicato capiendo*, upon pain of forfeiture of ten pounds. And thereupon after such proclamation had, and the said six days past and expired, then the said sheriff or other officer to whom such writ of *capias* shall be directed shall make return of the same writ of *capias* into the said Court of the King's Bench, of all that he hath done in the execution thereof, and whether the party named in the said writ have yielded his body to prison or not.

£10 forfeiture for not appearing upon the first *capias*.

5. And if upon the return of the said sheriff it shall appear, that the party or parties named in the said writ of *capias*, or any of them, have not yielded their bodies to the gaol and prison of the said sheriff or other officer, according to the effect of the same proclamation, that then every such person that so shall make default, shall for every such default forfeit to the Queen's Highness, her heirs and successors, ten pounds, which shall likewise be estreated by the said justices into the said Court of Exchequer, in such manner and form as fines and amerciaments there taxed and assessed are used to be.

A second *capias* may then be issued in like manner with £20 penalty.

6. And thereupon the said justices of the King's Bench shall also award forth one other writ of *capias* against the person or persons that so shall be returned to have made default, with such like proclamation as was contained in the first capias and a pain of twenty pounds, to be mentioned in the said second writ and proclamation, and the sheriff or other officer to whom the said writ of second capias shall be so directed shall serve and execute the said second writ in such like manner and form as before is expressed for the serving and executing of the said first writ of *capias*. And if the sheriff or other officer shall return upon the said second *capias*, that he hath made the proclamation according to the tenor and effect of the same writ, and that the party hath not yielded his body to prison according to the tenor of the said proclamation, that then the said party that so shall make default, shall for such his contempt and default forfeit to the Queen's Highness, her heirs and successors, the sum of twenty pounds, which said sum of twenty pounds the said justices of the King's Bench for the time being shall likewise cause to be estreated into the said Court of Exchequer in manner and form aforesaid.

A third *capias* may,

7. And then the said justices shall likewise award forth one other writ of *capias* against the said party, with such like proclamation and

pain of forfeiture as was contained in the said second writ of *capias*, and the sheriff or other officer to whom the said third writ of *capias* shall so be directed, shall serve and execute the said third writ of *capias* in such like manner and form as before in this Act is expressed and declared for the serving and executing of the said first and second writs of *capias*. And if the sheriff or other officer to whom the execution of the said third writ shall appertain do make return of the said third writ of *capias*, that the party upon such proclamation hath not yielded his body to prison according to the tenor thereof, that then every such party for every such contempt and default shall likewise forfeit to the Queen's Majesty, her heirs and successors, other £20, which sum of £20 shall likewise be estreated into the said Court of the Exchequer in manner and form aforesaid. And thereupon the said justices of the King's Bench shall likewise award forth one writ of *capias* against the said party with like proclamation and like pain of forfeiture of £20. And that also the said justices shall have authority by this Act infinitely to award such process of capias with such like proclamation and pain of forfeiture of £20 as is before limited against the said party that so shall make default in yielding of his body to the prison of the sheriff, until such time as by return of some of the said writs before the said justices it shall and may appear that the said party hath yielded himself to the custody of the said sheriff or other officer according to the tenor of the said proclamation. And that the party upon every default and contempt by him made against the proclamation of the said writs, so infinitely to be awarded against him, shall incur like pain and forfeiture of £20, which shall likewise be estreated in manner and form aforesaid.

CHAP. XI

if necessary, be issued with £20 penalty, and *ad infinitum* with £20 penalty in each case.

8. And be it further enacted by the authority aforesaid, that when any person or persons shall yield his or their body or bodies to the hands of the sheriff or other officer, upon any of the said writs of *capias*, that then the same party or parties that shall so yield themselves, shall remain in the prison and custody of the said sheriff or other officer, without bail, baston or mainprize, in such like manner and form to all intents and purposes as he or they should or ought to have done, if he or they had been apprehended and taken upon the said writ of *Excommunicato capiendo*.

§§ 8–10. Proceedings after surrender. When the surrender is made, imprisonment shall follow, as directed in the original writ.

9. And be it further enacted by the authority aforesaid, that if

CHAP. XI

The sheriff shall forfeit £40 for a false return.

any sheriff or other officer by whom the said writ of *capias* or any of them shall be returned as is aforesaid, do make an untrue return upon any of the said writs, that the party named in the said writ hath not yielded his body upon the said proclamations or any of them, where indeed the party did yield himself according to the effect of the same, that then every such sheriff or other officer, for every such false and untrue return, shall forfeit to the party aggrieved and damnified by the said return the sum of forty pounds, for the which sum of forty pounds the said party aggrieved shall have his recovery and due remedy by action of debt, bill, plaint, or information, in any of the Queen's courts of record, in which action, bill, plaint, or information, no essoin, protection, or wager of law shall be admitted or allowed for the party defendant.

Bishops may receive the submission of excommunicates who shall certify into Chancery, and receive the usual sheriff's writ.

10. Saving and reserving to all archbishops and bishops and all others having authority to certify any person excommunicated, like authority to accept and receive the submission and satisfaction of the said person so excommunicated in such manner and form heretofore used, and him to absolve and release, and the same to signify as heretofore hath been accustomed to the Queen's Majesty, her heirs and successors, into the high court of Chancery, and thereupon to have such writs for the deliverance of the said person so absolved and released from the sheriff's custody or prison, as heretofore they or any of them had, or of right ought or might have had, anything in this present statute specified or contained to the contrary in anywise notwithstanding.

§§ 11-13. Certain provisoes, &c. In jurisdictions exempt significavit by mittimus shall be issued to chief officer, who shall proceed as the sheriffs above.

11. Provided always, that in Wales, the counties palatines of Lancaster, Chester, Durham, and Ely, and in the Cinque Ports, being jurisdictions and places exempt, where the Queen's Majesty's writ doth not run, and process of *capias* from thence not returnable into the said Court of the King's Bench, after any *significavit* being of record in the said Court of Chancery, the tenor of such *significavit* by *mittimus* shall be sent to such of the head officers of the said county of Wales, counties palatines, and places exempt, within whose offices, charge, or jurisdiction the offender shall be resident, that is to say to the chancellor or chamberlain for the said county palatine of Lancaster and Chester; and for the Cinque Ports to the lord warden of the same; and for Wales and Ely and the county palatine of Durham to the chief justice or justiciar there. And thereupon every of the said justices and officers to whom such tenor of *significavit* with *mittimus* shall be directed and delivered,

shall by virtue of this statute have power and authority to make like process to the inferior officer and officers to whom the execution of process there doth appertain, returnable before the justices there at their next sessions or courts, two months at least after the *Teste* of every such process, so always as in every degree they shall proceed in their sessions and courts against the offenders as the justices of the said Court of King's Bench are limited by the tenor of this Act in term times to do and execute.

12. Provided also and be it enacted, that any person at the time of any process of *capias* aforementioned awarded, being in prison or out of this realm in the parts beyond the sea, or within age, or of *non sanae memoriae*, or woman *covert*, shall not incur any of the pains or forfeitures aforementioned which shall grow by any return or default happening during such time of non-age, imprisonment, being beyond the sea, or *non sanae memoriae*, and that by virtue of this statute the party aggrieved may plead every such cause or matter in bar of and upon the distress or other process that shall be made for levying of any of the said pains or forfeitures.

13. And that if the offender against whom any such writ of *Excommunicato capiendo* shall be awarded, shall not in the same writ of *Excommunicato capiendo* have a sufficient and lawful addition according to the form of the statute first of Henry the Fifth in cases of certain suits whereupon process of exigent are to be awarded, or if in the *significavit* it be not contained that the excommunication doth proceed upon some cause or contempt of some original matter of heresy, or refusing to have his or their child baptized, or to receive the Holy Communion as it commonly is now used to be received in the Church of England, or to come to divine service now commonly used in the said Church of England, or error in matters of religion, or doctrine now received and allowed in the said Church of England, incontinency, usury, simony, perjury in the Ecclesiastical Court, or idolatry, that then all and every pains and forfeitures limited against such persons excommunicate by this statute by reason of such writ of *Excommunicato capiendo* wanting sufficient addition, or of such *significavit* wanting all the causes aforementioned, shall be utterly void in law, and by way of plea to be allowed to the party aggrieved.

CHAP. XI

The penalties in default remitted in certain cases.

It is directed that every writ issued in the first instance shall contain the usual specification of offence.

14. And if the addition shall be with a *nuper* of the place, then in every such case at the awarding of the first capias with proclamation according to the form aforementioned, one writ of proclamation (without any pain expressed) shall be awarded into the county where the offender shall be most commonly resident at the time of the awarding of the said first *capias*, with pain in the same writ of proclamation to be returnable the day of the return of the said first *capias* with pain and proclamation thereupon, at some one such time and court as is prescribed for the proclamation upon the said first *capias* with pain. And if such proclamation be not made in the county where the offender shall be most commonly resident in such cases of additions of *nuper*, that then such offender shall sustain no pain or forfeiture by virtue of this statute for not yielding his or their body according to the tenor aforementioned, anything before specified to the contrary hereof in anywise notwithstanding.

CHAPTER XII

THE DEPRIVED CLERGY: ESTIMATES OF HISTORICAL WRITERS

THE evidence of the bishops' registers in regard to the deprived clergy is certainly the most trustworthy help to an estimate of the numbers that we are likely to get in the absence of a direct official return. It may not however be without interest to examine the figures which have come down to us in printed books from a period more or less contemporary. The numbers given by such writers as Dean Hook, Archdeacon Perry, Mr. Froude, Mr. Hore, and Mr. Lane vary very little, with the exception of the last-named, who speaks of an estimated 400 clergy deprived, but on what proof it does not appear. None of these writers, who otherwise vary from 177 to 192, make it clear within what limits the assessment is made. Does it for instance refer to the visitation of 1559, or to subsequent action as well? It is, at all events, clear that their ultimate authority is Strype, who wrote about 1720. This historian refers to three calculations, at which we will glance.

First comes the evidence of D'Ewes' *Journal*. Strype says [1], referring to D'Ewes [2]: 'by a calculation then (i.e. in Elizabeth's reign) taken of all the clergy in the land, of 9,400 ecclesiastical persons settled in their several promotions, but 177 left their livings rather than to renounce the pope and change their idolatrous Mass for the use of the English liturgy.' D'Ewes, who wrote his *Journal of all the Parliaments of Elizabeth* in 1631, is not a contemporary writer, and it will be pretty clear a little later that he depended for his numbers in this question on

Chap. XII

Estimate in modern histories of the number deprived.

Strype's three lists: i. D'Ewes'.

[1] *Ann.* i. 73.   [2] *Journal*, p. 23.

CHAP. XII Camden, who published the first volume of his *Annals of Queen Elizabeth* in 1615.

ii. Cotton MS. Titus C. 10, f. 172, i.e. Camden.

Strype's second reference is to a Cotton MS.: 'in one of the volumes of the Cotton Library (Titus C. 10), which volume seemeth once to have belonged to Camden, the whole number of the deprived is digested in this catalogue:—

Bishops	14
Deans	13
Archdeacons	14
Heads of Colleges . . .	15
Prebendaries	50
Rectors of Churches . . .	80
Abbots, Priors, and Abbesses . .	6
In all	192

Camden in his Annals little varies; only reckoning twelve deans and as many archdeacons.' We have discovered the folio referred to, and find that it is part of Camden's MS. collection which he got together as material for his works. The leaf in question consists chiefly of some remarks by a Romanist upon Elizabeth's religious policy, and at the foot in another hand, apparently, there comes in this short list which looks like a memorandum, and has no connexion with the rest of the MS. The numbers are bracketed together, and endorsed as 'abdicati primo ingressu E. R.' It will be noticed that the dignitaries are out of all proportion to the inferior clergy. But that is not the main point: the document is almost clearly Camden's memorandum written at the beginning of the seventeenth century for the estimate contained in his *Antiquities*, and, in proof of date, on the other side of the page is a reference to matters in Ireland for the year 1607. The 'E. R.' too gives the idea that the writer was writing when Elizabeth's reign had passed: otherwise *regni* would probably have been used instead of those initials.

Comparison of this list with

Before going on to Strype's third reference we may fitly complete Camden's evidence. The nearly contemporary

translation of his *Annals* runs thus: 'but certes as them- CHAP. XII
selves have certified, in the whole kingdom wherein are that in
numbered 9,400 ecclesiastical dignities (*promotiones ecclesi-* Camden's
asticae) they could find but eighty pastors of the Church, *Annals*.
fifty prebendaries, fifteen rectors of the college, twelve
archdeacons, and so many deans, six abbots and abbesses,
and all the bishops that were then in seance and were
fourteen in number[1].' These figures, added up, give a
total of 189, which is the number most frequently cited
by recent historians. It will be observed that it differs
from the Cotton MS. memorandum by three only, the
Annals subtracting one dean and two archdeacons, but
otherwise agreeing with the memorandum.

But where did Camden get his estimate from, whether Origin of
it should be 192 or 189? He refers it to 'themselves,' Camden's
which may mean the Romanist party or the ejected clergy. Sanders'
Camden, therefore, had seen some list which he quotes, *De Visibili*
and such a list is to be found in the seventh book of *Monarchia*.
Nicolas Sanders' *De Visibili Monarchia*, which was published at Louvain in 1571. Sanders had lectured at
Oxford under Mary as Professor of Law and of Divinity.
He was deprived, or resigned, when Elizabeth came to
the throne, and went abroad with Sir Francis Englefield,
who supplied him with frequent help until the book mentioned was published. A transcript of the larger part of
his list will be found at the end of this chapter. The
list gives some Scotch and Irish names, but after deducting
these the result is as follows and in the order here given:—

Bishops	14
Heads of Religious Houses . .	6
Deans	10
Archdeacons	12
Heads of Colleges	15
Prebendaries	47
Priests	90
In all	194

[1] Hearne's *Camden*, i. 47.

This list of Sanders we fully believe to be the source of all the enumerations quoted so far. The ten deans are immediately followed by three Irish deans, who might readily be included by a rapid counter. The same careless counting added in two Irish archdeacons, so making the archdeacons fourteen in all. The forty-seven prebendaries were perhaps raised to fifty as a round number. Sanders goes on to say that others canons had been deprived too. The ninety priests were probably reduced to eighty, because it was clear that some four or five had been reckoned twice by Sanders, and the deduction of these would give about eighty in all. D'Ewes' estimate of 177 very likely came from the same list in Sanders by his own calculation of the figures, or more probably from Camden, after deducting the abbess and prioress mentioned, and the fourteen bishops, perhaps, whom he does not specially name. But perhaps the most convincing thing to show the mutual interdependence of the lists is the fact that in every one of them the number of bishops is wrong. It ought to be fifteen, and the error can be traced to Sanders' list, in which Morgan of St. David's is omitted.

Clerke's criticism of Sanders. Sanders' seventh book, in which his list occurs, was attacked by Bartholomew Clerke, under the superintendence of Cecil and Parker. His work, dated 1573, is named *Fidelis servi subdito infideli responsio*. The list comes in for some examination. The writer finds fault with Sanders first of all for representing the bishops and others as enduring prison and death in prison. He says: 'vincula certe credo aliquos (si carceres vincula appelles) minime sapienter subiisse quod Romani primatus opinionem tenacius retinerent, verum mortem aliquos perpessos esse ob asserendum summi pastoris primatum, nunquam adhuc intellexi, nec te audisse suspicor. . . . Fuerunt fortasse aliqui, dum in carcere essent, vita functi: iidem etiam naturae, credo, cessissent si non fuissent incarcerati[1].' With regard to the numbers in the list Clerke makes a very important criticism: 'multi hic quasi exules et relegati

[1] O. 2.

a te recitantur qui hodie apud nos vivunt et valent, et non modo proborum civium sed Protestantium etiam piorum munere funguntur. . . . De numero qui alioqui valde exilis esset ita laborasti ut quos interserueris minime curares, et ne chartas satis implere minime videaris nec presbyteris parochialibus, nec clericis, nec ludimagistris supersedisti. Et inter eos etiam quosdam recensuisti qui nunquam ejecti, nunquam exules erant. Eorum hic nomina adderem, nisi odiosum esse cognoscerem, et illis valde ingratum qui indies tibi et tuae monarchiae male precantur[1].'

The sum of Clerke's charge, then, is that the list is both misleading and inaccurate. These charges are justified; for to begin with, Bonner was the only bishop who at the time of writing (1571) had died in prison, and in any case not one of the persons named had lost his life for refusing to abjure the pope. Some were put to death after, e.g. Laurence Vaux, but not until some time after the *De Visibili Monarchia* was published. We do not feel sure how far Clerke is right in saying that some of Sanders' deprived or exiled were still in possession of English benefices in 1571. Sanders' inaccuracy, however, is further evident in that he gives a few names twice over. But the matter is scarcely worth pursuing in detail, for Roman Catholic writers allow that Sanders was not always careful. Thus Mr. Bridgett says of Sanders' report to Cardinal Morone which is in the Vatican Archives[2]: ' Sanders tells of what he had himself seen, and what he had ascertained from the relation of others. There are a few inaccuracies in his narrative, as there will always be if a man tries to write down from memory and without the assistance of any documents the public events of which he has been an eye-witness, or in which he has been an actor.' The reference, of course, is not to the list which we are now considering, but the admission proves that Sanders was not always careful. Rishton, the continuator of Sanders'

Justification of such criticism.

---

[1] P. 4. Clerke was writing of course after the Bull of Excommunication of 1570, which stirred up a great deal of Protestant feeling. See the article on Clerke in *Dict. Nat. Biog.* xi. 45.

[2] *True Story*, &c., pref. x.

CHAP. XII *De Schismate Anglico,* is still more careless in the matter under consideration, and both from him and the admissions of Mr. Bridgett we gather that the Romanists at Douay and Louvain were somewhat inexact in regard to dates and numbers.

iii. Cardinal Allen.

Strype's third list is thus given: 'the answerer to the *English Justice* (supposed to be Cardinal Allen) mentions the deprived after this reckoning, viz. fourteen bishops (and in Ireland the Archbishop of Armagh, and an uncertain number of other bishops there), three elects, one abbot, four priors or superiors of religious convents, a dozen deans, fourteen archdeacons, above threescore canons of cathedral churches, not so few as an hundred priests, fifteen heads or rectors of colleges in Oxford and Cambridge, and above twenty doctors of divers faculties that fled the realm, or were in the realm imprisoned.' This is Strype's summary of a page from *Ad Persecutores Anglos.* The earliest form of this book was written about 1583, in criticism of a defence of Elizabeth's recent religious policy, entitled *The Execution of Justice in England.* The page in question is transcribed at the end of this chapter. Strype has omitted from his summary the 'two other English prelates, the one now dead and the other still surviving at Rome,' spoken of by the 'Answerer.' These must have been either Scott or Pate, who died in 1565, and Goldwell, who died at Rome in 1585. The three elects will be Thos. Wood[1], who must have been nominated to one of the sees still vacant in November, 1558, and probably Reynolds, Dean of Exeter, nominated to Salisbury. Goldwell of St. Asaph had been nominated to Oxford on November 9, 1558.

Origin of Allen's list.

But we find that this list also is dependent upon Sanders. The latter wrote in 1571, and the 'Answerer' has, it appears to us, simply taken his figures, bringing them down to 1583, and thus presenting a total of some 247. Thus the original (but erroneous) number of fourteen bishops is allowed to stand. To these Allen has added

[1] 'Priest and elected a bishop.' Fleet Prisoners in Harl. MS. 360, f. 7.

two exiled bishops, although he forgets a third; and he gives further three bishops elect, who are almost certainly included among the canons, and so are numbered twice over. The deans, archdeacons, and heads of colleges are those of Sanders. The canons and priests *may* have increased to the number given by 1583, but it is far from likely. The list, however, despite its inaccuracy, is valuable as showing that after twenty-five years' experience of the penal laws, the Romanists on the Continent were unable to prove anything like the wholesale ejection and punishment which some suppose to have taken place. I. W., *Priest*, in his *English Martyrology*, printed in 1608, gives twenty-one as the total number of those executed for religion between 1570 and 1582. Amongst these will be Allen's *plurimos martyrio coronatos*. He mentions no single martyr in Elizabeth's reign before 1570.

Having now examined Strype's three authorities, which seem to resolve themselves into one, we must look at a modern enumeration which has been very frequently quoted, and owing to its form has been twisted into a great deal more than it warrants upon examination. It is given in the appendix to Tierney's *Dodd*, vol. ii. no. xliv. It was made up by Tierney from the 'Lives of Clergymen' in Dodd's second folio volume. Tierney appears to have added a very few names that we have not noticed in Dodd. But what is Dodd's authority? He states it to be chiefly Anthony à Wood, Worthington's *Catalogue of Martyrs*[1], J. Bridgwater's *Concertatio Ecclesiae Catholicae in Anglia*, 1588. The last is the chief authority of Dodd. But here again through Bridgwater we are thrown back on Sanders, for just where Sanders gives no initial, there we find the same absence of initial in Dodd. So then the advance of Dodd over Sanders is simply this, that he has added some biographical details. Tierney then made the list more useful by a fresh classification and alphabetical arrangement. It is in the final shape given by Tierney that the list has been so much used of late

The list in Tierney's *Dodd*, and its origin.

[1] This book we have not been able to discover.

years by Roman Catholics. Their point is that the list containing about 200 names is evidently an enumeration of the higher clergy only—*ergo* an indefinite number of parish clergy who resigned, or were deprived, must be added in order to reach the sum total.

Fault must be found with Tierney at the outset for the misleading setting of his list. Twice over he speaks of those represented as opposing the Reformation *at the beginning of Elizabeth's reign*, and, taken in connexion with the text which the list is intended to illustrate, this might be supposed to refer to deprivations under the Supremacy Act of 1559. On examination, however, it is clear that names are given of those who were deprived or resigned long after. Thus Bristow, Fellow of Exeter, was not deprived until 1570. Zone, apparently a layman, was not ejected from his Cambridge professorship until about 1562. Some, e.g. Atslow, were never ordained at all. Others, e.g. Bavant, Stopes, Shaw, Wiggs, Meredith(b. 1547), were ordained abroad, after leaving England. Then again the register of the University of Oxford makes it clear that some of the Fellows of Colleges who are mentioned took degrees after 1559, and so by the terms of the two Supremacy Acts must have allowed the Queen's supremacy[1]. Thus Appleby proceeded M.A. in 1563, E. Atslow in 1560, Fitzsimons 1562. Alan Cope and R. Fenn proceeded B.C.L. in 1560, L. Atslow and T. Darrel B.A. in the same year. A few of those mentioned by Tierney, e.g. Gifford, are not in the Oxford register at all, and yet are referred to Oxford. Thus without going through the names more in detail here it will be seen that there are grave reasons for doubting their entire accuracy. At the best, the list gives the names of those who 'opposed the Reformation,' not at the beginning, but during the first twelve years of the reign [2].

Our general conclusion then is that the existing lists mainly depend on Sanders, who drew up his record in 1571, and in an inaccurate and exaggerated way gave the names

---

[1] Above, pp. 16 and 204.
[2] For biographical details of many of the deprived, see Mr. Jos. Gillow's *Literary and Biographical History*.

of all he knew or had heard of amongst the clergy and laity who had got into difficulties with the ecclesiastical authorities during those years. It will be necessary to try and get behind Sanders in order to compile a list from strictly contemporary authorities for the years 1558–1564.

I.

THE LIST OF NICOLAS SANDERS, 1571.

[Transcr. from *De Visibili Monarchia*, p. 688.]

[This list occurs in the seventh book of the *De Visibili Monarchia*. The general thesis of this particular book is 'Pontificem Romanum semper fuisse totius Ecclesiae Primatem,' and two-thirds of the whole treatise are devoted to working this out. It must be allowed that Sanders adopts a very comprehensive method when he concludes the argument of the seventh book with these words : ' Re igitur ab initio mundi repetita, universam et Patriarcharum ab Adamo usque ad Mosen, et Levitici generis sacerdotum ab Aarone usque ad Christum, et Pontificum Romanorum successionem a D. Petro usque ad Pium Quintum, qui nunc Romae in Petri Cathedra sedet, ordine perpetuo continuatam, velut sub unum Lectoris aspectum in hoc septimo libro subjiciam' (p. 221). The list itself occurs in a section which is thus headed: 'Quot et quanti tum espicopi tum alii, tam ecclesiastici quam nobiles et illustres in Anglia, Hibernia, et Scotia viri, dignitatem, fortunas, patriam, libertatem, ac denique vitam, Elizabetha apud Anglos regnante, atque haeresim profitente, amiserint, ut ne cogerentur Pontificis Romani Primatum abjicere atque abjurare' (p. 686). Then follows a page of history in which the English Reformation is described from this point of view, and the list succeeds on p. 688. We omit references to Scotland and Ireland, and the names of the laity given at the end.]

Qui autem pro Apostolicae Cathedrae Principatu confitendo, vel in vinculis domi, vel in exilio foris, partim usque ad mortem perstiterunt, partim usque ad hodiernum diem detinentur, hi sunt :

i. Episcopi Angli aut in vinculis, aut exilio vita defuncti.

Edmundus Bonnerus, Londinensis ; Joannes Vitus, Vintoniensis ; Cuthbertus Tonstallus, Dunelmensis ; Oglethorpus, Carleolensis ; Pateus, Vigorniensis; Baynus, Lichfeldensis; Thurlebeus, Elyensis ;

Polus, Petroburiensis; Burnus, Bathoniensis; Scottus, Cestriensis, in exilio defunctus.

 ii. Episcopi Angli adhuc in custodia detenti, aut exules, sed superstites.

Hethus, Eboracensis Archiepiscopus; Watsonus, Lincolniensis; Troblefildus, Exoniensis; Thomas Goldwellus, Asaphensis, Romae exulat.

 iii. Religiosorum ordinum Archimandritae, et Priores . . . ob fidem suis sedibus pulsi.

D. Feknamus, Monachorum D. Benedicti Abbas in carcere adhuc agit; Mauritius Chaceus, Cartusianorum Prior, cum suis omnibus Brugis in exilio agit; Wilsonus Cartusianorum de Monte Gratiae Prior; Catharina Palmera, Monialium D. Brigittae Abbatissa cum Hugone Huberto ejusdem ordinis generali Confessore, ac reliquis fratribus et sororibus suis locum exilii sui prope Antuerpiam in Brabantia sortitur; Elizabetha Cresnera, Monialium D. Dominici Priorissa cum suis apud Brugenses agit; Franciscani per inferiorem Germaniam dispersi in exilio agunt; Richardus Shelleus Ordinis D. Joannis in Anglia Prior, cum fratre suo Jacobo ejusdem ordinis milite, in exilio agit.

 iv. Decani Cathedralium in Anglia Ecclesiarum.

D. Henricus Colus, Ecclesiae Londinensis; D. Edmundus Stuardus, Ecclesiae Vintoniensis; D. Reginaldus, Ecclesiae Exoniensis; Robertsonus, Dunelmensis; Setholandus, Vigorniensis; D. Joannes Ramrigius, Lichfeldiensis; D. Joannes Harpsfildus, Nordovicensis; Henricus Joliffus, Bristoliensis; D. Joannes Boxollus, Vindelisoriensis; Daniel, Herfordensis.

 v. Archidiaconi vel vincti, vel exules.

D. Nicolaus Harpsfild, Cantuariensis; D. Dracottus, Eboracensis; Richardus Petreus, Bokingamiae; D. Chedseus Middlesexiae; Marvinus, Surriensis; Fitz Jacobus, Bathonensis; D. Albanus Langdalus de Lewis; Taylerus, Cicestriensis; Hodsonus, Lincolniensis; Joannes Hansonus, Richmundensis; Robertus Percevallus, Cestriensis; Robertus, Monensis in Wallia.

 vi. Studiosorum Collegiis, vel in Oxonio, vel in Cantabrigia Praefecti, partim vincti et vita defuncti, partim exules.

Belserus, Collegio D. Joannis in Oxoniensi Academia; Elius,

ejus successor in eodem Collegio; Slithurstus, Collegio S. Trinitatis; Henricus Henshaus, Lincolniensi Collegio; D. Georgius Bullocus, Collegio S. Joannis in Cantabrigia; D. Joannes Yongus, Collegio Penbrukensi; Edmundus Cosin, Collegio S. Catharinae; Thomas Pecok, Collegio Reginae; Gulielmus Taylerus, Collegio Christi; Thomas Redmannus, Collegio Jesu; Thomas Bayleus, Collegio de Clare; Laurentius Vausaeus, Collegio Mancestriensi; Gulielmus Martialis, Aulae S. Albani; Joannes Smithaeus, Collegio Regali in Oxonio; Hodgesonus Collegio Reginae in Oxonio.

vii. Canonici Cathedralium Ecclesiarum, ob sedis Apostolicae Primatum vel in custodia defuncti, vel adhuc vincti, aut exules.

Hillus **Ecclesiae Cantuariensis Canonicus**; Ardenus, Mauritius Clenok, Palmus, D. Setonus, D. Mortonus, Henricus Bouel in Ecclesia Suthwellensi ejusdem dioeceseos—**Ecclesiae Eboracensis**; D. Thomas Darbisherus, Willertonus, Cosinus, Moruinus—**Ecclesiae Londinensis**; Thomas Hidus, Langrigius, Bilsonus—**Ecclesiae Vintoniensis**; Saluinus, Dantonus, Tutinus, Nicolaus Marley—**Ecclesiae Dunelmensis**; D. Faucetus, Robertus Mannerus, Gulielmus Wilsus, Thomas Villerus—**Ecclesiae Lincolniensis**; Thomas Wilsonus, Gulielmus Colinwod—**Ecclesiae Cestriensis**; D. Heskinus, Cancellarius, D. Thomas Hardingus, Thesaurarius, Ricardus Dominicus, David Powellus, Faulerus—**Ecclesiae Sarisburiensis**; Joannes Bicardikus, Edouardus Cratfordus, Gilbertus Burnfordus, Egidius Capellus, Joannes Hemingus, Huchinsonus—**Ecclesiae Bathonensis**; Bemundus Cancellarius, Edouardus Godsaluus, Thomas Stapletonus—**Ecclesiae Cicestriensis**; Thomas Nutom, Joannes Blaxtonus, Gualterus Muggus—**Ecclesiae Exoniensis**; Ricardus Ludbius—**Ecclesiae Herefordensis**; Harcottus—**Ecclesiae Nordovicensis**; Gulielmus Dalby, Cancellarius **Ecclesiae Bristoliensis**; D. Ricardus Smithaeus, D. Treshamus—**Ecclesiae Oxoniensis**; Morganus Philippus Praecentor **Ecclesiae Menevensis**.

Non sic autem res accipienda est, velut hi soli Ecclesiarum Cathedralium Canonici quos hoc in loco ascripsi, ob sedis Romanae confessionem, patria, opibus, libertate, aut vita privati fuerint. Nec enim dubito quin alii praeterea valde multi hanc laudem meriti sint. Sed illos ego recensui quos aut ipse noveram, aut ab aliis hac dignitate motos esse acceperam. Presbyteri vero Parochiales, et alii clerici qui ob retinendae Sedis Apostolicae communionem, vel in vinculis defuncti, vel adhuc vincti, vel in exilium ire coacti sunt, multo difficilius enumerari possunt. Sed tamen ne Ordo ipse, si penitus praetermittatur, injuriam sibi factam existimet, eos hic adjungam de quibus me audire contigit.

> viii. Presbyteri in carcere aut defuncti, aut adhuc detenti, ob Primatus confessionem.

Edouardus Williamsonus, Gulielmus Sotton, Gretus, Hartus, Joannes Cubbidgus, Woddus, Jonsonus, Ramseius, Georgius London.

> ix. Presbyteri beneficiis suis exuti aut in exilio degentes ob Primatus Romani confessionem.

Clemens Burdettus, Edmundus Hargattus, Thomas Davys, Gregorius Bellus, Laurentius Webbus, Robertus Painus, [Nicolaus Langrigius,] Ricardus Adamus, Joannes Peritonus, Thomas Cranus, Ricardus Wodlock, Ricardus Jacobi, Thomas Haukins, Crocus, Grangerus, Gulielmus Giblettus, Coquus, Hugo Tenant, Thomas Palmerus, Thomas Atkinsonus, Pilus, Colinus, Redus, Durstonus, Edouardus Chamberus, Simon Bellostus, Kingus, Rogerus Bobettus, Robertus Jonus, Joannes Fezardus, Gulielmus Shepardus, Ricardus Bisshop, Joannes Berwikus, Martinus, Antonius Wilkinson, Courtmillus, Ricardus Prattus, Gulielmus Atkinsus, Heiwardus, Harperus, Josephus, Joannes Feltonus, Stephanus Markus, Joannes Oliverius, Gulielmus Greshoppus, Thomas Kirtonus, Edouardus Brumbrogus, Henricus Alwayus, Joannes Rastellus, Cuthbertus Vauxeus, Edmundus Brunus, Georgius Storcus, Gulielmus Smitheus, Grenwellus, Clemens, Petrus de Southwarmborough, Edouardus Taylerus, Gulielmus Woddus, Knightus, [Joannes Rastellus,] Joannes Danisterus, Havardus, Thomas Fremannus, Philippus, Joannes Fuccius, Anthonius Gardinettus, Joannes Bradshaus, Miniuerus, Robertus Kentus, Jaksonus, Henricus Gillus, Joannes Redshaus, Alanus Chenerie, Ricardus Wistus, Leonardus Stopius, Joannes Dalus, Edmundus Lysterus, Joannes Boltonus, Thomas Hamedinus, Henricus Pius, David de Skenthrist, Tomsonus.

Eos praeterea qui honestum locum in Collegiis utriusque Academiae sortiti, et eodem ob fidem Catholicam per hos duodecim annos, ejecti sunt, non minus trecentis fuisse vere dixerim, quos hic singulos recensere nolui, partim ne taedio lectorem afficerem, partim quia difficulter nomina singulorum addiscerem. Quos tamen aut publice legendo aliis praeivisse aut insignem literarii honoris gradum quandoque ascendisse intellexi, non putavi praetermittendos.

x. Professores.

Nicolaus Sanderus, qui tanquam Regius Professor Jus Canonicum suo jure in Oxonio publice praelegit, ei loco et muneri ob fidem conservandam renuntians.

Gulielmus Zonus in Cantabrigia juris civilis Regius Professor.

Georgius Ethrigius linguae Graecae in Oxonio Professor . . .

xi. Doctores S. Theologiae ob fidem, aut beneficiis privati, aut exules.

D. Babingtonus, D. Carterus, D. Sedgius, D. Nicolaus Mortonus, D. Carolus Parkerus, D. Ricardus Hallus, D. Gaspar Heiwoddus. D. Gulielmus Alenus, D. Thomas Stapletonus.

xii. Juris civilis et canonici Doctores aut in vinculis defuncti, aut adhuc vincti, aut exules.

D. Joannes Storaeus, D. Ricardus Micheus, D. Edmundus Windam, D. Joannes Pauleus, D. Gulielmus Knottus, D. Audoenus Ludovicus hodie in Duacensi Academia Regius Professor, D. Thomas Butlerus, D. Ricardus Vitus.

xiii. Doctores Artis Medicae in confessione Romani Primatus constantes.

D. Joannes Frierus pater in carcere mortuus, D. Joannes Frierus filius exulat Patavii, D. Nicolaus Carrus, Thomas Vavaserus, D. Joannes Clemens exul, D. Ricardus Smitheus, D. Edouardus Atslous.

xiv. Licentiati Theologiae.

Ricardus Bernardus, Gulielmus Wilsus, Thomas Dormannus, Ricardus Fleming, Gregorius Bellus, Joannes Martialis, Nicolaus Quemerford, Gulielmus Pomrellus, Thomas Darellus, Ricardus Bristous, Joannes Whitus.

xv. Ludimagistri, ob Primatus confessionem officio suo abdicati.

Fremannus S. Pauli in Urbe Londinensi, Joannes Harrisius in Bristoliensi, Benedictus in Sarisburiensi, Gulielmus Gooddus in Wellensi, Plumtreius in Lincolniensi, Joannes Fennus apud memoriam S. Edmundi, Joannes Potzus in Leicestrensi, Thomas Ivisonus in civitate Dunelmensi.

Chap. XII xvi. Magistri Musices, officio suo ob Primatus confessionem ejecti.

Sebastianus in Cathedrali Ecclesia Londinensi, Thornus in Metropoli Eboracensi, Prestonus in oppido Vindelisoriensi.

Omitto studiosorum plane maximam multitudinem qui ob Primatus Romani confessionem, partim rapti sunt in vincula, partim in exilium acti, partim suis collegiis ejecti. Caeterum ne soli clerici videantur istam in fide profitenda constantiam tenuisse, commemorabuntur etiam aliquot Illustrium Laicorum exempla in eodem genere.

[62 names follow (p. 702) of men, 15 of women, 14 of families who left the country.]

II.

The Summary in *Ad Persecutores Anglos*, p. 56.

After comparing the recent sufferings for religion with those of Mary's reign the writer goes on: 'Nos vero istis talibus, quatuordecim simul Episcopos opponimus, eosque excellentes et tanto munere dignissimos, et quos ipse libelli author paulo ante, animo licet pessimo, magnis laudibus in coelum extulit (et certe quoad eruditionem et sanctitatem nullis Europae Episcopis erant inferiores); qui omnes suis honoribus exuti, plerique etiam in carcerem conjecti, maximisque injuriis affecti fuerunt, una cum eximio illo confessore Archiepiscopo Armachano Hiberniae Primate, multisque aliis ejusdem insulae episcopis. Opponimus deinde duos alios ejusdem dignitatis Praesules Anglos, alterum jam mortuum, alterum Romae adhuc superstitem; tres quoque designatos Episcopos vita jam functos; quibus addimus Venerandum Abbatem Westmonasteriensem; quatuor religiosorum conventuum priores, tresque integros conventus fortunis omnibus spoliatos, et vel in ergastula detrusos vel e regni finibus exterminatos. Addimus deinde duodecim Decanos spectatae eruditionis, qui in Cathedralibus Angliae Ecclesiis secundas ab Episcopis obtinent; Archidiaconos quatuordecim; Canonicos Cathedralium Ecclesiarum supra sexaginta; Sacerdotes vero plus quam centum, omnes bono loco et existimatione, superioris Principis temporibus, ut alios omittam sacerdotes plurimos nostri hujus exilii creatos, et postea martyrio coronatos. Quibus adjicimus quindecim Rectores Collegiorum Oxoniensis Academiae et Cantabrigiensis, viros magnae certe in iis Academiis et in ipsa Republica authoritatis, quorum prudentia et pietate commoti precipui quique omnium scientiarum professores et Doctores in diversis facultatibus supra viginti, vel cum illis, vel non ita multo post eorum exemplum secuti, religionis causa partim in aliis regionibus peregrinantur exules, partim domi in carceribus detinentur vincti.'

III.

THE SUMMARY IN J. BRIDGWATER'S *Concertatio Ecclesiae Anglicanae* (1588).

[This list is printed on the fly leaf.]

Ecclesiastici.

Cardinalis unus.
Archiepiscopi tres martyres.
Episcopi consecrati 14 martyres.
Episcopi electi tres.
Abbas unus.
Priores religiosorum conventuum, 4.
Conventus integri, 4.

Decani Ecclesiarum Cathedralium, 13.
Archidiaconi, 14.
Canonici Cathedralium Ecclesiarum, supra 60.
Sacerdotes maxima ex parte illustres aut nobili loco nati, 350.

Academici.

Rectores Collegiorum, 15.
Doctores Theologiae, 45.
Licentiati Theologiae, 12.
Doctores Juris, 15.

Doctores Medicinae, 8.
Ludimagisti, 8.
Magistri Musices, 3.

[Saeculares, 257, etc.; Feminae, 101, etc.; Martyres, 110.]

IV.

THE LIST OF DODD (1737) AS CORRECTED BY TIERNEY (1839).

[Tierney's *Dodd*, vol. ii. App. xliv.]

'An imperfect catalogue of Deans, Archdeacons, and Chancellors who opposed the Reformation in the beginning of Queen Elizabeth's reign.

Deans.

Boxall, John, Windsor.
Cole, Henry, St. Paul's.
Daniel, Richard, Hereford.
Holland, Seth, Worcester.
Joliff, Henry, Bristol.
Ramridge, John, Lichfield.
Stuart, Edmund, Winchester.

THE ELIZABETHAN CLERGY

CHAP. XII

Archdeacons.

Fitz James, John, Bath.
Hanson, John, Richmond.
Harpsfield, John, London.
Harpsfield, Nich., Canterbury.
Hodgson, Dr., Lincoln.
Langdale, Alban, Lewes.
Mervyn, Edward, Surrey.
Perceval, Robert, Chester.
Peter, Richard, Buckingham.
Roberts, Dr., St. David's.

Chancellors.

Bremund, John, Chichester.
Burnford, Gilbert, Wells.
Dalby, William, Bristol.
Draycot, Anthony, Lichfield.
Heskins, Thomas, Sarum.
Martin, Thomas, Winchester.
Story, John, Oxford.

An imperfect catalogue of the Heads of Colleges, Fellows, Prebendaries, and other dignified Ecclesiastics who opposed the Reformation in the beginning of Queen Elizabeth's reign.

Heads of Colleges.

Baily, Thomas, Clare Hall, Camb.
Baker, Philip, King's Coll., Camb.
Belsire, Alex., St. John's, Oxford.
Bullock, George, St. John's, Camb.
Chedsey, William, Corp. Christ., Oxford.
Cole, Arthur, Magd. Coll., Oxford.
Cosins, Edmund, Catherine Hall, Oxford.
Coveney, Thomas, Magd. Coll., Oxford.
Dugdale, James, Univ. Coll., Oxford.
Ely, William, St. John's Coll., Oxford.
Gervase, James, Merton Coll., Oxford.
Henshaw, Henry, Lincoln Coll., Oxford.
Hodgson, Dr., Queen's Coll., Oxford.
Marshal, William, Alban Hall, Oxford.
Moss, William, Trin. [Hall], Camb.
Neale, John, Exeter Coll., Oxford.
Palmer, Thomas, Glo'ster Hall, Oxford.
Peacock, Thomas, Queen's Coll., [Camb.].
Philips, Morgan, St. Mary's Hall, Oxford.
Redman, Thomas, Jesus Coll., Oxford.
Slythurst, Thomas, Trin. Coll., Oxford.
Smith, John, Oriel Coll., Oxford.
Taylor, William, Christ's Coll., Camb.
Wright, William, Balliol Coll., Oxford.
Young, John, Pembroke Hall, Camb.

Fellows of Colleges in Oxford.

Appleby, Ambrose, Merton.
Atkins, Anthony, Merton.
Atslow, Edward, New.
Atslow, Luke, New.
Bramston, Thos., St. John's.
Bursthard, John, New.
Catagre, John, New.
Cope, Alan, Magdalen.

Darrel, Thomas, New.
Dawkes, Robert, Merton.
Doleman, Thomas, All Souls.
Dorman, Thomas, All Souls.
Fenn, Jas., C.C.C.
Fenn, Robert, New.
Fitzsimons, Leond., Trinity.
Fowler, John, New.
Giffard, Robert, Merton.
Hyde, David, Merton.
Ingram, John, New.
Knott, William, New.
Marshal, John, New.
Meredith, Jonas, St. John's.
Noble, John, New.
Potts, John, Merton.
Poyntz, Robert, St. John's.
Rastal, John, New.
Scott, Thos., Trinity.
Shaw, Henry, St. John's.
Shelley, Richard, New.
Sheprey, William, C.C.C.
Stapleton, Thos., New, and Preb. of Chichester.
Stopes, Leon., St. John's.
White, Richard, New.
Wiggs, William, St. John's.
Windon, Ralph, St. John's.
Windsor, Miles, C.C.C.
Wright, John, Magdalen.

The reader may judge how defective this catalogue is, from what is observed by Mr. Wood, the Oxford historian. He tells us that twenty-three Fellows of New College only refused to subscribe to Queen Elizabeth's Injunctions. As for the nonconformists in other colleges, we have no satisfactory account of them: and still less of the number that opposed the Reformation in the University of Cambridge.

Prebendaries.

Allen, Wm., York.
Arden, John, York.
Bicherdyk, John, Wells.
Bilson, Richard, Wells.
Blaxton, —, Christ Church, Oxford.
Bovel, Henry, Southwell.
Capel, Giles, Wells.
Collingwood, Wm., Chester.
Cratford, Edward, Wells.
Dalton, —, Durham.
Derbyshire, Thos., St. Paul's.
Dominick, Rich., Sarum.
Faucet, —, Lincoln.
Fowler, —, Sarum.
Godsalve, Edward, Chichester.
Harcourt, —, Norwich.
Harding, Thomas, Sarum.
Henning, John, Wells.
Hill, —, Canterbury.
Hutchinson, Robert, Wells.
Johnson, Robert, York.
Langridge, —, Winchester.
Lilly, George, St. Paul's.
Ludby, Richard, Hereford.
Mannors, Robert, Lincoln.
Marley, Nicholas, Durham.
Morton, Nicholas, York.
Powel, David, Sarum.
Salvin, —, Durham.
Tresham, Wm., Ch. Ch., Oxford.
Tute, —, Durham.
Villiers, Thomas, Lincoln.
Willerton, —, St. Paul's, London.
Wills, Wm., Lincoln.
Wilson, Thomas, Chester.

CHAP. XII

Other dignified Ecclesiastics.

Barret, John, D.D., Carmelite.
Bavant, John, D.D., Professor.
Bell, Gregory, Licentiate Div.
Bernard, Richard, D.D.
Bristowe, Richard, Lic. Div.
Browborough, Edward, D.D.
Butler, Thos., D.D.
Carter, William, D.D.
Davison, —, D.D.
Fleming, Richard, D.D.
Hall, Richard, D.D.
Hart, —, Legum Doctor.
Haywood, Gaspar, D.D.
Lewis, Owen, Legum Professor.
Mather, —, D.D.
Matthews, —, D.D.
Michy, Richard, Legum D.
Neale, Thomas, D. Professor.
Nicholson, Richard, D.D.
Palmer, George, Legum D.
Parker, Charles, D.D.
Parul, John, Legum D.
Paul, John, Legum D.
Pendleton, Henry, D.D.
Pomrel, William, Licentiate D.
Quemerford, Nicholas, Lic. Div.
Sanders, Nicholas, Legum Prof.
Seaton, John, D.D., Professor.
Sedge, —, D.D.
Sedgwick, Thomas, D.D., Professor.
Smith, Richard, D.D., Vice-Chancellor, Oxford.
Tempest, Robert, Legum Doctor.
Tenant, Stephen, D.D.
Vaux, Cuthbert, Lic. Div.
Vaux, Richard, D.D.
Walley, Robert, D.D.
Webb, Laurence, Legum D.
Weedon, Nicholas, D.D.
White, John, D.D.
Williamson, —, D.D.
Windham, Edmund or William, D.D.
Wood, Richard, D.D.
Zoon, William, Legum D., Professor.

Superiors of Religious Houses and Schools.

Bennet, —, Master of Salisbury School.
Chauncey, Maurice, Prior of the Carthusians at Sheen, with his monks.
Feckenham, John, Abbot of Westminster and twenty-eight monks.
Fenn, John, Master of School at St. Edmundsbury.
Fox, Stephen, Guardian of Franciscans at Greenwich, with his friars.
Freeman, —, Master of St. Paul's School.
Good, Wm., Master of School at Wells.
Harris, John, Master of School at Bristol.
Hubert, Hugh, Confessor of Sion House.
Hyde, Thomas, Master of Winchester School.
Iveson, Thomas, Master of School at Durham.

Palmer, Catherine, Abbess of Sion.
Peryn, William, Prior of Dominicans in Smithfield, with his friars.
Plumtree, —, Master of School in Lincoln.
Potts, John, Master of School in Leicester.
Shelley, Sir Richard, Prior of St. John's of Jerusalem.
Vaux, Laurence, Warden of Manchester Coll. Church.

'To these [concludes Tierney] may be added many more of less note, whose names I have met with in private records.'

CHAPTER XIII

THE DEPRIVED CLERGY: EVIDENCE OF REGISTERS

Chap. XIII
An investigation of the registers is necessary.

THE main purpose we have had before us in this inquiry has been to discover the number of the clergy who were deprived during the first six years of Elizabeth's reign for refusing to acquiesce in the settlement of religion. We have seen from a survey of the extant lists and estimates that the traditional numbers are unsatisfactory: can we reach a more precise conclusion? At this point, then, we turn to the episcopal registers, which do not seem to have been systematically consulted with the special purpose of getting out such a list for all the dioceses of England and Wales. This search we have now completed, thanks to the kind help of the bishops' registrars, who in all cases gave us free and ready access to the documents that we wished to see.

Nature and extent of their evidence.

But what did we expect to find? It is well known that the lists of institutions to vacant benefices have been carefully kept in most dioceses from the thirteenth or fourteenth century onwards. The entries do not merely give the name of the clerk instituted, but in most cases that of his predecessor as well, and the cause of the vacancy, whether *per mortem naturalem* A.B. *ultimi et immediati incumbentis*, or *per cessionem*, or *per resignationem*, or *per deprivationem*. The last is sometimes varied by *per amotionem* or *destitutionem*, or else by the combination of two of these three nouns. It was, then, from the entries in which deprivation was assigned as the reason of vacancy that we hoped to make up a full list of all who, from whatever cause, were deprived in the period under review.

For eleven of the twenty-five English and Welsh dioceses of the sixteenth century we were able to obtain complete lists, which will be found at the end of the chapter. Elsewhere we were not so fortunate. Thus the records required have disappeared entirely in the dioceses of Bristol, Bangor, Llandaff, St. Asaph. At Lincoln there is a lamentable gap from 1547 to 1595. At York the usual register appears to be wanting for the critical years 1558 to 1565, in which latter year it begins, but is in a bad state of preservation. Happily the lacuna is made up to some extent by two books of institutions, the one labelled 1547–1553, the other 1553–1571. In the latter, however, there is a gap from September, 1558, to May 24, 1561. At Worcester there is a curious omission of all entries between November, 1563, and the year 1571. At Ely there is no record between June, 1559, and October, 1562. The same is true of Carlisle between November, 1558, and 1561. For the remaining extant lists the commencing dates are as follows: Durham, May 22, 1560; Hereford, February 3, 1560; Salisbury, May 7, 1560; Winchester, March 26, 1561.

At first sight, then, we have no very sufficient reward for the labour of our search, if we can only present complete lists for the following eleven dioceses: Bath and Wells, Canterbury, Chester, Chichester, Exeter, Gloucester, London, Norwich, Peterborough, Rochester, and St. Davids. But we can supplement the lists from other sources, and so approach completeness. For the gaps in Hereford, Salisbury, and Winchester, due to the vacancy of the sees, we have full *sede vacante* information at Canterbury, so that those three dioceses are rendered complete. From the same source we can make up similar omissions during the period of vacancy for those dioceses which have no register extant, viz. Bangor, Bristol, Lincoln, Llandaff, St. Asaph. We hoped to find some aid in the bishops' certificates at the Public Record Office, but where they covered the years with which we are concerned, the information was so meagre that we gained little. At this point we turned to the lists of Crown presentations for

Supplementary evidence at Lambeth, and in bishops' certificates, and Crown presentations.

Chap. XIII

Elizabeth's reign preserved amongst the Lansdowne MSS. These appear to have been taken from the Patent Rolls, and are very numerous. The Crown had in its own right a very large amount of patronage, and claimed also to present to all livings in episcopal gift during the vacancy of the see. In this way the Crown presented to some 583 vacant benefices between the beginning of the reign and Lady Day, 1561, when all the sees except Bristol and Gloucester (April 19, 1562) had been filled up. From March 25, 1561, to July 18, 1563, a similar period, the number of Crown presentations falls to 343. The value of this very full list consists in the fact that, in at least half the cases, the name of the predecessor and the reason of vacancy are fully stated. Accordingly we were able to make very useful additions of institutions, or at all events presentations, for the dioceses where the registers fail us, and to find the particulars of many deprivations.

The list of deprived resulting from these combined materials.

From the materials thus described we first drew up a catalogue of all those who, for whatever cause, were stated by these returns to have been deprived. In order to ensure its completeness we added in all names of persons stated by Sanders to have been deprived[1]. It seemed to us that in this way we should approximate to the extreme possible number of those ejected from their cures during the early years of Elizabeth.

This list needs careful pruning.

Reflexion, however, will at once show that this extreme upward limit cannot fail to be fallacious. The number is 480[2]. Are we to assert that so many were actually deprived for refusing to conform to the settlement of religion? Assuredly not. It does not, for instance, follow from an entry of institution in any register *post deprivationem A.B.* that the said A.B. was deprived for Roman sympathies. Of course the probability of such a cause would be somewhat high in the first year or two of the reign, but it lessens as time goes on; and, as is well known, the deprivations, in and after 1564, were mainly of puritan clergy. Again, there may have been a long gap between

[1] For his list see above, p. 225. [2] See the lists in the Appendix, p. 252.

the deprivation and institution, so that some institutions of 1559 or 1560 may have occurred after deprivation that took effect in the reign of Mary. In fact from the visitors' report of 1559, and elsewhere[1], we find that many livings had been vacant for some time[2]. Then, again, in the list of names given by Sanders in 1571, very slight inspection proves that some of his deprived were never clergymen at all; others conformed at first, and afterwards (sometimes years after) saw fit to change their opinions. In fact his list contains some whom we now should call *perverts*; that is to say, after an acquiescence which may or may not have been feigned, they at last renounced the Church of England for union with Rome. Other names given by Sanders we cannot verify from the registers, though some doubtless correctly belong to the years 1558-1564.

It is clear, then, that having found the extreme possible number of deprived clergymen warranted by our evidence, we have now to eliminate from this total those wrongfully included, either as being improperly designated by Sanders

Method of its reduction.

---

[1] See the return of 1564, p. 245.

[2] See above, p. 82. In this connexion a letter of Archbishop Sandys to Cecil in 1571 may be quoted (MSS. Add. 32091, f. 242). He refers to the diocese of York. 'Oftentimes where there are 1,000 or 1,500 people in a parish there is neither parson nor vicar, but only a stipend of £7 or £8 for a curate. And because that is too little to find a man in these days, such cures are commonly (lacuna) for avoiding of that extremity served either with a (lacuna) or the curate of the next parish. This is (lacuna) general inconvenience throughout the whole realm (lacuna) more common in these parts.'

A good deal of capital has been made of Bishop Cox' return for Ely in 1561 as quoted by Strype (*Parker*, i. 72), in which the Bishop says, 'Miseranda sane et deploranda hujus dioeceseos facies,' etc. This return is in the British Museum (Add. MSS. 5813, f. 105 (85). It gives thirty-four benefices as vacant out of 152. The next return of 1563 (Harl. 594, f. 196) shows that of 129 parishes mentioned in Ely diocese only nineteen are vacant. Of these nineteen one is on lease, two vacant post mortem, and the remainder 'for exility of the living.' The fact is that 'exility of living' was a very general cause of vacancy, and is often so noted at the time, e.g. C.C.C. returns for Bath and Wells, 1561. See further, p. 245. The lament of Cox in 1561 does not mean that this diocese or any other was unserved by clergy, rather it refers to the 53 (not 57) incumbents who were non-resident, so that 53 + 34 benefices had no resident clergyman. His list immediately appended by him to his complaint shows that there were 103 priests and seven deacons belonging to the diocese.

as clergymen, or as having been deprived after 1564. In this way we subtract twenty-four, whose names are given below[1] in our third list. Of the remaining 456 there are about eighty that we cannot identify for certain[2]. It is impossible to judge the proportion of these eighty that should be included within our six years. Striking them all off for the moment as uncertain we still have about 376. Of these there are 108 italicised in our first list below[3] who acquiesced at first, and then were deprived, either for perversion to Rome or some other fault. For making such a distinction we have a certain amount of evidence, and if our materials were fuller the 108 would be augmented. Thus we have the lists of signatures alluded to above, which prove that in five dioceses some at all events signed in 1559 and were deprived later. Then Canon Dixon has kindly drawn our attention to the diocesan returns of 1561, which refer to the southern province only. These lists, preserved at C. C. C., Cambridge, are very full and give the names of incumbents, and often furnish other particulars. From these names and particulars we find that at least thirty-five of the 108 referred to above were in possession of their benefices in that year. These then must have acquiesced at first, as did the signatories of 1559; and if we had these signatures and returns complete for all the dioceses and not for some only, it is at all events probable that we should find amongst the residuum a large number who signed and conformed and were then deprived. Besides the signatures and returns we have the Register of the University of Oxford, which shows that some of the deprived took degrees in the University after May, 1559, and therefore by the terms of the Supremacy Act and the Assurance of Supremacy must have acknowledged the supremacy, the Injunctions, and the Prayer Book. Some of the Cambridge men, too, we can similarly distinguish by the aid of Cooper's *Athenae Cantabrigienses*. The net result, then, from these various sources of information is to show that at the very least some 108 conformed to the

---

[1] See p. 269. [2] See p. 266. [3] See p. 252.

settlement, and were afterwards, but before November, 1564, CHAP.XIII deprived of their benefices.

We have thus eliminated or distinguished a large proportion of the 480. We must now anticipate one or two objections that may be made to our deductions. It will be said, for instance, that on our own confession the registers are imperfect, and that a full return of deprivations in Wales, in Bristol, and in the large diocese of Lincoln, would bring up our 480 to a much higher figure. No doubt the extreme limit we have reached would have to be raised, but we much doubt whether the increase would be large. In this connexion it is interesting to notice that despite all the prophecies of wholesale deprivation which were made in the first half of 1559[1], no contemporary proof exists of the fulfilment of such prediction. Stapleton and other Romanist writers of the time make no point of wholesale deprivation[2]. Indeed, so far as we have noticed, Sanders in 1571 was the first to take up the question of numbers, and we have seen all that his utmost vigilance was able to effect[3]. There is, then, no tradition that a large number left their benefices in the early years of the reign, either generally or in the dioceses where the registers fail us. It may be mentioned too that the returns of 1561 show remarkably few vacant benefices in Wales, and few in proportion in Lincoln, though more in Bristol[4]. This would scarcely be the case if a large number of incumbents had been turned out for refusing to conform. In the admitted difficulty[5] of finding suitable clergymen to fill vacant posts at that time, it is very noticeable that so few benefices are returned as void. But even if we could grant that the gross number of deprived should be raised considerably, a reduction would still have to be made. Thus, it must be repeated, we have the visitation signatures of only five dioceses, and these

Objections considered:
i. In completeness of the registers.

[1] See above, p. 41.
[2] See, however, the note on p. 251.
[3] Cap. xii.
[4] The actual numbers are: Bangor 3, St. Asaph 0, Llandaff 9, Bristol 38 out of 254, Lincoln 38 out of 727. Compare with these London 67, Peterborough 20 out of 250, Worcester 28 out of 199.
[5] See Strype, *Ann.* i. 182.

CHAP. XIII

ii. The large number of men ordained.

not quite perfect; the signatures in the remaining dioceses would certainly in like manner include some on our list who would, by the fact of signing, be proved to have acquiesced at the beginning of the reign. It must further be remembered that the C. C. C. returns of 1561 do not extend to the province of York; a like return for the four northern dioceses would probably reveal the names of some still in possession who now are returned as deprived.

Another objection, sometimes made[1], is based on the very large number of ordinations which appear in Parker's register during the first year or two of his primacy. It is argued that such an excessive number of deacons and priests would have been needless had not the vacancies been very numerous. The supposition is, we presume, that all these candidates for ordination had titles in the Canterbury and perhaps the London dioceses. The difficulty, however, may be soon dismissed, for an examination[2] of the names given shows that many of the newly ordained

---

[1] For instance by the late Mr. Pocock, *Guardian*, November, 1892.

[2] Parker appears to have delegated ordination to one of his suffragans, usually Berkeley of Bath and Wells, or Bullingham of Lincoln: indeed from his register he cannot be proved to have ordained priests and deacons certainly as far as 1570, whatever the reason may be. There are 239 cases of ordination as deacon, priest, or deacon and priest between December 22, 1559, and January, 1563. As a rule the number ordained on each occasion is not large. The difficulty relates to the great ordination in March, 1560, when there were 120 deacons, 37 priests, 6 deacons and priests. Parker himself was to have ordained on March 3, according to a notice in English preserved in the Register at Lambeth (f. 219). On March 10 he commissioned Bullingham to act for him. Now in no case is the diocese appended to a name in the list of those ordained on that date, and the assumption of Mr. Pocock and others is based on this silence. We have rearranged all the names in alphabetical order, and thus discover that the diocese is affixed to at least eleven of these deacons when ordained as priests on some subsequent occasion next month or later in the year. Most of these eleven belong to dioceses in which there was as yet no bishop, for on March 10, 1560 there were only eleven bishops in possession of sees. At the same time it must be allowed that one or two of the eleven belong to Bangor and London, for which dioceses there were bishops consecrated in Dec. 1559. But further, we make out that nineteen of the deacons ordained in March, 1560, were instituted to benefices in all parts of England before 1563, and that for a few of the priests ordained on that occasion the diocese is specified in previous lists, when they were ordained deacons in the February or December preceding.

deacons and priests served their first cures in distant dioceses. In a word, the ordinations at Lambeth were not merely for Canterbury, nor yet for London, but for all parts of England. And indeed had so large a number of ordination candidates been forthcoming for just one or two dioceses, how could this be reconciled with the known difficulty already alluded to of finding suitable candidates, a difficulty which is mentioned more than once by Strype?

It will perhaps be objected too that our list contains no names of unbeneficed clergy, and that the omission is serious. 'Curates' in our modern sense of the word were not numerous in the sixteenth century, and therefore in any case the number deprived could not have been large. In the returns of 1561 it is quite the exception to find vacancies where a cure was served or assisted by a stipendiary curate. At all events we have found no tradition or hint in contemporary writers of any deprivation amongst the unbeneficed clergy.

iii. The case of curates.

A more important objection is that resignation may frequently have been prompted by unwillingness to accept the new *régime*. It is very easy to assert this motive, and its disproof involves no little labour. We have gone fairly into all available evidence, with the result that the contention vanishes. First of all, in glancing through the writings of Sanders, Dorman, Rastall, Stapleton and others who were active contemporary writers in opposition to the Elizabethan settlement, we have not noticed any assertion of the kind, beyond that contained in Sanders' list already quoted[1]. In the next place, after making a careful alpha-

iv. The asserted probability of resignation for conscience sake.

---

[1] Sanders, *De Visibili Monarchia*, 1571, answered by G. Acworth, *De Visibili Romanarchia*, 1573, and by Bartholomew Clerke, *Fidelis servi subdito infideli responsio*, 1573 (produced under the superintendence of Lord Burleigh and Archbishop Parker; see above, p. 220); Dorman's *Proof of certain Articles in Religion*, 1564, answered by Alex. Nowell in his *Reproof*, 1565, and vindicated in Dorman's *Disproof*, 1565; Rastall's *Confutation of a Sermon pronounced by M. Juell*, 1564. Rastall was attacked by W. Fulke in a book entitled *D. Heskins, D. Sanders, and M. Rastall, accounted three pillars and Archpatriarchs of the Popish Synagogue . . . overthrown and detected of their several blasphemous heresies*, 1579. On the fly-leaf of this last work occurs a useful (but imperfect) list

betical list of nearly all the extant institutions between the years 1559 and 1563 or 1564, we do not notice that any of those who resigned appear[1], for certain, on the contemporary lists of recusants given above, or on the subsequent list of Sanders[2]; nor are they, generally speaking we believe, men known to have disliked the settlement. But we are able to go a little farther. It has been stated, in reliance, we presume, on the difficulty of disproving the assertion, that this supposed number of those who resigned for conscience sake was considerable[3]. If this be so, the number of resignations during Elizabeth's early years ought to be out of all proportion to those of the last years of Mary. This is the fairest and perhaps the easiest method of comparison in order to settle the question. We have taken for our purpose some four or five dioceses in different parts of England, and the result, on a review of the whole comparison, is that the average annual number of resignations in these dioceses at the end of Mary's reign was 73½, and during the early years of Elizabeth 53; so that on the whole the resignations are fewer under the altered state of affairs[4]. In order to insure the point, we had a calculation made of all the presentations on the Patent Rolls for 1556, 1557, and 1559 to 1563[5]. The list embraces presentations to Crown benefices throughout all England, but the cause of vacancy

of books published abroad and directed against the Elizabethan settlement. The list notes which have been as yet answered. Stapleton's earliest work was *The Fortress of the Faith*, 1565. It was followed by the *Counterblast*, directed against Horne! See note, p. 251.

[1] There is a difficulty, of course, in regard to the identification of such common names as Wood, Smith, &c. It is possible that some of those who bear such familiar titles in Sanders' catalogue ought to be identified with their namesakes on our list of institutions. The assertion of the text is borne out, however, by the large number of unusual names in Sanders which we cannot trace amongst those who resigned.

[2] For these lists see pp. 179 and 225.

[3] The statement has frequently been made, and quite recently it has been repeated in a correspondence in the *Manchester Guardian*, November, 1897.

[4] For the figures see the comparative table, p. 245.

[5] The calculation was made by the Rev. George Hennessy, author of the *Novum Repertorium Parochiale Londinense*. Mr. Hennessy has made lists of all the Patent Roll institutions from the earliest times. See below, p. 247.

is not always stated. The average ascertained resignations for 1556 and 1557 are 9½, and for the first five years of Elizabeth 8. But once more: there exists in the Public Records Office a list[1] of vacant benefices which internal evidence assigns to the year 1564. In this the reason of vacancy is generally but not always given. From the list we reckon that out of 427 benefices void at that time, 140 were so *propter exilitatem*; 141 *per mortem*; 26 *per cessionem*; 36 only *per resignationem*; 3 were sequestered. The remaining 81 have no reason whatever assigned for vacancy. We submit, therefore, that in face of all this combined evidence from official returns, in addition to the argument from the silence of contemporary writers, the assertion of any extensive resignation for conscience sake must be finally abandoned.

COMPARATIVE TABLE OF INSTITUTIONS[2].

Year ending March 25.	Causes of Vacancy.			Total.
	Death.	Resignation.	Other causes.	
1557.				
Bath and Wells ...	15	12	2	29
Canterbury	8	8	7	23
Durham	8	3	—	11
London	31	41	5	77
Norwich	73	34	23	130
1558.				
Bath and Wells ...	10	2	2	14
Canterbury.........	23	15	8	46
Durham	5	1	—	6
London	49	21	8	78
Norwich	79	32	25	136

[1] The reference is S. P. Dom. Eliz. Addenda xii. 108. The list shows (what was noted above, p. 239) that *propter exilitatem* was a constant reason of vacancy at this time.

[2] See above, p. 244. We have reckoned these numbers from the bishops' registers to Lady Day in each year. We have not counted institutions in which particulars of the vacancy are omitted. Under the head of 'other causes' will be chiefly comprehended deprivation and cession.

THE ELIZABETHAN CLERGY

Year ending March 25.	Causes of Vacancy.			Total.
	Death.	Resignation.	Other causes.	
1559.				
Bath and Wells ...	15	1	0	16
Canterbury.........	16	4	1	21
Durham	12	2	—	14
London	71	11	3	85
1560.				
Bath and Wells ...	17	0	1	18
Canterbury.........	16	4	7	27
London	40	10	17	67
Norwich	68	15	3	6
1561.				
Bath and Wells ...	23	5	2	30
Canterbury.........	29	14	18	61
Durham	4	3	6	13
London	36	27	19	82
Norwich	57	25	2	84
1562.				
Bath and Wells ...	4	9	1	14
Canterbury.........	15	12	19	46
Durham	5	2	1	8
London	18	17	11	46
1563.				
Bath and Wells ...	23	8	3	34
Canterbury.........	12	5	13	30
Durham	5	4	4	13
London	31	19	26	76
1564.				
Bath and Wells ...	9	2	3	14
Canterbury.........	19	6	12	37
Durham	7	3	3	13
London	22	11	12	45

Patent Roll presentations for the whole of England.			Death.	Resignations.	Otherwise.	Not stated.	Total.
March 25, 1556, to March 24, 1557, on account of			10	10	5	166	191
,, 1557 ,, 1558		,,	16	9	0	242	267
Nov. 17, 1558, to Nov. 16, 1559		,,	22	3	8	179	212
,, 1559 ,, 1560		,,	30	14	48	131	223
,, 1560 ,, 1561		,,	14	8	7	161	190
,, 1561 ,, 1562		,,	9	7	3	106	125
,, 1562 ,, 1563		,,	10	5	2	38	55
,, 1563 ,, 1564		,,	7	8	1	95	111

All available evidence, therefore, upon which we have been able to lay our hands seems to give 480 as the total ascertainable number of deprivations *from all causes* between November 17, 1558, and the same day of that month in 1564. Of this number twenty-four have to be subtracted as having been improperly introduced. Of the remainder at least 108 can be proved to have acquiesced in the settlement for a longer or shorter period; and 35 of these 108 were in possession of their benefices as late as 1561. Of the 348 now remaining, 80 are given on Sanders' authority, and cannot be certainly identified in the registers, though doubtless some of the names are accurate enough. Thus, the list comes fairly below 300, and of these an uncertain proportion were, in all probability, deprived for other offences than refusal to acknowledge the settlement of religion. On the whole, then, we cannot believe that many more than 200 were deprived for such refusal within the limits that we have taken. It is, of course, disappointing that we cannot give an exact number, but we have at all events shown that when Elizabeth came to the throne no wholesale turning out of the clergy took place. Comparatively few were deprived at once. The majority acquiesced in the settlement, at all events outwardly, and a proportion of these seem to have changed their attitude, and to have been ejected as time went on.

Conclusion.

CHAPTER XIV

SUMMARY OF THE INQUIRY

WE have now completed our survey of the first six years of Elizabeth's reign from the special point of view proposed. We have examined the relation of the clergy to the settlement of religion during that period, and have attempted to estimate the number of those deprived for their refusal to conform. It may be convenient to sum up in a few short paragraphs the chief facts that, we hope, have been established.

i. At the outset of the reign, the clergy, as a body, were hostile to any change in the existing state of affairs so far as the Church was concerned. This hostility was shown by the protest of Convocation, and by the resolute opposition maintained by the bishops in parliament.

ii. The Supremacy and Uniformity Acts which were before parliament during the spring of 1559, together with the revived and amended Edwardine Injunctions, formed the basis of the settlement which was ready by Midsummer. Under the Supremacy Act the Privy Council were empowered to administer an oath admitting the supremacy, and for refusing to take this oath the bishops, with one exception, were, in conformity with the Act, deprived.

iii. Meanwhile under the same Act a royal visitation of both provinces was arranged, and a summary form of oath was prepared by the visitors, in which the Supremacy, the Prayer Book, and the Injunctions were sworn to. This oath was administered throughout the country during August, September, and October, 1559. We have a list of absentees in the North, and a list of those who took the oath survives for five dioceses in the South. These seem to prove that nearly half the clergy absented themselves from the visitation. Very few, however, were deprived by the visitors in the North. There is no evidence for the number then ejected in the South, except a vague reference in one of Jewel's letters.

iv. A permanent ecclesiastical commission, erected in accordance with the Supremacy Act, began its work, apparently, in the first week of November, 1559. It took cognizance at that time of all cases of refusal to acknowledge the settlement which had been referred to it by the visitors. This was the first work of the commissioners, and they continued to meet at intervals until July, 1562, when a fresh commission was named. They were entrusted with all manner of spiritual jurisdiction, but no record of their proceedings exists, save in fragments and allusions. They do not appear to have carried out their powers of punishment and deprivation with much rigour, and from the surviving lists of prisoners it is certain that very few people, either clerical or lay, were imprisoned in London on account of religion by this commission. Some, however, were by them placed in custody, including eight of the deprived bishops.

First ecclesiastical commission established, 1559.

v. What proportion of those who evaded subscription during the visitation of 1559 were induced by the commissioners and other authorities to take the oath in the months that followed cannot be ascertained. The impression left is that no great diligence was used to enforce subscription. The metropolitical visitation of 1560, continued into 1561, did not administer the oath, but inquired into the working of the Uniformity Act, bringing pressure to bear on those who ignored that Act. On the whole a tolerable state of conformity was discovered in the province of Canterbury.

Metropolitical visitation of the South, 1560 1.

vi. In the North the sees were vacant until 1561, and no effort was made to tender the oath after October, 1559. Meanwhile in May of that year a commission was issued to the Council of the North to deal with those who had not taken the oath in 1559. An episcopal visitation therefore tendered the oath in conjunction, probably, with some of

Visitation of the North, 1561.

the Council of the North. It was probably only partially successful, and in 1562 the Council was constituted a kind of ecclesiastical commission for the North, but we have no record of its proceedings.

New ecclesiastical commission. July 20, 1562.

vii. So far there had been more show of vigour than of rigour. In the middle of 1562 fears were aroused by the condition of affairs in France. Disorders in that country seems to have raised hopes in the minds of those who had signed reluctantly, and of those who had evaded the oath so far. Many of the deprived clergy were celebrating Mass, &c., in private. Hence a new commission was issued in July, 1562, with new procedure, viz. restraint and surveillance, but still proceedings were mainly *in terrorem*.

Penal Statutes of 1563.

viii. Thus the new commission failed to awe the recalcitrant clergy. In 1563 there was much fear of papal sympathy. A new parliament acknowledged that the penal laws had not been pressed. Hence the Assurance of Supremacy Act was passed, and marks a new stage. The oath could now be applied by more elaborate local machinery to those already deprived, as well as to those in office. Recusancy was after a second refusal to incur a traitor's death. The bishops might administer the oath to the clergy without assessors, and spiritual censures were made more sure by the *de excommunicato capiendo* Act. There were however no deaths under the Assurance Act for some time to come. It was hoped that the cases of imprisonment inflicted by these two acts would prove a deterrent sufficiently strong to render the extreme penalty needless. On the whole the operation of the severe penal laws of 1563 was not rigorously pressed, nor were any local commissions for the execution of the Act issued before November, 1564.

Sanders' list of the deprived.

ix. Looking back over the first six years of the reign there is no contemporary evidence of the number of the clergy who were actually deprived during the period. An attempt was made by Nicholas Sanders to draw up such a list in 1571. This list exhibits many inaccuracies. To it, however, may be traced all subsequent attempts to estimate the deprivations. As Sanders' catalogue is inaccurate it is necessary to abandon it and the calculations derived from it[1].

x. A complete search of all extant episcopal registers and other official documents proves that the extreme ascertainable number of the clergy deprived *for all causes* between November 17, 1558, and November 17, 1564, is about 400. To these may be added eighty more whose names are preserved by Sanders, but are not to be identified in official authorities. From this extreme possible number, 480, large deductions have to be made. Against such subtraction must be set a certain proportion to be added for those dioceses where the registers fail us. On a review of the whole evidence it is impossible to conclude that many more than 200 were deprived within the period contemplated (1558-1564).

---

[1] Since the note on p. 243 was written, we have read through *An Addition with an Apology to the causes of burning of Paul's Church*, prefixed to Pilkington's *Confutation*, 1563. The *Addition* says 'some [clergymen] they deprive from their livings, some they commit to prison.' At the end of the volume certain Romanist questions are propounded and answered. In the fourth of these it is stated: 'the bishops be in prison and put from all their livings, and a great number of the clergy have lost all their livings.' Pilkington in his answer to the questions does not notice the point of numbers. The sentence in the *Addition* would go to prove that the 'great number' is more or less rhetorical. With the lapse of half a century the 'some' of the *Addition* was still further multiplied. Parsons in his *Three Conversions of England*, 1603, speaks of the ejected clergy as 'a multitude of learned witnesses, not to speak of infinite others of less degree' (p. 264). His authority is the list of Sanders. The *Supplication of the Lay Catholics to the King's Majesty*, 1604, quoted in the Appendix to *The Fiery Trial of God's Saints*, 1612, says: 'about 1,000 of them abandoned their livings rather than they would change their religion.'

[NOTE: For Bishop Stanley of Sodor and Man see the remarks of Prof W. E. Collins 'The English Reformation' p. 65 *note*. See too above, p. 88.]

APPENDIX I

LISTS OF CLERGYMEN DEPRIVED, 1558-1564.

FIRST LIST[1].

Name with date of successor.		Cure and date of institution.
J. Abowen	. R. 64	Mount Bures, Lon. 63.
R. Adams	S. R. 60	Sparsholt, Win.
J. Alford	. R. 64	Stondon, Lon.[2]
W. Allen.	S.	Prin. St. Mary's Hall, Ox.[3]
T. Alston.	. R. 63	East Langdon, Cant. 45.
Simon Anderson	. R. 61	Hingham, Norw. 56.
Griffin ap David	. R. 62	Stowe, Her. 52.
Amb. Appleby .	S.	Fell. of Merton Coll., Ox.[4]
R. Appletoft	. R. 61	Offton, Norw. 56[5].

[1] This list contains the names of all those known to have been deprived for any reason whatever during these six years. Those in italics are proved, on the evidence given in the footnotes, or by the date of their institution annexed in the second column, to have acquiesced in the settlement for a longer or shorter period. The date in the first column refers to the year in which the successor was instituted.

Abbreviations used :—

    R. = Diocesan Register. Cf. p. 236.
    S. 59 = Signed in 1559. Cf. p. 102.
    Abs. 59 = Absent from the Visitation, 1559. Cf. p. 83.
    S. = Sanders. Cf. p. 225.
    C. C. C. = The Corpus Christi returns. Cf. pp. 160, 240.
    Rest. = Restored. Cf. p. 74.
    Res. = Resigned.
    Fasti / Ath. = Wood's *Fasti* and *Athenae* (Bliss).
    Gutch = His edition of *Wood's Annals*.
    Boase = *Register of Oxford University*, vol. i.
    D. N. B. = *Dictionary of National Biography*.

[2] S. 59. [3] Res. 1560; ordained abroad 61 or 62.
[4] B.A. 60; M.A. 63. [5] S. 59.

LISTS OF CLERGYMEN DEPRIVED, 1558-1564

Name with date of successor.		Cure and date of institution.
T. Arden . . .	R. 61	Preb. III Worc. 58.
	R. 62	Preb. Bartonshaw, Her. 59.
	R. 61	Hartlebury, Worc.
		Preb. York, 56.
Nich. Aspinall . .	R. 64	Stepney, Lon. 62.
W. Assheley . . .	R. 63	Moreton Corbett, C. and L. 39 [1].
Ant. Atkins . . .	S.	Fell. Merton Coll., Ox. [2]
J. Atkinson . . .	R. 59	Whiston, Yk. 54.
T. Atkinson . .	S. R. 59	Sedbergh, Ch. 54.
W. Atkinson . . .	R. 63	Shalford, Lon. [3]
F. Babington . .	S. R. 63	Holsworthy, Ex. 62 [4].
T. Bailey . . .	S.	Master Clare, Camb. 58 [5].
J. Baker . . .	R. 60	Stamford Rivers, Lon. 53 [6].
P. Baker . . .	S.	Prov. King's, Camb. 59.
J. Balkeye . . .	R.	Hargrave, Norw. 56.
N. Bamford . . .	R. 64	Fenny Bentley, C. and L.
		Bentley, Lich. 61.
W. Barrett . . .	R. 61	Longford, 56.
R. Barslow . . .	R. 62	Braintree, Lon. 56 [7].
J. Bartlett . . .	R. 61	Stortford, Lon. 56 [8].
G. Barton . . .	R. 61	St. Swithin, Lon.
		? Hollesworth, Ex. 63.
Rob. Barton . . .	R. 62	Corringham, Lon. 58 [9].
W. Barton . . .	R. 61	Snitterfield, Worc. 57.
G. Basset . . .	R. 60	Sowton, Ex.
Ralph Bayne . .		Bishop of Cov. and Lich. 54.
G. Bell . . .	S. R.	Beaulieu, Win. 55.
		East Ilsley, Sar. 54.
A. Belsire .	S.	Pres. St. John's Coll., Ox. 55.
		IV Canon of Ch. Ch.
		R. Hanborough [10].
E. Benigfeld . . .	R. 62	Preb. St. Endellion, Ex.
J. Bent . . .	R. 63	Tichencote, Pet. 56 [11].
L. Bilson . . .	R. 62	Preb. Sarum [12].
		Preb. Winton.
		Preb. Wells.
		Kingsworthy, Win. 58.

[1] S. 59.   [2] Dep. 59 (Gutch, ii. 137, 146).   [3] S. 59.   C.C.C. 61.
[4] D.D. 60.   Extra hoc regnum Angliae sine licentia regia fugit (Reg.).
[5] See Mullinger, ii. 177, at Douay.   [6] S. 59.   [7] S. 59.   C.C.C. 61.
[8] S. 59.   [9] S. 59.   [10] Gutch, ii. 143.   Died as Rector, 1567.
[11] C.C.C. 61.   [12] Called by Tierney, *R.* Bilson.

Name with date of successor.		Cure and date of institution.
J. Blaxton	S. R. 59	Archd. Brecon, 54.
		Preb. Ex.
		Bratton, Ex.
R. Blunston	R. 59	Ordsall, Yk. 54.
R. Blythman	R. 61	Preb. Wells [1].
R. Bolbelt or Bobbet	R. 64	Donhead St. Mary, Sar.
		Cokeley, Norw. 63.
E. Bonner	59	Bp. of London, 54.
G. Bourne	R. 60	Bp. Bath and Wells, 54.
H. Bovell	S. R. 62.	Preb. Southwell, 59.
J. Bowen	R.	*See* Abowen.
J. Boxall	R. 60. S.	Dean of Windsor, 57.
		Preb. Bath and Wells.
T. Bradley	R. 64	Tudingham, Norw. 54 [2].
R. Bramborough	R. 63. S. ?	Cherington, 48 [3].
T. Bramston	S.	Fell. St. John's, Ox. [4]
T. Bromhedd	R. 60	Hawkesbury, Gl. 56.
J. Bryckebecke, or Byrtebecke	R. 63	Gt. Canfield, Lon. 45 [5].
T. Buckmaster	R. 63	Twickenham, Lon. 62.
G. Bullock	R. S.	Master St. John's, Camb. 54 [6].
T. Burbank	R. 64	Preb. Sarum. 46 [7].
C. Burdett	S. R. 60	Englefield. Sar. 42.
G. Burnford	R. 61. S.	Preb. Bath and Wells, 54.
W. Burton	R. 59	Braddon, Pet. 44.
W. Burye	R. 59	St. Nich. Hospital, Richmond [8].
R. Buttell	R. 63	Cokeley, Norw [9].
T. Byam	R. 62	Preb. Brondesbury, Lon. 60 [10].
J. Byckerdyke	R. 59. S.	Preb. Ely and Wells ?
T. Byrche	R. 62	St. Laurence, I. of W., Win.
R. Calner	R. 60	Scole, Norw [11].
R. Carr, LL.D	R. 59	Mast. Magd. Coll., Camb. 46.
		Preb. Chulmleigh, Ex.
R. Carrier	R. 64	Hastingley, Cant. 57.
H. Carter	R. 62	Denton, Norw. 54 [12].
W. Carter, D.D	S. R. 61	Arch. Northumberland, Durh. 58 [13].
S. Caston	R. 64	Little Stambridge, Lon. 58 [14].
Dominic Chane	R. 61	Winnall, Win.

[1] M. A. 60.   [2] S. 59. C.C.C. 61.   [3] C.C.C. 61.   [4] B.A. 62 (Gutch, ii. 145).   [5] Abs. in 61. C.C.C.   [6] Also Munden, Linc. and Preb. Durh. see Mullinger, ii. 177).   [7] B.A. 60.   [8] Abs. 59.   [9] C.C.C. 61.   [10] C.C.C. 61.   [11] S. 59.   [12] S. 59. C.C.C. 61.   [13] Dep. 59.   [14] S. 59. C.C.C. 61.

LISTS OF CLERGYMEN DEPRIVED, 1558-1564

Name with date of successor.		Cure and date of institution.
W. Chedsey, D.D.	S. R. 59	Pres. Corp. Christ., Ox. 58.
	R. 60	Archd. Middlesex, Lon. 56.
	R. 59	Preb. IV Ox. 57.
W. Chell	R. 58	Precentor, Her. 54 [1].
A. Chenerie	S. [2]	
T. Chyddalton	R. 62	Worfield, Cov. and Lich.
R. Clare a̅s Dominick	R. 60	Stratford Tony, Sar. 54 [3].
		Preb. Sar.
Ant. Clerke, B.D.	R. 63	Preb. Firle, Chich. 50.
	R. 60	East Dean, Chich. 58.
		? Lanynton, Chich. 60.
R. Clif, D.D.	R.	Boldon, Dur. 41.
Rob. Coates	R. 62	Great Haukesley, Lon. Ap. 59.
And. Cole	R. 64	Sculthorpe, Norw [4].
H. Cole	S. R. 59	Dean, St. Paul's, 56.
	R. 59	Wrotham, Cant. 58.
T. Collyer	R. 59	Uppingham, Pet. 54.
J. Collyns	R. 62	Inkpen, Sar. [5]
Rob. Collyns	S. R. 60	Preb. VI Cant. 54.
J. Collinson	R. 60	Eccles. Norw. 41.
T. Coltesmore	R. 61	Poynings, Chich.
J. Colvyer	R. 62	Hilston, Yk.
R. Conwaw	R. 62	Loddington, Pet. 53.
J. Cook	S. ? R. 62	? Cliddesden, Win.
W. Cook	R. 59	Preb. Kilsby, Linc. 54 [6].
R. Coplet	R. 62	Walton on the Hill, Win.
Edm. Cosyn	S.	Mast. Cath. Hall, Camb. 53 [7].
Rob. Cosyn	R. 59	Preb. Mora, Lon. 59.
	R. 60	Treasurer, Lon. 58.
R. Cotton	R. 62	Braughing, Lon. Dec. 59 [8].
T. Coveney, M.B.	S.	Pres. Magd. Coll., Ox. [9]
T. Cradocke	R. 61	Widford, Lon.
E. Cratford a̅s Stratford	S. R.	Preb. Bath and Wells.
	R. 61	Lydeard St. Lawrence, Bath and Wells.
T. Crofte	R. 62	Lanteglos, Ex. 58 [10].
H. Cumberford	R. 61	Norbury, Cov. and Lich.
	R. 60	Precentor, Cov. and Lich. 55.
	R. 60	Yelvertoft, Pet.

[1] Dep. 59. C.C.C. 61. [2] Cf. S. P. Dom. Eliz. xviii. 7. [3] Res. 59. [4] S. 59.
[5] C.C.C. 61. [6] Longland rest. [7] Res. 59.
[8] C.C.C. 61. [9] Gutch, ii. 142. Deprived for not being in orders; Bloxam, iv. 137. [10] C.C.C. 61.

Name with date of successor.		Cure and date of institution.
W. Dalbye	S. R. 60	Preb. and Chanc., Bristol, 58.
R. Dalton (Dr.)	S. R. 60	Preb. VII Dur. 41.
	R. 60	Billingham, Dur. 44.
Emeric Dande	R. 64	Oakington, Ely, 59.
Edm. Daniel	R. 60	Preb. V Worc.[1]
	R. 59	Kingsland, Her. 58.
	S. R. 58	Dean, Her. 58[2].
T. Darbyshire	R. 60	Archd. Essex, Lon. 58.
	S. R. 60	Preb. Tottenham, London, 43.
	R. 60	St. Magnus, Lon.
	R. 60	Fulham, Lon.
T. Darrel	S.	Fell. New Coll., Ox.[3]
Rob. Davyes	R. 62	Shenfield, Lon. Apr. 59[4].
T. Davys	S.	R. Hardwick[5].
Rob. Dawks	S.	Fell. Merton Coll., Ox.[6]
T. Dobeson	R. 59	Austwick, Ch.
T. Doleman	S.	Fell. All Souls Coll., Ox.[7]
R. Dominick		See Clare.
T. Dorman	S.	Fell. All Souls Coll., Ox. 54[8].
Geoff. Downe	R. 61	Preb. Morton, Gl.
Ant. Draycot	S.	Chanc., C. and L.
	R. 60	Preb. Longdon, C. and L. 56.
	R. 60	Wirksworth, C. and L.
	R. 61	Checkley, C. and L.
	R. 60	Preb. Bedford Major, Linc. 39.
	R. 60	Archd. Hunts, Linc. 43.
	R. 60	Cottingham, Pet.
	R. 60	Kettering, Pet.
R. Drury	R. 59	Preb. North Newbald, Yk.
		Preb. Barnby, 58.
J. Dugdale	S. R. 61	Master Univ. Coll., Ox. 58[9].
	R.	Archd. St. Albans, Lon. 57.
Mich. Dunning	R. 59	Preb. Milton Eccl., Linc. 58.
R. Durdane	R. 61	Shalford, Win. 57[10].
— Durston	S.	? J. Durston, Fell. Oriel, 34.
		Master at Eton[11].
Dd. Edwards	R. 64	Llandegla, St. Asaph's[12].
Jas. Ellis	R. 62	Chiddingfold, Win.

[1] Called also R. Daniel; but cf. Le Neve, i. 477.   [2] Dep. 59.
[3] B.A. 60.   [4] S. 59. C.C.C. 61.   [5] B.D. 59. Dep. 62. Boase.
[6] Dep. 59.   [7] ? Dep. 59. Burrows.   [8] Dep. 59. Burrows.
[9] Dep. 61. Boase.   [10] C.C.C. 61.   [11] Dep. 61.   [12] C.C.C. 61.

LISTS OF CLERGYMEN DEPRIVED, 1558-1564

Name with date of successor.		Cure and date of institution.	App. I
E. Elmsley	R. 62	Llandowror, St. Dd's.	
W. Elye	S. R. 63	Pres. St. John's Coll., Ox. 59[1].	
	R. 61	Norton, Cant. 56.	
		Freckenham, Cant. 58.	
Rob. Eyre	R. 64	Upton Lovell, Sar. 48[2].	
J. Farler	R. 63	Wonsington, Win.	
R. Fawcett	R. 60	Preb. Cant.[3]	
	R. 60	Lyminge, Cant. 59.	
	S.	Preb. Linc.[4]	
Rob. Fawcett	R. 64	Shalford with Bromley, Win. 57[5].	
Jas. Fenn	S.	Fell. Corp. Christ. Coll., Ox.[6]	
Rob. Fenn	S.	Fell. New Coll., Ox.[7]	
J. Fezard	S.	Donhead St. Mary, Sar. 58.	
J. Fitz James	S. R. 60	Archd. Taunton, Bath and Wells.	
	R. 64	Chew Magna and Dinder, Bath and Wells, 54.	
Leon. Fitzsimons	S.	Fell. Trin. Coll., Ox.[8]	
— Fowler	S.	Preb. Sar.[9]	
J. Fowler	S.	Fell. New Coll., Ox.[10]	
		Wonston, Win. 60.	
Ant. Gardinet	S.	? Ant. Garnet, Master of Balliol, 60-63.	
J. Gardyner	R. 62	Willoughby, C. and L. 48[11].	
Oliver Garnell	R. 60	Graine, Cant.	
R. Gatskall	R. 63	Purley, Sar. 54.	
Jas. Gervase	S.	Warden, Merton Coll., Ox.[12]	
Rog. Gifford[13]	S.	Fell. Merton Coll., Ox.	
Hugh Glasier	R. 59	Preb. Cant.	
J. Glasyer	R. 60	Archd. Her. 57.	
	R. 62	Freshwater, Win. 49.	
		Erwarton, Norw. Dec. 59.	
E. Godshalfe	S. R. 63	Preb. Ferring, Chich.	
		? Stoke Dawborn, Win. 61.	
T. Goldwell	R. 59	Bp. St. Asaph.	
W. Good	R. 63	Middle Chinnock, Bath and Wells, 56[14].	
	S.	Master of School at Wells.	

[1] Dep. 63. *Fasti*, 153. [2] C.C.C. 61. [3] Dep. 60. *Ath.* 207. [4] C.C.C. 61. [5] *See* Durdame. [6] B.A. 60. [7] B.C.L. 60. [8] B.A. 60. M.A. 62. [9] ? same as next. [10] M.A. 60. Trans mare. C.C.C., 61. [11] S. 59. [12] D.C.L. 60. [13] Tierney wrongly, *Rob.*; cf. Boase, i. 232. [14] Resigned 60 ?

S

Name with date of successor.		Cure and date of institution.
J. Goodman	. R. 60	Dean, Bath and Wells, 53 [1].
Roland Gosnell	. R. 60	Oldbury, Her. 39.
	R. 62	Tenbury, Her. 55.
J. Grete	S. R. 60	Wootton St. Lawrence, Win.
Hugh Hall	. R. 62	Hamstall Ridware, C. and L.
J. Hall	. R. 64	Wooler, Dur. 61.
R. Halse	. R. 60	Preb. Ex.
	R. 60	Broad Clyst, Ex.
	R. 60	Thurlestone, Ex.
T. Handcock	. R. 63	Purley, Sar. 63.
J. Hanson or Hansom	S. R. 59	Archd. Richmond, Ch. 54 [2].
	R. 60	Rochdale, Ch.
– Harcourt	. S.	Preb. Norw.
T. Harding	S. R. 59	Treasurer, Sar. 55.
	R. 59	Bishopstone, Sar.
	R. 59	Preb. Win. 54.
J. Hargravys	. R. 62	Blackburn, Ch.
E. Harman	. R. 60	Ashley, Win.
J. Harpsfeld	. R. 61	Preb. Ex. 58.
	S. R. 59	Archd. Lon. 54.
	R. 60	Preb. Mapesbury, Lon. 58.
	R. 60	Dean Norw. 58.
Nich. Harpsfeld	S. R. 59	Archd. Cant. 54.
	R. 59	Preb. IV Cant. 58.
	R. 60	Saltwood, Cant.
	R. 59	Preb. Harleston, Lon. 54.
J. Harris	. S.	Master of school at Bristol.
J. Harris [3].	. S.	
J. Harrison	. R. 59	Archd. Stow, Linc. 54 [4].
T. Harvye	. R. 64	Hendon, Lon. 62.
Oliver Haver	. R. 60	Burgh, Norw. 58 [5].
T. Haward	S. R. 59	Llandilo Fawr, St. Dd's. 54.
Chr. Hawkes	. R. 61	Bircholt, Cant.
Nich. Heath	. R. 60	Archbp. Yk. 55.
H. Henshaw	. S.	Rect. Linc. Coll., Ox. 58.
R. Hertborn	. R. 62	Long Newton, Dur. 55.
T. Heskyns	S. R. 59	Chanc. Sar. 58 [6].
Fras. Hiberden	. R. 61	Bishopstone, Chich. 55.
Rob. Hill	. S.	Preb. Cant.
	R. 60	Old Romney, Cant. 57.

[1] Dep. 60. Turner restored. [2] Abs. 59. [3] Not ordained. Dodd, 160. Douay D. 141. [4] Elmer rest. ? [5] S. 59. [6] Dep. 59. Cooper, 419.

LISTS OF CLERGYMEN DEPRIVED, 1558-1564

Name with date of successor.		Cure and date of institution.
	R. 60	Lydd, Cant. 58.
	R. 58	Preb. Win.
Giles Hillings	R. 61	Preb. St. Decumans, Bath and Wells.
	R. 61	Skilgate and Winsford, Bath and Wells, 42.
Owen Hodgson	R. 59	Archd. Linc. 59.
	R. 60	Preb. Langford Manor, Linc. 57.
Hugh Hodshon	R. 61	Skelton, Carlisle[1].
	S. R. 61	Prov. Queen's Coll., Ox. 58.
— Holland	R. 61	Preb. Combe IX Bath and Wells[2].
Seth Holland	S. R. 60	Dean Worc. 57.
J. *Hopper*	R. 62	Reed, Lon. 56[3].
J. Howell	R. 60	Manordivy, St. Dd's.
P. Howell	R. 62	Locking, Bath and Wells, ? 59.
T. Huddleston	R. 59	Hockerton, Yk.
Hugh Hudson	R. 62	Titchwell, Norw. 47.
J. Hudson	R. 59	Doncaster, Yk.
Maur. Hughes	R. 60	Goring, Chich. 58.
G. Hunter	R. 60	Preb. Leighton Eccl., Linc. 58[4].
Rob. Hutchyns, or Hutchinson	S. R. 60	Preb. Henstridge, Bath and Wells.
Hugh Huchonson	R. 62	St. Oswald, Dur.
T. *Hybbots*	R. 59	Willersey, Gl.[5]
		Inckberge, Worc. 59.
Dd. Hyde	S.	Fell. Merton Coll., Ox.[6]
T. Hyde	R. 61	Preb. Norton Epis., Linc. 55.
	R. 60	Preb. Win. 54.
	S.	Master of Win. School, 52.
J. Jakeson	S ? R. 59	Bulmer, Yk.[7]
G. Indolen	R. 61	Preb. Fittleworth, Chich.
H. Johnson	R. 61	Broadwas, Worc. 48.
	R. 61	Kinwarton, Worc.
H. Joliffe	S. R. 59	Dean, Bristol, 54.
	R. 60	Preb. IV Worc. 42.
— Jones	R. 63	Yatton, Bath and Wells.
Geoff. Jones	R. 64	White Notley, Lon. 38[8].
		St. Mary Woolchurch.
Griff. Jones	R. 64	Kilken, St. Asaph[9].
J. Kerrell	R. 60	Priston, Bath and Wells, 58.

[1] Abs. 59.   [2] ? the same as the next.   [3] S. 59. C.C.C. 61.
[4] R. Gill rest.   [5] C.C.C. 61.   [6] Dep. 59. *Ath.* i. 456.   [7] Abs. 59.
[8] S. 59. Abs. C.C.C. 61.   [9] C.C.C. 61.

App. I	Name with date of successor.		Cure and date of institution.
	R. Key	R. 62	Condover, C. and L. 52 [1].
	G. Kiddall	R. 63	Preb. Oxton, S'well, 60.
	T. King	S. R. 61	East Camel, Bath and Wells, after 41.
	T. Kingeston	R. 60	Aldham, Lon.
		R. 60	St. Anne and St. Agnes, Lon.
	J. Knight	R. 60	Gt. Chart, Cant. 58.
		R. 61	Preb. Ipthorne, Chich. 58.
	R. Lache	R. 64	Gimingham, Norw. 31 [2].
	J. Laiken	R. 64	Master Jesus Coll., Camb. 62.
			Duxford St. Peter, Ely [3].
	G. Lambe	R. 62	Preb. North Leverton, S'well, 59.
	J. Lamb	R. 60	Kentisbere, Ex. 54.
	Alban Langdale, D.D.	S. R. 59	Archd. Chichester, 55.
		R. 59	Buxted, Chich.
	J. Langland	R. 62	Trowbridge, Sar. 59.
	Peter Lanridge	S. R. 59	Preb. Win.
	Alban Latwicke	R. 63	Merowe, Win. [4]
	J. Lawrence	R. 64	Archd. Wilts, Sar. 54.
	J. Lawson	R. 61	Eastry, Cant. 58.
	J. Leder	R. 61	Nevendon, Lon. 57.
	E. Legge	R. 64	Wigmore, Her. 60.
	T. Lenge	R. 63	Over Stowey, Bath and Wells, 60.
	J. Lewett	R. 64	Selmeston, Chich. 61.
	J. Lloyd? See J. Pryce		
	A. Lofthouse	R. 62	Sedgefield, Dur. 60.
	J. Lovell	R. 64	Ramsey, Lon. 60.
	Arth. Lowe	R. 63	Preb. Fridaythorpe, Yk. 54.
	H. Maddock	R. 64	Shellow Bowells, Lon. 54 [5].
	T. Makinge	R. 62	Bepton, Chich. 18 (sic).
	W. Mancley	R. 62	Hamstall Ridware, C. and L. 57.
	Rob. Mannors	S.	Preb. Linc. [Ketton 58.]
	Nich. Marley	S. R. 61	Preb. IX Dur. 41.
		R. 60	Pittington, Dur. 58.
	J. Marshall	S.	Fell. New Coll., Ox.
	R. Marshall, D.D.	R. 62	Westbourne, Chich.
		R. 61	Preb. Neasden, Lon.
		R. 59	Dean Ch. Ch., Ox., 53.
	W. Marshall	S.	Prin. Alban Hall, Ox. 47.

[1] S. 59.   [2] S. 59. C.C.C. 61.   [3] Res. 63.   [4] C.C.C. 61.
[5] S. 59.

LISTS OF CLERGYMEN DEPRIVED, 1558-1564

Name with date of successor.		Cure with date of institution.	App. I
W. Massenger . . .	R. 60	Preb. Holywell, Lon. 57.	
	R. 62	Preb. Cons. per Mare, Lon. 57.	
T. Mawndevil . . .	R. 61	Preb. Gates, Chich.	
— Mere	R. 62	Chislet, Cant.	
Edm. Mervyn . .	S. R. 59	Archd. Surrey, Win. 54.	
	R. 60	Sutton, Win.	
T. Moorefylde . . .	R. 63	Little Sampford, Lon. 44 [1].	
H. Morgan . . .	R. 60	Bp. St. Dd's. 54.	
J. Morren	R. 60	Preb. Wedland, Lon. 58.	
	R. 60	Copford, Lon. 58.	
	R. 60	St. Martin's Ludgate, Lon. 58.	
	R. 60	Asheldean, Lon.	
	R. 60	Orsett, Lon.	
Rees Morrice . .	R. 62	Llangunllo, St. Dd's.	
		Llanghan, 62.	
W. Mosse, D.C.L. .	S.	Master Trin. Hall, Camb. [2]	
		Reg. Prof. Civil Law, Ox. 54.	
W. Moyle . .	R. 60	St. Leonard's Shoreditch, Lon. 56	
W. Mugge	S. R. 61	Preb. Ex.	
	R. 60	Newton St. Cyres, Ex. 57.	
J. Noble . . .	S.	Fell. New Coll., Ox. [3]	
H. Norman .	R. 62	Reigate, Win. 57.	
W. Northfolke .	R. 61	Hanbury, Worc.	
Baldwin Norton	R. 62	Preb. Langtoft, Yk. 59.	
		Downham, Lon. 50 [4].	
T. Nutcombe . .	S. R. 60	Subdean, Ex.	
Owen Oglethorpe, D.D. .	R. 60	Bp. Carlisle, 57.	
	R. 59	Romald Kirk, Ch. 41.	
G. Ottwaye	R. 60	South Weld, Lon. Feb. 59.	
T. Packard .	R. 61	Preb. Bargham, Chich.	
	R. 60	Rype, Chich. 56.	
G. Palmer, LL.D.	S. R. 59	Preb. North Muskham, S'well., 58.	
	R. 59	Preb. Wetwang, Yk. 58.	
T. Palmer . .	S.	Prin. Glo'ster Hall, Ox. 58.	
J. Parfay . .	R. 62	Preb. Moreton Parva, Her. 56.	
	R. 60	Cradley, Her.	
E. Parratt . . .	R. 62	Preston, Cant. 58.	
R. Pate . . .	R. 59	Bp. Worcester, 55.	
	R. 59	Bothal, Dur.	

[1] Abs. in C.C.C. 61.   [2] *Ath.* ii. 140.   [3] B.A. 59. Dep. 62.
[4] C.C.C. 61.

Name with date of successor.		Cure and date of institution.
Rob. Payne	S.	Fell. New Coll., Ox. 47–59.
		R. Saham Toney, 58–63.
T. Peacock	R. 59	Preb. VII Ely, 56.
	S.	Pres. Queens' Coll., Camb. 56.
Edm. Pearce	R. 63	Hampstead Marshall, Sar.
Rob. Persevall	S. R. ?	Archd. Ch. 54[1].
	R. 59	Ripley, Yk.
J. Perye	R. 63	Titchfield, Win. 58[2].
J. Peryn	R. 59	Plymouth, Ex.
W. Petrose	R. 59	Wrotham, Cant. 58.
J. Philips	S. ? R. 59	Llangan, St. David's, 54.
Morgan Philips	R. 61	Preb. Ex.
	R. 62	Preb. Ex.
	R. 60	Harberton, Ex. 53[3].
	R. 59	Precentor, St. Dd's. 54.
	S.	Prin. St. Mary Hall, Ox.
D. Pole	R. 59	Bp. Pet. 57.
	R. 59	Wadenhoe, Pet.
W. Pomrel	S.	B.A. New Coll., Ox. 58[4].
J. Porter	R. 60	Crundale, Cant.
R. Porter	R. 59	Archd. Bucks. 54.
J. Potts	S.	Fell. Merton Coll., Ox.[5]
	S.	Master of School in Leicester.
Rob. ap Powell	R. 60	Preb. Hewyd, St. Dd's.
Rob. Poyntz	S.	Fell. St. John's, Ox.[6]
R. Pratt	S.	Master at Eton[7].
J. Precy	R. 63	Preb. Warminster, Sar. 61.
J. Pryce (? or Lloyd).	R. 59	Preb. Llanywith, St. Asaph, 59.
W. Pulleyn	R. 62	Farnsfield, York.
		Billsthorp, Yk. 61.
Rob. Pursglove	R. 60	Suffragan Bishop of Hull.
		Preb. Oxten, S'well, 58.
	R. 61	Archd. Notts, Yk. 53.
Ralph Pyckeringe	R. 63	Shustoke, C. and L.
Nich. Quemerford[8]	S.	
J. Ramridge	R. 58	Archd. Derby, C. and L. 58.
	S.	Dean, C. and L.
	R. 61	Longford, C. and L.
R. Ramsey	R. 60	Quennington, Gl. 46.

[1] Abs. 59. [2] C.C.C. 61. [3] Abs. C.C.C. 61. [4] *Ath.* ii. 118.
[5] M.A. 62, Wood. Dep. 63, Gutch, ii. 150. [6] M.A. 60. [7] Dep. 61.
[8] B.A. 63.

Name with date of successor.		Cure and date of institution.
W. Ramsey a⸍s Slatter	S ? R. 62	Timberscombe, Bath and Wells, 54.
J. Rastall	S.	Fell. New Coll., Ox. 49 [1].
Mich. Raymond	R. 60	Kemerton, Gl. 41 ?
T. Raynar	R. 59	Ashton Favell, Linc.
J. Redman	R. 59	Edersham, Ch.
T. Redman	S.	Master Jesus Coll., Camb. 59 [2].
R. Redworth	R. 64	Farley, Win. 60 [3].
R. Reed	S.	Fell. Ex. Coll., Ox. [4]
J. Reve	R. 63	Altarnon, Ex. 58 [5].
Rob. Reynolds, D.D.	R. 59	Preb. Milton Eccl., Linc. 55.
	R. 60	Farley, Win. [6]
T. Reynolds	R. 60	Dean, Ex. 55.
	R. 60	Holsworthy, Ex.
	S.	Warden of Merton Coll., Ox. 45.
Rob. Richards	R. 63	East Brent, Bath and Wells, 60.
G. Roberts	S.	Archd. St. Dd's.
	R. 59	Archd. Anglesey, Bangor, 58.
T. Robertson, D.D.	R. 59	Dean, Dur. 57.
J. Robinson	R. 63	Shustoke, C. and L. 36.
Giles Saintbarbe	R. 60	Chilton Cantelow, Bath and Wells, 55.
Lancelot Salkeld	R. 59	Dean, Carlisle, 53.
R. Salvyn	R. 61	Hinderwell, Yk.
Ant. Salwyn	S. R. 59	Preb. XI Dur. 58.
	R. 60	Sedgefield, Dur. 58.
Nich. Sanders, LL.D.		Fell. New Coll., Ox. 50 [7].
Cuth. Scott		Bp. Chester, 56.
	R. 59	Beeford, Yk. 49.
T. Scott	S.	Fell. Trin. Coll., Ox. [8]
T. Securis	R. 63	North Stoneham, Win. 58.
W. Senden	R. 61	Iden, Chich.
J. Sergeant	R. 61	Peper-Harrow, Win.
J. Seton, D.D.	S. R. 59	Harting, Chich.
	R. 60	Preb. Ulleskelf, Yk. 54.
J. Sewell	R. 63	Strumpshaw, Norw. 55 [9].
Rob. Shawe	R. 61	Naunton, Gl. 59.
	R. 61	Preb. VI Worc. 58.
Rob. Shelmerdine	R. 61	Morton Bagot, Worc.
	R. 62	Spernall, Worc.

[1] Res. 60.   [2] Dep. 59.   [3] C.C.C. 61.   [4] B.C.L. Feb. 59.
Dep. 59, Boase.   [5] C.C.C. 61.   [6] C.C.C. 61.   [7] Res. 59.
[8] Proctor, 60.   [9] S. 59.

Name with date of successor.		Cure and date of institution.
Simon Sheparde	R. 64	Preb. Waltham, Chich.
W. Sheprey	S.	Fell. C.C.C., Ox.[1]
T. Sigiswicke, D.D.	R. 60	Stanhope, Dur. 58.
	S. R. 61	Reg. Prof. Div., Camb. 57.
T. Slany	R. 62	Preston, Cant. 57.
Slatter, *see* Ramsey.		
T. Slithurst	S. R. 59	Pres. Trin. Coll., Ox. 56.
	R. 60	Canon, St. Geo., Windsor, 54.
J. Smerte	R. 61	Preb. Ex. 57.
J. Smith	R. 62	Treasurer, Chich. 55.
		Prov. Oriel Coll., Ox. 50 [2].
R. Smith	S.	Vice-Chanc., Ox.
	R. 60	Reg. Prof. Div., Ox.
	R. 59	Preb. VIII Ox. 54.
	R. 63	Preb. Twyford, Lon. 54.
T. Snarpon	R. 64	Wedmore, Bath and Wells, 59.
Simon Southcrue	R. 60	Hinton, Gl.
Tristram Spackman	R. 61	Nateley-Scures, Win.
W. Squier	R. 64	Cricket-Thomas, Bath and Wells.
T. Stafford	R. 62	Westfield, Chich. 58.
J. Standish	R. 59	Archd. Colchester, Lon. 58.
Jas. Stanley	R. 63	Washbrook, Norw.[3]
T. Stapleton	S. R. 63	Preb. Woodhorn, Chich.
	S.	Fell. New Coll., Ox.
J. Stephenson	R. 62	Preb. Tachbrook, C. and L. 58 [4].
Edm. Steward	S. R. 59	Dean, Win. 54.
	R. 60	Preb. Offley, C. and L. 34.
J. Stomeinge	R. 64	Clanfield, Win.
Rob. Stoopes	R. 56	Preb. Sneating, Lon. 56.
	R. 62	Barkstede, Norw.
L. Stopes	S.	Fell. St. John's Coll., Ox.[5]
Stratford, *see* Cratford.		
R. Summerscall	R. 59	Burnsall, Yk.
W. Sutton	S.	Master at Macclesfield.
Tristram Swaddle	R. 60	Preb. Rugmere, Lon.[6]
	R. 62	Stepney, Lon. 58.
W Sylvester	R. 60	Preb. Wistow, Yk. 41.
J. Symes	R. 60	Yeovil, Bath and Wells.
R. Symnell	R. 61	Boxted, Lon. 55 [7].
H. Symondes	R. 62	Hendon, Lon. Feb. 59 [8].

[1] *Ath.* i. 668. B.A. 60. [2] Res. 64. [3] S. 59. C.C.C. 61. [4] S. 59.
[5] Ordained abroad. *Fasti,* 154. [6] S. 59 (three times). [7] S. 59.
[8] C.C.C. 61.

LISTS OF CLERGYMEN DEPRIVED, 1558-1564

Name with date of successor.		Cure and date of institution.
Edm. Tarver	R. 61	Cudworth, C. and L.
J. Taversham	R. 59	Newark, Yk.
— Taylor	R. 59	Archd. Lewes, Chich.
R. Taylor	R. 59	Westwick, Norw. 55 [1].
Rob. Taylor	R. 61	Maresfield, Chich.
Roger Taylor	R. 63	Kettilberston, Norw. 56 [2].
Tristram Taylor	R. 63	Stawleigh, Bath and Wells, 60.
W. Taylor	S. R. 59	Master Ch. Coll., Camb. 57.
	R. 61	Preb. South Muskham, S'well, 59.
	R. 59	North Burton, Yk. 57 [3].
	R. 60	Preb. Fenton, Yk. 58.
T. Thirlby	.	Bp. Ely, 54.
Rob. Thompson	S. R. 62	Beaumont, Carlisle.
J. Thorneton	R. 62	Twickenham, Lon. 49.
	R. 59	Settrington, Yk.
W. Thurbane	R. 59	Wrotham, Cant. 58.
J. Towton	R. 60	Preb. VIII Dur. [4]
W. Treshes	R. 60	Preb. Middleton, Chich. [5]
W. Tresham, D.D.	R. 60	Chanc., Chich.
	R. 60	Preb. Asgarby, Linc. 41.
	S. R. 60	Preb. II Ox. 46 ?
	R. 59	Bugbroke, Pet. 42.
Cuth. Tunstall	R. 61	Bp. Dur. 30.
Jas. Turberville	R. 60	Bp. Ex. 55.
Elizeus Umfrye	R. 64	Stanford, Yk.
T. Valence	R. 64	Preb. Bracklesham, Chich.
W. Valentine	R. 59	Harrowden, Pet. 58.
Cuth. Vaux [6]	S.	
Laur. Vaux	S.	Warden Manch. Coll. Church [7].
T. Villiers	S.	Preb. Linc. [8]
W. Wakelyn	R. 59	Alresford, Win. [9]
P. Walker	R. 62	Tendring, Lon. Oct. 59 [10].
And. Warbreton	R. 62	Charlecote, Worc.
T. Washington	R. 62	Fledborough, Yk. [11]
T. Watson	R. 60	Bp. Linc. 57.
Laur. Webb, LL.D.	S.	Ordained 57 [12].
J. White, D.D.	S. R. 61	Bp. Win. 56.

[1] ? S. 59. [2] S. 59. C.C.C. 61. [3] Abs. 59. [4] J. Cuttinge on Pat. Roll. [5] Probably the following. [6] M.A. Ox. 60. [7] Ath. i. 384. [8] G. Dodds rest. [9] C.C.C. 61. [10] S. 59. Abs., C.C.C. 61. [11] Abs. 59. [12] Res. 59.

266   THE ELIZABETHAN CLERGY

App. I

Name with date of successor.		Cure and date of institution.
R. White	S.	Fell. New Coll., Ox.[1]
T. White . . .	R. 63	Sturmer, Lon. 58[2].
J. Whyteheare . .	R. 63	Portsea, Win.[3]
R. Whitley? . .	R. 60	Sedlescombe, Chich.
R. Willanton or Willerton	S. R. 59	Preb. St. Pancras, Lon. 58.
	R. 60	Harringay, Lon.
W. Wills . . .	S.	Preb. Linc. [Hungate] 56[4].
J. Wilson . .	R. 61	Aldrington, Chich.
T. Wilson . .	S.	Preb. Ch.[5]
	R. 62	Arncliffe, Yk.
R. Windam . .	S.	Fell. St. John's Coll., Ox.[6]
R. Wingfield . .	R. 63	Gt. Henney, Lon. 62.
		Langford, Sar.[7]
T. Wood . .	R. 60	Preb. XI Cant.
	R. 59	High Ongar, Lon.
	R. 60	Harlington, Lon. 54.
W. Wood . . .	S. R. 60	Newtimber, Chich. 54.
W. Wright, S.T.B. .	S. R. 59	Master Ball. Coll., Ox. 55.
J. Wylton . .	R. 63	Widford, Lon. 61.
J. Yates .	R. 59	Ormside, Carlisle.
T. Yaxley .	R. 62	East Donyland, Lon. 55.
	R. 64	Wyvenhoe, Lon. 54.
J. Yonge, D.D. .	S. R. 59	Master Pemb. Coll., Camb. 53.
	R. 59	Preb. I pars bor., Ely.
W. Zone .	S.	Reg. Prof. Civ. Law, Camb. 61[8].

SECOND LIST.

NAMES GIVEN ON SANDERS' AUTHORITY BUT NOT CERTAINLY IDENTIFIED [9].

Name.	Cure and date of institution.
H. Always	
S. Bellost	? S. Bellyster, M.A. Oxon. 42.
T. Bennet	Master of Salisbury School.
R. Bernard or Berner . .	? (1) R. Barnard, M.A. Oxon. 57.
	Or (2) Preb. Wells, 51.

[1] B.A. 60. Dep. 64. [2] S. 59. Abs. C.C.C. 61. [3] C.C.C. 61.
[4] C.C.C. 61. [5] Abs. 59. [6] Dep. 59. [7] C.C.C. 61.
[8] ? layman.
[9] Suggested identifications are marked with a query.

LISTS OF CLERGYMEN DEPRIVED, 1558-1564

Name.	Cure and date of institution.
J. Berwick	? M.A. Oxon. 56.
R. Bishop	? M.A. Oxon. 47.
J. Bolton	
J. Bradshaw	? B.A. Oxon. 64.
J. Bremund	Chancellor, Chich.[1]
Edm. Brown	
J. Bursthard	Fell. New Coll., Ox.
Giles Capel	Preb. Bath and Wells [White Lakington].
J. Catagre	Fell. New Coll., Ox.[2]
E. Chamber	B.D. Oxon. 58. Master at Eton?
— Clement	
Alan Cope	Fell. Magd. Coll., Ox.[3]
— Courtmill	
T. Crane	? N. Crane, Vicar of Deptford, Roch. 62.
— Crook	
J. Cubbidge	
J. Dale	
J. Danister	
— Davison, D.D.[4]	
J. Fenn	Master of School at St. Edmundsbury.
J. Felton	
R. Fleming	
J. Fox	? Preb. of Shipton, Sar. 63.
T. Freeman	Master of St. Paul's School. ? Denford, Pet. 61.
— Giblet	? W. Giblet, Fell. New Coll. 49-60. Ord. Douay, 80.
— Gill	
— Grenville	
— Greshop	J. Greshop, M.A. 58.
Hamden	
Edm. Hargat	
— Harper	

[1] Sanders has Bemundus. J. Beaumont was sixth Prebendary of Westminster, *after* 1560.   [2] In possession, 1564.   [3] B.C.L. 60. Ordained abroad after 60 (*Ath.*).   [4] ? And. Davison. *Fasti*, 121.

App. I Name.	Cure and date of institution.
J. Hart, LL.D.[1]	
T. Hawkins	
Gaspar Haywood, D.D.	? Fell. Merton Coll., Ox.[2]
J. Heming	Preb. Bath and Wells.
T. Iveson	Master of School at Durham. ? St. George, York, 62.
R. Jacoby	
Rob. Jones	
— Joseph	
Owen Lewis	Legum Prof.[3]
G. London	? B.D. Ox. 39.
R. Ludby	Preb. Hereford.
Edm. Lyster	
St. Marks	? Fell. Ex. Coll., Ox. B.D. 59.
— Mather, D.D.	
— Matthews, D.D.	
— Miniver	
Nich. Morton	Preb. York.
R. Nicholson, D.D.	
W. Nott	Fell. New Coll., Ox.
J. Oliver	
C. Parker, D.D.	
H. Pendleton, D.D.	Of B.N.C., Ox.
J. Periton	
J. Pile	
H. Pius	
T. Plumtree	Master of School in Lincoln.
Dd. Powell	Preb. Salisbury.
J. Redshaw	
— Sedge, D.D.	
W. Shepard	
W. Smith	
G. Story	? Fell. Or. Coll., Ox. 49.
E. Taylor	

[1] Ordained abroad (Dodd).   [2] Ordained abroad, 61 (*Ath.* 663).
[3] Ordained abroad (Gutch, ii. 145).

Name.	Cure and date of institution.
H. Tenant[1]	
— Thompson	
Rob. Walley, D.D.[2] . . .	
J. White	
Ant. Wilkinson . . .	
Edm. or W. Windham, D.D. .	
R. Wist	
R. Wood, D.D.	
R. Woodcock	

THIRD LIST.

NAMES IMPROPERLY INCLUDED IN THE PERIOD.

Name.		Cure and date of institution.
E. Atslow . . .	S.	Fell. New Coll., Ox.[3]
L. Atslow . . .	S.	Fell. New Coll., Ox.[4]
B. Baynes	R. 61	Eaglescliffe, Durh. 55[5].
R. Bristowe . . .	S.	Fell. Ex. Coll., Ox. 67[6].
T. Butler	S.	LL.D. of New Coll., Ox.[7]
Arth. Cole . .	R. 63	Preb. Twyford, Lon. 54[8].
	R. 60	Canon, St. Geo. Windsor, 43.
	S.	Pres. Magd. Coll., Ox. 55.
W. Collingwood . .	S.	Preb. Chester, 57[9].
G. Etheridge . . .	S.	Prof. Greek, Ox. 48[10].
J. Ingram .	S.	Fell. ? New Coll., Ox.[11]
R. Johnson .	S.	Preb. York, 56[12].
G. Lilly . .	S.	Preb. St. Paul's [Cantlers][13].
T. Martin . . .	S.	Chancellor, Winch.[14]
R. Marton . . .	R. 62	Colebrook, Ex.[15]
Jonas Meredith . .	S.	Fell. St. John's, Ox.[16]

[1] Tierney gives Stephen Tenant, D.D. So Douay Diary, 4. [2] *T.* Walley was Proctor, 1563. B.C.L. 62. [3] M.A. 60. M.D. 65. [4] B.A. 60. M.A. 65. [5] A layman (Reg.). [6] M.A. 62. Res. 69. [7] Not in orders. [8] Died 1558 (Boase). [9] Died 60 (Le Neve). [10] A layman (*D.N.B.*). [11] A layman (Gutch, ii. 145). [12] Died 59 (Cooper). [13] Cf. Bonner's Reg. f. 469. Lilly died in 59. [14] D.C.L. 55. A layman. [15] C.C.C. 61, aet. sixteen years. [16] B.A. 69.

Name.		Cure and date of institution.
R. Michy, or Mitch (Cooper), LL.D.	S.	(No particulars given [1].)
J. Neale . . .	S.	Rect. Ex. Coll., Ox. 60 [2].
H. Shaw . .	S.	Fell. St. John's, Ox. [3]
R. Shelley .	S.	Fell. New Coll., Ox. [4]
J. Story . .	S.	Chancellor, Ox. [5]
R. Tempest, LL.D. . .	S.	(No particulars given [6].)
Nich. Weedon, D.D., or Wendon (Cooper)	S.	Archd. Suff. 59 [7]. Preb. Nor. 61.
W. Wigges . .	S.	Fell. St. John's, Ox. [8]
M. Windsor . .	S.	Fell. C.C.C., Ox. [9]
J. Wright . . .	S.	Fell. Magd. Coll., Ox. 53 [10].

[1] A layman? [2] M.A. 60. Dep. 70. [3] *Fasti*, 186. B.A. 66. M.A. 70. [4] Gutch, ii. 145. B.A. 65. Dep. 67. [5] A civilian (*Ath.* i. 386). [6] A layman. [7] Res. 70. [8] B.A. 66. [9] B.A. 63. M.A. 66. [10] B.D. 65. Dean of Divinity 1560, 1564–66. R. of Horsington. 1580. Bloxam, iv. 136.

APPENDIX II

List of Institutions after Deprivation, 1558-1564.

Note :—*The following lists are taken from the extant episcopal registers, supplemented in certain cases by other contemporary official documents as noted. The date annexed is that of institution. In the case of the deprived it was not always possible to ascertain this. The persons deprived are printed in italics. Those in brackets were designated* ultimus incumbens *in the register, and their identification has been made from Crown Presentations or other mentions in the register.*

DIOCESE OF BANGOR.

I. Dignitaries.

J. Salisbury, 59.	Archd. of Anglesey.	*G. Roberts*, 58.

II. Incumbents.

(The register does not exist.)

DIOCESE OF BATH AND WELLS.

I. Dignitaries.

Gilb. Berkeley, 60.	Bishop.	*Gilb. Bourne*, 54.
W. Turner, 60.	Dean.	*J. Goodman*, 53.
J. Lancaster, 60.	Archd. Taunton.	*J. Fitz James*, 54.
H. Sommer, 60.	Preb. Ilton.	*J. Boxall*.
R. Hughes (rest.), 60.	Preb. Henstridge.	*Rob. Hutchyns*.
Griffin Williams, 60.	Preb. Combe VIII.	
Edm. Edwards, 61.	Preb. Combe IX.	*S. Holland*.
J. Pratt, 61.	Preb. St. Decuman's.	*Giles Hilling*, 54.
H. Parry, 64 ?	Preb. Haselbeare.	*Gilb. Burnford*, 55.

?	?	E. Cratford.
?	Preb. Dinder.	Bart. Blythman.
T. Ellis (schoolmaster), 63.	Preb. Combe IV.	?
R. Argentine, 64.	Preb. Combe VI.	?

II. Incumbents.

J. Coles, 60.	Priston.	*J. Kerell*, 58.
R. Plompton, 60.	Yeovil.	*J. Symes*, 47.
T. Maister, 60.	Chilton Cantelow.	[*Giles Saintbarbe*, 55.]
W. Woodroff, 61.	Lydeard St. Lawrence.	*E. Cratford ats Stratford?*
J. Cowche, 61.	Cossington.	*Bart. Blythman?*
J. Leage, 61.	Skilgate and Winsford.	*Giles Hillings*, 42.
Rog. Cocks, 61.	East Camel.	*T. King? after* 41.
T. Snarpon, 62.	Locking.	*P. Howell?*
P. Jones, 62.	Timberscombe.	[*W. Ramsey ats Slatter.*]
Fras. Newton, D.D., 63.	East Brent.	[*Robt. Richards*, 60.]
W. Bennett, 63.	Middle Chinnock.	[*W. Good*, 56.]
J. Lambert, 63.	Over Stowey.	[*T. Lenge*, 60.]
J. Fishepoole, 63.	Stawleigh.	[*Tristram Taillour*, 60.]
T. Kingman, 63.	Yatton.	[—*Jones.*]
J. Bodie, 64.	Burnet.	
G. Spaggott, 64.	Wedmore Vicarage.	[*T. Snarpon*, 59.]
Sampson Newton, 64.	Chew Magna and Dinder.	[*J. Fitz James*, 54.]
Amitus Metforde, 64.	Cricket-Thomas.	*W. Squier.*

DIOCESE OF BRISTOL.

I. Dignitaries.

G. Carewe, 59 (rest.).	Dean.	*H. Joliffe*, 54.
Arth. Sawle, 60.	Preb. I and Chancellor.	*W. Dalbye*, 58.

II. Incumbents.

(The Register does not exist.)

DIOCESE OF CANTERBURY.

I. Dignitaries.

J. Butler, 59.	Preb. VII.	*Hugh Glasier*, 42.
T. Becon, 59.	IV Preb.	*Nich. Harpsfeld*, 58.
E. Geste, 59.	Archd. Canterbury.	*Nich. Harpsfeld*, 54.
J. Bale, 60.	XI Preb.	*T. Wood*, 54.
Alex. Nowell, 60.	VI Preb.	*Rob. Coleyns*, 54.
H. Goodricke, 60.	XII Preb.	*R. Fawcett*, 54.

II. Incumbents.

And. Peerson, B.D., 59.	Wrotham.	[*H. Cole*, 58.]
J. Steward, 60.	Old Romney.	*Rob. Hill*, 57.
Alex. Nowell, 60.	Saltwood.	*Nich. Harpsfeld*.
J. Hardyman, 60.	Lydd.	*Rob. Hill*, 58.
And. Peerson, 60.	Great Chart.	*J. Knight*, 58.
W. Painter, 60.	Graine.	*Oliver Garnell*.
W. Awchar, 60.	Lyminge.	*R. Fawcet*, 59.
Adr. Waterdale, 60.	Crundale.	*J. Porter*.
Robt. Carrier, 61.	Bircholt.	*Christ. Hawkes*.
J. Appleby, 61.	Norton.	*W. Elye, B.D.*, 56.
P. Lymiter, 61.	Eastry.	*J. Lawson*, 58.
Jas. Perce, 62.	Chislet.	— *Mere*.
W. Russell, 62.	Preston.	*T. Slany*, 57.
J. Gunyer, 63.	East Langdon.	*T. Alston*.

DIOCESE OF CARLISLE.

I. Dignitaries.

Sir T. Smith, 59.	Dean.	*Lancelot Salkeld, rest.* 53.
J. Best, 60.	Bishop.	*Owen Oglethorpe*, 57.

II. Incumbents.

T. Atkinson, 59 [1].	Ormside.	*J. Yates* [2].
H. Dacre, 61.	Skelton.	*Hugh Hodshon*.
H. Haselhead, 62.	Beaumont.	*Rob. Thompson*.

---

[1] Restored by the visitors, August, 1559.
[2] No means of finding date exists at Carlisle.

App. II

DIOCESE OF CHESTER.

I. Dignitaries.

Rob. Rogers, ?	Archd. Chester.	*Rob. Persevall*, 54.
Chris. Goodman, 59 [1].	Archd. Richmond.	*J. Hanson*, 54.
W. Birche, 60.	Cardl. at Manchester.	?
W. Downhan, 61.	Bishop.	*Cuthbert Scott*, 56.

II. Incumbents.

R. Baldwyn, 59 [1].	St. Nicholas' Hospital, Richmond.	*W. Burye.*
E. Sandys, D.D., 59 [1].	Edersham.	*J. Redman.*
W. Soorye, 59 [1].	Sedbergh.	*T. Atkinson.*
W. Soorye, 59 [1].	Austwick.	*T. Dobeson.*
J. Best, 59 [2].	Romald-Kirk.	*Owen Oglethorpe*, 41.
— Huntingdon, 60.	Rochdale.	*J. Hanson.*
J. Hilton, 62.	Blackburn.	*J. Hargravys.*

DIOCESE OF CHICHESTER.

I. Dignitaries.

R. Tremayne, 59.	Archd. Chichester.	*Alban Langdale, D.D.*, 55.
E. West, 59.	Archd. Lewes.	*T. Tayler*, 58.
Aug. Bradbury, 60.	Chancellor.	*W. Tresham*, 59.
R. Wright, 60.	Preb. Middleton.	*W. Tresham*, 59.
David Spenser, 61.	Preb. Fittleworth.	*G. Indolen.*
E. Foster, 61.	Preb. Ipthorne.	*J. Knight.*
Edm. Weston, LL.B., 61.	Preb. Gates.	*T. Mawndevil.*
J. Richardson, 61.	Preb. Bargham.	*T. Packard.*
Aug. Bradbridge, 62.	Treasurer.	*J. Smyth*, 55.
Laur. Nowell, 63.	Preb. Ferring.	*E. Godshalfe.*
Chris. Lancaster, 63.	Preb. Firle.	*Anth. Clerke*, 50.
W. Overton, 63.	Preb. Woodhorn.	*T. Stapleton.*
R. Kytson, 64.	Preb. Bracklesham.	*T. Valence.*
Robt. Erewakers, 64.	Preb. Waltham.	*Simon Sheparde.*

[1] Restored by the visitors, August, 1559.
[2] Bishop of Carlisle, 1560.

II. Incumbents.

R. Farnden, 59.	Buxted.	A. Langdale.
Aristotle Webbe, 59.	Barcombe.	?
G. Forbes, 59.	Harting.	J. Seton.
J. Wells, 60.	Rodmell.	?
Rob. Norman, 60.	East Dean.	Ant. Clerke, 58.
E. Tyckerydal ? 60.	Newtimber.	W. Wood, 54.
W. Harward, 60.	Cowfold.	?
T. Blewet, 60.	Rogate.	?
J. Bucke, 60.	Rype.	T. Packarde, 56.
Fras. Coxe, 60.	Horsted-Keynes.	?
T. Trencham, 60.	Sedlescombe.	R. Whitley ?
Rob. Browne, 60.	Goring.	Maur. Hughes, 58.
T. Molder, 61.	Iden.	W. Senden.
F. Sharp, 61.	Bishopstone.	Fras. Hiberden, 55.
J. Inglishe, 61.	Aldrington.	J. Wilson.
T. Mawdsley, 61.	Maresfield.	Rob. Taylor.
J. Soresby, 61.	Poynings.	T. Coltesmore ?
R. Byrddocke, 62.	Westfield.	T. Stafford, 58.
J. Igulden, M.A., 62.	Bepton.	T. Makinge, 18.
H. Wilsha, 62.	Westbourne.	R. Marshall.
T. Mawdisley, 63.	'Michynge.'	?
Robt. Parrys, 64.	Selmeston.	J. Lewett.

DIOCESE OF COVENTRY AND LICHFIELD.

I. Dignitaries.

Laur. Nowell, 59.	Archd. Derby.	J. Ramridge, 58.
E. Leeds, 60.	Precentor.	H. Comberford, 55.
T. Walkenden, 60.	Preb. Longdon.	A. Draycott, 56.
T. Bentham, 60.	Bishop.	R. Bayne, 54.
T. Yale, 60.	Preb. Offley.	E. Steward, 34.
Aug. Barneker, 62.	Preb. Tachbrook.	J. Stephenson, 58.

II. Incumbents.

J. Hyron, 60.	Wirksworth.	Anth. Draycott.
E. Lyngarde, 61.	Crudworth.	Edm. Tarver.
P. Morweyn, 61.	Longford.	J. Ramridge.
P. Morwyng, 61.	Norbury.	H. Comberford.
T. Bolte, 61.	Checkley.	A. Draycott.
H. Baxter, 62.	Condover.	R. Key, 52.
Hum. Blarney, 62.	Worfield.	T. Chyddalton, 45.

App. II

T. Hancoke, 62.	Willoughby.	*J. Gardyner*, 48.
T. Bradshawe, 62.	Hamstall Ridware.	*Hugh Hall.*
Thrustan Tyleston, 63.	Moreton Corbett.	[*W. Assheley*, 39.]
Nich. Haighe, 63.	Shustoke.	*Ralph Pyckeringe.*
Robt. Woodhouse, 64.	Fenny Bentley.	*Nich. Bambford.*

DIOCESE OF DURHAM.

I. Dignitaries.

Rob. Horne, D.D., 59.	Dean.	*Dr. T. Robertson*, 57.
J. Rudd, 59.	Preb. X.	*G. Bullock*, 54.
J. Henshaw, 59.	Preb. XI.	*Ant. Salwyn*, 58.
Adam Sheppard, 60.	Preb. VIII.	*J. Towton*[1], 41.
T. Sampson[2], 60.	Preb. VII.	*R. Dalton*, 41.
W. King, 61.	Archd. Northumberland.	*W. Carter*, 58.
T. Horton, 61.	Preb. IX.	*Nich. Marley*, 41.
Jas. Pilkington, D.D., 61.	Bishop.	*Cuthbert Tunstall*, 30.

II. Incumbents.

W. Harrison[3], 59.	Bothal.	*Rob. Pace or Pates.*
Edm. Bene, 60.	Stanhope.	*Dr. T. Sigiswicke*, 58.
G. Clif, B.D., 60.	Billingham.	*Dr. Robt. Dalton*, 44.
Adam Lofthouse, 60.	Sedgefield.	*Ant. Salwyn*, 58.
Roger Watson, D.D., 60.	Pittington.	*Dr. Nich. Marley*, 58.
W. Garnet, LL.B., 61.	Eaglescliffe.	*Brian Baynes (gen.)*, 55.
E. Bancke, 62.	Long Newton.	*R. Hertborn*, 55.
Ralf Skynner, 62.	Sedgefield.	*A. Lofthouse*, 60.
T. Pentland, 62.	S. Oswald, Durham.	*Hugh Hochonson, B.D.*
Rob. Rollie, ?	Boldon.	*R. Clif, D.D.*, 41.
Adam Ecke, 64.	Woler.	*J. Hall*, 61.

[1] J. Tutting on Pat. Roll.   [2] Verbi Dei Minister.
[3] Restored by the visitors, August, 1559.

DIOCESE OF ELY.

App. II

I. Dignitaries.

E. Gascon, 59.	Preb. VII.	T. Peacock, 56.
T. Barwicke, 59.	Preb.	?
Rob. Wisdom, 59.	Archd. Ely.	J. Boxall, 56.
J. Ebden, 59.	Preb. VII.	J.Byckerdike, res.1559?
J. Pory, 60.	Preb. I pars bor.	J. Yonge, 54.
Rob. Wisdom, 60.	Dean and Preb. I.	J. Boxall, 54.
R. Cox.	Bishop.	T. Thirlby, 54.

II. Incumbents.

Dr. Launcelot Ridley, 59.	Stretham and Thetford.	[W. Marshall, s. 59.]
Geo. Chatbourne, 64.	Duxford St. Peter.	J. Laiken.
Vincent Goodwyne, 64.	Oakington.	Emeric Dande, 59.

DIOCESE OF EXETER.

I. Dignitaries.

R. Tremayne, 60.	Preb. Cutton.	J. Blaxton, 56.
Rob. Fyssher, 60.	Preb.	R. Halse.
W. Alley, 60.	Bishop.	Jas. Turberville, 55.
Gregory Dodds, 60.	Dean.	T. Reynolds, 55.
R. Gammon, 60.	Subdean.	T. Nutcombe, 58.
R. Argentyne, D.D., 61.	Preb.	J. Harpsfeld, 58.
J. Smyth, LL.D., 61.	Preb.	W. Mugge.
Rob. Williams, or Goldsmith, 61.	Preb.	Morgan Philips.
E. Reley, B.D., 61.	Preb.	J. Blaxton.
R. Bagnall, 61.	Preb.	J. Smerte, 57.
T. Hooper, 61.	Preb.	J. Huntington, 60.
Edm. Morecrofte, 62.	Preb.	Morgan Philips.

II. Incumbents.

Ralph Newton, 59.	Plymouth.	J. Peryn.
W. Rawson, 59.	Preb. Chulmleigh.	R. Carr.
R. Holland, 60.	Broad Clyst.	R. Halse.
T. Kent, 60.	Holsworthy.	T. Reynolds, D.D.
J. Hopkyns, 60.	Harberton.	Morgan Philips, 53.
J. Tuttley, 60.	Thurlestone.	R. Halse.
Chris. Bodlegh, 60.	Newton St. Cyres.	Walt. Mugge, 57.

278   THE ELIZABETHAN CLERGY

App. II

Ant. Dillon, 60.	Bratton.	*J. Blaxton*, 54.
J. Huntington, 60.	Sowton.	*Greg. Basset.*
T. Carter, 60.	Kentisbere.	*J. Lamb*, 54.
H. Redinge, 62.	Colebrook.	*R. Marton.*
W. Launder, 62.	Lanteglos.	*T. Crofte*, 58.
Ralph Hortopp, 62.	Preb. St. Endellion.	*Edm. Benigfeld.*
E. Reley, 63.	Altarnon.	*J. Reve*, 58.
Robt. Bracher, 63.	Anstey and 'Blasye.'	?
G. Barton, 63.	Holsworthy.	*F. Babington*, 62 [1].

DIOCESE OF GLOUCESTER.

I. Dignitaries.

Walter Jones, 59.	Preb. V.	?
J. Lytlegrome, 60.	Preb. of Morton.	*Geoff. Downe.*

II. Incumbents.

R. Hunt, 59.	Willersey.	*T. Hybbots.*
R. Warret, 60.	Quennington.	*R. Ramsey.*
Hugh Kerke, 60.	Hawkesbury.	*T. Bromhedd*, 56.
W. Clynton, 60.	Kemerton.	*Mich. Raymond*, 41 ?
W. Linsecum, 60.	Hinton.	*Simon Southcrue.*
Hugh Evance, 61.	Naunton.	*Rob. Shawe*, 59.
J. Rogers, 63.	Cherington.	*R. Bramborough*, 48.

DIOCESE OF HEREFORD.

I. Dignitaries.

Walter Jones, 58.	Precentor.	— *Chell*, 54.
H. Elize, 58.	Dean.	*R. Daniel*, 58.
Rob. Crowley, 60.	Arch. Hereford.	*J. Glasyer*, 57.
J. ap. Owen, 62.	Preb. Bartonsham.	*T. Arden*, 59.
Ralf Griffin, 62.	Preb. Moreton Parva.	*J. Parfay*, 56.

II. Incumbents.

T. Taylor, 59.	Kingsland.	*E. Daniel*, 48.
T. Grenewich, 60.	Cradley.	*J. Parfay.*
R. Sherar, 60.	Oldbury.	*Roland Gosnell*, 39.
W. Mappe, 62.	Tenbury.	*Roland Gosnell*, 55.
Hugh ap. Rice, 62.	Stowe.	[*Griffin ap. David*, 52.]
R. Palfrey, 64.	Wigmore.	*E. Legge*, 60.

[1] Extra hoc regnum Angliae sine licentia regia fugit.

DIOCESE OF LINCOLN.

I. Dignitaries.

J. Longland, 59.	Preb. of Kilsby.	W. Cook, 54.
J. Aylmer, 59.	Archd. Stow.	J. Harrison, 54.
Nich. Bullingham, 59.	Archd. Lincoln.	Owen Hodgson, 59.
J. Longland, 59.	Archd. Bucks.	R. Porter, 54.
R. Barber, 59.	Archd. Beds.	Mich. Dunning, 58.
W. Bill, 59.	Preb. of Milton Ecclesia.	Rob. Reynolds, 55.
R. Gill, 60.	Preb. of Leighton Ecclesia.	G. Hunter, 58.
Nich. Bullingham, 60.	Bishop.	T. Watson, 57.
J. Watson, 60.	Preb. Langford Manor.	Owen Hodgson, 57.
Chris. Shorthouse, 60.	Preb. of Asgarby.	W. Tresham, 41.
T. Goodwin, 60.	Preb. Bedford Major.	Ant. Draycot, 39.
Rob. Beaumont, 60.	Archd. Hunts.	Ant. Draycot, 43.
T. Lark, 61.	Preb. of Norton Episcopi.	T. Hide, 55 [1].

II. Incumbents.

J. Lunde, 60.	Munden.	G. Bulloke.
R. Barnes, 60.	Houghton.	?
W. Fishe, 61.	Moulton.	?
R. Stevenson, 61.	Aylton (? Elton).	?
T. Godwyne, 62.	Lutterworth.	?

(There is a large gap in the Register.)

DIOCESE OF LLANDAFF.

(The Register does not exist.)

DIOCESE OF LONDON.

I. Dignitaries.

J. Hodgkins, 59.	Preb. Harlesden.	N. Harpsfield, 54.
W. Alley, 59.	Preb. St. Pancras.	R. Willanton, 58.
W. May, 59.	Dean.	H. Cole, 56.
J. Veron, 59.	Mora.	Robt. Cousyn, 54.

[1] Act Book gives Gervase Fishbourne, March 28, 1559, p. m.

280   THE ELIZABETHAN CLERGY

App. II
—

J. Mullens, 59.	Archd. London.	*J. Harpsfield*, 54.
J. Pulleyn, 59.	Archd. Colchester.	*J. Standish*, 58.
E. Grindal, 59.	Bishop.	*E. Bonner*, 53.
David Padye, 56.	Sneating.	*Robt. Stoopes*, 56.
W. Saxey, 60.	Treasurer.	*Robt. Cosen*, 58.
Alexr. Nowell, 60.	Archd. Middlesex.	*W. Chedsey*, 56.
T. Watts, 60.	Preb. Totenhall.	*T. Darbyshire*, 43.
T. Cole, 60.	Arch. Essex.	*T. Darbyshire*, 58.
J. Pilkington, 60.	Preb. Mapesbury.	*J. Harpsfield*, 58.
T. Penny, 60.	Preb. Newington.	*J. Boxhall*, 58.
D. Kempe.	Archd. St. Albans.	*J. Dugdale*, 57.
Alex. Nowell, 60.	Preb. Wildland.	*J. Morren*, 58.
T. Cole, 60.	Preb. Rugmere.	*Tristram Swaddle.*
Nich. Fleming, 61.	Preb. Neasdon.	*R. Marshal.*
J. Atherton, 62.	Preb. Consumpta per Mare.	*W. Massenger*, 57.
M. Hutton, 62.	Preb. Brondesbury.	*T. Byam*, 60.
Robt. Greenacres, 63.	Preb. Twyford.	*Arth. Cole*, 54.

II. **Incumbents.**

T. Cole, 59.	High Ongar.	*T. Wood*, 54.
T. Horton, 60.	St. Magnus.	*T. Darbyshire.*
E. Layfeld, 60.	Fulham.	*T. Darbyshire.*
J. Pulleyn, 60.	Copford.	*J. Morren*, 58.
J. Veron, 60.	St. Martin's, Ludgate.	*J. Morren*, 58.
H. Zulley, 60.	Harlington.	*T. Wood*, 54.
J. Stather, 60.	Asheldam.	*J. Morren.*
R. Harrington, 60.	Harringay.	*R. Willerton.*
Robt. Foster, 60.	Stamford Rivers.	*J. Baker*, 53.
E. Brichell, 60.	Orsett.	*J. Morren.*
N. Karvile, 60.	South Weld.	*G. Ottwaye, Feb.* 59.
J. Dane, 60.	St. Leonard's, Shoreditch.	*W. Moyle*, 56.
W. Hande, 60.	Aldham.	*R. Kingeston*, 55.
W. Marshe, 60.	St. Anne and St. Agnes.	*R. Kingeston.*
W. Bretton, 60.	Keldon.	*J. Baker*, 47.
T. Sympson, 61.	Stortford.	*J. Bartlett*, 56.
J. Wylton, 61.	Widford.	*T. Cradocke.*
Chris. Rame, 61.	Boxted.	*R. Symnell*, 55.
R. Laverock, 61.	Nevendon.	*J. Leder*, 57.
W. Lyvinge, 61.	St. Swithin.	*G. Barton.*
W. Leaper, 62.	Braintree.	*Robt. Barslowe*, 56.
T. Woode, 62.	Twickenham.	*J. Thorneton*, 49.

Nich. Aspinall, 62.	Stepney.	*Tristram Swaddell*, 58. App. II
R. Salisbury, 62.	Tendring.	*P. Walker*, Oct. 59.
T. Skotte, 62.	Gt. Horkesley.	*Robt. Coates, Ap.* 59.
Geoff. Foster, 62.	Corringham.	*Rob. Burton*, 58.
G. Wilson, 62.	East Donyland.	*T. Yaxley*, 55.
R. Preston, 62.	Reed.	*J. Hopper*, 56.
R. Peacock, 62.	Downham.	*Baldwin Norton*, 50.
W. Lyon, 62.	Braughing.	*R. Cotton, Dec.* 59.
T. Buckmaster, 62.	Twickenham.	*T. Wood.*
W. Newhouse, 62.	Shenfield.	*Robt. Davyes, Ap.* 59.
T. Harvye, 62.	Hendon.	*H. Symondes, Feb.* 59.
Geoff. Phillips, 63.	Sturmer.	*T. White*, 58.
W. Kyndehed, 63.	Shalford.	*W. Atkinson, Sep.* 59.
Jas. Norreys, 63.	Twickenham.	*T. Buckmaster*, 62.
Griffin Evans, 63.	Little Sampford.	*T. Moorefylde*, 44.
H. Palmer, 63.	Widford.	*J. Wylton*, 61.
W. Inman, 63.	Great Canfield.	*J. Bryckebecke*, 45.
J. Colynson, 63.	Great Henny.	*R. Wingfield*, 62.
Baptist Willoughby, 63.	Great Stanmore.	
J. White, 64.	Shellow-Bowels.	*Hugh Maddock*, 54.
Reubens Hart, 64.	Little Stambridge.	*Steph. Caston*, 58.
Adam Richardson, 64.	White Notley.	*Geoff. Jones*, 38.
W. Fering, 64.	Standon.	*J. Allforde*, 59.
W. Betts, 64.	Wivenhoe.	*T. Yaxley*, 54.
R. Lawrence, 64.	Hendon.	*T. Harvye*, 62.
J. Philpot, 64.	Stepney.	*Nich. Aspinall*, 62.
H. Reginald, 64.	Ramsey.	*J. Lovell*, 60.
T. Clerke, 64.	Mount-Bures.	*J. Abowen*, 63.

DIOCESE OF NORWICH.

I. Dignitaries.

J. Salisbury, 60.	Dean.	*J. Harpsfield*, 58.

II. Incumbents.

E. Rust, 59.	Westwick.	*R. Taylor*, 55.
J. Worth, 60.	Burgh.	*Oliver Haver*, 58.
R. Johnson, 60.	Scole.	*R. Calner.*
T. Reede, 60.	Eccles.	*J. Collinson*, 41.
Nich. Wemnouthe, 61.	Offton and Little Bricett.	*R. Appletoft*, 56.
R. Wingfilde, 61.	Langford.	
J. Powlye, 61.	Hingham (Berroughe).	*Simon Anderson*, 56.
J. Hancocke, 62.	Titchwell.	*Hugh Hudsonne*, 47.

App. II

J. Porter, 62.	Denton.	*H. Carter*, 54.
Nich. Locke, 62.	Barkestede.	*Rob. Stopes.*
T. Warwick, 63.	Strumpshaw.	*J. Sewell*, 55.
Edm. Reve, 63.	Hargrave.	*J. Balkeye*, 56.
J. Benston, 63.	Kettilsberston.	*Roger Taylor*, 56.
J. Mychelfield, 63.	Washbrook.	*Jas. Stanley*, 54.
R. Bobbett, 63.	Cokeley.	*Robt. Buttell.*
Jas. Lyng, 64.	Gimingham.	*R. Lache*, 31.
W. Woode, 64.	Tudingham.	*Thurstan Bradley*, 54.
Laur. Yelverton, 64.	Skulthorpe.	*And. Cole.*

DIOCESE OF OXFORD.

I. Dignitaries.

G. Carew, 59.	Dean.	*R. Marshall, D.D.*, 53.
T. Kent, 59.	4th Preb.	*Alex. Belsire*, 46.
R. Bankes, 59.	6th Preb.	*W. Chedsey, D.D.*, 54.
R. Bankes, 59.	8th Preb.	*R. Smyth, D.D.*, 54.
J. Calfhill, 60.	2nd Preb.	*W. Tresham,* ? 46.

II. Incumbents.

(The Register notes no deprivations.)

DIOCESE OF PETERBOROUGH.

I. Dignitaries.

Edm. Scamler, D.D., 59.	Bishop.	*D. Pole*, 57.
W. Latimer, D.D., 59.	Dean.	*J. Boxall, D.D.*, 57.

II. Incumbents.

Ralph Phillip, 59.	Bradden.	*W. Burton*, 44.
W. Yale, 59.	Harrowden.	[*W. Valentyne*, 58.]
Geoff. Parishe, 59.	Wadenhoe.	*Bp. Pole.*
Bernard Brandon, D.D., 59.	Uppingham.	*T. Collyer*, 54.
W. Archbold, 59.	Bugbrooke.	*W. Tresham, D.D.*, 42.
Gilb. Leyborne, 60.	Cottingham.	*Ant. Draycot.*
W. Todde, 60.	Kettering.	*Ant. Draycot.*
W. Walkenden, 60.	Yelvertoft.	*H. Comberford.*

			App. II
W. Thorpe, 61.	Cottesmore.	?	
W. Howell, 61.	Dingley.	?	
T. Stronghenkin, 62.	Desborough.	?	
W. Cuthbarte, 62.	Loddington.	*R. Conwaw*, 53.	
R. Russell, 63.	Tilkencote.	*J. Bent*, 56.	

DIOCESE OF ROCHESTER.

I. Dignitaries.

(None.)

II. Incumbents.

R. Lovelace, 60.	'Mapescombe.'	?
J. Dawlyn, 60.	Lullingstone.	?

DIOCESE OF ST. ASAPH.

I. Dignitaries.

Rob. Whettell, 59.	Preb. of Llanyfydd.	[*J. Parfue*, 56.]
R. Davys, 60.	Bishop.	*T. Goldwell*, 54.
T. Smythe, 60.	? Preb. of Llansantffraid.	?

II. Incumbents.

David Yale, 64.	Llandegla.	*David Edwards.*
T. Brereton, 64.	Kilken.	*Griff. Jones.*

DIOCESE OF ST. DAVID'S.

I. Dignitaries.

T. Young, 59.	Precentor.	*Morgan Philips*, 54.
— Constantine, 59.	Archd. Brecon.	*J. Blaxton*, 54.
T. Young, 60.	Bishop.	*H. Morgan*, 54.
W. Leche, 60.	Preb. of Hewyd.	*Rob. ap. Powell.*
W. Downham, 60.	Arch. St. David's.	?

II. Incumbents.

— Vaughan, 59.	Llangan.	*J. Philips*, 54.
J. ap. Owen, 59.	Llandilo Fawr.	*T. Haward, LL.B.*, 54.
T. Lloyd ap. Jones, 60.	Manordivy.	*J. Hoell.*

App. II

Giles Shears, 62.	Kidwelly.	?
Morgan Jones, 62.	Llandowror.	E. Elmsly.
Rob. Jones, 62.	Llangunllo.	Rees Morrice.
Ralph Savyer, 64.	Roberston.	?

DIOCESE OF SALISBURY.

I. Dignitaries.

T. Lancaster, 59.	Treasurer.	T. Harding, 55.
H. Parry, 59.	Chancellor.	T. Heskyns, 58.
Arth. Salle, 59.	Preb. of Beaminster.	J. Blackeston.
E. Barnard, 59.	Preb. of Grantham.	J. Boxall.
J. Jewel, 60.	Bishop.	J. Capon, 39.
W. Benett, 63.	Preb. Warminster.	J. Precy, 61.
H. Securys, 64.	Preb. Beaminster, 2.	T. Burbank, 46.
Giles Lawrence, 64.	Archd. Wilts.	J. Lawrence, 54.

II. Incumbents.

J. Dysleye, 59.	Bishopstone.	T. Harding.
Martin Morland, 60.	East Ilsley.	G. Bell, 54.
Hanmet Hayde, 60.	Stratford Tony.	R. Clare a̔s Dominick, 54.
J. Houseman, 60.	Englefield.	Clem. Burdett, 42.
T. Webbe, 62.	Trowbridge.	J. Langland, 59.
J. Greenway, 62.	Inkpen.	J. Collyns.
T. Handcock, 63.	Purley.	R. Gatskell, 54.
T. Flint, 63.	Hampstead Marshall.	Edm. Pearce.
T. Mountayne, 63.	Purley.	T. Handcock, 63.
W. Moseley, 64.	Dunhead St. Mary.	Roger Bolbelt.
Godfrey Cobin.	Upton Lovell.	Robt. Eyre, 48.

SOUTHWELL MINSTER.

G. Ackworth, 59.	Preb. North Muskham.	G. Palmer, 58.
Goddard Kiddall, 60.	Preb. Oxten.	Rob. Pursglove, 58.
G. Powes, 61.	Preb. South Muskham.	W. Tayllor, 59.
Walter Jones, 62.	Preb. Normanton.	H. Bovell, 59.
J. Taverham, 62.	Preb. North Leverton.	G. Lambe, 59.
J. Pratt, 63.	Preb. Oxten.	G. Kiddall, 60.

DIOCESE OF WINCHESTER.

I. Dignitaries.

W. Overton, 58.	Preb.	Rob. Hyll.
T. Langley, 59.	Preb. I.	Peter Lanridge.
J. Warner, M.D., 59.	Dean.	Edm. Steward, 54.
J. Watson, 59.	Archd. Surrey.	Edm. Mervyn, 54.
Walt. Wright, 59.	Preb.	T. Harding.
Mich. Pennigar, 60.	Preb.	T. Hyde, 56.
Rob. Horne, 61.	Bishop.	J. White, 56.
J. Ebdenne, 62.	Preb. VII.	Laur. Bilson, 51.

II. Incumbents.

W. Wakelyn, 59.	Alresford.	W. Wakelyn.
J. Coxe, 59.	Compton.	?
Mich. Pennygar, 59.	Crawley.	?
Rob. Leyborne, 60.	Falley.	Rob. Reynolds.
H. Parry, 60.	Sutton.	Edm. Marvyn.
J. Abrall, 60.	Sparsholt.	R. Adams.
G. Leyceter, 60.	Wootton St. Lawrence.	J. Grete.
J. Cook, 60.	Ashley.	E. Harman.
T. Lancaster, 61.	Sherfield-English.	W. Baker.
J. Lacock, 61.	Winnall.	Dominic Chane.
W. Weke, 61.	Nateley-Scures.	Tristram Spackeman.
R. Robarts, 61.	Katerington.	
Rob. Vaser, 61.	Shalford.	R. Durdame, 57.
Mt. Standley, 61.	Great Bookham.	?
R. Clere, 61.	Peper-Harow.	J. Sergeant, 58.
R. Skynner, 62.	Reigate.	H. Norman, 57.
? 62.	Walton on the Hill.	Rob. Coplet.
J. Evanne, 62.	Chiddingfold.	Jas. Ellis.
J. Champion, 62.	Freshwater.	J. Glasyer, 49.
J. Warweke, 62.	Beaulieu.	Greg. Bell, 55.
Nich. Fox, 62.	Wootton, I. of W.	?
J. Archarde, 62.	St. Lawrence, I. of W.	T. Byrche.
J. Alen, 62.	Cliddisdon.	J. Cooke.
J. Cardele, 63.	Titchfield.	J. Perye, 58.
R. Elys, 63.	Mickleham.	?
G. Hanssard, 63.	Merowe.	Alban Latwicke.
Nich. Sawe, 63.	Portsea.	J. Whytcheare.
W. Hyde, 63.	North Stoneham.	T. Securis, 58.
Robt. Leybourne, 63.	'Wonsington.'	J. Farler.
Steph. Chescome, ? 63.	King's Worthy.	Laurence Bilson, 58.
J. Turck, 64.	Farley.	R. Redworth, 60.
Hugh Traybonne, 64.	Shalford with Bromley.	Robt. Fawcett, 57.
J. Abrall, 64.	Clanfield.	J. Stomeinge.

286   THE ELIZABETHAN CLERGY

App. II

ST. GEORGE'S, WINDSOR.

G. Whithorne, 59.	Canon.	W. Chedsey, 54.
H. Ryley, B.D., 60.	Canon.	T. Slythurst, 54.
Edm. Johnson, 60.	Canon.	Arth. Cole, 43.
G. Carewe, 60.	Dean.	J. Boxall, 57.

DIOCESE OF WORCESTER[1].

I. Dignitaries.

E. Sandys, 59.	Bishop.	R. Pate, 55.
J. Pedder, 60.	Dean.	Seth Holland, 57.
Aug. Brodebridge, 60.	Preb. IV.	[H. Jolife, 42.]
Rob. Avis, 60.	Preb. V.	Edm. Danyell.
T. Herte, 61.	Preb. I.	W. Norfolk, 58.
Liberius Bierd, 61.	Preb. III.	T. Arden, 58.
T. Norley, 61.	Preb. X.	W. Turnbull, 58.
T. Norley, 61.	Preb. VI.	Rob. Shaw, 58.

II. Incumbents.

Nich. Jackson, 61.	Kinwarton.	H. Johnson.
W. Tomlynson, 61.	Hanbury.	W. Northfolke.
Nich. Shepherd, 61.	Hartlebury.	T. Arden.
R. Barnes, 61.	Broadwas.	H. Johnson, 48.
J. Peder, B.D., 61.	Snitterfield.	W. Barton, 57.
Rob. Cleyfield, 61.	Morton-Bagot.	Rob. Shelmerdyne, 51.
T. Penford, 62.	Spernall.	Rob. Shelmerdyne.
Nich. Smyth, 62.	Charlecote.	And. Warbreton.
T. Clerke, 62.	Kenwarton.	H. Johnson.

DIOCESE OF YORK.

I. Dignitaries.

Roger Askame, 59.	Peb. of Wetwang.	G. Palmer, 58.
Fras. Newton, 59.	Preb. of North Newbald.	[R. Drury ?]
J. Stokes, 60.	Arch. York.	G. Palmer, 43.
T. Young, 60.	Archbishop.	Nich. Heath, 55.
Edm. Scambler, 60.	Preb. of Wistow.	[W. Sylvester, 41.]
T. Wilson, 60.	Preb. of Fenton.	W. Taylor, 58.

[1] There is a gap in the Registers between 1563 and 1570.

INSTITUTIONS AFTER DEPRIVATION, 1558–1564

G. Bullen, 60.	Preb. of Ulleskelf.	J. Seton, 54.
W. Day, 61 [1].	Arch. Notts.	Robt. Pursglove, 53.
T. Thackham, 62.	Preb. Langtoft.	Baldwin Norton, 59.
R. Maister, 63.	Preb. Fridaythorpe.	Arth. Lowe, 54.

II. Incumbents.

Oliver Columben, 59 [2].	Stanford.	Eliz. Umfrye.
Chris. Sugden, B.D., 59 [2].	Newark.	J. Faversham.
Ant. Blake, 59 [2].	Doncaster.	J. Hudson.
Ant. Blake, 59 [2].	Whiston.	J. Atkinson.
Ant. Holgate, 59 [2].	Burnsall.	R. Summerscall.
W. Denman, 59 [2].	Ordsall.	Rob. Blunston.
Rob. Wisdom, 59 [2].	Settrington.	J. Thornton.
T. Atkinson, 59 [2].	Elwick.	G. Clife.
G. Tailor, 59 [2].	Bulmer.	J. Jakeson.
Marm. Pulleyn, 59 [2].	Ripley.	Rob. Persivall.
J. Adams, 59 [2].	Hockerton.	T. Huddleston.
Nich. Halgh, 59.	North Burton.	[W. Taillor, 57.]
T. Dixon, 59 [2].	Etton.	?
T. Reader, 59.	Beeford.	[Cuthbert Scott, 49.]
T. Lakyn, 59.	Bolton.	?
Fras. Scarthe, 61.	Hinderwell.	[R. Salvyn.]
Rob. Pole, 62.	Kirby in Cleveland.	W. Bury.
T. Smythe, 62.	Hilston.	J. Colvyer.
Ralf Bylby, 62.	Fledborough.	T. Washington, 58.
J. Sye, 62.	Farnsfield.	W. Pulleyn.
Ant. Toppam, 62.	Arncliffe.	T. Wilson.

[1] Presented by the Crown, December 23, 1559.

[2] Restored during the Northern Visitation of August and September, 1559. See S. P. Dom. Eliz. x.

APPENDIX III

INSTITUTIONS AFTER DEPRIVATION, NOVEMBER 18, 1564–1570.

App. III

NOTE :—*This list contains the names of those who were instituted after deprivation to about the beginning of 1570. As we took out such entries where the Registers are extant, it seemed that the list might be useful for other inquiries, and accordingly we inserted it here.*

DIOCESE OF BATH AND WELLS.

J. Brydgwater, 66.	Porlock.	*Rob. Brocke*, 33.
W. Jones, 67.	Cucklington.	*Chris. Dewe*, 58.
R. Woodfall, 69.	Christon.	*R. Schore*, 65.

DIOCESE OF CANTERBURY.

J. Shepard, 65.	Godmersham.	*T. King.*
Chris. Yaxle, 65.	Horsley.	*R. Daniel*, 49.
H. Delbricke, 66.	Orpington.	*Maur. Clenocke*, 57.
W. Lesley, 67.	St. John's Thanet.	*J. Wood*, 63.
T. Knell, 69.	Lyminge.	*W. Hawkins.*

DIOCESE OF CHESTER.

Rob. Hebblethwayt, 65.	Croft.	*Ant. Green*, 58.
W. Langley, 69.	Prestwich.	*W. Langley* (sic).

DIOCESE OF CHICHESTER.

Anth. Garrawaye, 66.	Iford.	*Rob. Holloway.*
T. Northoll, 66.	Stopham.	*— Martin.*
W. Miller, 66.	Wartling.	*Peter Horsey.*
Tim. Grene, 66.	Birdford.	*W. Elliot.*
Roger Hale, 66.	Horsted Magna.	*Fras. Coxe*, 60.
J. Peverill, 67.	Bodiham.	*R. Symons.*
St. Chatfeilde, 67.	Pett.	*W. Garret*, 60.
W. Hawkins, 67.	Oving.	*W. Smith.*
W. Wright, 68.	Crawley.	*Roger Hall.*

DIOCESE OF COVENTRY AND LICHFIELD.

Robt. Wodeharne, 65.	Fenny Bentley.	Nich. Bambford.
T. Dabenen, 66.	Stretton le Dale.	G. Greame?
T. Barnes, 66.	Uttoxeter.	Arth. Blunt, 62.
R. Astlyn, 67.	Leamington Priors.	H. Stevens, 63.
Hugh Asburie, 67.	Elford.	T. More, 62.
Hum. Steile, 67.	Madeley.	Ralph Hales, 57.
E. Sandes, 70.	Tatbury.	Edm. Barber.
H. Smythe, 70.	Solihull.	J. Bavand.
Robt. Aston, 70.	Standen.	?

DIOCESE OF DURHAM.

T. Marshall, 64.	Hartwisle.	Nich. Crawhall.
Ralph Graye, 65.	Welpington.	W. Restley, 56.
T. Benyon, 65.	Embleton.	T. Palmer.
Ralph Levir, 66.	Archd. Northumberland.	W. Kynge, 58.
J. Mackbrey, 66.	Billingham.	G. Clyf, 60.
Leon. Pilkington, 67.	Preb. VII.	W. Byrche, 62.
Ralph Levir, 67.	Preb. IV.	W. Tod.
R. Longworth, D.D., 67.	Preb. VIII.	T. Levir, 63.
T. Clerke, 67.	Barwick.	J. Blackhall.
W. Duxfield, 70.	Mitford.	Roger Venie, 61.

DIOCESE OF ELY.

W. Lucas, 69.	Carlton and Willingham.	Rob. Kent.
Rob. Holborne, 70.	Elsworth.	Phil. Baker, D.D.
Rob. Willan, 70.	Little Wilbraham.	J. Walker.

DIOCESE OF EXETER.

T. Phillips, 65.	Seaton.	T. Mychell, 60.
E. Relie, 65.	Stockleigh Pomeroy.	R. Argentine, 61.
T. Washington, 66.	Michaelstow.	R. Aldridge, 63.
Chr. Bodlegh. 66.	Subdean.	T. Nutcombe.
P. Buggens, 67.	Awton Gifford.	Rob. Leugher, 62.

290   THE ELIZABETHAN CLERGY

App III

DIOCESE OF HEREFORD.

Robt. Phillis, 70. | Pembridge. | *Phil. Baker* [?66].

DIOCESE OF LONDON.

W. Thorneton, 64.	Broomfield.	*W. Ferynge*, 63.
Robt. Brecher, 65.	Langham.	*Otto Rumpelli*, 46.
J. Cardynall, 65.	Gestingthorp.	*Chr. Hill*, 59.
W. Womocke, 65.	Olton Beauchamp.	*Chr. Hill*, 48.
J. White, 65.	Barkeway.	*T. Chambers*, 64.
Robt. Heron, 66.	Aveley.	*R. Bradshaw.*
Bart. Busfield, 66.	St. Christopher Stocks.	*J. Lythall*, 64.
J. Orvice, 66.	Terling.	*T. Carwardyn*, 60.
Thurstan Shawe, 66.	Theydon on the Hill.	*Chr. Threadare*, 59.
W. Burde, 66.	Chishall Magna.	*W. Pulleyn*, 54.
J. Frampton, 66.	Cressing.	*J. Calye*, 51.
Chr. Knight, 67.	Steeple.	*Hugh. Joanes*, 60.
J. Smith, 67.	Norton, nr. Baldock.	*T. Serlbye*, 62.
A. Semper, 66.	St. Mary Stannings.	*J. Owgan*, 64.
W. Lyvinge, 67.	St. Mary Abchurch.	*G. Barton*, 61.
R. Mathewe, 67.	St. Michael Cornhill.	*J. Philpott*, 63.
T. Mortyboyes, 67.	St. Alphage Cripplegate.	*Robt. Sheriff*, 64.
T. Dunne, 67.	Shenfield.	*W. Newhouse*, 62.
R. Porder, 68.	St. Peter Cornhill.	*J. Gough*, 60.
W. Aylewarde, 68.	St. Leonard Shoreditch.	*Nich. Daniels*, 63.
J. Hedlam, 68.	Braughing.	*W. Lyon*, 62.
T. Clough, 68.	Elmedon.	*Ant. Toppam*, 54.
J. Beryman, 68.	Shelley.	*R. Hutton*, 58.
Rob. Hudson, 68.	Yeldham Magna.	*G. Raynolds*, 63.
Nich. Nichols, 68.	St. Martin Pomeroy.	*G. Barton*, 60.
R. Smith, 68.	St. Margaret Pattens.	*Nich. Standen*, 66.
J. Douglas, 68.	Northwolde.	*J. Cormett*, 53.
J. Sympson, 69.	St. Botolph Bishopsgate.	*E. Turner.*
W. Chapman, 70.	Black Notley.	*T. Daukes*, 64.
W. Womocke, 70.	Gestingthorp.	*J. Cardinall*, 65.

DIOCESE OF NORWICH.

Cuthbert Hyndmer, 65.	Reydon.	*Leon. Howlett*, 61.
R. Gaseley, 65.	Beddingham.	*Rob. Randall.*
R. Tenett, 66.	Carlton Colville.	*J. Gough*, 60.

INSTITUTIONS AFTER DEPRIVATION, 1564-1570   291

			App. III
W. Daglas, 67.	Walpole.	R. *Bowling*.	
W. Baldwyne, 67.	Brandeston.	W. *Goodfellow*.	
T. Howlett, 68.	Groton.	H. *Browne*.	
J. Treman, 68.	Bentley.	*Peter Welles*.	
H. Bancke, 68.	Gt. Finborough.	[*Gilb. Alcock*.]	
Jas. Eache, or Conyers, 68.	Wickham-Skeith.	*J. Evans*.	
H. Hutchinson, 68.	Henley.	*T. Ridinges*.	
G. Conyers, 68.	Bintree.	*R. Walker*.	
W. Hattonne, 68.	Stody.	W. *Hatton* (sic).	
Steph. Nevinson, 69.	Stiffkey.	W. *Frost*.	
Jas. Love, 69.	East Harling.	*T. Moore*.	
R. Twynne, 69.	Hopton.	?	
W. Hornbye, 69.	Rogdon.	*T. Tie*.	
R. Fortune, 69.	Reedham.	*Rob. Barney*.	
J. Kiffen, 70.	Stanstead.	*J. Combes*.	
J. Park, 70.	Lackford.	*J. Helme*.	

DIOCESE OF OXFORD

Rob. Scholfelde, 69.	Hardwick.	*Griffin Gough*.

DIOCESE OF PETERBOROUGH.

Peter Conwey, 65.	Alderton.	?
T. Palmer, 66.	Merebashbie.	?
R. Rayner, 66.	Southwich.	? 60.
T. Sharrocke, 67.	Badby Newenham.	? 61.

DIOCESE OF ROCHESTER.

Nich. Bishoppe, 65.	Stoke.	*Robt. Cragge*, 61.
W. Darell, 65.	Cowling.	*E. Haydon*.

DIOCESE OF ST. DAVID'S[1].

Phil. Sidney (Scholar), 65.	Preb. Llangunlo.	*T. Bulkley*.
T. ? 65.	Castle Emleyn.	*J. Butler*.

[1] The book ends 1565.

APP. III

DIOCESE OF SALISBURY.

Edm. Becke, 65.	Inkpen.	*J. Greenway*, 61.
J. William, or Gunter, 65.	Wookey.	*Roger Griffith*, 55.
J. Pyerse, 65.	Newbury.	?
T. Davye, 65.	Whaddon.	*J. Carell.*
Jas. Procter, 65.	Malmesbury St. Paul.	*J. Skinner.*
Nich. Rogers, 65.	Dunhead St. Mary.	*J. Fezarde*, 55.

DIOCESE OF WINCHESTER.

Bernard Blacher, 65.	Elsfield.	*W. Hinckersfield.*
R. Foxe, 65.	Hursley.	*J. Hynton.*
T. Ladlowe, ? 66.	Farley.	*W. Smythe.*
R. Wythen, 66.	Ewhurst.	*Aristotle Webb.*

DIOCESE OF YORK.

G. Aplebie, 65.	Tickhill.	*Rob. Elden.*
Chr. Harrison, 65.	Bossall.	*Ant. Grene*, 62.
T. Robinsone, 65.	Kirk-Sandall.	*Lancelot Tailor.*
J. Overton, 66.	Yedingham.	*C. Cherleson*, 59.
Peter Challoner, 66.	Stainton.	*T. Holden.*
W. Waistnes, 67.	Headon.	*J. Swynscoe*, 61.
W. Crake, 67.	Folkton.	*J. Thompson*, 62.
J. Wilson, 68.	Ilkey.	*J. Pullen*, 54.
G. Mitchell, 68.	Cowesby.	*Ant. Grene*, 47.
J. Chetam, 69.	Colwick.	*Oliver Haywoode.*

INDEX

ABBREVIATIONS.

abs. = absentee, 1559.
rec. = recusant.
Ch. = Christopher.
R. = Richard.

dep. = deprived.
sig. = signatory, 1559.
E. = Edward.
T. = Thomas.

inst. = instituted.
H. Henry.
W. = William.

J. = John.

A.

Abadam, J., sig., 109.
Abbot, Rob., sig., 118.
Abell, J., sig., 120.
Abowen, J., dep., 252, 281.
Abrall, J., inst., 285.
Abṙtt, W., sig., 109.
Acworth, George, writer, 243; inst., 284.
Acton, T., sig., 124.
Ad Persecutores Anglos, its account of deprivations, 222, 230.
Adams, J., restored, 89, 287.
— R., dep., 228, 252, 285.
— T., sig., 124.
Adamson, Philip, sig., 109.
Adde, J., sig., 120.
Adran, J., sig., 109.
Akers, J., sig., 109.
Albon, J., sig., 109.
Alcock, Gilbert, dep., 291.
— R., sig., 124.
— T., sig., 120.
Aldridge, R., dep., 289.
Alem, Rob., sig., 109.
Alexander, Rob., sig., 102.
Alford, J., sig., 102; dep., 252, 281.
— W., sig., 124.
Allaman, H., sig., 102.
Allen, Gervase, sig., 120.
— James, sig., 120.
— J., sig., 102, 109, 124; inst., 285.
— Rob., sig., 102.
— W., dep., 229, 233, 253.
Alley, W., inst., 277, 279.

Allmark, R., sig., 118.
Alms; the clergy to give part of their revenues to the poor, 50.
Alms-boxes to be placed in churches, 55.
Alpden, Rob., sig., 120.
Alrad, J., sig., 102.
Alsop, J., sig., 120.
— Rob., sig., 120.
— W., sig., 120.
Alston, T., dep., 252, 273.
Altars, removal of, 63.
Always, H., dep., 228, 266.
Ambros, Elizeus, abs., 87.
Amgar, R., sig., 109.
Anderson, Simon, dep., 252, 281.
Anderton, J., sig., 102.
Andrew, J., sig., 102, 124.
— Rob., sig., 109.
Annullyng, J., sig., 118.
Ap David, Griffin, dep., 252, 278.
Apeleye, Rob., abs., 83.
Apowell, Hugh, abs. 87.
— Rob., dep., 262, 283; *see also* Powell.
ap Owen, J., inst., 278, 283.
Appleby, Ambrose, M.A., 224; dep., 232, 252.
— G., inst., 292.
— J., inst., 273.
Appletoft, R., sig., 109; dep., 252, 281.
Appryce, E., sig., 102.
— Hugh, inst., 278.
— Philip, sig., 102.
Ap Richart, Hugh, sig., 120.
Archarde, J., inst., 285.
Archbold, W., inst., 282.

Arden, T., dep., 78, 161, 227, 253, 278, 286; lurking in Herefordshire, 184, 200, 233. (N.B., called also *John* Arden.)
Argentine, R., inst., 272, 277; dep., 289.
Armitage, T., sig., 109.
Armour, J., sig., 102.
Arnolds, J., sig., 124.
Arsleye, W., abs., 83.
Arundel, H., E. of, Visitor for the South, 101.
— Sir Nicholas, Visitor for the South, 101.
Asburie, Hugh, inst., 289.
Asche, W., sig., 109.
Ashebury, Ch., sig., 102.
Asheby, Rob., sig., 117.
— W., sig., 124.
Ashelake, T., sig., 120.
Ashley, W., sig., 120; dep., 253, 276.
Ashton, J., sig., 103.
— Rob., sig., 102.
Assheworth, Laurence, sig., 109.
Ashwyn, J., sig., 124.
Askam, Anthony, abs., 83.
— Roger, inst., 286.
Askew, Sir Francis, Visitor for the South, 97.
Aspinall, Nicholas, sig., 124; inst., 281; dep., 253, 281.
Asplen, T., sig., 118.
'Assurance of Supremacy' Act, its provisions, 188; compared with the Supremacy Act, 188; the text, 202.
Astley, W., sig., 120.
Astlyn, R., inst., 289.
Aston, Rob., sig., 120; inst., 289.
— T., sig., 120.
Atherton, J., inst., 280.
Athowe, T., sig., 109.
Atkins, Anthony, dep., 136, 232, 253; restricted to bounds, 180.
— T., sig., 120.
— Walter, sig., 117.
— W., dep., 228.
Atkynson, H., sig., 102.
— J., sig., 109; dep., 89, 253, 287.
— T., dep., 89, 228, 253, 274; restored, 89, 273, 287; imprisoned, 185; sig., 124.
— W., sig., 102; dep., 253, 281.
Atslowe, Edward, rec., 183, 224; M.A., 224; Dr. of Medicine, 229; deprived of Fellowship, 232, 269.
— Luke, B.A., 1560, 224; deprived of Fellowship, 232, 269.
Augier, T., sig., 109.
Averell, H., sig., 120.
Avis, Rob., inst., 286.

Awchar, W., inst., 273.
Awdley, J., sig., 120.
— N., sig., 102.
— Rob., sig., 109.
Awgest, T., sig., 103.
Aylewarde, W., inst., 290.
Aylmer, J., inst., 279.
Aynsworthe, Francis, sig., 117.
— G., sig., 109.
Ayre, J., sig., 103.
Ayslabye, J., sig., 124.

B.

Babington, Dr. . . . , dep., 229.
— F., dep., 253, 278.
— W., sig., 120.
Bache, J., sig., 120.
Bacheler, E., sig., 109.
Backehouse, J., abs., 87.
— Raphael, sig., 109.
Bacon, Sir Nicholas, his Protestant leaning, 3; Visitor for the South, 94, 95.
— Rob., sig., 103.
— W., sig., 120.
Bactar, J., sig., 103.
Badcok, H., sig., 109.
Badnall, T., sig., 120.
Bagaley, Nicholas, sig., 120.
Bagley, Rob., abs., 83.
Bagnall, R., inst., 277.
Baily, Matthew, sig., 125.
— T., dep., 227, 232, 253.
Baitsoms, Rob., sig., 125.
Bakelar, T., sig., 109.
Baker, J., sig., 103; rec., 185; dep., 253, 280, 285.
— P., dep., 253, 289, 290.
— R., sig., 103.
— Rob., sig., 125.
Bakewell, T., sig., 120.
Baldwyn, R., sig., 120; restored, 89, 274.
— W., inst., 291.
Bale, J., inst., 273.
Balgaye, J., sig., 103.
Balkeye, J., dep., 253, 282.
Ballard, Rob., abs., 87.
— W., sig., 109.
Bamford, N., dep., 253, 276, 289.
Ban, Roger, sig., 125.
Banester, Nicholas, rec., 182.
— T., sig., 109.
— W., sig., 120.
Bancroft, James, sig., 125.
Bangor, Bishop of; *see* Meyrick, R.
— diocese, records of, 237.
Bank, E., inst., 276.
— H., inst., 291.

INDEX

Banks, E., sig., 103.
— H., sig., 125.
— R., inst., 282.
Banrenson, J., sig., 120.
Banyard, T., sig., 109.
Bapster, J., sig., 125.
Bapthorpe, Rob., sig., 78.
Barber, Edmund, sig., 120; dep., 289.
— R., sig., 125; inst., 279.
Barker, Adam, sig., 109.
— E., sig., 103.
— Philip, sig., 125.
— T., sig., 109.
— W., sig., 103, 154; abs., 87.
Barley, Oliver, sig., 154.
— W., sig., 120.
Barlowe, Alexander, sig., 120.
— Geoffrey, sig., 125.
— William, Bishop of Chichester, confirmed, 156; his efforts for the oath, 157.
Barnage, Rob., sig., 109.
Barnard, E., inst., 284; *see also* Bernard.
Barnbye, T., abs., 83.
Barne, J., sig., 109.
— T., abs., 83.
Barneker, Aug., 275.
Barnes, R., inst., 279, 286.
— T., sig., 120; inst., 289.
— W., sig., 120.
Barney, Rob., dep., 291.
Barrett, J., sig., 109; dep., 234.
— W., sig., 109; dep., 253.
Barrowe, Anthony, abs., 86.
Barslowe, Rob., sig., 103; dep., 253, 280.
Barthylmew, Roger, sig., 120.
Bartleton, T., sig., 103.
Bartlett, J., dep., 253.
Barton, G., abs., 86; inst., 278; dep., 253, 280, 290.
— Hugh, abs., 86.
— James, abs., 83.
— Rob., sig., 117; dep., 253, 281.
— W., dep., 253, 286.
Bartram, Rob., sig., 125.
Barwicke, T., inst., 277.
Baskerville, Sir James, Visitor for the South, 101.
Bass, J., sig., 118.
Basset, Gregory, lurking in Hereford, 184. 200; dep., 253, 278.
Bate, Hugh, sig., 120.
Bath and Wells, Bishop of; *see* Bourne, G.; Berkeley, G.
— diocese, visitation of, 160, 159, 160. deprivations and institutions in, 288.
Battye, Charles, sig., 109.
— J., sig., 125.

Bavant, John, rec., 224; dep., 234. 289.
Baven, R., abs., 87.
Baxter, H., sig., 120; inst., 275.
— Ralph. sig., 120.
— W., sig., 109.
Baydyll, G., sig., 103.
Bayforth, W., sig., 109.
Baymine, J., sig., 109.
Baynbryg. Geoffrey, sig., 103.
— W., sig., 109.
Baynbriggs, T., sig., 109.
Bayne, Ralph, Bishop of Coventry and Lichfield, opposes Supremacy Act. &c., 5, 8; entangled in the public disputation, 32; is deprived, 35, 225, 253, 275.
Baynes, Brian, dep., 86, 269, 276.
— R., sig., 125.
Bays, W., sig., 125.
Beacon, T., Visitor for the South, 101.
Beare, J., sig., 109.
Beaumont, Rob., inst., 279.
Beecham, T., sig., 103.
Beche, W., sig., 120.
Becke, Barth., sig., 125.
— Edm., inst., 292.
Becket, J., sig., 109.
Beckewith, Ch., abs., 87.
Becon, T., inst., 273.
Bedall, J., sig., 125.
Bedford, Francis, Earl of, Visitor for the South, 94, 95, 98.
Bede, Rob., sig., 118.
Bees, W., sig., 120.
Bell, David, abs., 87.
— E., abs., 86.
— Gregory, dep., 228, 229, 234, 253, 284, 285.
— T., sig., 125.
— W., abs., 83, 86.
Beller, P., sig., 125.
Bellost, Simon, dep., 228, 268.
Bellowes, T., sig., 109.
Belsire, Alex., dep., 136, 226, 232, 253, 282; restricted to bounds, 170.
Bemund, J., *see* Bremund.
Bendall, J., sig., 103.
Bendrysche, H., sig., 110.
Bene, Edm., inst., 276.
Benedict, . . . , dep., 229.
Benger, Sir T., Oxford Visitor, 130.
Benhere, Aug., sig., 155.
Benigfeld, E., dep., 253, 278.
Bennett, Edm., sig., 120.
— E., sig., 120.
— J., sig., 103.
— Nich., sig., 125.
— R., sig., 110, 118.
— T., dep., 234.

296 INDEX

Bennett, W., sig., 120; dep., 79; inst., 272, 284.
Benson, J., abs., 86.
— T., sig., 110.
Benston, J., inst., 282.
Bent, J., dep., 253, 283.
Bentley, W., sig., 125.
Bentham, T., Bishop of Coventry and Lichfield, Visitor for the South, 97; consecrated bishop, 157; inst., 275.
Bentley, J., sig., 125.
— Ralph, sig., 103.
Benyon, T., inst., 289.
Berkeley, Gilbert, Bishop of Bath and Wells; consecrated. 157, 271.
— Sir Maurice, Visitor for the South, 98.
Bernard, Rob., dep., 229, 234, 266.
— T., sig., 155; *and see* Barnard.
Bernercape, T., sig., 120.
Berwick, J., dep., 228, 267.
Bery, W., sig., 125; *and see* Bury.
Berydge, W., sig., 125.
Beryman, J., inst., 290.
Besakell, J., abs., 83.
Besfeld, J., sig., 103.
Best, J., Bishop of Carlisle, preaches for the Visitors, 75 *note*; consecrated, 166, 273; commissioner for the North, 167; his visitation of Carlisle, 168, 169; inst., 273, 274.
— R., sig., 103.
— Rob., sig., 110.
Bettreton, J., sig., 120.
Betts, W., inst., 281.
Beverley, Rob., sig., 110.
Beulay, Gregory, sig., 103.
— T., sig., 103.
Bible, the, to be set up in churches, 48; reading thereof to be encouraged, 49.
Bibliography of the Supremacy controversy, 243 *note*, 251 *note*.
Bibney, James, sig., 103.
Bierd, Liberius, inst., 286.
Bill, Dr. W., Cambridge Visitor, 132; ecclesiastical commissioner, 147; inst., 279.
Bilson, Laurence or Richard, dep., 227, 233, 253, 285.
Bingay, W., sig., 103.
Birch, Ralph, sig., 103.
— T., sig., 103; dep., 3 *note*, 254, 285.
— W., inst., 274; dep., 289.
Byrchley, Roger, sig., 103.
Bishop, Gregory, sig., 110.
— Nicholas, inst., 291.
— R., dep., 228, 267.
— W., sig., 103.
Bishops, deprivations of, 30, 220; in the Parliament of 1559, 31; imprisonment of, 144, 145, 175, 192 195; consecration of the new, 156, 157, 166; vacant sees, 157, 158, 165, 166; their release from prison, 193, 194.
Blacher, Bernard, inst., 292.
Blackborne, Edm., sig., 103.
— J., sig., 103.
— R., sig., 110.
Blackhall, J., dep., 289.
Blakhede, R., sig., 103.
Blake, Anthony, restored, 89, 287.
Blakemeyre, H., sig., 120.
Blakwyn, R., sig., 154.
Blamefeld, Stephen, sig., 110.
Bland, Ch., sig., 103.
— E., sig., 117.
— R., sig., 117.
Blands, Gibisert, sig., 125.
Blarney, Hum., inst., 275.
Blaxton, J., dep., 161, 227, 233, 254, 277, 278, 283, 284; restrained to bounds, 181; lurking in Hereford, 200.
Blennerhasset, E., sig., 154.
Blewet, T., inst., 275.
Blithe, G., abs., 78.
Blount, Sir R., Visitor for the South, 97.
Bolton, J., dep., 228, 267.
Blunston, R., preaches for the Visitors, 75 *note*; dep., 89, 254, 287.
Blunt, Arthur, dep., 289.
Blythe, W., sig, 120.
Blythman, B., dep., 254, 272.
Bobett, or Bolbett, Roger, dep., 228, 254, 284; inst., 282.
Bodie, J., inst., 272.
Bodlegh, Ch., inst., 277, 289.
Bolte, T., sig., 120; inst., 275.
Bolton, W., sig., 125.
Bowlton, J., sig., 125.
Bond, W., sig., 103.
Boneham, R., sig., 110.
Boninton, Edm., sig., 117.
Bonner, Edm., Bishop of London, opposes Supremacy Act, &c., 5, 8; is dep., 34, 225, 254, 280; imprisoned, 144, 145, 185, 193, 194; suspected of treason, 145, 195; excommunicated, 190; refuses the oath in prison, 195; dies, 195.
Bordman, E., sig., 103.
Borough, R., sig., 103.
Borrow, Edm., sig., 110.
— R., sig., 110.
— T., abs., 83.
Borthe, H., sig., 120.
Bossall, Rob., sig., 110.
Boste, W., sig., 110.
Botswayne, W., sig., 110.
Bourne, Gilbert, Bishop of Bath and

INDEX

Wells, deprived of Presidency of Wales, 31; absent from Parliament of 1559, 31; returns to his see, 38; is dep., 38, 144, 226, 254, 271; imprisoned, 144; restricted to bounds, 194, 196; dies, 196.
Bousfield, Barth., inst., 290.
Bovell, H., sig., 125; rec., 185; dep., 227, 233, 254, 284.
Bower, Humphrey, sig., 118.
— Ralph, sig., 120.
Bowes, R., Visitor for the North, 71.
Bowling, R., dep., 291.
Bowman, Rob., sig., 110.
— Stephen, abs., 86.
Bowmne, R., sig., 120.
Bownell, J., sig., 103.
Bownes, Edm., sig., 110.
Bowoirs, W., sig., 125.
Bowyer, Andrew, sig., 120.
Boxall, J., imprisoned, 146; dep., 226, 231, 254, 271, 277, 280, 282, 284, 286.
Boylston, Roger, sig., 125.
Boynton, T., sig., 117.
Boys, W., rec., 77; restricted to bounds, 180.
Boyse, E., Visitor for the South, 101.
Braban, J., sig., 103.
Bracher, Rob., inst., 278, 290.
Bradbridge, Aug., inst., 274, 286.
Bradbury, Aug., inst., 274.
Bradley, Thurstan, sig., 110; dep., 254, 282.
Bradocke, T., sig., 120.
Bradshaw, J., sig., 120; dep., 228, 267, 290.
— T., inst., 276.
Braithwayte, Michael, abs., 87.
Braker, H., sig., 103.
Bramborough, R., dep., 254, 278.
Bramston, T., dep., 232, 254.
Brancker, W., sig., 110.
Brandlinge, Ralph, abs., 86.
Brandon, Bernard, inst., 282.
Bratchard, Rob., sig., 103
Braye, J., sig., 125.
Bredkerke, H., sig., 103.
Bremund, J., dep., 227, 232, 267.
Brereton, T., inst., 283.
Bretland, T., sig., 110.
Brett, Ralph, sig., 120.
— Rob., sig., 103.
Bretton, W., sig., 103, 117; inst., 280.
Brettyn, Humphrey, sig., 125.
Brewerton, R., sig., 110.
Brian, T., sig., 103.
Brichell, E., inst., 280.
Bridger, R., sig., 118.
Bridgwater, J., his account of numbers deprived, 223, 231; inst., 288; sig., 154.
Briggs, R., sig., 118.
Brightyre, J., sig., 110.
Briskowe, R., sig., 125.
Bristol diocese, records of, 237.
Bristowe, R., dep., 131, 224, 229, 234, 269.
Brivyll, T., sig., 118.
Brock, Ralph, sig., 120.
— Rob., abs., 87; dep., 288.
Brodebente, James, abs., 83.
Brodley, W., sig., 117.
Brogden, W., abs., 83.
Broke, Adam, sig., 120.
— James, abs., 87.
Bromhedd, T., dep., 254, 278.
Brond, Simon, sig., 117.
Broughton, J., sig., 110.
Brown, Edm., dep., 228, 267.
— George, Visitor for the North, 71-73.
— H., dep., 291.
— J., sig., 103, 110, 125.
— Rob., sig., 103, 118, 125; inst., 275.
— T., sig., 103, 118.
— Walter, sig., 125.
Brownhall, Roger, sig., 154.
Brownsmyth, W., sig., 110.
Brownying, W., sig., 118.
Browyne, Sylvester, sig., 120.
Brudenell, Edm., Visitor for the South, 97.
Brunborough, or Browborough, Edm., rec., 180; dep., 228, 234.
Brune, Stephen, sig., 121.
Bryan, W., sig., 121.
Bryckebeche, J., dep., 254, 281.
Bryggs, T., sig., 103, 110.
Brymley, W., sig., 121.
Bucke, J., inst., 275.
Buckmaster, T., inst., 281; dep., 254, 281.
Buggens, P., inst., 289.
Bukkes, J., sig., 110.
Buknal, W., sig., 118.
Bulhey, J., sig., 110.
Bulkley, T., abs., 87; dep., 291.
Bull, J., sig., 110.
— W., sig., 125.
Bullen, G., inst., 287.
Bullingham, N., Bishop of Lincoln, has charge of Bourne, 194, 196; inst., 279.
Bullock, G., rec., 79; dep., 89, 136, 226, 232, 254, 276, 279; is abroad, 184.
Bulter, J., sig., 121.
Burbank, T., dep., 254.
Burde, W., inst., 290.

298   INDEX

Burdett, Clement, rec., 182; dep., 228, 254, 284.
Burgyn, J., abs., 83.
Burnam, Rob., sig., 110.
Burne, W., sig., 118.
Burnett, R., sig., 110, 117.
Burnford, G., dep., 227, 232, 254, 271.
Bursthard, J., dep., 232, 267.
Burton, Rob., sig., 103.
— T., sig., 121.
Burton, W., sig., 110; rec., 183; dep., 254, 282.
Burtonton, Edm., sig., 121.
Burwyk, James, sig., 110.
Bury, R., sig., 103.
— W., abs., 87; dep., 83, 89, 254, 274, 287.
Burywey, W., sig., 110.
Bushby, Humphery, sig., 103.
Buson, E., sig., 125.
Busshe, J., sig., 110.
— W., sig., 103.
Butler, J., inst., 273; dep., 291.
— T., sig., 121; dep., 229, 234, 269.
Buttell, R., dep., 254, 282.
Butterton, R., sig., 121.
Butterworthe, E., sig., 125.
Byam, T., dep., 254, 280.
Byas, Rob., abs., 83.
Bycher, W., sig., 110.
Byckerdyke, J., sig., 110; dep., 227, 233, 254, 277.
— Marmaduke, sig., 103.
Byeryll, R., sig., 103.
Byckley, T., sig., 155.
Bylby, Ralph, inst., 287.
Bylcliffe, Thurstan, sig., 125.
Byncks, Rob., sig., 110.
Byngley, Rob., sig., 125.
Bynonson, F., sig., 103.
Byrd, H., sig., 110.
— T., sig., 121.
Byrrdocke, R., inst., 275.
Bywell, J., sig., 110.

C.

Cabt..., Edm., sig., 154.
Cachard, J., sig., 110.
Calfhill, J., inst., 282.
Callaway, Sir W., Visitor for the South, 101.
Calley, J., sig., 103; dep., 290.
Calner, R., sig., 110; dep., 254, 281.
Calson, R., sig., 104.
Calverd, W., abs., 83.
Cambridge University endorses the five articles, 1559, 3; visitation of, 44, 132; writ for the same, 133.
Camden's account of numbers dep., 218.

Campyon, Sylvester, sig., 103.
Canterbury, Archbishop of; see Parker, M.
— diocese, Visitation of, 1560, 160; deprivations and institutions in, 273, 288.
Cantrell, W., sig., 125.
Capel, Giles, dep., 227, 233, 267.
Capon, J., dep., 284.
Capperson, J., sig., 125.
Cardele, J., inst., 285.
Cardynall, J., inst., 290; dep., 290.
Carell, J., Visitor for the South, 101; dep., 292.
Carewe, G., Dean of Bristol and Oxford, has charge of Bourne, 196; inst., 272, 282, 286.
— Matthew, sig., 110.
—, Sir Peter, Visitor for the South, 98, 100.
Carlelley, Rob., sig., 121.
Carlisle, Bishop of; see Oglethorpe, O.; Best, J.
— diocese, Visitation of, 1561, 168; recusancy in, 199; records of, 237; deprivations and institutions in, 273.
Carre, N., dep., 136; Dr. of Medicine, 229.
—, R., dep., 254, 277.
Carrier, R., inst., 273; dep., 254.
Cartell, W., sig., 121.
Carter, H., sig., 110; dep., 254, 282.
—, T., inst., 278.
—, W., sig., 121; dep., 79, 229, 234, 254, 276; restricted to bounds, 180.
Catagre, J., dep., 136, 232, 267.
Carton, T., sig., 110.
Cartwright, J., sig., 121.
— T., sig., 125.
Carvar, R., sig., 125.
Carwardyn, T., dep., 290.
Caryngton, Roger, sig., 121.
Caslyn, T., sig., 125.
Caston, Stephen, sig., 103; dep., 254, 281.
Catechism to be taught in church, 59.
Caterall, Stephen, sig., 104.
Caterbanke, W., sig., 121.
Catton, H., sig., 125.
Cave, Sir Ambrose, Visitor for the South, 97; ecclesiastical commissioner, 147.
—, Francis, ecclesiastical commissioner, 147.
Cawappe, E., sig., 121.
—, Ralph, sig., 121.
Cawerden, Sir T., Visitor for the South, 101.
Cawse, J., sig., 110.
Cawscon, Anthony, sig., 104.

INDEX

Cayle, T., abs., 83.
Cecil, Sir W., Visitor for the South, 97; Cambridge Visitor, 132.
Chace, or Chauncey, Maurice, prior, dep., 226, 234.
Chadfounte, Charles, sig., 104.
Chadwyck, J., sig., 110.
Challoner, Peter, inst., 292.
Chamber, E., dep., 228, 267.
— T., sig., 104.
Chambers, T., dep., 290.
Champion, or Champernowne, Sir Arthur, Visitor for the South, 99, 100.
Champion, J., inst., 285.
Chandos, Edmund, Lord, Visitor for the South, 98.
Chane, Dominic, dep., 254, 285.
— J., sig., 110.
Channey, Edmund, sig., 104.
Chapleyn, Thurstan, sig., 121.
Chapman, Ch., sig., 110.
— G., sig, 104.
— J., sig., 118.
— Rob., sig., 117.
— W., sig., 110; inst., 290.
Charleton, Alan, abs., 87.
— W., abs., 87.
Chatbourne, G., inst., 277.
Chatfeilde, Stephen, inst., 288.
Chedsey, W., engaged in the public disputation, 32, 175; dep., 136, 226, 232, 255, 280, 282, 286; imprisoned, 175, 185.
Chekeryng, Rob., sig., 117.
Chell, W., dep., 255, 278.
Chelton, Nich., sig., 121.
Chenerie, Alan, dep., 228, 255.
Cherleson, C., dep., 292.
Chescome, Stephen, inst., 285.
Chester, Bishop of; see Scott, Dr. Cuthbert; Downham, W.
— cathedral, state of in 1559, 82.
— diocese, deprivations and institutions in, 274, 288.
Chester, T., sig., 125.
— Sir William, ecclesiastical commissioner, 147.
Cheston, T., abs., 78.
Chetam, J., inst., 292.
Cheyney, J., sig., 125.
Chichester, Bishop of; see Barlow, W.
— diocese, deprivations and institutions in, 274, 288.
Chichester, Sir John, Visitor for the South, 98, 100.
Chomley, E., sig., 125.
— Randall, ecclesiastical commissioner, 147.
Choyse, J., sig., 125.
Christyan, J., sig., 117.

Chyddalton, T., dep., 255, 275.
Chyese, W., sig., 125.
Chyld, J., sig., 104.
— Roger, sig., 104.
Church, the, her independence of the Crown asserted, 3; Crown rights under the Supremacy Act, 7, 13, 14; Church goods, the goods of the poor, 50.
Church, J., sig., 117.
— Nich., sig., 110.
Churcheley, W., sig., 121.
Churches, repairs to, 51.
Claibourne, T., sig., 110.
Clapham, R., sig., 104.
Clapton, Martin, sig., 110.
Clare, alias Dominick, R., rec., 180; dep., 227, 233, 255, 284.
Clarke, Alexander, sig., 118.
— Ant., dep., 255, 274, 275.
— J., sig., 104, 117, 125.
— Ralph, sig., 121.
— Rob., sig., 104.
— T., abs., 87; sig., 125; inst., 281, 286, 289.
— W., sig., 118, 121, 125.
Clay, J., sig., 110.
Cleyfield, Rob., inst., 286.
Clayton, Ch., Registrar to Visitors' deputies, 81.
— Laurance, sig., 104.
— Nich., sig., 121.
— Oliver, sig., 104.
— Ralph, sig., 121.
— Roger, sig., 104.
Clegg, R., sig., 110.
Clement, . . ., dep., 228, 267.
— J., Dr. of Medicine, 229.
— T., sig., 121; abs., 78.
Clenok, Maurice, dep., 227, 288.
Clerke, B., writer, 220.
Clergy, the, on Elizabeth's accession, 1, 248; opposed to reform, 2, 3; their stubborn attitude, 41; cloistered clergy leave the country, 45; discipline of, 49, 65; to give alms to the poor, 50; to be respected, 56; their marriage, 57; their apparel, 57; numbers of deprived, 217 et seq., 236 et seq., 249, 251 note.
Cleving, Rob., abs., 83.
Clife, G., rec., 79; inst., 276; dep., 89, 287, 289.
— R., sig., 121; dep., 255, 276.
Clough, T., sig., 117; inst., 290.
Clynton, W., inst., 278.
Clypsham, E., sig., 125.
— Martin, sig., 104.
Coates, Rob., dep., 255, 281.
Cobham, Lord, Visitor for the South, 101.

Cobham, J., sig., 110.
Cobin, Geoffrey, inst., 284.
Cocket, G., sig., 125.
Cocks, R., sig., 125.
— Rog., inst., 272.
— W., sig., 125.
Cockeson, T., abs., 83.
Cockyn, Sir T., Visitor for the South, 97.
Coke, Sir Anthony, Cambridge Visitor, 132.
— Rob., sig., 110, 121.
Coker, Roger, sig., 104.
Cokerell, G., sig., 104.
Cokke, James, sig., 110.
Colborne, G., sig., 104.
Cole, Andrew, sig., 110; dep., 255, 282.
— Arthur, dep., 232, 267, 280.
— H., engaged in the public disputation, 32; imprisoned, 146, 185; dep., 226, 231, 255, 273, 279; proceedings against, 197.
— J., sig., 121.
— T., inst., 280.
Coles, Humphrey, Visitor for the South, 99.
— J., inst., 272.
— Rob., sig., 104.
Colin, . . . dep., 228.
— W., sig., 110.
Colisman, W., sig., 110.
Coll, Leonard, sig., 104.
Colliar, N., sig., 104.
Collier, T., dep., 255, 282.
Collyns, J., dep., 255, 284.
— Rob., dep., 255, 273.
Colynson, J., inst., 281; dep., 255, 281.
Collynwood, T., sig., 125.
— W., abs., 86, 87; dep., 227, 233, 269.
Collys, W., sig., 110.
Colman, H., sig., 118.
Coltesmore, T., dep., 255, 275.
Columbell, R., sig., 104.
Columben, Oliver, restored, 89, 287.
Colvyer, J., dep., 255, 287.
Combes, J., dep., 291.
Commissioners, ecclesiastical, power to appoint, 7, 14, 137; as judges of heresy, 20; commission of May 23, 1559, 34; to control the press, 61; the First Commission, 42, 137; its duties, 139, 148; its headquarters in London, 139; proceedings of first commission, 140; proceedings with regard to Supremacy Oath, 142, 153, 157; text of the commission, 147; the Northern commissions, 165; Second Commission, 174; abstract of its duties, 178.

Communion, Holy, admittance to, 54.
Company, R., sig., 110.
Compton, N., sig., 104.
Conal, W., sig., 119.
Coningford, J., sig., 110.
Constantine, . . . , inst., 283.
Conwaw, R., dep., 255, 283.
Conwey, Peter, inst., 291.
Conyers, G., inst., 291.
— T., sig., 110.
Cook, Sir Anthony, Visitor for the South, 94; ecclesiastical commissioner, 147; Eton Visitor, 162.
— J., sig., 110; inst., 285; dep., 255, 285.
— R., sig., 110, 117, 121.
— W., dep., 279.
Cooper, T., sig., 110.
Copage, J., abs., 81.
Cope, Alan, rec., 183; B.C.L., 1560, 224; dep., 232, 267.
Coote, W., sig., 110.
Copland, J., sig., 104.
— Nicholas, abs., 87.
Coplet, R., sig., 255, 285.
Copman, Albert, sig., 104.
Copschef, J., sig., 104.
Copysette, Roger, sig., 121.
Coram Rege Rolls searched for proceedings against recusants, 197.
Cordall, Walter, sig., 104.
Corker, N., sig., 110.
— T., sig., 110.
— W., sig., 125.
Cormett, J., dep., 290.
Cormoth, J., sig., 104.
Cornwall, H., sig., 110.
— T., sig., 104.
Cory, Robert, sig., 119.
Coscleye, W., abs., 83.
Coshey, Ralph, sig., 125.
Cosyn, Edm., dep., 136, 227, 232, 255.
— J., sig., 110.
— Robert, dep., 227, 255, 279, 280.
Cotton, J., sig., 110.
— Nicholas, sig., 125.
— R., dep., 255, 281.
— T., sig., 121.
Cottrell, Dr. . . . , Visitor of Salisbury Cathedral, 159.
— J., sig., 155.
Cotyer, Ralph, sig., 125.
Council of the North, the, its powers of dealing with recusancy, 168, 170.
Courtmill, . . . , deprived, 228, 267.
Coveney, T., sig., 118; dep., 132, 232, 255.
Coventry and Lichfield, Bishop of, *see* Bayne, Ralph; Bentham, T.

Coventry and Lichfield, diocese, number of parishes, 98; deprivations and institutions in, 275, 289.
Cowche, J., inst., 272.
Cowke, W., sig., 104.
Cowper, R., sig., 121.
— T., sig., 125.
— Walter, sig., 110.
— W., abs., 83.
Coxe, Francis, inst., 275; dep., 288.
— J., inst., 285.
— Richard, Bishop of Ely, his Parliamentary sermon, 3; Oxford Visitor, 130; ecclesiastical commissioner, 142; consecrated bishop, 156, 277; a letter of his quoted, 157; has charge of Watson, 196.
Coxall, J., sig., 104.
Cradocke, T., dep., 255, 280.
Cragge, Rob., dep., 291.
Crake, W., inst., 292.
Crakell, W., sig., 125.
Crakinthorpe, Mighell, abs., 87.
Crample, Oliver, sig., 110.
Crane, G., sig., 121.
— J., sig., 121.
— ? Nich., dep., 267.
— Thomas, dep., 228, 267.
Cranforth, J., rec., 79.
Crany, W., sig., 117.
Cratford, *alias* Stratford, E., dep., 227, 233, 255, 272.
Crawforth, R., abs., 86.
— W., sig., 117.
Crawhill. Nich., dep., 289.
Cresner, Elizabeth, prioress, dep., 226.
Cressye, Robert, officer of the Archdeacon of Nottingham, 75.
Creton, James, abs., 83.
Crickett, T., inst., 272.
Croft, Brian, sig., 104.
— T., dep., 255, 278.
— Vincent, abs., 83.
Croftes, Sir James, Visitor for the North, 71.
— Robert, sig., 125.
Crook, . . ., dep., 228, 267.
Crosier, J., sig., 111.
Crosley, T., sig., 111.
Crosse, Aug., sig., 155.
— W., sig., 111.
Crow, W., sig., 121.
Crowes, Laurence, sig., 111.
Crowley, Rob., inst., 278.
Crown rights over the Church by the Supremacy Act, 7, 13, 14; presentations, 238.
Cruke, T., sig., 125.
Cruse, J., sig., 121.
Cubbidge, J., dep., 228, 267.

Cumberford, H., dep., 3 *note*. 255, 275, 282; restricted to bounds, 181.
Cumberland, Henry, E. of, not appointed a Visitor, 72; shelters recusants, 168, 184.
Cundall, Ralph, sig., 111.
Curates, deprivations of, 243.
Cursson, G., sig., 125.
Curtes, Robert, sig., 111.
Cuthbert, Ch., sig., 125.
— W., inst., 283.

D.

Dabenen, T., inst., 289.
Dacre, H., inst., 273.
— J., abs., 86.
Dacres of Gilsland, Lord, not appointed a Visitor, 72; shelters recusants, &c., 80 *note*, 168.
Dacye, J., abs., 84.
Daddesburye, Hugh, sig., 111.
Dakyn, Ralph, sig., 125.
Dalby, W., dep., 227, 232, 256, 272.
Dale, E., sig., 111.
— J., rec., 182; dep., 228, 267.
Dalisson, Roger, abs., 84.
Dalton, Rob., dep., 79, 233, 256, 276; rec., 157; restricted to bounds, 181.
Damer, Emericus, sig., 117.
Dande, Emeric, dep., 256, 277.
Dane, J., abs., 87; inst., 280.
Daniel, Edm. (*or* R.), sig., 104; rec., 182; dep., 226, 231, 256, 278, 286, 288.
— J., sig., 119.
Daniels, Nich., dep., 290.
Danister, J., dep., 228, 267.
Dannel, Rob., sig., 104.
Danton, . . ., dep., 227.
Danver, W., sig., 104.
Darbishire, T., imprisoned, 146; dep., 227, 233, 256, 280; is abroad, 184.
Darby, G., sig., 104.
Darlaye, J., sig., 111.
Darrel, T., B.A., 1560, 224; dep., 229, 233, 256.
— W., inst., 291.
Davies, R., Bishop of St. Asaph; consecrated, 157, 283; Visitor for the South, 101.
— R., sig., 111.
— Rob., sig., 104; rec., 180; dep., 256, 281.
— Thomas, dep., 228, 256.
— W., sig., 119.
Davison, Dr. . . ., dep., 234, 267.
— James, abs., 87.
— R., sig., 104.
— Roger, sig., 125.

302 INDEX

Davy, E., sig., 119.
— Rob., sig., 104.
— T., abs., 87 ; sig., 292.
Dawkes, Rob., dep., 136, 233, 256; restricted to bounds, 180.
— T., dep., 290.
Dawlyn, J., inst., 283.
Dawson, Adam, abs., 87.
— Ralph, sig., 121.
— W., sig., 111.
Day, William, Commissioner for the North, 172 ; inst., 287.
Daygle, T., sig., 121.
Dead, prayers for the, 64.
Deane, Andrew, sig., 117.
— J., sig., 104.
— Reginald, abs., 84.
Debank, J., sig., 125.
— Rob., sig., 119.
de la Hide, David, rec., 180.
Delbricke, H., inst., 288.
Dend, W., sig., 125.
Denham, E., letter from, 198.
— R., sig., 125.
Denman, W., restored, 89, 287.
Denny, Edmund, sig., 111.
Denston, W., sig., 111.
Dent, Rob., sig., 125.
Denton, J., rec., 3 *note*.
Derby, Edward, Earl of, Visitor for the North, 71, 72.
Desham, Baldwin, sig., 104.
Dewe, Ch., dep., 288.
D'Ewes, Simon, his account of deprived clergy, 217.
Dewsnap, W., sig., 125.
Deyre, J., sig., 125.
— P., sig., 111.
Dickenson, E., abs., 87.
— J., sig., 121.
— Laur., abs., 84.
— T., abs., 87.
Dickson, Ch., sig., 111.
— J., abs., 88.
— R., sig., 111.
— Rob., sig., 111.
— T., abs., 88 ; inst., 287.
Digbie, Leonard, sig., 125.
Dighton, Rob., sig., 155.
Dillon, Anthony, inst., 278.
Dobson, T., dep., 89, 256, 274.
— W., sig., 104.
Dobyson, T., sig., 117.
Dodds, Gregory, inst., 277.
Dodpont, V., sig., 104.
Dolman, T., dep., 136, 233, 256.
Dominick, R.; *see* Clare.
Donatson, R., sig., 111, 112.
Donell, T., sig., 104.
Dounaye, Vincent, abs., 84.

Donnekley, W., sig., 119.
Dorman, Edm., sig., 125.
— T., dep., 136, 229, 233, 243, 256.
Dormer, T., rec., 183.
Dosyn, H., sig., 119.
Douglas, J., inst., 290.
— W., inst., 291.
Dowle, W., sig., 154.
Downabi, W., sig., 111.
Downe, Anthony, sig., 121.
Downes, Geoffrey, rec., 78 ; dep., 256, 278.
— T., sig., 111.
Downham, T., sig., 121.
— W., Bishop of Chester, consecrated, 166 ; inst., 274, 283.
Dowson, R., sig., 111.
— W., abs., 88.
Drakcoferd, T., sig., 121.
Draycot, Anthony, imprisoned, 175, 185 ; dep., 226, 232, 256, 275, 279, 282.
— J., assists recusants, 184 ; imprisoned, 184, 185.
Drury, R., sig., 121 ; dep., 256, 286.
Dryng, T., sig., 126.
Ducks, Ch., abs., 88.
Dudley, Arthur, abs., 87 ; sig., 121.
— Dion., sig., 121.
— G., abs., 76.
— Lord Rob., opposes Uniformity Act, 8 ; not appointed a Visitor, 97.
Dugdale, James, dep., 232, 256, 280.
Dukker, Ralph, sig., 111.
Dumont, P., sig., 111.
Dunche, Andrew, sig., 111.
Dunne, T., inst., 290.
Dunning, Mich., dep., 256, 279.
Durdane, R., dep., 256, 285.
Durham, Bishop of; *see* Tonstall, C. Pilkington, James.
— diocese, recusancy in, 157, 165, 166, 169, 199 ; visitation of, 168, 169 ; records of, 237 ; deprivations and institutions in, 276, 289.
Durham, J., abs., 84 ; rec., 180.
Durston, . . ., dep., 228, 256.
Duxfield, W., inst., 289.
Dycheffelde, Roger, sig., 119.
Dycher, James, sig., 121.
— J., sig., 121.
Dye, Edmund, sig., 111.
Dyer, J., sig., 104.
— Ralph, sig., 126.
— Sir T., Visitor for the South, 99.
— W., sig., 104.
Dylke, T., sig., 121.
Dymock, Sir E., Visitor for the South, 97.
Dysleye, J., inst., 284.

INDEX

E.

Eache, or Conyers, Jas., inst., 291.
Ebden, J., inst., 277, 285.
Ebbs, T., sig., 111.
Ecke, Adam, inst., 276.
Eckersall, W., sig., 111.
Edderych, T., sig., 111.
— alias James, W., sig., 111.
Edgecombe, Sir R., Visitor for the South, 98.
Edlyngsun, W., sig., 119.
Edmonds, Rob., sig., 104.
Educational duties of University Visitors, 134.
Edwards, David, dep., 256, 283.
— Edm., inst., 271.
— R., sig., 121.
— W., sig., 111.
Eglate, R., sig., 126.
Eiton, T., sig., 121.
Eland, E., sig., 104.
Elden, Rob., dep., 292.
Elizabeth's ecclesiastical policy, 2, 4, 7, 156; its mild character, 192.
Ellerkar, J., abs., 88.
Elliot, W., dep., 288.
Ellis, H., inst., 278.
— James, dep., 256, 285.
— Percival, sig., 126.
— R., inst., 285.
— Stephen, abs., 84.
— T., inst., 272.
— W., abs., 84; dep., 89; sig., 111.
Ellison, Cuthbert, abs., 86.
Elmyn, J., sig., 111.
Elmsley, E., dep., 257, 284.
Elsley, E., sig., 111.
Eltringham, Ralph, abs., 86.
Ely, Bishop of; see Thirlby, T.; Cox, R.
— diocese, number of cures in 1559, 97; records of, 237; deprivations and institutions in, 277, 289; state of, in 1561, 239 note².
Ely, William, dep., 161, 226, 232, 257, 273; lurking in Herefordshire, 184, 200.
Emerson, Geoffrey, sig., 111.
Ems, Alexander, sig., 111.
Englefield, Sir Francis, a friend of Sanders, 219.
Enssken, Stephen, sig., 104.
Erasmus' Paraphrases to be set up in churches, 48.
Erewakers, Rob., inst., 274.
Erle, John, rec., 181.
Estofte, Ch., Visitor for the North, 71, 73; Commissioner for the North, 172.
Estobye, W., sig., 104.

Ethridge, G., dep., 229, 269.
Eston, J., sig., 126.
Eton, Visitation of, 1559, 44, 133; 1561, 162.
Eton, Ch., sig., 104.
Etwold, J., sig., 117.
Eudus, Hugh, sig., 111.
Evanne, J., inst., 285.
Evans, Griffith, inst., 281.
— Hugh, sig., 104; inst., 278.
— J., dep., 291.
Evers, W., Lord, Visitor for the North, 71, 72.
Evett, James, sig., 119.
Evinggam, James, sig., 126.
Excommunication of recusants, 190, 197, 198; ancient law of, 190; the bill providing for execution of writs, 191, 210.
Exeter, Bishop of, see Turberville, James.
— diocese, Visitation of, 1561, 161; recusancy in, 199; deprivations and institutions in, 277, 289.
Exhibitioners to be supported by the clergy, 51.
Eyre, Rob., dep., 257, 284.
— T., sig., 126.

F.

Famma, Edmund, sig., 111.
Farent, J., sig., 126.
Farewell, W., sig., 111.
Farler, J., dep., 257, 285; cp. Fowler, J.
Farmar, J., sig., 126.
— alias Oxford, Matthew, sig., 111.
— T., sig., 121.
Farmery, J., sig., 126.
Farnden, R., inst., 275.
Farquharson; see Pharkson.
Farrold, Bernard, sig., 111.
Farthing, J., sig., 104.
Fascet, Alexander, sig., 111.
Faucet, Dr. . . . , dep., 227, 233.
— R., dep., 257, 273.
— Rob., dep., 257, 285.
— W., sig., 111; and see Forset.
Fawpcet, Reynold, sig., 111.
Fayrhayre, J., sig., 111.
Feckenham, J., Abbot of Westminister, opposes Supremacy Act, 5; suspected of treason, 145; imprisoned, 146; dep., 226, 234.
Feld, Laurance, sig., 104.
Fell, James, sig., 119.
— R., sig., 121.
Feltham, J., sig., 111.
Felton, J., dep., 228, 267.
Fenne, G., sig., 111.

Fenne, James, dep., 233. 257.
— J., dep., 229, 234, 267.
— Rob., rec., 183; B.C.L., 1560, 224; dep., 233, 257.
Fennymore, J., sig., 104.
Fenton, J., sig., 121.
Ferdinand the Emperor, intercedes for the bishops, &c., 193, 194.
Fering, W., inst., 281; dep., 290.
Ferne, Stephen, sig., 111.
Ferrer, J., sig., 111.
Feyrust, R., sig., 126.
Fezard, J., dep., 228, 257, 292.
Fildhows, R., sig., 121.
Finch, Sir T., Visitor for the South, 101
Fishe, J., abs., 84.
— W., inst., 279.
Fishborn, Brian, sig., 126.
— Gervase, sig., 126.
— R., abs., 84.
Fisher, G., abs., 84.
— J., abs., 84; sig., 104, 111, 155.
— Rob., inst., 277.
— W., sig., 119, 126.
Fishpool, J., inst., 272.
Fitzherbert, Sir T., assists recusants, 184; imprisoned, 285.
Fitz James, J., dep., 226, 232, 257, 271, 272.
Fitzsimons, Leonard, dep., 233, 257.
Fitzwilliams, Sir W., Visitor for the South, 98.
Fleett, W., sig., 104.
Fleetwood, W., Visitor for the South, 97.
Fleming, H., sig., 121.
— Nicholas, inst., 280.
— R., dep., 229, 234, 267.
Fletchur, E., sig., 121.
— R., sig., 111.
Flint, R., sig., 111.
— T., inst., 284.
Flivet, Charles, sig., 126.
Folberin, J., sig., 117.
Forbes, G., inst., 275.
Ford, Ralph, sig., 111.
Forester, T., sig., 104.
Forman, Rob, sig., 126.
Forset, Alexander, sig., 111; *and see* Fawcet.
Forster, Giles, sig., 126.
— T., sig., 104.
Fortune, R., inst., 291.
Foster, . . ., assists Bishop Horne, 163.
— E., inst., 274.
— Geoffrey, inst., 281.
— Sir J., deputy for the Visitors, 80.
— J., abs., 86.
— Rob., sig., 119; inst., 280.
— W., sig., 121.
Fothergill, Roger, sig., 126.

Foward, H., sig., 126.
Fowler, . . ., dep., 233, 257.
— Brian, receives Bishop Poole, 196.
— J., dep., 233, 257; *cp*. Farler, J.
Fowne, Leonard, sig., 126.
Fox, Jas., sig., 121.
— J., sig., 111; dep., 228, 267.
— Nicholas, rec., 180; inst., 285.
— R., inst., 292.
— Stephen, dep., 234.
— T., sig., 121.
Foxcroft, W., sig., 126.
Frampton, J., sig., 104; inst., 290.
Franch, T., sig., 111.
Franklyn, T., sig., 104.
Frauncis, J., sig., 104.
— T., sig., 104.
Frecke, T., sig., 111.
Freman, Oliver, sig., 126.
— Rob., sig., 126.
— T., dep., 228, 229, 234, 267.
Frere, J., sig., 121.
Frettwell, T., sig., 111.
Friar, J. (father and son), Drs. of Medicine, 229.
Frost, W., sig., 117; dep., 291.
Fugall, T., abs., 84.
Fydell, *v*. Harcourt and Robins, 22.
Fykays, W., sig., 111.
Fyldisend, W., sig., 121.
Fynche, J., sig., 117.
Fynkel, H., sig., 117.
Fytto, J., sig., 126.
Fytton, Sir E., surrogate for the Visitors, 81.

G.

Gaisley, R., sig., 111.
Gainson, Robert, sig., 121.
Gale, Ch., sig., 105.
— J., sig., 117.
Galte, F., sig., 111.
Gamble, J., sig., 126.
Gammon, R., inst., 277.
Ganull, G., sig., 121.
Gardiner, E., sig., 119.
— J., sig., 104; dep., 257, 276.
— Rob., abs., 88.
— T., sig., 121, 155.
Gardinet, Anthony, dep., 228, 257.
Gargate, W., abs., 87.
Gargrave, Sir T., Visitor for the North, 71, 72, 75, 77; Commissioner for the North, 167.
Garlec, J., sig., 121.
Garnell, Oliver, dep., 257, 273.
Garnett, R., sig., 111.
— W., abs., 84; inst., 276.
Garrard, Giles, sig., 104.

Garrawaye, Anthony, inst., 288.
Garett, R., sig., 111.
— W., sig., 121 ; dep., 288.
Gartfolde, R., sig., 111.
Gascon, E., inst., 277.
Gascoigne, Sir J., Visitor for the South, 97.
— W., abs., 88.
Gaseley, R., inst., 290.
Gates, Sir H., Visitor for the North, 71, 72, 75, 77, 81 ; Commissioner for the North, 167.
Gatskall, R., dep., 257, 284.
Gaudyn, T., sig., 104.
Gavyn, J., sig., 126.
Gawber, G., sig., 117.
Gaytes, *alias* Yatts, T., sig., 111.
Gegewycke, N., sig., 117.
Gerne, Ch., sig., 112.
Gerrard, Gilbert, ecclesiastical commissioner, 147.
— W., Visitor for the South, 101 ; sig., 111.
Gervase, James, dep., 232, 257.
Geste, E., inst., 273.
Gibbon, W., sig., 119.
Gybbons, W., sig., 112.
Giblett, W., rec., 180; dep., 228, 267.
Gibson, G., sig., 112.
— J., sig., 112.
— R., sig., 112.
Gifford, Rob., rec., 224 ; dep., 233, 257.
Gilbert, T., sig., 121.
Giles, Laurence, sig., 119.
— T., sig., 105.
Gill, H., dep., 228, 267.
— R., sig., 105 ; inst., 279.
Gilpin, Dr. Bernard, preaches for the Visitors, 75 *note*, 80 *note*; deputy for them, 80, 81.
Glascoikn, W., sig., 105.
Glascok, T., sig., 105.
Glasier, Hugh, dep., 257, 273.
— J., dep., 257, 278, 285.
— Rob., sig., 111.
Glave, Matthew, sig., 119.
Gledle, Hugh, abs., 84.
Gloucester diocese, visitation of 1560, 159 ; deprivations and institutions in, 278.
Glowgate, Edm., sig., 111.
Glyn, J., sig., 105.
Goddall, J., sig., 126.
Godshalfe, E., dep., 227, 233, 257, 274.
Godwyn, J., sig., 121.
— T., sig., 155.
Goldbure, T., sig., 111.
Goldsmith, Randolf, sig., 121.
Goldwell, T., Bishop of St. Asaph, absent from Parliament of 1559, 31 ;

is deprived, 35, 226, 257, 283 ; leaves England, 145 ; his treason at Rome, 187 ; dies, 222.
Golstun, T., sig., 121.
Good, W., dep., 229, 234, 257, 272.
Goodfellow, W., sig., 111 ; dep., 291.
Goodman, Ch., inst., 274.
— J., sig., 105 ; dep., 258, 271.
Goodmayn, Gabriel, ecclesiastical commissioner, 185.
Goodricke, H., inst., 273.
— R., Visitor for the South, 95 ; Oxford Visitor, 130 ; ecclesiastical commissioner, 147.
Goodwyn, Ch., sig., 126.
— H., sig., 117.
— T., sig., 111 ; inst., 279.
— Vincent, inst., 277.
Goshawk, W., sig., 111.
Gosling, Geoffrey, sig., 121.
— J., sig., 111.
Gosnell, Roland, dep., 258, 278.
— T., sig., 121.
Gough, Griffin, sig., 119 ; dep., 291.
— Hugh, sig., 119.
— J., sig., 112 ; dep., 290.
Gouttrell, W., sig., 112.
Gowland, J., abs., 84.
Gowle, W., abs., 84.
Grace, Rob., sig., 126.
Granger, C., dep., 228.
— W., sig., 109.
Graunge, Gregory, sig., 112.
Gravener, W., sig., 105.
Gray, J., Lord, Visitor for the South, 94.
— Ralph, inst., 289.
— Rob., sig., 126; rec., 184.
— T., sig., 126.
— W., abs., 88 ; dep., 89 ; sig., 105.
Greame, G., dep., 289.
Great, Rob., sig., 126.
— W., sig., 126.
Green, Anthony, dep., 292.
— Ch., sig., 121.
— Edm., sig., 121.
— James, sig., 112.
— J., abs., 84.
— Nicholas sig., 126.
— R., sig., 126.
— Tim., inst., 288.
Greenacres, Rob., inst., 280.
Greenway, J., inst., 284 ; dep., 292.
Grenewich, T., inst., 278.
Grenes, W., sig., 126.
Greete, J., rec., 185; dep., 228, 258, 285.
— W., sig., 126.
Gregill, J., rec., 3 *note*; sig., 105.
Gregory, . . ., dep., 161.
Grening, Charles, sig., 105.
Grenville, . . ., dep., 228, 267.

Greshop, W., dep., 228, 267.
Gresley, Laurence, Visitor for the South, 97.
Grewe, E., sig., 112.
Greyne, T., abs., 84.
Griffin, Ralph, sig., 119; inst., 278.
Griffynson, Ch., sig., 112.
Griffith, J., sig., 105.
— Roger, dep., 292.
Grindall, Edm., Bishop of London, consecrated, 156; has charge of Watson, 194; inst., 280.
— J., abs., 88.
Grove, J., sig., 126.
Grymsby, W., sig., 112.
Guest, Edm., Bishop of Rochester, consecrated, 157.
Guild-funds to be put in the alms-boxes, 56.
Gunyer, J., inst., 273.
Gyppes, W., sig., 105, 112.
Gyttyns, R., sig., 121.

H.

Hadcocke, R., sig., 126.
Haddon, Walter, Cambridge Visitor, 132; ecclesiastical commissioner, 147.
Hagger, J., abs., 84.
Haighe, Nicholas, inst., 276, 287.
— W., sig., 121.
Hale, J., sig., 105.
— Roger, inst., 288.
— T., sig., 112, 119, 126.
— W., sig., 105.
Halen, Rob., sig., 121.
Hales, Humphrey, Visitor for the South, 101.
— Ralph, dep., 289.
Halewell, R., sig., 105.
Hall, Hugh, sig., 258, 276.
— J., sig., 105; dep., 258, 276.
— R., dep., 229, 234.
— Roger, dep., 288.
— T., abs., 86; sig., 112.
Halman, T., abs., 86.
Halme, T., sig., 126.
Halsall, H., abs., 88.
— R., abs., 88.
Halse, R., rec. 180; dep., 258, 277.
Halstyd, G., sig., 112.
Halyday, Ch., sig., 126.
Hamden, T., dep., 228, 268.
Hamerson, ..., rec., in Hereford, 200.
Hamet, J., sig., 105.
Hammersley, T., sig., 126.
Hand, ..., H., sig., 154.
Hande, W., inst., 280.
Handcok, James, sig., 112.
— J., sig., 112; inst., 281.

Handcocke, T., sig., 126; inst., 276, 284; dep., 258, 284.
Hancoks, J., sig., 122.
Hanson, J., rec., 184; dep., 89, 226, 232, 258, 274.
Hanssard, G., inst., 285.
Hapwode, R., sig., 105.
Harall, W., sig., 122.
Harbarbard, R., sig., 122.
Harcoks, Edm., sig., 112.
Harcourt, ..., deprived, 227, 233, 258.
Harde, R., abs., 84.
Hare, Edm., sig., 154.
Harding, T., sig., 122; rec., 180; dep., 227, 223, 258, 284, 285.
— W., sig., 105.
Hardy, J., sig., 112.
Hardyman, J., inst., 273.
Hargatt, Edmund, dep., 228, 268.
Hargrave, Rob., sig., 117.
Hargravys, J., dep., 258, 274.
Harlam, J., sig., 112.
Harley, T., sig., 119.
Harman, E., dep., 258, 285.
— J., sig., 105.
Harper, ..., dep., 228, 268.
Harpham, T., sig., 126.
Harpsfeld, J., engaged in the public disputation, 32; abs., 95; imprisoned, 146; dep., 226, 232, 258, 277, 280, 281.
— Nicholas, abs., 95; imprisoned, 146; dep., 226, 232. 258, 273, 279.
Harrington, James, Visitor for the South, 97.
— R., inst., 280.
Harris, J., dep., 229, 234, 258.
— R., abs., 88.
— T., sig., 122.
— W. sig., 126.
Harrison, Ch., inst., 292.
— G., sig., 112.
— J., abs., 84, 87; sig., 112; dep., 258, 279.
— R., sig., 112.
— Rob., sig., 117.
— W., deputy for the Visitors, 80; restored, 89, 276; sig., 112, 155.
Hart, J., dep., 234, 268.
— R., rec., 81; restricted to bounds, 181; dep., 228.
— Reubens, inst., 281.
— T., inst., 286.
— W., abs., 84.
Hartburn, R., dep., 86, 258, 276.
Hartley, Bernard, sig., 112.
Harvey, Dr. H., Visitor for the North, 71, 72, 75, 77, 81.
— T., inst., 281; dep., 258, 281.
Harwar, Nich., sig., 126.

INDEX

Harward, W., sig., 105; inst., 275.
Harwood, W., sig., 105.
Haselhead, H., inst.. 273.
Hastings, H., Lord, Visitor for the South, 97.
— Bernard. sig., 122.
Hatkyns, W., sig., 154.
Hatton, Augustine, sig., 119.
— R., sig., 105, 122; dep., 290.
— Rob., sig., 105.
— W., dep., 291; inst., 291.
Havard, or Haward, T., dep., 161, 258, 268, 283; lurking in Hereford, 184, 200.
Haver, Oliver, dep., 258, 281.
Hawardyn, J., sig., 119.
Hawes, E., sig., 122.
— H., sig., 117.
— W., sig., 126.
Hawkar, H., sig., 105.
Hawkes. Chr., dep., 258, 273.
— Rob., sig., 105.
Hawkins, T., dep., 228, 268.
— W., inst., 288; dep., 288.
Hawson, J., abs., 88.
Hay, J., sig., 112.
Haycon, R., sig, 126.
Hayde, Hanmet, inst., 284.
Haynes, T., Commissioner for the North, 172.
Hayward, J., sig., 122.
— R., abs., 84.
Haywood, Gaspar, dep., 228, 229, 234, 268.
— Oliver, dep., 292.
Heath, Nicholas, Archbishop of York, opposes Supremacy Act, &c., 5, 8; resigns Chancellorship, 31; in the Parliament of 1559, 31; is deprived, 36, 226, 258, 286; imprisoned, 144; suspected of treason, 145; excommunicated, 190; restricted to bounds, 194; dies, 195.
Hede, J., sig., 112.
Hedlam, J., inst., 290.
Helds, J., sig., 126.
Hellyer, J., sig., 112.
Helme, J., abs., 88; dep., 291.
Heming, or Henning, J., dep., 227, 233. 268.
Hensham, H.. sig., 122.
Henshaw. H., rec., 185; dep., 227, 232, 258.
— Hugh, sig.. 119.
— J., inst., 276.
— W., sig.. 105.
Henson, Roger, sig., 122.
Hensworth, T., sig., 105.
Henton, W., sig., 105.
Hentyer, T., sig., 112.

Herde, J., sig., 126.
Hereford, Bishop of; *see* Scory, J.
— diocese, recusancy in, 157, 161, 162, 164, 199; visitation of, 161; records of, 237; deprivations and institutions in, 276, 290.
Heresy, how to be determined, 20.
Herling, E., abs., 84.
Herod, G., sig., 122.
Heron, Rob., inst., 290.
Hertford, H., E. of, Visitor for the South, 101.
Heskyns, T., dep., 227, 232, 258, 284.
Hethcott. W., sig., 126.
Hether, W., sig.. 122.
Hewett, Rob., sig., 112.
— T., sig., 126.
Heworthe, J., abs., 84.
Heyber, Oliver, sig., 112.
Heydock, T., sig.. 122.
Heydon, Sir Christopher, Visitor for the South, 94.
— E., dep., 291.
Heyly, Hugh, sig., 112.
Heylyn, Rob., sig., 122.
Heyton, J., sig., 122, 126.
— Ralph, sig., 112.
— W., sig.. 112.
Hiberden, Fras., dep., 258, 275.
Hill, Ch., dep., 290.
— H., sig., 112.
— J., sig., 105, 126.
— Ralph, sig., 117.
— R., sig., 105, 122, 126.
— Rob., rec., 182; dep., 227, 233, 258, 273, 285.
— Sir Rowland, ecclesiastical commissioner, 147.
— T., sig., 112. 126.
— W., abs., 88; sig., 105, 117.
Hillings, Giles, dep., 259, 271, 272.
— W., sig., 126.
Hilton, G., sig., 122.
— H., sig., 155.
— J., sig., 112; inst., 274.
Hinckersfield, W., dep., 292.
Hindmere. Reg., abs., 88.
Hobbey, T., Visitor for the South, 101.
Hobson, G., sig., 126.
Hocston, R., sig., 126.
Hodges, J., Registrar to the Northern Visitors, 74.
Hodgkins, T., inst., 279.
Hodgson, Hugh, abs., 87; dep., 136, 227, 259. 273.
— Owen, dep., 80, 226, 232, 258, 279.
— R., abs., 87.
— T., sig., 112.
Hodson, H., sig., 105.
— J., sig., 119.

Hodson, Roger, sig., 122.
Hoggyns, R., sig., 122.
Holborne, Rob., inst., 289.
Holden, T., dep., 292.
Holgate, Anthony, restored, 89, 287.
Holland, R., inst., 277.
— Rob., sig., 117.
— Seth, dep., 226, 231, 259, 271, 286.
— T., sig., 105.
Holloway, R., dep., 288.
Hollwey, J., sig., 112.
Hollynshed, R., sig., 122.
Holmes, W., abs., 84.
Holone, Edm., sig., 122.
— R., sig., 122.
Holt, Arlot, sig., 112.
— J., sig., 105.
Holtby, W., sig., 112.
Holwey, J., sig., 122.
Homilies, the reading of, 48, 56.
Hongon, Anthony, sig., 112.
Hooper, T., inst., 277.
Hopkyn, R., sig., 126.
Hopkyns, J., inst., 277.
— Stephen, rec., 183.
Hopkinson, E., sig., 105,
— T., abs., 84.
Hopper, J., sig., 105 ; dep., 259, 281.
Hopton, Avinus, Visitor for the South, 95.
Horleston, J., restored, 89.
Horne, Rob., Bishop of Winchester, Visitor for the South, 95 ; Cambridge Visitor, 132 ; Eton Visitor, 162 ; his letters quoted, 162, 163 ; tenders the Oath to Bonner, 195 ; instituted, 276, 285.
— W., sig., 119.
Hornbye, W., inst., 291.
Hornse, N., sig., 112.
Horsey, Peter, dep., 288.
Horsnayle, J., sig., 105.
Horton, Humphrey, sig., 122.
— T., inst., 276, 280.
Hortopp, Ralph, inst., 278.
Horwarms, W., sig., 126.
Horwood, J., sig., 119.
Hoskyn, T., sig., 105.
Hoskyns, . . . , rec., 184.
Hossert, W., sig., 112.
Houghton, Roger, sig., 122.
— W., abs., 84.
Houldam, W., sig., 112.
Houseman, J., sig., 105 ; inst., 284.
Hovell, J., sig., 112.
How, W., sig., 105.
Howard, T., Viscount, Visitor for the South, 98.
Howbyn, Laurence, sig., 122.
Howell, J., dep., 259, 283.

Howell, P., dep., 259, 272.
— W., sig., 117 ; inst., 283.
Howlett, Leon., dep., 290.
— T., inst., 291.
Howorthe, J., sig., 112.
Howse, Rob., sig., 112.
Howson, Fras., sig., 126.
Howys, J., sig., 122.
Huainson, Laurence, abs., 84.
Hubank, J., sig., 119.
Hubbard, P., sig., 112.
Hubert, Hugh., confessor, exiled, 226, 234.
Huddleston, T., dep., 89, 259, 287.
— W., sig., 126.
Hudson, E., sig., 126.
— H. (junr.), sig., 126.
— Hugh, dep., 259, 281.
— J., dep., 89, 259, 287.
— R., sig., 112.
— Rob., inst., 290.
— W., sig., 112.
Hughes, J., sig., 105.
— Maurice, dep., 259, 275.
— R., inst., 271.
Hughson, T., sig., 112.
Hull, T., sig., 112.
Hulley, T., sig., 122.
Hulme, R., sig., 126.
— Rob., sig., 122.
Humfrey, Elisha, sig., 126.
Hunt, R., inst., 278.
— T., sig., 112, 122.
Hunter, G., dep., 259, 279.
Huntingdon, . . . , inst., 274.
— Francis, E. of, Visitor for the South, 97.
— J., sig., 105 ; inst., 278.
— T., abs., 84.
Hurst, James, sig., 105.
Hussey, H., sig., 122.
Hutchyn, H., sig., 126.
Hutchinson, H., inst., 291.
— Hugh, dep., 259, 276.
— P., sig., 112.
— Rob., dep., 227, 233, 259, 271.
Hutton, M., inst., 280.
Huyck, Dr. T., Visitor for the South, 95 ; ecclesiastical commissioner, 147, 185.
Huyson, J., abs., 84.
Hybbots, T., dep., 259, 276.
Hycess, Edm., sig., 112.
Hyckman, Nich., sig., 126.
Hycks, James, sig., 105.
Hyde, David, dep., 233, 259.
— T., rec., 182 ; dep., 227, 234, 259, 279, 285.
— W., inst., 285.
Hygdon, Rob., sig., 122.
Hyggyns, J., sig., 122.

INDEX

Hylon, Humphrey, sig., 126.
Hymners, G., abs., 86.
Hynd, T., sig., 117.
Hyndehed, W., inst., 281.
Hyndmer, or Hyndmershe, Cuthbert, sig., 112; inst., 290.
Hynman, James, sig., 126.
Hynthton, H., sig., 126.
Hynton, J., dep., 292.
Hyron, J., inst., 275.

I.

Ide, W., sig., 112.
Ifel, J., sig., 119.
Igulden, J., inst., 275.
Images, reverence of, to be discouraged, 47, 58.
Imprisonment under the Religious Acts, 144-146, 150, 175-177, 185.
Indolen, G., dep., 259, 274.
Ingham, Rob., sig., 109.
Inglishe, J., inst., 275.
Inglott, Edm., sig., 112.
Ingram, J., dep., 233, 269.
'Injunctions,' the, of 1559, 43, 45, 46.
Inman, J., sig., 116.
— W., inst., 281.
Institutions, lists of. kept from early times, 236; after deprivations, 238; under Mary and Elizabeth, compared, 244-247.
Irby, Ambrose, sig., 112.
Isack, E., Visitor for the South, 101.
Iveson, T., dep., 229, 234, 268.

J.

Jackson, ..., dep., 228.
— Brian, abs., 84.
— E., sig., 112.
— J., abs., 84; sig., 112; dep., 89, 259, 287.
— Nich., inst., 286.
— Ralph, sig., 105.
— R., sig., 105.
Jaclyn, Rob., sig., 105.
Jacoby, R., dep., 228, 268.
Jagger, Francis, abs., 88.
Jake, J., abs., 84.
James, E., sig., 122.
— Rob., sig., 105.
— W., sig., 112; *see also* Edriche.
Jareake, W., sig., 126.
Jeffrison, T., rec., 79.
Jekler, Rob., sig., 112.
Jellow, Simon, sig., 112.
Jenkinson, W., sig., 105, 126.
Jennynges, ..., Vicar of Bingley, denies Royal Supremacy, 77.
Jennynges, T., sig., 105.
Jerves, W., sig., 105.
Jevans, David, sig., 119.
Jewell, J., Bishop of Salisbury, Visitor for the South, 99, 100; his letters quoted, 99, 100, 130, 145, 174; consecrated bishop, 157; inst., 284.
Jobber, W., sig., 122.
Johns, Geoffrey, sig., 105.
Johnson, ..., dep., 228.
— Edm., inst., 286.
— G., sig., 126.
— H., sig., 105; rec., 183; lurking in Hereford, 200; dep., 259, 286.
— James, abs., 84.
— Jonas, sig., 117.
— Ralph, sig., 119.
— R., inst., 281.
— Rob., dep., 233, 269.
— T., sig., 126.
— W., sig., 126.
Joliffe. H., dep., 226, 231, 259, 272, 286.
Joly, W., sig., 105.
Jolybrande, Nich., sig., 119.
Jone, ..., Cambridge Professor, ejected, 224.
Jones, ..., dep., 259, 268, 272.
— Geoffrey, dep., 259, 281.
— Griff., dep., 260, 283.
— Hugh, dep., 290.
— Morgan, inst., 284.
— P., inst., 272.
— Rob., dep., 228; inst., 284.
— Walter, Commissioner for the North, 172; sig., 105; inst., 278, 284.
— W., inst., 288.
Jonson, E., sig., 105.
— J., sig., 105.
Joseph, ..., dep., 228, 268.
Joye, Charles, sig., 112.
Jurden, E., sig., 122.
Jyer ..., J., sig., 117.

K.

Katty, J., sig., 105.
Keat, Raff, rec., 183.
Kellett, Hugh, abs., 88.
Kempe, D., sig., 105; inst., 280.
— J., sig., 113.
Kennes, Miles, sig., 127.
Kent, Rob., sig., 117; dep., 228, 289.
— T., inst., 277, 282.
Kerke. Hugh, inst., 278.
Kerrell, J., dep., 260, 272.
Ketill, R., sig., 106.
Keye, H., abs., 84
— R., sig., 122; dep., 260, 275.
Kiddall, Goddard, inst., 284; dep., 260, 284.
Kiffen, J., inst., 291.

King, Gregory, sig., 127.
— J., sig., 106.
— R., sig., 119.
— T., dep., 228, 260, 272, 288.
— W., inst., 276; dep., 289.
King's Bench cognizant of non-conformity, 188, 203, 205; of excommunications, 191, 211.
Kingman, T., inst., 272.
Kingsmill, R., Visitor for the North, 72; for the South, 101.
Kingeston, T., dep., 259, 280.
— W., sig., 127.
Kynsey, Rob., abs., 88.
Kirkebecke, J., abs., 87.
Kirkbie, Barth.. sig., 122.
Kirklye, Rob., sig., 113, 119.
Kyrkman, G., sig., 113.
Kirton, T., dep.. 228.
Kitchen, Antony, Bishop of Llandaff, opposes Supremacy Act., &c., 5, 8; takes the oath, 35.
— Ch., sig., 106.
Kneeling, regulations respecting, 62.
Knell, T., inst., 288.
Knight, Ch., inst., 290.
— J., dep., 228, 260, 273, 274
— Rob., sig., 127.
Knyppe, E., abs., 87.
Knyston, R., sig., 122.
Knollys, Edm., sig., 127.
- Sir Francis, Visitor for the South, 97; ecclesiastical commissioner, 147.
— T., sig., 113.
Knott, W., dep., 136, 229, 233.
Kyashe, T., sig., 127.
Kylbury, P., sig., 113.
Kymberleyns, Fras , sig., 122.
Kytson, R., inst., 274.

L.

Lache, R., sig., 113; dep., 260, 282.
Lacock, J., inst., 285.
Lacy, J., sig., 106.
Ladd, Rob., abs., 88.
Ladlowe, T., inst., 292.
Laifeld, E., inst., 280.
Laiken, J., dep., 277.
— T., sig., 155; Commissioner for the North, 172.
Lakynby, James, abs., 86.
Lakers, W., sig., 113.
Lambe, G., abs., 76, 88; dep., 260, 284.
— James, sig., 106.
— J., dep., 260, 278.
— T., sig., 113.
Lambert, J., sig., 127; inst., 272.
Lamson, James, sig., 113.
Lancashire, Rob., sig., 122.
— W., sig., 122.

Lancastell, *alias* Hewster, Roger, sig., 122.
Lancaster, Ambrose, sig., 119.
— Ch., inst., 274.
— J., inst., 271.
— T., inst., 284, 285.
Lane, G., abs., 84.
— J., sig., 122.
— Martin, sig., 122.
— Sir Rob., Visitor for the South, 97.
Lancham, G., sig., 122.
Langdale, Dr. A., engaged in the public disputation, 32; abs., 78; restricted to bounds, 182; dep., 226, 232, 260, 274, 275.
Langfellowe, R., abs., 88.
Langhorn, W., sig., 106.
Langland, J., dep., 260, 284.
Langley, J., sig., 113.
— T., inst., 285.
— W., inst., 288; dep., 288.
Langridge, Nicolas, dep., 228.
— Peter, dep., 227, 233, 269, 285.
Langton, Fras., sig., 122.
— P., sig., 113.
— Rob., sig., 127.
Lanman, J., sig., 113.
Lanmett, J., sig., 127.
Larch, T., sig., 122.
Lark, T., inst., 279.
Larvile, N., inst., 280.
Latham, Ch., sig., 117.
Latimer, W., restored, 89; inst., 282.
Latwicke, Alban, dep., 260, 285.
Launder, W., inst., 278.
Laverock, R., sig., 106; inst., 280.
Law, Owen, sig., 106.
— J., sig., 106.
Lawrence, Edm., sig., 106.
— Giles, inst., 284.
— J., dep., 260, 284.
— R., inst., 281.
Laws, Geoffrey, sig., 113.
Lawson, J., dep., 260, 273.
— W., sig., 106.
Laxe, James, sig., 127.
Lay, T., sig., 119.
Laynge, Dychard, sig., 127.
Laynning, T., sig., 113.
Leage, J., inst., 272.
Leaper, W., inst., 280.
Leasbie, T., sig., 127.
Leche, W., inst., 283.
Ledbury, . . . , rec., in Hereford, 200.
Ledem, G., sig., 106.
Leder, J., sig., 106, 117; dep., 260, 280.
— R., sig., 106.
Lee, G., sig., 122.
— W., abs., 88.
Leedes, . . . , Visitor of Canterbury, 160.

INDEX

Leedes, E., sig., 117; inst., 275.
Legewyn, W., sig., 113.
Legge, E., dep., 260, 278.
Legh, Edm., sig., 117.
— J., sig., 127.
Leghtoman, E., sig., 106.
Leicester, G., inst., 285.
— Oliver, abs., 84.
Leither, T., abs., 84.
Leke, J., sig., 106.
Leman, T., sig., 113.
Le Marynel, T., sig., 106.
Lemyng, T., abs., 88.
Lench, W., sig., 106.
Lenge, T., dep., 260, 272.
Lesley, W., inst., 288.
Leson, Anthony, sig., 122.
Letherland, H., sig., 127.
Lettock, J., excommunicated, 197.
Levagies, Launcelot, abs., 87.
Leveson, J., sig., 122.
Levir, Ralph, inst., 289.
— T., dep., 289.
Lewen, Gilbert, abs., 86.
Lewes, Ch., abs., 86.
— Owen, dep., 229, 234, 268.
— W., rec., 183.
Lewett, J., dep., 260, 275.
Leyborne, Gilbert, inst., 282.
— Rob., inst., 285.
Leyke, T., sig., 122.
— W., sig., 127.
Licensing of preachers, 49; printing. 61.
Like, T., sig., 122.
Lilly, G., dep., 233, 269.
Linchon, N., sig., 113.
Lincoln, Bishop of; see Watson, T., Bullingham, N.
— diocese, number of parishes, 98; records of, 237; deprivations and institutions in, 279.
Linsecum, W., inst., 278.
Litany, regulations concerning, 52.
Littlegrome, J., inst., 278.
Llandaff, Bishop of; see Kitchen, Anthony.
— diocese, records of, 237.
Lloyd, E., sig., 106.
— J., sig., 122.
— ap Jones, T., inst., 283.
Locke, Nicholas, sig., 113; inst., 282.
Lodge, Geoffrey, abs., 84.
Lofthouse, Adam, sig., 113; inst., 276; dep., 260, 276.
Lokett, J., sig., 113.
Lolly, R., sig., 106.
London, Bishop of; see Bonner, Edm.; Grindall, Edm.
— diocese, number of clergy in 1559,
96; deprivations and institutions in, 279, 290.
London, George, dep., 228, 268.
Long, G., sig., 117.
— Stephen, sig., 113.
Longford, J., sig., 122.
Longland, J., sig., 155; inst., 279.
Longleye, W., abs., 88.
Longworth, J., sig., 113.
— R., inst., 289.
Lord, Griffith, sig., 122.
— W., sig., 117.
Lougher, Rob., 289.
Louvain, recusants at, 193, 200.
Love, James, inst., 291.
— Philip, sig., 106.
— Rob., sig., 113.
Lovelace, R., inst., 283.
— W., Visitor for the South, 99, 100.
Lovell, J., dep., 260, 281.
Lovett, T., sig., 113, 127.
Lowe, Arthur, abs., 78, 88; dep., 260, 287.
Lucas, W., inst., 289.
Lucy, T., Visitor for the South, 97.
Ludby, R., dep., 227, 233, 268.
Luddington, T., abs., 84.
— J., sig., 117.
Lunde, J., inst., 279.
Lupton, T., sig., 113.
Luson, W., Preb. Hereford, supports recusants, 181.
Luter, Roger, sig., 122.
Lydyatt, T., sig., 122.
Lye, T., sig., 122.
Lyghtfoot, Humphrey, sig., 122.
Lymiter, P., inst., 273.
Lynch, W., sig., 106.
Lyne, Bartholomew, sig., 113.
Lyng, James, inst., 282.
Lyngarde, E., inst., 275.
— J., sig., 122.
Lynne, T., sig., 113.
Lyon, W., inst., 281; dep., 290.
Lysby, J., inst., 290.
Lyster, Edm., dep., 228, 268.
— J., abs., 84.
— Rob., sig., 113.
Lythall, ..., dep., 290.
Lytton, G., sig., 113.
Lyving, W., sig., 106; inst., 280, 290.

M.

Mably, R., sig., 113.
Mackbrey, J., sig., 106; inst., 289.
Machell, Philip, abs., 84.
Madford, E., sig., 122.
Maddock, Hugh, sig., 106; dep., 260, 281.
— Lewis, sig., 106.
— W., sig., 113.

INDEX

Madis, Gregory, sig., 113.
Mady, J., sig., 106
Magistrates empowered to enforce use of Prayer-book, 27; their powers under penal laws of 1563, 188, 199, 203.
Mainwaring, J., sig., 122.
— R., sig., 106, 155.
Maister, R., inst., 287.
— T., inst., 272.
Makyn, R., sig., 113.
— T., dep., 260, 275.
Malan, Patrick, sig., 106.
Malberye, J., abs., 84.
Malbon, Hamlet, sig., 119.
Malet, Fras., abs., 84.
— H., sig., 106, 155.
— J., Visitor for the South, 99.
Malevery, H., abs., 84.
Mandeville, T., dep., 268, 274.
Maneley, W., dep., 260.
Mann, G., sig., 106.
Mannell, H., sig., 113.
Manners, Rob., rec., 182; dep., 227, 233, 260.
Mansfield, J., sig., 127.
Manus, R., sig., 113.
— Rob., sig., 113.
Mappe, W., inst., 278.
Marcall, T., sig., 113.
Marc, H., sig., 117.
— Nicholas, sig., 122.
Margeson, Hugh, sig., 117.
Marke, R., sig., 113.
— Stephen, dep., 228, 268.
Markyk, J., sig., 106.
Markindale, T., abs., 84.
Marler, T., sig., 122.
Marley, Nicholas, rec., 79, 157; restricted to bounds, 181; dep., 227, 233, 260, 276.
— Stephen, rec., 79.
Marris, T., sig., 122.
Marrow, T., Visitor for the South, 97.
Marsden, J., sig., 106.
Marser, T., sig., 113.
Marshall, J., abs., 84; sig., 122, 127; dep., 136, 229, 233, 260.
— Randall, sig., 117.
— R., abs., 86; rec., 184; dep., 136, 260, 275, 280, 282; sig., 154.
— Rob., abs., 88.
— Roger, rec., 78, 179.
— T., inst., 289.
— W., abs., 84; inst., 280; sig., 106, 113, 117; dep., 227, 232, 260, 277.
Marson, Ch., sig., 127.
Marston, T., sig., 127.
Martin, . . . , dep., 228, 288.
— Gregory, sig., 113.

Martin, F., sig., 106; dep., 232, 269.
— W., sig., 106, 127.
Marton, R., dep., 269, 278.
Martyr, Peter, his work at Oxford, 130; letter to, 174.
Mary, Queen of Scots, plots in her favour hasten the Penal Laws, 187.
Mason, Anthony, sig., 117.
— G., sig., 106, 154.
— Sir J., Oxford Visitor, 130; sig., 106.
— T., sig., 113.
— W., sig., 106.
Mass, the doctrine of, in 1554 and 1559, 3.
Massenger, W., dep., 261, 280.
Master, D., Oxford Visitor, 130.
Mastroder, Edm., sig., 119.
Massy, Bernard, sig., 122.
— W., sig., 122.
Mateson, Ralph, sig., 122.
Mathe, W., sig., 113.
Mather, Dr. . . . , dep., 234, 268.
Mathew, J., sig., 127.
— Oliver, sig., 113.
— R., inst., 290.
Matthews, Dr. . . . , dep., 234, 268.
Matys, Rob., sig., 127.
Maund, T., sig., 113.
Mawdsley, T., inst., 275.
Mawen, N., abs., 86.
Maxon, H., sig., 106.
Maxwell, Anthony, abs., 84.
May, W., Cambridge Visitor, 132; ecclesiastical commissioner, 147; inst., 279; nominated Archbishop of York, 166.
Maydwell, J., sig., 113.
Maynman, J., sig., 127.
Meij, J., sig., 117.
Melton, Alan, sig., 113.
Mendons, Philip, sig., 119.
Menel, Sergeant, takes the oath, 168.
Menevar, . . . , rec., in Hereford, 200; dep., 228, 268.
Mere, . . . , dep., 261, 273.
Meredith, Jonas, dep., 233, 269; ordained abroad, 224.
Mericke, Edm., sig., 122.
— W., sig., 127.
Merman, J., sig., 113.
Merre, E., sig., 113.
Merriman, Ralph, sig., 106.
Merton, W., sig., 122.
Mervyn, Edm., dep., 226, 232, 261, 285.
Merycoke, . . . , sig., 113.
Metcalf, . . . , assists recusants, 184.
— G., sig., 127.
Meyhoe, T., sig., 119.

Meyrick, Roland, Bishop of Bangor; Visitor for the South, 101; consecrated, 156.
Michy, R., dep., 229, 234, 270.
Middleton, J., sig., 117, 127.
— Rob., abs., 84.
— T., sig., 127.
Mildmay, Sir Walter, Visitor for the South. 97.
Miller, J., sig., 122.
— N., sig., 113.
— W., sig., 106; inst., 288.
Miracles, reverence of, to be discouraged, 47.
Mitchell, Charles, sig., 119.
— G., inst., 292.
— J., sig., 119.
— T., dep., 289.
Mychellield, J., inst., 282.
Mody, W., sig., 113.
Mohunt, Reginald, Visitor for the South, 99.
Moke, T., sig., 106.
Molder, T., inst., 275.
Moley, R., sig., 113.
Mollyneux, Anthony, abs., 88.
Monnson, G., sig., 127.
Montacute, Lord, opposes Supremacy Act, &c , 5, 8; a recusant put in his care, 182.
Moore, T., dep., 291.
Moorefylde, T., dep., 261, 281.
More, Giles, sig., 106.
More. H., rec., 79.
— Miles, sig., 106.
— R., sig., 113.
— Rob., sig., 122.
— T., dep., 289.
— W., abs., 84; sig., 119, 122.
Morecrofte, Edm., inst., 277.
— E., abs., 88.
Morehall, J., sig., 122.
Moreton, J., sig., 123, 127.
Morgan, H., Bishop of St. David's, summoned to London, 37; dep., 261, 283.
— Philip, rec., 184.
Morland, Martin, inst., 284.
Morley, Lord, opposes Uniformity Act, 8.
— Geoffrey, abs., 78.
— Rob., sig., 113.
Morleys, David, sig., 119.
Morpeth, J., sig., 106.
Mortlake, Rob., sig., 106.
Morren, J., lurks in Cheshire, 184; dep., 3 note, 227, 261, 280.
Morris, . . . , sig., 119.
— Rees, dep., 261, 284.
— R., sig., 127.

Morris, Rob., sig., 123.
— W., sig., 117; abs., 84.
Moreson, T., sig., 119.
Morton, Nicholas, dep., 227, 229, 233, 268.
— Rob., sig., 113.
— W., Surrogate for the Visitors. 81.
Mortyboyes, T., inst., 290.
Morweyn, P., inst., 275.
Moscley, W., inst., 284.
Mosse, W., dep., 136, 232, 261.
Motte, Rob., sig., 127.
Mountague, T., sig., 106; inst., 284.
Mountain, E., Visitor for the South, 97.
Moutrye, James, Lord, Visitor for the South, 98.
Mower, T., sig., 123.
Mownforth, T., sig., 127.
Mowre, Rob., sig., 122.
Mowse, W., abs., 76.
Moyle, W., dep., 261, 280.
Mugge, Walter, dep., 161, 227, 261, 277; restricted to bounds, 181; lurking in Hereford, 200.
Mullins, J., inst., 280.
Mundye, W., sig., 106.
Murake, Rob., sig., 113.
Murffett, W., sig., 106.
Murrey, J., abs., 87.
— Lancelot, abs., 87.
Music in churches, 60.
Myle, Hamlet, sig., 127.
Mynteyng, R., sig., 127.

N.

Nappe, Simon, sig., 118.
Neale, J., dep., 131, 232, 270.
— T., dep., 234.
— W., sig., 106.
Nedham, J., sig., 123.
Neham, W., sig., 113.
Nelson, Rob., abs., 88.
Neto, Hugh, sig., 106.
Nettelt, T., sig., 106.
Nevard, W., sig., 106.
Neve, Marmaduke, sig., 118.
Nevell, Edm., sig., 106.
Nevill, G., abs., 87.
— Sir H., Visitor for the South, 98.
— Sir T., Visitor for the South, 97.
Nevinson, Dr. Stephen, Visitor for the South, 97; of Canterbury, 160; inst., 291.
Newby, Anthoney, sig., 127.
Newhouse, W., inst., 281; dep., 290.
Newsome, J., abs., 84.
Newton, Francis, inst., 272, 286.
— Ralph, sig., 113; inst., 277.

Newton, Sampson, inst., 272.
Neytol, J., sig., 106.
Nicholas, H., sig., 113.
Nichols, J., sig., 123.
— Nicholas, inst., 290.
— R., sig., 123.
— Simon, sig., 113.
Nicolson, James, abs., 87.
— R., dep., 234, 268.
Noble, J., dep., 233, 261.
Nicson, T., sig., 123.
Norfolk, T., Duke of, Visitor for the South, 94, 95.
Norfolk, J., abs., 84.
— W., rec., 184; dep., 261, 286.
Norley, T., inst., 286.
Norman, H., dep., 261, 285.
— Rob., inst., 275.
— W., sig., 123.
Normavell, J., abs., 84.
Norreys, James, inst., 281.
— Rob., sig., 127.
Norryson, James, sig., 106.
North, E., Lord, opposes Uniformity Act, 8; Visitor for the South, 94, 95.
Northampton, W., Marquis of, Visitor for the South, 97.
Northends, R., sig., 127.
Northoll, T., inst., 288.
Northumberland, T., Earl of, Visitor for the North, 71, 72.
Norton, Baldwin, rec., 184; dep., 261, 281, 287.
— Sir George, Visitor for the South, 99.
— J., sig., 113.
Norwich diocese, number of clergy in 1559, 96; deprivations and institutions in, 281, 290.
Norwood, Rob., sig., 119.
Nott, Rob., sig., 127.
— W., dep., 268.
Nottingham, proceedings of the Visitors at, 74.
Nowell, Alex., Visitor for the South, 97, 101; Visitor for Oxford, 130; Visitor of Canterbury, 160; inst., 273, 280.
— Laur., inst., 274, 275.
— Rob., Visitor for the South, 101.
Nowelly, J., sig., 113.
Nowglass, J., sig., 106.
Nudde, Rob., sig., 113.
Nutcombe, T., 227, 261, 277, 289.
Nuttall, Ch., sig., 113.
— T., sig., 106.
Nutte, W., abs., 84.
Nutthide, Rob., abs., 87.
Nyells, Rob., sig., 113.

O.

Oath of Supremacy, from whom required, 14–16, 39, 40, 188–9, 207; its form, 15, 45, 77; tendered to the Bishops, 33; tendered to the Magistrates, &c., 35, 170; official explanation of, 62; not pressed at Oxford, 131; powers of the Ecclesiastical Commissioners, 142, 153, 157; the Northern commission, 167, 172; tendered to the laity, 169, 170, 188, 189, 201; feigned subscriptions, 198.
Obell, T., sig., 119.
Obrey, J., sig., 127.
Ocley, Roger, sig., 113.
Ofspryng, G., sig., 127.
Ogle, T., abs., 86.
Oglethorpe, Owen, Bishop of Carlisle; opposes Supremacy Act, &c., 5, 8; at the Coronation, 30; his recognizances taken, 32; is fined, 33; is deprived, 35, 225, 261, 273, 274; dies, 38.
Okam; see Raky.
Okeley, R., sig., 123.
Olde, W., sig., 123.
Oldman, J., sig., 127.
Oliver, J., abs., 88; dep., 228, 268.
Ollerton, W., sig., 123.
Olverley, J., sig., 127.
Ordinations, number of Archbishop Parker's, 242.
Ornaments, Church, orders regarding, 28, 54, 59.
Orpe, T., sig., 123.
Orrell, W., sig., 127.
Orvyce, J., inst., 290.
Osborn, W., sig., 119.
Osome, Rob., sig., 106.
Oswald, rec., in Hereford, 200.
Othye, E., abs., 84.
Otford, Rob., abs., 84.
Otley, Roger, sig., 123.
Oton, J., abs., 84.
Ottwaye, G., dep., 261, 280.
— Rob., sig., 123.
Otwell, W., sig., 106.
Overton, James, sig., 127.
— J., inst., 292.
— W., inst., 274, 285.
Owen, David, abs., 84.
Owgan, J., dep., 290.
Owsley, W., sig., 119.
Oxford, J., Earl of, Visitor for the South, 94, 95.
Oxford diocese, number of parishes, 98; visitation of, 1561, 161; deprivations and institutions in, 282, 291.
Oxford University endorses the five

articles, 1559, 3; Visitation of, 130, 163; opposed to reform, 130.
Oxford, M.; *see* Farmer.

P.

P..., R. (*sic*), sig., 123.
Pacher, R., sig., 113.
Pachet, Rob., sig., 113.
Packard, T., dep., 261, 274, 275.
Padye, David, inst., 280.
Page, J., sig., 113.
Pagett, T., sig., 127.
Painter, Rob., sig., 114.
Painter, W., sig., 114; inst., 273.
Palfrey, R., inst., 278.
Palles, Sir Hugh, Visitor for the South, 101.
Palmer, Ambrose, sig., 113.
— Catherine, abbess, dep., 226, 235.
— George, dep., 234, 261, 284, 286.
— H., inst., 281.
— R., sig., 123.
— T., sig., 114; inst., 291; dep., 136, 228, 232, 261, 289.
Palmes, G., rec., 78; proceedings against, 197; dep., 227.
Papal Supremacy, doctrine of, in 1559, 3; to be preached against, 47; penalties for holding, 188.
Papists; *see* Recusants.
Papenry, Hugh, sig., 127.
Parfay, J., rec., 184; dep., 261, 278, 283.
Parishe, Geoffrey, inst., 282.
Parke, H., sig., 114.
— J., sig., 127; inst., 291.
Parker, Charles, dep., 229, 234, 268.
— J., sig., 106.
— Matthew, Archbishop of Canterbury; archbishop-elect, 38; Cambridge Visitor, 132; consecrated archbishop, 156; his activity, 160; Eton Visitor, 162; scrupulous of enforcing penalties, 192; his ordinations, 242.
— N., sig., 114.
— Ralph, sig., 123.
— Rob., sig., 106.
— T., sig., 106, 127.
Parkers, Ch., sig., 106.
Parkhurst, J., Bishop of Norwich; Letter from, 175.
Parkynson, T., sig., 118.
Parr, R., abs., 88.
— Rob., sig., 106.
Parratt, E., dep., 261.
Parry, H., Visitor for the South, 99, 100; inst., 271, 284, 285.
— J., sig., 118.

Parry, Sir Thomas, Visitor for the South, 94; Oxford Visitor, 130.
Parrys, Rob., inst., 275.
— T., sig., 106.
Parson, Rob., sig., 118.
Parul, J., dep., 234.
Passe, R., dep., 86.
Passefont, T., sig., 114.
Paternoster, Rob., sig., 114.
Pate, R., Bishop of Worcester; opposes Supremacy Act, &c., 5, 8; is deprived, 35, 225, 261, 286; imprisoned, 144, 145; dies, 222.
Pates, R., Visitor for the South, 101.
— Rob., dep., 89, 276.
Patteson, J., sig., 114.
Paul, J., dep., 229, 234, 270.
Payne, Rob., dep., 228, 262.
Peacock, R., inst., 281.
— Rob., Commissioner for the North, 172.
— T., dep., 136, 227, 232, 262, 277; sig., 114.
Pearce, Edm., dep., 262, 284.
— J., inst., 292.
Peerson, And., inst., 273.
— E., sig., 107.
— H., sig., 127.
— J., abs., 84.
— Rob., sig., 114.
Pechen, Lambert, sig., 107.
Pecke, J., sig., 114.
Pedder, J., inst., 286.
— Meleus, sig., 114.
Peell, Rob., sig., 114.
Pell, W., sig., 127.
Pembroke, W., E. of, Visitor for the South, 98.
Penal enforcement of Liturgical enactments, 3, 8, 23-27; of Supremacy Act, 15-18 (*see also* Imprisonment); penal laws of 1563, 186.
Pendlebury, P., sig., 123.
Pendleton, H., dep., 234.
— W., sig., 123.
Penford, T., inst., 286.
Penn, W., sig., 123.
Pennel, W., sig., 107.
Pennigar, Michael, inst., 285.
Penyngton, G., sig., 127.
Penny, T., inst., 280.
Pentland, T., inst., 276.
Pepper, Roger, sig., 114.
Percy, Alan, abs., 84; sig., 114.
— Sir Henry, Visitor for the North, 71, 72; Commissioner for the North, 167.
— James, inst., 273.
— T., Registrar to the Northern Visitors, 74, 75, 77.

Periton, J., dep., 228, 268.
Perkyn, W., sig., 123.
Pernby, T., sig., 118.
Perne, Andrew, sig., 118.
Perpointe, W., abs., 84.
Perseval, James, sig., 123.
— J., sig., 127.
— Rob., dep., 88, 89, 226, 232, 262, 274, 287.
Perstell, T., sig., 123.
Perye, J., dep., 262, 285.
Peryn, J., dep., 262, 277.
— W., dep., 235.
Pese, W., sig., 123.
Peter, R.; *see* Porter, R.
Peterborough diocese, Visitation of, 1560, 159; deprivations and institutions in, 282, 291.
Peterson, Rob., abs., 86.
Petrose. W., dep., 262.
Peverill, J., inst., 288.
Pharkson, T., sig., 114.
Pheron, Rob., sig., 107.
Philip V does not assist the Catholics, 37.
Phillip, Ralph, abs., 88; inst., 282.
Phillips, Geoffrey, inst., 281.
— J., dep., 262, 283.
— Morgan, Bp. of St. David's; absent from Parliament, 1559, 31; dep., 37, 227, 232, 262, 277, 283.
— T., inst., 289.
Phillis, Rob., inst., 290.
Philpot, J., inst., 281; dep., 290.
Pickard, W., abs., 85.
Pickering. Ralph, dep., 262, 276.
Picto, Rob., sig., 114.
Pile, J., dep., 228, 268.
Pilkington, James, Bishop of Durham; preaches for the Visitors, 75, *note*; Cambridge Visitor, 132; consecrated bishop, 166; Commissioner for the North, 167; his letters to Cecil, 168; inst., 276, 280.
— Leon., inst., 289.
Pinner, James, sig., 107.
Pirrey, E., abs., 88.
Pius, Henry, dep., 228, 268.
Place, R., abs., 87.
Plandon, Andrew, sig., 118.
Plante, Rob., abs., 88.
Plompton. R., inst., 272.
Plumtree, T., dep., 229, 234, 268.
Pockeson, J., abs., 88.
Poisegate, J., abs., 85.
Pokyse, J., sig., 107.
Pole, or Poole, D., Bishop of Peterborough; abs. from Parliament, 1559, 31; summoned to London, 37; dep., 38, 144, 226, 262, 282; restricted to London, 145, 179, 196; dies, 196.
Pole, Rob., inst., 287.
Pollard, Sir J., Visitor for the South, 99.
— W., sig., 127.
Polson, J., sig., 107.
Pomrel, W., dep., 229, 234, 262.
Ponder, Roger, sig., 107.
Pope, appeals to, under Supremacy Act, 21-2; his designs against England, 198, *note*².
Pope, W., sig., 119.
Porder, R., inst., 290.
Port, R., sig., 123.
Porter, J., sig., 107; rec., 182; inst., 282; dep., 262, 273.
— R., dep., 226, 232, 262, 279.
— W., abs., 87; sig., 123.
Pory, J., inst., 277.
Pott, Sir J., Visitor for the South, 101.
— J., sig., 114.
— Philip, sig., 127.
Potts, J., dep., 229, 233, 235, 262.
Powell, David, dep., 227, 233, 268.
— Roger, sig., 114.
— T., sig., 114; Visitor of Gloucester, 159.
— W., sig., 119; *see also* Ap. Powell.
Powes, W., sig., 123.
Powlye, J., inst., 281.
Powtrell, T., sig., 127.
Poxleye, E., sig., 107.
Poyntz, R., dep., 233, 262.
Pratt, J., inst., 271, 284.
— R., sig., 114; dep., 228, 262.
Prayer-book; its revision, 2 (*see also* Uniformity Act); Magistrates to enforce its usage, 9 *and note*, 26-7; reluctance to use, 82, *note*¹; accepted generally in 1560, 164.
Preachers, licensing of, 49, 135; for the Visitors, 75, 95.
Preaching; *see* Sermons.
Precy, J., dep., 262, 284.
Presberi, H., sig., 127.
Prester, T., sig., 114.
Prestland, P., abs., 88.
Preston, ..., choirmaster, dep., 230.
— J., sig., 127.
— R., sig., 107; inst., 281.
— Roger, sig., 127.
— T., abs., 85; sig., 123.
Price, H., abs., 85.
— J., dep., 262.
— Lewis, sig., 119, 154.
Primer, Edward VI's, to be used, 58.
Printing forbidden except by licence, 61.
Processions in church abolished, 52.
Proctor, James, sig., 155; inst., 292.

INDEX

Proctor, J., sig., 114.
— Rob., sig., 118.
Prod, W., sig., 123.
Prowett, Stephen, sig., 114.
Public worship, enforced attendance at, 26.
Pullay, H., sig., 127.
Pulleyn, J., inst., 280; dep., 292.
— Marmaduke, restored, 89, 287.
— W., dep., 262, 287, 290.
Pulpits to be placed in churches, 55.
Punder, T., sig., 114.
Purkin, W., abs., 85.
Pursglove, Rob., rec., 78; restricted to bounds, 179; dep., 262, 284, 287.
Purzaunt, J., sig., 107.
Pychyll, J., sig., 127.
Pye, T., sig., 114.
Pyks, T., sig., 114.
Pynder, Edm., sig., 107.
Pytts, J., sig., 115.

Q.

Quemerford, Nich., dep., 229, 234, 262.

R.

Raben, Matthew, sig., 114.
Raby, Radaud, sig., 114.
Radoss, Ralph, sig., 123.
Raignold, J., abs., 85.
Raky, *alias* Okam, Miles, sig., 114.
Rame, Ch., inst., 280.
Ramridge, J., imprisoned, 146; dep., 226, 231, 262, 275; restricted to bounds, 181.
Ramsey, ..., dep., 228.
— R., dep., 262, 278.
— *alias* Slatter, W., dep., 263, 272.
Rand, Rob., sig., 154.
Randal, J., sig., 114.
— Rob., dep., 290.
Randolf, Rob., sig., 114.
Ranys, J., abs., 86.
Rastall, J., rec., 180; dep., 228, 233; 263; writes, 243.
Ratcliffe, Geoffrey, sig., 127.
— J., abs., 87.
Ratlyns, Ch., sig., 127.
Ravis, W., sig., 123.
Ravyn, G., sig., 127.
Rawdon, J., sig., 107.
Rawlyn, J., sig., 107.
Rawlins, W., sig., 107.
Rawson, W., inst., 277.
Raymond, Mich., dep., 263, 278.
Rayne, G., abs., 86.
Rayner, Ch., abs., 85.

Rayner, R., inst., 291.
— T., dep., 263.
Reader, T., inst., 287.
Reaz, Laurence, sig., 107.
Recusants, given every opportunity to sign, 77, 96, 143; restricted to certain bounds, 176; list of, 179; feeling of the country against, 187; the Penal laws of 1563, 186; proceedings against, 197; harboured in the country, 80 *note*, 168, 184, 196, 200.
Redfern, Anthony, sig., 107.
Redford, Aemerus, sig., 118.
Redinge, H., inst., 278.
Redman, J., dep., 89, 263, 274.
— T., dep., 136, 227, 232, 263; restricted to bounds, 181.
Redshaw, J., dep., 228, 268.
— Rob., abs., 88.
Redworth, R., dep., 263, 285.
Redwycke, J., sig., 114.
Reed, J., sig., 114.
— R., dep., 228, 263.
— T., sig., 114; inst., 281.
Reginald, H., inst., 281.
Registers, parish, regulations concerning, 50.
Reley, E., inst., 277, 278, 289.
Relff, J., sig., 118.
Relics, reverence of, to be discouraged, 47.
Remyngton, W., sig., 127.
Renerl, J., sig., 114.
Restley, W., dep., 289.
Reve, Edm., inst., 282.
— J., dep., 263, 278.
Reynolds, G., dep., 290.
— Rob., dep., 263, 279, 285.
— T., dep., 136, 222, 226, 263, 277.
Rich, Lord, opposes Uniformity Act, 8.
— W., sig., 107.
Richard, P., sig., 119.
Richards, Rob., dep., 263, 272.
Richardson, Adam, inst., 281; sig., 107.
— J., abs., 85; sig., 107, 114; inst., 274.
— R., sig., 127.
— Rob., sig., 107.
— W., sig., 123.
Rieters, G., sig., 114.
Ridinges, T., dep., 291.
Ridley, Launcelot, inst., 277.
Ringrose, Rob., abs., 85.
Riverney, T., abs., 87.
Rix, W., sig., 114.
Roberts, G., dep., 226, 232, 271.
— R., inst., 285.
Robertson, T., rec., 79, 184 (here called *Robinson*), dep., 226, 263, 276.

Robyns, Humphrey, sig., 123.
Robinson, Abraham, abs., 85.
— E., sig., 127.
— G., abs., 86; sig., 107.
— James, sig., 114.
— J., abs., 87, 88; sig., 114, 118; dep., 263, 276.
— Lancelot, sig., 114.
— T., inst., 292.
Robinsonnes, R., sig., 127.
Robson, J., sig., 107.
— R., sig., 107.
— T., sig., 107.
Rochester, Bishop of; see Guest, Edm.
— diocese, Visitation of, 1560, 160; deprivations and institutions in, 283, 291.
Rochester, E., sig., 114.
Rod, W., sig, 114, 127.
Roderaon, R., sig., 123.
Rodlay, J., sig., 119.
Rods, T., sig., 127.
Roger, Laurence, sig., 123.
— R., sig., 107.
Rogers, J., inst., 278.
— Nich., inst., 292.
— Rob., inst., 274.
Rogerson, T., sig., 107, 114.
Rogges, Francis, sig., 114.
Rok, T., sig., 114.
Rokeby, John, Commissioner for the North, 172.
— W., abs., 85.
Rokesby, J., Member of the Council for the North, 77.
Rollie, Rob., inst., 276.
Rood, H., sig., 123.
Roper, H., abs., 88.
Rothewell, James, sig., 107.
— W., sig., 119.
Rotliff, T. sig., 107.
Rouley, W., sig., 123.
Rowbe, J., sig., 123.
Rowe, Rob., sig., 107.
Rowghton, W., sig., 114.
Rowlinge, Arthur, abs., 85.
Ruckwode, T., sig., 114.
Rudd, J., abs, 85; restored, 89; sig., 114; inst., 276.
Rughsyche, Humphrey, sig., 107.
Rumpell, Otto, dep., 290.
Runce, R., sig., 114.
Rushbroke, W., sig., 107.
Rushton, G., sig., 114.
— R., sig., 123.
Russell, J., sig., 123.
— Laurance, sig., 114.
— R., sig., 114; inst., 283.
— Sir T., Visitor for the South, 101.
— Walter, rec., 183.

Russell, W., inst., 273.
Rust, E., sig., 114; inst., 281.
— W., sig., 107.
Ruston, Rob., sig., 114.
Rutland, H., E. of, Visitor for the South, 97; Commissioner for the North, 167.
Rydavure, W., sig., 123.
Ryddysdall, J., sig., 107.
Ryder, T., sig., 123.
Rydyngs, T., sig., 114.
Ryley, E., sig., 107.
— H., inst., 286.
— T., sig., 107.
Rynger, H., sig., 114.
Rypham, Rob., sig., 127.

S.

Sacheverell, J., assists recusants, 184; imprisoned, 184, 185.
Sackforde, T., ecclesiastical commissioner, 147.
Sackville, Sir R., Visitor for the South, 101.
Sadler, J., sig., 107, 123.
— Sir Ralph, Visitor for the South, 94.
— T., sig., 114.
Sadleyer, H., sig., 119.
Saint, Nicholas, sig., 128.
St. Asaph, Bishop of; see Davies, R.; Goldwell, T.
— diocese, Visitation of, 1560, 159; records of, 237; deprivations and institutions in, 283.
Saintbarbe, Giles, dep., 263, 272.
St. David's, Bishop of; see Morgan, H.; Young, T.
— diocese, Visitation of, 1560, 159; deprivations and institutions in, 283, 291.
St. John, J., Lord, Visitor for the South, 98.
— Oliver, Lord, Visitor for the South, 97.
St. Leger, Sir J., Visitor for the South, 98, 100.
Sale, W., sig., 123.
Salebanke, W., sig., 114.
Salisbury, Bishop of; see Jewell, J.
— Cathedral visited by Dr. Cottrell, 159.
— diocese, Visitation of, 1560, 159; records of, 237; deprivations and institutions in, 284, 292.
Salisbury, J., sig., 127; inst., 271, 281.
— R., inst., 281.
Salheld, Lancelot, sig., 80; dep., 263, 273.
Salle, Arthur, inst., 284.
Salter, W., sig., 114.

INDEX

Saltunstall, Gilbert, sig., 114.
Salvyn, Anthony, rec., 79, 157; restricted to bounds, 182; dep., 227, 233, 263, 277.
— J., Visitor for the South, 95.
— R., rec., 79; dep., 263, 287.
Sampson, T., inst., 276.
Samuell, W., sig., 155.
Sanders, Nicolas, his account of the deprived clergy, 219, 225; his history, 219; dep., 229, 234, 263.
Sandford, Brian, sig., 123.
— Ch., abs., 85.
Sandys, Edwin, Bishop of Worcester; Visitor for the South, 71, 72, 75-77, 81; restored, 89, 274; consecrated bishop, 156, 286.
— E., inst., 289.
Sankey, J., sig., 114.
Sapcote, W., sig., 127.
Sare, J., abs., 86.
Satten, Rob., sig., 123.
Saunders, H., rec., 183.
Saunderson, T., sig., 107.
— W., sig., 127.
Savage, G., sig., 127.
— J., sig., 128.
Savyer, Ralph, inst., 284.
Sawar, R., sig., 128.
Sawdill, J., sig., 128.
Sawe, Nicholas, inst., 285.
Sawle, Arthur, inst., 272.
Saxey, W., abs., 76; inst., 280.
Say, Rob., sig., 107.
Scales, J., abs., 87.
Scambler, Edm., Bishop of Peterborough, preaches for the Visitors, 75, note; surrogate for them, 81; inst., 282, 286.
Scargyll, Francis, sig., 118.
Scarthe, Francis, inst., 287.
Schepey, Hugh, sig., 123.
— R., sig., 128.
Scherar, R., sig., 123.
Scholfelde, Rob., inst., 291.
Schore, R., dep., 288.
Scorbrugg, J., sig., 114.
Scory, J., Bishop of Hereford, confirmed, 156; his projected visitation, 158, 161; his letters quoted, 161.
Scotch priests take low wages, 201.
Scott, Alan, sig., 119.
— Cuthbert, Bishop of Chester; opposes Supremacy Act, &c., 5, 8; in the Parliament of 1559, 31; is entangled in the public disputation, 32, 33; is dep., 35, 226, 263, 274, 287; imprisoned, 144, 185; escapes, 192; is restricted to bounds, 192; escapes to Belgium, 193; dies, 193, 222.

Scott, J., sig., 114.
— T., inst., 281; dep., 233, 263.
Scanton, Rob., sig., 114.
Searle, T., sig., 114.
Seaton, John, rec., 78; restricted to bounds, 181; dep., 227, 234, 263, 275, 287.
— W., sig., 115.
Sebastian, . . . , choirmaster, dep., 230.
Securys, H., inst., 284.
— T., dep., 263, 285.
Sedge, Dr. . . . , dep., 229, 234, 268.
Sedgwick, T., dep., 79, 234, 264, 276; restricted to bounds, 179.
Seele, W., sig., 123.
Selbye, Oliver, abs., 86.
Sell, Leon, abs., 88.
Seller, James, abs., 88.
Selvin, J., sig., 114.
Seman, Rob., sig., 114.
— T., sig., 114.
Senden, W., dep., 263, 275.
Sergeant, J., dep., 263, 285.
— T., sig., 115.
Serlbye, T., dep., 290.
Sermons, regulations concerning, 47.
Sewell, J., sig., 115; dep., 263, 282.
— R., preaches for the Visitors, 75 note; abs., 85.
— W., sig., 128.
Seyllank, Hugh, sig., 128.
Seymour, Sir H., Visitor for the South, 101; assists Bishop Horne, 163.
— J., abs., 86; sig., 107.
Shakylton, T., sig., 115.
Shalfild, Rob., abs., 87.
Sharp, Edm., sig., 119.
— F., inst., 275.
— Rob., sig., 115.
Sharrocke, T., inst., 291.
Shaw, H., abs., 85; dep., 233, 270; ordained abroad, 224; sig., 128.
— J., sig., 119.
— Ralph, sig., 123.
— Rob., sig., 115; rec., 183; dep., 263, 278, 286.
— Thurstan, inst., 290.
Shears, Giles, inst., 284.
Sheffield, Lord, opposes the Uniformity Act, 8.
— T., sig., 118.
Sheldon, Hugh, sig., 123.
— J., sig., 123.
— W., Visitor for the South, 101.
Shelley, Sir R., Prior, dep., 226, 233, 235, 270.
Shelton, Geoffrey, sig., 123.
Shelmerdine, Rob., rec., 183; dep., 286.
Sheppard, Adam, inst., 276.
— James, sig., 115.

Sheppard, J., inst., 288.
— Nicholas, inst., 286.
— T., sig., 123.
— W., abs., 86; sig., 107; dep., 228, 268.
Sheprey, W., dep., 233, 264.
Sherar, R., inst., 278.
Sherard, A., sig., 123.
— T., sig., 123.
Sherbroke, Cuthbert, sig., 115.
Sherburn, J., sig., 107.
Sheriff, Rob., dep., 290.
Sherman, J., sig., 115.
— T., sig., 123.
Shrygley, W., sig , 123.
Sherwyn, Rob., sig., 123.
Shevyn, Ralph, sig., 119.
Shew, R., sig., 107.
Shipman, T., abs., 85.
Shirm, J., sig., 107.
Shorthouse, Ch., inst., 279.
Shrewsbury, Francis, Earl of, opposes Supremacy Act, &c., 5, 8 ; Visitor for the North, 71, 72.
Shute, Rob., sig., 154.
Sidney, Philip, inst., 291.
Sifton, W., sig., 115.
Silles, Peter, abs., 85.
Silvester, Nicholas, sig., 123.
— T., sig., 107.
— W., dep., 264, 286.
Simmerley, G., sig., 128.
Simony, penalties for, 56.
Simpson, Ch., abs., 88.
— George, rec., 180.
— J., abs., 85 ; sig., 108, 115, 128; inst., 290.
— Marband, sig., 108.
— M., sig., 108.
— Pat, sig., 128.
— T., sig., 108, 128 ; inst., 280.
Singleton, T., abs., 88 ; sig., 115.
Skarlett, J., sig , 115.
Skelton, J , sig., 115.
— W., abs., 85.
Skenthrist, David de, dep., 228.
Skinner, J., Registrar to Ecclesiastical Commission, 140, 151.
— J., dep., 292.
— Ralf, inst., 276.
— R., inst., 285.
Skoyle, J., sig., 115.
Skydmore, J., supports recusants, 181.
Skypp, R., sig., 115.
Skypwith, Roger, sig., 128.
Slany, R., sig., 123.
— T., dep., 264, 273.
Slater, James, sig., 114.
— W., sig., 123.
Slatter, W ; see Ramsey, W.
Slynger, Geoffrey, sig., 119.

Slithurst, T., dep., 136, 227, 232, 264, 286.
Smart, J., dep., 264, 277.
Smethe, R., sig., 115.
Smeythman, T., sig., 128.
Smith, Alexander, sig., 107.
— Ch., sig., 115.
— Edm., sig., 128.
— E., sig., 128.
— F., sig., 128.
— Fras., sig., 128.
— G., sig., 118.
— H., sig., 115, 128 ; inst., 289.
— J., sig., 107, 115, 128 ; inst., 277, 290 ; dep., 132, 136, 232, 264, 274.
— Nicholas, sig., 115 ; inst., 286.
— R., sig., 107, 123, 128 ; dep., 136, 227, 234, 264, 282.
Smyth, R., Dr. of Medicine, 229.
— Rob., sig., 107, 115.
— Sir T., Prayer-book conferences at his house, 2 ; Visitor for the South, 94 ; Oxford Visitor, 130 ; ecclesiastical commissioner, 147 ; inst., 273.
— T., abs., 87, 88; sig., 123, 128 ; inst., 283, 287.
— W., sig., 107, 118, 123 ; dep., 228, 269, 288, 292.
Smythson, W., abs., 85 ; sig., 128.
Snape, R., sig., 123.
Snarpon, T., dep., 264, 272 ; inst., 272.
Snell, R., abs., 76.
Snowdon, W., sig., 123.
Snowe, Nicholas, sig., 123.
Snytall, R., abs., 85.
Sodor, Bishop of, abs., 88, 251 *note.*
Somerset, T., imprisoned, 185.
Sommer, H., inst., 271.
Soorye, W., restored, 89, 274.
Soresby, J., inst., 275.
Sotheran, H., sig., 115.
Soto, his work at Oxford, 130.
Southcote, J., ecclesiastical commissioner, 147.
Southcrue, Simon, dep., 264, 278.
Southwarmborough, P. de, dep., 228.
Southwell Minster, deprivations and institutions, 284.
Southwell, T., sig., 115.
Sowdley, J., sig., 107.
Sowre, Ellis, sig., 128.
Sowthill, H., abs., 85.
Spackman, Tristram, dep., 264, 285.
Spaggott, G., inst., 272.
Sparke, T., abs., 86.
Speght, James, sig., 118.
Spells, . . . , sig., 115.
Spenser, David, inst., 274.
— Milo, sig., 115.
— R., sig., 119, 128.

Sprotte, Rob., sig., 107.
Spurgyn, Rob., sig., 115.
Spynk, J., sig., 115.
Squyer, J., sig., 107.
— R., sig., 107.
— W., dep., 264, 272.
Stacy, J., sig., 115.
Stafford, Leon., abs., 85.
Stalinge, Rob., abs., 85.
Stampe, E., abs., 85.
Stanbancke, J., sig., 107.
— W., sig., 123.
Stanclyff, P., sig., 115.
Standen, Nich., dep., 290.
Standish, J., sig., 128; dep., 264, 280.
— Thurstan, sig., 119.
Standley, M., inst., 285.
Stanely, T., abs., 85.
Stanley, H., sig., 115.
— James, sig., 115; dep., 264, 282.
— J., sig., 118, 123.
— T., abs., 88, 251 *note*.
Stapleton, R., abs., 85; sig., 115.
— Rob., sig., 115.
— T., dep., 136, 227, 229, 233, 264, 274.
Starker, Emericus, sig., 115.
Stather, J., inst., 280.
Staworthe, J., sig., 107.
Stayns, E., sig., 107.
Steile, Humphrey, inst., 289.
Stele, T., sig., 123.
Stemple, T., sig., 154.
Stene, W., sig., 107.
Stenett, N., sig., 118.
Sterne, Edm., sig., 115.
Stethe, E., sig., 118.
Stetten, H., sig., 123.
Stevens, H., dep., 289.
Stevyns, Rob., sig., 115.
Stevensone, James, sig., 123.
— J., sig., 128; dep., 264, 275.
— Martin, abs., 85.
— R., inst., 279.
— W., abs., 86.
Steward, Edm., dep., 226, 231, 264, 275, 285.
— J., inst., 273.
Steuardson, P., sig., 115.
Sthone, T., sig., 119.
Stocker, W., sig., 128.
Stocks, Alexander, sig., 108.
— Nicholas, sig., 128.
Stokes, J., sig., 115; Commissioner for the North, 172; inst., 286.
— Rob., sig., 108.
Stokton, Rob., sig., 108.
Stomeinge, J., dep., 264, 285.
Stone, L., sig., 108.
Stopes, Leon., rec., 224; dep., 228, 233, 264.

Stopes, Rob., dep., 264, 280, 282.
Store, W., sig., 108.
Storer, Anthony, sig., 115.
Storey, G., dep., 228, 269.
— J., proceedings against, 197; dep., 229, 232, 270.
— T., sig., 128.
Stratford; *see* Cratford.
Stretham, Edm., sig., 108.
Stringer, W., abs., 88.
Stronghenkin, T., inst., 283.
Strype's authorities for the numbers deprived, 217, 222.
Stubbes, Edm., abs., 85.
Sturge, Gilbert, sig., 128.
Stynton, Reuben, sig., 123.
Suddall, H., abs., 88; sig., 108, 155.
Sugden, Christopher, restored, 89, 287; sig., 128.
Summerscale, R., dep., 89, 264, 287.
Sunday, observance of, 53.
Superstition rife in the S.W. of England, 1559, 99.
Supremacy Act, the (*see also* 'Assurance of Supremacy Act'), 4-7; its various titles, 4, 6; its provisions, 7; text of, 9; records of proceedings under, 34; is liberally interpreted, 43.
Susanne, W., sig., 115.
Sutton, Rob. sig., 123.
— W., proceedings against, 197; dep., 228, 264.
Swadell, Tristram, sig., 108; restricted to bounds, 183; dep., 264, 280, 281.
Swane, T., abs., 85.
— W., sig., 108.
Swayne, R., abs., 88.
Swetlad, T., sig., 128.
Swettonham, Randolf, sig., 123.
— T., sig., 123.
Swycar, J., sig., 115.
Swyft, Nicholas, sig., 154.
Swynscoe, J., dep., 292.
Sye, J., inst., 287.
Symes, J., rec., 185; dep., 264, 272.
Symnell, R., sig., 108; dep., 264, 280.
Symon, W., sig., 123.
Symond, T., sig., 108.
Symonds, H, sig., 115; dep., 264, 281.
— James, sig., 107.
Symons, R., dep., 288.

T.

Tailboys, W., sig., 154.
Tailfurth, J., sig., 124.
Talbot, W., sig., 108.
Talybut, H., sig., 115.
Tarlleton, Rob., sig., 124.

Tarver, Edm., dep., 265, 275.
Taskworth, J., sig., 118.
Tassell, Geoffrey, sig., 115.
Tassye, T., abs., 88.
Tatem, Ch., sig., 108.
Taverham, J., inst., 284.
Taversham, J., dep., 89, 265, 287.
Taw, Edm., sig., 108.
Taylor, E., dep., 228, 269.
— G., abs., 85 ; restored, 89, 287; sig., 128.
— H., sig., 128.
— Hugh, sig., 108.
— J., sig., 115, 128.
— Lancelot, dep., 292.
— N., sig., 115.
— R., sig., 108, 115, 128; dep., 226, 265, 281.
— Rob., dep., 265, 275.
— Roger, dep., 265, 282.
— T., sig., 115; inst., 278.
— Tristram, dep., 265, 272.
— W., abs., 85 ; sig., 118, 124; dep., 136, 227, 232, 265, 284, 286, 287; is abroad, 184.
Teachers to be duly qualified, 59.
Teesdale, Marmaduke, abs., 85.
— Rob., abs., 86.
Tempest, Rob., dep., 234, 270.
Tempol, Ralph, sig., 124.
Tenant, Hugh, dep., 228, 269.
— R., sig., 128.
— Stephen, dep., 234, 269 note[1].
Tenett, R., inst., 290.
Teyrre, Ralph, sig., 108.
Thackham, T., inst., 287.
Thæpe, W., sig., 128.
Thaxter, Rob., sig., 115.
Thembylthorp, Edm., sig., 115.
Thewles, W., Master of Durham School, 79; restricted to bounds, 180.
Thimelby, Sir R., Visitor for the South, 97.
Thirkell, R., sig., 128.
Thirkylby, Simon, sig., 128.
Thyrketyll, Rob., sig., 115.
Thirland, T., sig., 154.
Thirlby, T., Bishop of Ely ; opposes the Uniformity Act, 8; in the Parliament of 1559, 31 ; dep., 36, 225, 265, 277; imprisoned, 144; suspected of treason, 145; excommunicated, 190 ; restricted to bounds, 194, 195 ; dies, 195.
Thomas, J., sig., 108.
— Walter, sig., 108.
Thomlinson, Roger, abs., 88.
Thompson, E., sig., 108, 128.
— J., sig., 155 ; dep., 292.
— R., sig., 108 ; abs., 85.

Thompson, Rob., sig., 108, 115; abs., 87; dep., 265, 273.
— Roger, rec., 180 ; dep., 228.
— T., abs., 86 ; sig., 128.
Thorn, ..., choirmaster, dep., 230.
Thorneys, T., sig., 128.
Thornley, J., abs., 85.
Thorneton, H., sig., 115.
— J., dep., 89, 280, 287.
— W., inst., 290.
Thorpe, T., sig., 128.
— W., sig., 115 ; inst., 283.
Threadare, Ch., dep., 290.
Threlket, Roland, abs., 87.
Throder, Ch., sig., 115.
Throgmorton, J., Visitor for the South, 101.
Thurbane, W., dep., 265.
Thurguy, Rob., sig., 118.
Thurland, E., abs., 85.
— T., abs., 85.
Thurlow, J., sig., 115.
Thurman, Rob., sig., 128.
Thurston, G., sig., 115.
— W., sig., 115.
Thynne, Sir J., Visitor for the South, 99.
Thyrlyng, N., sig., 115.
Thystylthwayte, Cyprian, sig., 108.
Thwaites, E., sig., 116.
— J., abs., 85.
Tie, Ch., sig., 118.
— T., dep., 291.
Tierncy, ..., his work criticised, 131, 224; his account of numbers deprived, 223.
Tithes, payment of, 51.
Tobman, W., abs., 88.
Todd, Nicholas, sig., 124.
— W., sig., 128 ; inst., 282 ; dep., 289.
Tofte, W., sig., 108.
Toller, J., sig., 115.
Tomlynson, W., inst., 286.
Toppam, Anthony, sig., 108; inst., 287; dep., 290.
Torleton, W., sig., 124.
Tott, J., sig., 124.
Touneys, T., sig., 120.
Towneley, W., sig., 120.
Townrawe, W., sig., 128.
Towreson, W., abs., 88.
Towson, R., abs., 87.
Towton, J., rec., 79 ; dep., 227, 265, 276.
Toyler, J., sig., 128.
Traybonne, Hugh, inst., 285.
Treman, J., inst., 291.
Tremayne, R., inst., 274, 277.
Trencham, T., inst., 275.

INDEX

Tresham, W., dep., 132, 136, 227, 233, 265, 274, 279, 282.
Trowell, Rob., sig., 108.
Trowtbecke, E., abs., 86.
Trygarny, Griffin, sig., 118.
Tryket, Stephen, sig., 115.
Trylenter, H., sig., 124.
Tuefeld, Emery, sig., 154.
Tuddenham, J., sig., 115.
Tudman, H., sig., 115.
Tugnye, W., sig., 115, 116.
Tukyson, Hugh, sig., 124.
Tull, J., sig., 108.
Tunstall, Cuthbert, Bishop of Durham; absent from Parliament of 1559, 31, 37; summoned to London, 37; commissioned to consecrate new primate, 37; dep., 38, 225, 265, 276; dies, 38.
— J., abs., 88.
Turberville, James, Bishop of Exeter; opposes Supremacy Act, &c., 5, 8; dep., 37, 226, 265, 277; imprisoned, 144; released, and restricted to bounds, 194; dies, 195.
Turck, J., inst., 285.
Turnbull, W., dep., 286.
Turner, Edm., sig., 124.
— E., sig., 108; dep., 290.
— Geoffrey, sig., 116.
— G., sig., 124.
— J., sig., 124.
— Rob., abs., 85.
— W., sig., 118; inst., 271.
Tute, ..., dep., 233.
Tuttley, J., inst., 277.
Tuttyn, J.; *see* Towton, J.
Twenge, Rob., abs., 85.
Twentyman, T., abs., 87.
Twynne, R., inst., 291.
Twysse, T., sig., 124.
Tyckerydal, E., inst., 275.
Tylar, Hugh, sig., 120.
Tylestan, Thrustan, inst., 276.
Tyleard, J., sig., 118.
Tylney, Hugh, sig., 116.
— J., sig., 108, 118.
Tyndall, Edmund, abs., 85.
— Humphrey, sig., 128.
Tyrer, Edmund, sig., 128.
Tyrril *v.* Chetwood and Woodhall, 21.
Tyrwhitt, Sir Rob., Visitor for the South, 97.
Tyson, J., sig., 128.

U.

Ufton, T., sig., 128.
Umfrey, Edm., sig., 118.
— Elizeus, dep., 89, 265, 287.
Underhill, J., sig., 124.

Underward, J., sig., 108.
Underwood, J., sig., 116.
— R., sig., 116.
— T., sig., 124.
Uniformity Act, the, 7; its various titles, 8; its provisions, 8; text of, 22; proceedings under, 160, 163, 165, *et seq.*
Universities, the (*see also* Cambridge *and* Oxford), Visitation of, 44, 130.
Urlkar, Roger, sig., 116.
Urtaye, Rob., sig., 116.
Ustler, Ch., abs., 85.
Uttley, W., sig., 116.
Uxton, Rob., sig., 116.

V.

Valle, P., sig., 108.
Vane, or Vannes, Peter, abs., 78, 87.
Vaser, Rob., inst., 285.
Vassy, Massacre of, its effect in England, 174.
Valence, T., dep., 265, 274.
Valentine, W., dep., 265, 282.
Vaughan, ..., inst., 283.
— J., Commissioner for the North, 172.
— R., sig., 154.
Vaux, Cuthbert, dep., 228, 234, 265.
— Laurence, rec., 181; dep., 227, 235, 265; put to death, 221.
Vaux, R., dep., 234.
Vavasour, T., abs., 85; Dr. of Medicine, 229.
Venie, Roger, dep., 289.
Veron, J., inst., 279, 280.
Vicarary, J., sig., 116.
Villa Garcia, J. de, at Oxford, 131; dep., 136.
Villiers, T., dep., 227, 233, 265.
Visitation, the Metropolitical, 1560-1, 156.
— Royal, arrangements for, 41; the scheme founded on that of 1 Edw. VI, 42; articles of inquiry, 65; Visitation of the Northern Province, 71; method of procedure, 73; duties of the Visitors, 73, 90-92; letters patent appointing the Visitors, 89; proceedings of the Southern Visitors, 94; of the Universities, 44, 130; writ for the Cambridge Visitation, 133; duties of the Visitors, 134; conclusion of visitation, 141.
Vollkyll, W., sig., 116.
Vyncent, T., sig., 116.

W.

Wade, J., sig., 120.
Wadforthe, J., abs., 88.

Waikefyld, Ralph, sig., 128.
— Stephen, sig., 124.
Wainwrighte, Ch., abs., 88.
Waistnes, W., inst., 292.
Waite, R., sig., 124.
Waker, Edm., sig., 124.
Waklyn, J., sig., 108.
— W., dep., 265, 285; inst., 285.
Walkenden, T., inst., 275.
— W., sig., 124; inst., 282.
Walker, E., sig., 120.
— James, sig., 124.
— J., abs., 88; sig., 116; dep., 289.
— P., sig., 108; dep., 265, 281.
— R., abs., 85, 88; sig., 108, 124; dep., 291.
— Roger, abs., 85.
— T., sig., 124.
— W., sig., 124.
Walkwyd, J., sig., 128.
Walkys, R., sig., 124.
Walldon, T., sig., 116.
Wallett, J., sig., 116.
Walley, Rob., dep., 234, 269.
Wallrond, Rob., sig., 116.
Walsingham, J., sig., 116.
Walter, R., sig., 124.
Walton, J., sig., 124.
— Rob., sig., 116.
— W., sig., 124.
Wamoke, James, sig., 116.
Waoter, Edm., sig., 116.
Warbar, T., sig., 108.
Warbreton, Andrew, dep., 265, 286.
Ward, J., sig., 124.
— R., abs., 88; sig., 124, 128.
— W., sig., 116, 118, 128.
Wardman, H., sig., 116.
Warner, J., sig., 120; inst., 285.
Warren, Gilbert, sig., 116.
Warren, J., abs., 78.
Warret, R., inst., 278.
Warton, R., sig., 124.
Warwake, J., inst., 285.
— T., inst., 282.
Washington, T., dep., 85, 265, 287; sig., 128; inst., 289.
— W., sig., 124.
Waterdale, Adr., inst., 273.
Watling, J., sig., 116.
Watmough, E., sig., 128 (*and see* Whatmo).
Watson, J., abs., 86; sig., 108, 116, 120, 128; inst., 279, 285.
— Michael, sig., 155.
— Ralph, sig., 109.
— R., sig., 120.
— Rob., sig., 124, 128.
— Dr. Roger, deputy for the Visitors, 81; inst., 276.

Watson, T., Bishop of Lincoln, the first bishop to suffer, 30; not in Parliament of 1559, 31; entangled in the public disputation, 32; dep., 226, 265, 279; released from prison, 36; imprisoned, 144, 145, 193, 196; restricted to bounds, 194, 196; his death, 144, 196.
— T., abs., 85; sig., 116.
— W., abs., 86; Commissioner for the North, 172.
Watts, Peter, sig., 116.
— T., inst., 280.
Waynehouse, J., abs., 85.
Weale, J., sig., 108.
Webbe, Aristotle, inst., 275; dep., 292.
— G., sig., 124.
— Laurence, dep., 228, 234, 265.
— Nich., sig., 124.
— T., sig., 120; inst., 284.
Webster, E., sig., 128.
— R., sig., 116, 118.
— Rob., sig., 116, 128.
— T., sig., 128.
Weddysburghe, Rob., sig., 124.
Weedon, Nicholas, dep., 234, 270.
Weke, W., inst., 285.
Wellche, J., sig., 128.
Wells, J., sig., 108; inst., 275.
— Peter, dep., 291.
Welshaw, H., sig., 124.
Welltham, P., sig., 108.
Wemnouthe, Nich., inst., 281.
Wendlocke, R., sig., 124.
Wendy, T., Cambridge Visitor, 132.
Wentworth, T., Lord, Visitor for the South, 94.
Wering, Humphrey, sig., 124.
Werynton, J., sig., 124.
West, Edm., sig., 128.
— E., inst., 274.
— Leonard, sig., 124.
— R., sig., 155.
Westcrope, Ralph, abs., 85.
Westmills, J., sig., 128.
Westminster, Abbot of; *see* Feckenham, J.
Weston, Edm., inst., 274.
— Rob., Visitor for the South, 101; ecclesiastical commissioner, 147; visits Coventry and Lichfield, 159.
Wetherall, W., abs., 85.
Wethestall, Gilbert, sig., 128.
Wetwot, Othivell, sig., 118.
Wever, R., sig., 124.
Wharton, Lord, opposes Uniformity Act, 8.
— Percival, restored, 89.
Whatmo, Hugh, sig., 128 (*and see* Watmough).
Wheatley, James, abs., 85.

Whelpdarnell, J., sig., 128.
Whettell, Rob., inst., 283.
Whitbroch, W., sig., 108.
Whytbee, T., restored, 89; sig., 116.
White, Gabriel, sig., 154.
— J., Bishop of Winchester; opposes Supremacy Act, 5; entangled in public disputation, 32; released from prison, 36; dies, 38; is deprived, 225, 229, 234, 265, 285.
— J., sig., 116; inst., 281, 290; dep., 269.
— R., dep., 229, 233, 266.
— T., sig., 108, 118; dep., 266, 281.
— W., sig., 108.
Whitehead, David, Oxford Visitor, 130.
— W., dep., 79.
Whytcheare, J., 266, 285.
Whithorne, G., inst., 286.
Whiting, J., sig., 108.
Whitlock, R., sig., 128.
Whitley, R., dep., 266, 275.
Whyteyn, Ralph, sig., 108, 129.
Whyttynton, J., sig., 116.
Whytwell, J., sig., 116.
Whorwood, R., sig., 124.
Wiclife, Anthony, abs., 84.
Widdowson, W., sig., 108.
Wielde, R., sig., 124.
Wiggs, W., dep., 233, 270; ordained abroad, 224.
Wightman, J., sig., 124.
Wilcocks, R., sig., 129.
Wild, Edm., sig., 124.
Wyldblod, J., sig., 124.
Wyldman, Geoffrey, sig., 109.
Wyldy, Rory, sig., 124.
Wilkinson, Anthony, sig., 116; dep., 228, 269.
— Ch., sig., 124.
— Rob., sig., 116.
— T., sig., 118.
Willan, Rob., inst., 289.
Willens, T., sig., 116.
Willantan, or Willerton, R., rec., 95; dep., 227, 233, 266, 279, 280.
Wyllanton, T., rec., 179.
William, or Gunter, J., inst., 292.
Williams, Griffin, inst., 271.
— J., Lord, Visitor for the South, 101.
— J., sig., 129.
— or Goldsmith, Rob., inst., 277.
— Roger, sig., 116.
Williamson, E., sig., 116; dep., 228, 234.
— G., sig., 78.
Willis, J., sig., 116.
Willoughby, W., Lord, Visitor for the South, 97.
— Baptist, inst., 281.

Willoughby, J., sig., 116.
Wills, or Wells, W., sig., 128; dep., 227, 229, 233, 266.
Wilsha, H., inst., 275.
Wilson, Ch., sig., 116.
— G., sig., 124; inst., 281.
— H., sig., 116.
— Humphrey, sig., 116.
— J., sig., 116, 129; dep., 266, 275; inst., 292.
— R., sig., 124.
— T., abs., 85; sig., 108, 116, 124; dep., 227, 233, 266, 287; inst., 286.
— W., sig., 129.
Wilton, J., dep., 266, 281; inst., 280.
Winchester, Bishop of; see White, J.
— diocese, Visitation of, 162, 163; records of, 237; deprivations and institutions in, 285, 292.
— W., Marquis of, opposes Uniformity Act, 8; Visitor for the South, 100.
Winck, W., rec., 182.
Windham, Sir Edm., Visitor for the South, 94.
— Edm., or W., dep., 229, 234, 269.
— or Windon, Ralph, dep., 233, 266.
Windsor, Miles, dep., 233, 266, 270.
Wingfield, R., dep., 266, 281; inst., 281.
— Rob., Visitor for the South, 97.
Wisdom, Rob., restored, 89, 277, 287.
Wist, R., dep., 228, 269.
Witte, Roger, sig., 129.
Wolff, Edm., sig., 120.
Wollaston, H., sig., 124.
Wollverston, Edm., 129.
Womocke, W., inst., 290.
Wond, T., sig., 129.
Wood, . . ., rec., 77.
— J., dep., 288.
— Marmaduke, sig., 109.
— Matthew, abs., 88; sig., 116.
— R., abs., 85; dep., 234, 269.
— T., imprisoned, 146, 185; bishop elect, 222; dep., 228, 266, 273, 280; inst., 280.
— W., sig., 154; dep., 228, 266, 275; inst., 282.
Wooddall, H., abs., 88.
Woddye, J., abs., 88.
Woodfall, R., inst., 288.
Wodeharne, Rob., inst., 289.
Woodhouse, J., sig., 129.
— Rob., inst., 276.
— Sir W., Visitor for the South, 94.
Woodley, W., sig., 109.
Woodlock, R., dep., 228, 269.
Woodroff, Thurstan, sig., 124.
— W., inst., 272.
Woodthorpe, J., sig., 108.

Woodyard, W., sig., 116.
Woollen, R., sig., 109.
Worcester, Bishop of; *see* Pate, R.; Sandys, Edw.
— diocese, Visitation of, 1561, 161; recusancy in, 199; records of, 237; deprivations and institutions in, 286.
Wormmall, E., abs., 85.
Worsley, R., Visitor for the South, 101.
Worth, J., inst., 281.
Worthynton, E., sig., 109.
Wotton, T., Visitor for the South, 101.
Wrexhay, W., sig., 124.
Wright, Arthur, sig., 109.
— J., sig., 124, 129; dep., 233, 270.
— R., sig., 129; inst., 274.
— T., abs., 85; sig., 129.
— Walter, sig., 155; inst., 285.
— W., sig., 109; dep., 136, 232, 266; inst., 288.
Wrightson, J., sig., 118.
Wrigley, . . ., rec., 77.
— Ralph, sig., 124.
Wroth, Sir T., Visitor for the South, 94.
Wroughton, Sir W., Visitor for the South, 99.
Wybram, W., abs., 88.
Wyckham, T., sig., 116.
Wyclyn, W., sig., 124.
Wydd, J., sig., 124.
Wydder, W., sig., 120.
Wyley, P., sig., 109.
Wyllat, Ralph, sig., 120.
— Walter, sig., 116.
Wyncopp, Rob., sig., 116.
Wynder, James, sig., 116.
Wyneslowe, Ralph, abs., 88.
Wyngrene, Edm., abs., 85.
Wyngseans, R., sig., 116.
Wynne, J., sig., 124.
Wynschent, Alexander, sig., 109.
Wythin, Cuthbert, sig., 129.
— R., inst., 292.
Wytwyll, J., sig., 124.

Y.

Yale, David, inst., 283.
— T., Visitor of Peterborough, &c., 159, 160; inst., 275.
— W., inst., 282.
Yarrowe, Miles, abs., 85.
Yate, Alexander, sig., 109.
— J., sig., 120.
— Laurence, sig., 120.
Yates, J., dep., 89, 266, 273.
Yatts, *see* Gaytes.
Yaxle, Ch., inst., 288.
Yaxley, T., dep., 266, 281.
Yelverton, Laurence, inst., 282.
Ylkins, . . ., abs., 88.
Ylston, T., sig., 129.
Yonge, Hugh, sig., 109.
— J., sig., 129; dep., 136, 227, 232, 266, 277.
— Rob., rec., 183; sig., 129.
— T., Bishop of St. David's, and Archbishop of York; Visitor for the South, 101; instituted, 283, 286.
— T., sig., 120.
Yonger, Humphrey, sig., 116.
— J., sig., 116.
Yoppe, Nicholas, sig., 124.
York, Archbishop of; *see* Heath, N.; Yonge, T.
— diocese, livings vacant in 1559, 82 *note*[2]; recusancy in, 199; records of, 237; deprivations and institutions in, 286, 292; want of clergy in, 239 *note*[2].
Yorkshire, the oath shirked in, 169, 170.
Yoyle, Francis, sig., 116.

Z.

Zone, W., dep., 229, 234, 266.
Zouche, George, Lord, Visitor for the South, 97, 98.
Zulley, H., inst., 280.

THE END.

OXFORD
PRINTED AT THE CLARENDON PRESS
BY HORACE HART, M.A.
PRINTER TO THE UNIVERSITY

SELECT LIST
OF
Standard Theological Works
PRINTED AT
THE CLARENDON PRESS, OXFORD.

THE HOLY SCRIPTURES, ETC.	page 1
FATHERS OF THE CHURCH, ETC.	,, 4
ECCLESIASTICAL HISTORY, ETC.	,, 5
ENGLISH THEOLOGY	,, 6
LITURGIOLOGY	,,

1. THE HOLY SCRIPTURES, ETC.

HEBREW, etc. *Notes on the Text of the Book of Genesis.* By G. J. Spurrell, M.A. *Second Edition.* Crown 8vo. 12s. 6d.

—— *Notes on the Hebrew Text of the Books of Samuel.* By S. R. Driver, D.D. 8vo. 14s.

—— *Treatise on the use of the Tenses in Hebrew.* By S. R. Driver, D.D. *Third Edition.* Crown 8vo. 7s. 6d.

—— *The Psalms in Hebrew without points.* Stiff covers, 2s.

—— *A Commentary on the Book of Proverbs.* Attributed to Abraham Ibn Ezra. Edited from a MS. in the Bodleian Library by S. R. Driver, D.D. Crown 8vo, paper covers, 3s. 6d.

—— *Ecclesiasticus* (xxxix. 15–xlix. 11). The Original Hebrew, with Early Versions and English Translation, &c. Edited by A. E. Cowley, M.A., and Ad. Neubauer, M.A. 4to. 10s. 6d. net.

—— —— Translated from the Original Hebrew, with a Facsimile. Crown 8vo, stiff covers, 2s. 6d.

—— *The Book of Tobit.* A Chaldee Text, from a unique MS. in the Bodleian Library; with other Rabbinical Texts, English Translations, and the Itala. Edited by Ad. Neubauer, M.A. Crown 8vo. 6s.

—— *A Hebrew and English Lexicon of the Old Testament*, with an Appendix containing the Biblical Aramaic, based on the Thesaurus and Lexicon of Gesenius, by Francis Brown, D.D., S. R. Driver, D.D., and C. A. Briggs, D.D. Parts I–VI. Small 4to. 2s. 6d. each.

—— *Hebrew Accentuation of Psalms, Proverbs, and Job.* By William Wickes, D.D. 8vo. 5s.

—— *Hebrew Prose Accentuation.* By the same Author. 8vo. 10s. 6d.

—— *The Book of Hebrew Roots*, by Abu 'l-Walîd Marwân ibn Janâh, otherwise called Rabbi Yônâh. Now first edited, with an appendix, by Ad. Neubauer. 4to. 2l. 7s. 6d.

ETHIOPIC. *The Book of Enoch.* Translated from Dillmann's Ethiopic Text emended and revised, and edited by R. H. Charles, M.A. 8vo. 16s.

Oxford: Clarendon Press. London: HENRY FROWDE, Amen Corner, E.C.

GREEK. *A Concordance to the Septuagint and the other Greek Versions of the Old Testament, including the Apocryphal Books.* By the late Edwin Hatch, M.A., and H. A. Redpath, M.A. In six Parts, imperial 4to, 21s. each.

—— *Essays in Biblical Greek.* By Edwin Hatch, M.A., D.D. 8vo. 10s. 6d.

—— *Origenis Hexaplorum quae supersunt; sive, Veterum Interpretum Graecorum in totum Vetus Testamentum Fragmenta.* Edidit Fridericus Field, A.M. 2 vols. 4to. 5l. 5s.

—— NEW TESTAMENT. *Novum Testamentum Graece.* Antiquissimorum Codicum Textus in ordine parallelo dispositi. Accedit collatio Codicis Sinaitici. Edidit E. H. Hansell, S.T.B. Tomi III. 8vo. 24s.

—— *Novum Testamentum Graece.* Accedunt parallela S. Scripturae loca, etc. Edidit Carolus Lloyd, S.T.P.R. 18mo. 3s.

On writing paper, with wide margin, 7s. 6d.

—— *Appendices ad Novum Testamentum Stephanicum,* jam inde a Millii temporibus Oxoniensium manibus tritum; curante Gulmo. Sanday, A.M., S.T.P., LL.D. I. Collatio textus Westcottio-Hortiani (jure permisso) cum textu Stephanico anni MDL. II. Delectus lectionum notatu dignissimarum. III. Lectiones quaedam ex codicibus versionum Memphiticae Armeniacae Aethiopicae fusius illustratae. Extra fcap. 8vo, cloth. 3s. 6d.

—— *Novum Testamentum Graece juxta Exemplar Millianum.* 18mo. 2s. 6d. On writing paper, with wide margin, 7s. 6d.

—— *The Greek Testament,* with the Readings adopted by the Revisers of the Authorised Version, and Marginal References:—

(1) 8vo. *Second Edition.* 10s. 6d.
(2) Fcap. 8vo. *New Edition.* 4s. 6d.
(3) The same, on writing paper, with wide margin, 15s.

—— *The Parallel New Testament,* Greek and English; being the Authorised Version, 1611; the Revised Version, 1881; and the Greek Text followed in the Revised Version. 8vo. 12s. 6d.

—— *Outlines of Textual Criticism applied to the New Testament.* By C. E. Hammond, M.A. *Fifth Edition.* Crown 8vo. 4s. 6d.

—— *A Greek Testament Primer.* An Easy Grammar and Reading Book for the use of Students beginning Greek. By E. Miller, M.A. *Second Edition.* Extra fcap. 8vo, 2s.; cloth, 3s. 6d.

LATIN. *Libri Psalmorum Versio antiqua Latina, cum Paraphrasi Anglo-Saxonica.* Edidit B. Thorpe, F.A.S. 8vo. 10s. 6d.

—— *Old-Latin Biblical Texts:* No. I. The Gospel according to St. Matthew, from the St. Germain MS. (g_1). Edited with Introduction and Appendices by John Wordsworth, D.D. Small 4to, stiff covers, 6s.

—— *Old-Latin Biblical Texts:* No. II. Portions of the Gospels according to St. Mark and St. Matthew, from the Bobbio MS. (k), &c. Edited by John Wordsworth, D.D., W. Sanday, M.A., D.D., and H. J. White, M.A. Small 4to, stiff covers, 21s.

—— *Old-Latin Biblical Texts:* No. III. The Four Gospels, from the Munich MS. (q), now numbered Lat. 6224 in the Royal Library

Oxford: Clarendon Press.

at Munich. With a Fragment from St. John in the Hof-Bibliothek at Vienna (Cod. Lat. 502). Edited, with the aid of Tischendorf's transcript under the direction of the Bishop of Salisbury), by H. J. White, M.A. Small 4to, stiff covers, 12s. 6d.

Nouum Testamentum Domini Nostri Iesu Christi Latine, secundum Editionem S. Hieronymi. Ad Codicum Manuscriptorum fidem recensuit Iohannes Wordsworth, S.T.P., Episcopus Sarisburiensis. In operis societatem adsumto Henrico Iuliano White, A.M. 4to.

    Fasc. I. *Euangelium secundum Matthaeum.* 12s. 6d.
    Fasc. II. *Euangelium secundum Marcum.* 7s. 6d.
    Fasc. III. *Euangelium secundum Lucam.* 12s. 6d.
    Fasc. IV. *Euangelium secundum Iohannem.* 10s. 6d.

OLD-FRENCH. *Libri Psalmorum Versio antiqua Gallica e Cod. ms. in Bibl. Bodleiana adservato, una cum Versione Metrica aliisque Monumentis pervetustis.* Nunc primum descripsit et edidit Franciscus Michel, Phil. Doc. 8vo. 10s. 6d.

ENGLISH. *The Books of Job, Psalms, Proverbs, Ecclesiastes, and the Song of Solomon. According to the Wycliffite Version of Hereford and Purvey.* With Introduction and Glossary by W. W. Skeat, Litt.D. 3s. 6d.

The New Testament. According to the same Version. 6s.

―――― *The Holy Bible.* Revised Version*.

    Cheap Editions for School Use.
    Revised Bible. Pearl 16mo, cloth boards, 10d.
    Revised New Testament. Nonpareil 32mo, 3d.; Brevier 16mo, 6d.; Long Primer 8vo, 10d.

* The Revised Version is the joint property of the Universities of Oxford and Cambridge.

ENGLISH. *The Oxford Bible for Teachers,* containing the Holy Scriptures, together with a new, enlarged, and illustrated edition of the *Oxford Helps to the Study of the Bible,* comprising Introductions to the several Books, the History and Antiquities of the Jews, the results of Modern Discoveries, and the Natural History of Palestine, with copious Tables, Concordance and Indices, and a series of Maps. Prices in various sizes and bindings from 7s. 6d. to 2l. 2s.

―――― *Helps to the Study of the Bible,* taken from the *Oxford Bible for Teachers. New, Enlarged, and Illustrated Edition.*

    Pearl 16mo, stiff covers, 1s. net.
    Nonpareil 8vo, cloth boards, 2s. 6d. net.
    Large Type edition, long primer 8vo, cloth boards, 5s.

―――― *The Psalter, or Psalms of David, and certain Canticles,* with a Translation and Exposition in English, by Richard Rolle of Hampole. Edited by H. R. Bramley, M.A. With an Introduction and Glossary. Demy 8vo. 1l. 1s.

―――― *Studia Biblica et Ecclesiastica.* Essays in Biblical and Patristic Criticism, and kindred subjects. By Members of the University of Oxford. 8vo.

    Vol. I. 10s. 6d. Vol. II. 12s. 6d.
    Vol. III 16s. Vol. IV. 12s 6d.

―――― *The Book of Wisdom:* the Greek Text, the Latin Vulgate, and the Authorised English Version; with an Introduction, Critical Apparatus, and a Commentary. By W. J. Deane, M.A. 4to. 12s. 6d.

2. FATHERS OF THE CHURCH, ETC.

St. Athanasius : *Orations against the Arians.* With an account of his Life by William Bright, D.D. Crown 8vo. 9s.

—— *Historical Writings, according to the Benedictine Text.* With an Introduction by W. Bright, D.D. Crown 8vo. 10s. 6d.

St. Augustine : *Select Anti-Pelagian Treatises, and the Acts of the Second Council of Orange.* With an Introduction by William Bright, D.D. Crown 8vo. 9s.

St. Basil : *The Book of St. Basil on the Holy Spirit.* A Revised Text, with Notes and Introduction by C. F. H. Johnston, M.A. Crown 8vo. 7s. 6d.

Canons *of the First Four General Councils of Nicaea, Constantinople, Ephesus, and Chalcedon.* With Notes by W. Bright, D.D. Second Edition. Crown 8vo. 7s. 6d.

Catenae *Graecorum Patrum in Novum Testamentum.* Edidit J. A. Cramer, S.T.P. Tomi VIII. 8vo. 2l. 4s.

Clementis Alexandrini *Opera, ex recensione Guil. Dindorfii.* Tomi IV. 8vo. 3l.

Cyrilli *Archiepiscopi Alexandrini in XII Prophetas.* Edidit P. E. Pusey, A.M. Tomi II. 8vo. 2l. 2s.

—— *in D. Joannis Evangelium.* Accedunt Fragmenta Varia necnon Tractatus ad Tiberium Diaconum Duo. Edidit post Aubertum P. E. Pusey, A.M. Tomi III. 8vo. 2l. 5s.

Cyrilli *Commentarii in Lucae Evangelium quae supersunt Syriace.* E mss. apud Mus. Britan. edidit R. Payne Smith, A.M. 4to. 1l. 2s.

—— The same, translated by R. Payne Smith, M.A. 2 vols. 8vo. 14s.

Ephraemi Syri, *Rabulae Episcopi Edesseni, Balaei, aliorumque Opera Selecta.* E Codd. Syriacis mss. in Musco Britannico et Bibliotheca Bodleiana asservatis primus edidit J. J. Overbeck. 8vo. 1l. 1s.

Eusebii Pamphili *Evangelicae Praeparationis Libri XV.* Ad Codd. mss. recensuit T. Gaisford, S.T.P. Tomi IV. 8vo. 1l. 10s.

—— *Evangelicae Demonstrationis Libri X.* Recensuit T. Gaisford, S.T.P. Tomi II. 8vo. 15s.

—— *contra Hieroclem et Marcellum Libri.* Recensuit T. Gaisford, S.T.P. 8vo. 7s.

Eusebius' *Ecclesiastical History,* according to the text of Burton, with an Introduction by W. Bright, D.D. Crown 8vo. 8s. 6d.

Evagrii *Historia Ecclesiastica,* ex recensione H. Valesii. 8vo. 4s.

Irenaeus : *The Third Book of St. Irenaeus, Bishop of Lyons, against Heresies.* With short Notes and a Glossary by H. Deane, B.D. Crown 8vo. 5s. 6d.

Patrum Apostolicorum, *S. Clementis Romani, S. Ignatii, S. Polycarpi, quae supersunt.* Edidit Guil. Jacobson, S.T.P.R. Tomi II. 8vo. 1l. 1s.

Philo. *About the Contemplative Life ; or, the Fourth Book of the Treatise concerning Virtues.* Critically edited, with a defence of its genuineness. By Fred. C. Conybeare, M.A. 8vo. 14s.

Reliquiae Sacrae *secundi tertiique saeculi.* Recensuit M. J. Routh, S.T.P. Tomi V. 8vo. 1l. 5s.

Scriptorum *Ecclesiasticorum Opuscula.* Recensuit M. J. Routh, S.T.P. Tomi II. 8vo. 10s.

Socrates' *Ecclesiastical History,* according to the Text of Hussey, with an Introduction by William Bright, D.D. Crown 8vo. 7s. 6d.

Sozomeni *Historia Ecclesiastica.* Edidit R. Hussey, S.T.B. Tomi III. 8vo. 15s.

Tertulliani *Apologeticus adversus Gentes pro Christianis.* Edited, with Introduction and Notes, by T. Herbert Bindley, B.D. Crown 8vo. 6s.

——— *de Praescriptione Haereticorum ; ad Martyras ; ad Scapulam.* Edited, with Introduction and Notes, by T. Herbert Bindley, B.D. Crown 8vo. 6s.

Theodoreti *Ecclesiasticae Historiae Libri V.* Recensuit T. Gaisford, S.T.P. 8vo. 7s. 6d.

3. ECCLESIASTICAL HISTORY, ETC.

Adamnani *Vita S. Columbae.* Edited, with Introduction, Notes, and Glossary, by J. T. Fowler, M.A., D.C.L. Crown 8vo, half-bound, 8s. 6d. net.

Baedae *Historia Ecclesiastica.* A New Edition. Edited, with Introduction, English Notes, &c., by C. Plummer, M.A. 2 vols. Crown 8vo. 21s. net.

Bedford (W.K.R.). *The Blazon of Episcopacy.* Being the Arms borne by, or attributed to, the Archbishops and Bishops of England and Wales. With an Ordinary of the Coats described and of other Episcopal Arms. *Second Edition, Revised and Enlarged.* With One Thousand Illustrations. Sm. 4to, buckram, 31s. 6d. net.

Bigg. *The Christian Platonists of Alexandria.* By Charles Bigg, D.D. 8vo. 10s. 6d.

Bingham's *Antiquities of the Christian Church, and other Works.* 10 vols. 8vo. 3l. 3s.

Bright. *Chapters of Early English Church History.* By W. Bright, D.D. *Second Edition.* 8vo. 12s.

Burnet's *History of the Reformation of the Church of England.* A new Edition, by N. Pocock, M.A. 7 vols. 8vo. 1l. 10s.

Cardwell's *Documentary Annals of the Reformed Church of England ;* being a Collection of Injunctions, Declarations, Orders, Articles of Inquiry, &c. from 1546 to 1716. 2 vols. 8vo. 18s.

Councils *and Ecclesiastical Documents relating to Great Britain and Ireland.* Edited, after Spelman and Wilkins, by A. W. Haddan, B.D., and W. Stubbs, D.D. Vols. I and III. Medium 8vo, each 1l. 1s.
Vol. II, Part I. Med. 8vo, 10s. 6d.
Vol. II, Part II. *Church of Ireland ; Memorials of St. Patrick.* Stiff covers, 3s. 6d.

Fuller's *Church History of Britain.* Edited by J. S. Brewer, M.A. 6 vols. 8vo. 1l. 19s.

London: HENRY FROWDE, Amen Corner, E.C.

Gibson's *Synodus Anglicana.* Edited by E. Cardwell, D.D. 8vo. 6s.

Hamilton's (*Archbishop John*) *Catechism*, 1552. Edited, with Introduction and Glossary, by Thomas Graves Law, Librarian of the Signet Library, Edinburgh. With a Preface by the Right Hon. W. E. Gladstone. Demy 8vo. 12s. 6d.

Hussey. *Rise of the Papal Power, traced in three Lectures.* By Robert Hussey, B.D. *Second Edition.* Fcap. 8vo. 4s. 6d.

Jackson. *The Church of St. Mary the Virgin, Oxford.* By T. G. Jackson, M.A., R.A. With Twenty-four full-page Illustrations, and numerous Cuts in the Text. Demy 4to, half-bound, 36s. net; or in vellum, gilt top and morocco labels &c., 42s. net.

John, *Bishop of Ephesus. The Third Part of his Ecclesiastical History.* [In Syriac.] Now first edited by William Cureton, M.A. 4to. 1l. 12s.

—— *The same.* translated by R. Payne Smith, M.A. 8vo. 10s.

Le Neve's *Fasti Ecclesiae Anglicanae.* Corrected and continued from 1715 to 1853 by T. Duffus Hardy. 3 vols. 8vo. 1l. 1s.

Noelli (A.) *Catechismus sive prima institutio disciplinaque Pietatis Christianae Latine explicata.* Editio nova cura Guil. Jacobson, A.M. 8vo. 5s. 6d.

Ommanney. *A Critical Dissertation on the Athanasian Creed.* By G. D. W. Ommanney, M.A. 8vo, 16s.

Records of the Reformation. *The Divorce,* 1527–1533. Mostly now for the first time printed from MSS. in the British Museum and other Libraries. Collected and arranged by N. Pocock, M.A. 2 vols. 8vo. 1l. 16s.

Reformatio *Legum Ecclesiasticarum.* The Reformation of Ecclesiastical Laws, as attempted in the reigns of Henry VIII, Edward VI, and Elizabeth. Edited by E. Cardwell, D.D. 8vo. 6s. 6d.

Shirley. *Some Account of the Church in the Apostolic Age.* By W.W. Shirley, D.D. *Second Edition.* Fcap. 8vo. 3s. 6d.

Stubbs. *Registrum Sacrum Anglicanum.* An attempt to exhibit the course of Episcopal Succession in England. By W. Stubbs, D.D. Small 4to. *Second Edition.* 10s. 6d.

4. ENGLISH THEOLOGY.

Bradley. *Lectures on the Book of Job.* By George Granville Bradley, D.D., Dean of Westminster. Crown 8vo. 7s. 6d.

—— *Lectures on Ecclesiastes.* By the same. Crown 8vo. 4s. 6d.

Bull's *Works, with Nelson's Life.* Edited by E. Burton, D.D. 8 vols. 8vo. 2l. 9s.

Burnet's *Exposition of the XXXIX Articles.* 8vo. 7s.

Butler's *Works.* Divided into Sections; with Sectional Headings; an Index to each volume; and some occasional Notes; also Prefatory Matter. Edited by the Right Hon. W. E. Gladstone. 2 vols. Medium 8vo. 1l. 8s.

Comber's *Companion to the Temple;* or a Help to Devotion in the use of the Common Prayer. 7 vols. 8vo. 1l. 11s. 6d.

Cranmer's *Works.* Collected and arranged by H. Jenkyns, M.A., Fellow of Oriel College. 4 vols. 8vo. 1l. 10s.

Enchiridion Theologicum *Anti-Romanum.*
Vol. I. Jeremy Taylor's Dissuasive from Popery, and Treatise on the Real Presence. 8vo. 8s.
Vol. II. Barrow on the Supremacy of the Pope, with his Discourse on the Unity of the Church. 8vo. 7s. 6d.
Vol. III. Tracts selected from Wake, Patrick, Stillingfleet, Clagett, and others. 8vo. 11s.

Greswell's *Harmonia Evangelica.* Fifth Edition. 8vo. 9s. 6d.

Hall's *Works.* Edited by P. Wynter, D.D. 10 vols. 8vo. 3l. 3s.

Heurtley. *Harmonia Symbolica: Creeds of the Western Church.* By C. Heurtley, D.D. 8vo. 6s. 6d.

Homilies *appointed to be read in Churches.* Edited by J. Griffiths, D.D. 8vo. 7s. 6d.

Hooker's *Works,* with his Life by Walton, arranged by John Keble, M.A. *Seventh Edition.* Revised by R. W. Church, M.A., Dean of St. Paul's, and F. Paget, D.D. 3 vols. medium 8vo. 1l. 16s.

—— *the Text* as arranged by J. Keble, M.A. 2 vols. 8vo. 11s.

Jackson's (Dr. Thomas) *Works.* 12 vols. 8vo. 3l. 6s.

Jewel's *Works.* Edited by R. W. Jelf, D.D. 8 vols. 8vo. 1l. 10s.

Martineau. *A Study of Religion: its Sources and Contents.* By James Martineau, D.D. Second Edition. 2 vols. Crown 8vo. 15s.

Patrick's *Theological Works.* 9 vols. 8vo. 1l. 1s.

Pearson's *Exposition of the Creed.* Revised and corrected by E. Burton, D.D. *Sixth Edition.* 8vo. 10s. 6d.

—— *Minor Theological Works.* Edited with a Memoir, by Edward Churton, M.A. 2 vols. 8vo. 10s.

Sanderson's *Works.* Edited by W. Jacobson, D.D. 6 vols. 8vo. 1l. 10s.

Stillingfleet's *Origines Sacrae.* 2 vols. 8vo. 9s.

—— *Rational Account of the Grounds of Protestant Religion;* being a vindication of Archbishop Laud's Relation of a Conference, &c. 2 vols. 8vo. 10s.

Wall's *History of Infant Baptism.* Edited by H. Cotton, D.C.L. 2 vols. 8vo. 1l. 1s.

Waterland's *Works,* with Life, by Bp. Van Mildert. *A new Edition,* with copious Indexes. 6 vols. 8vo. 2l. 11s.

—— *Review of the Doctrine of the Eucharist,* with a Preface by the late Bishop of London. Crown 8vo. 6s. 6d.

Wheatly's *Illustration of the Book of Common Prayer.* 8vo. 5s.

Wyclif. *A Catalogue of the Original Works of John Wyclif.* By W. W. Shirley, D.D. 8vo. 3s. 6d.

Wyclif. *Select English Works.* By T. Arnold, M.A. 3 vols. 8vo. 1l. 1s.

—— *Trialogus.* With the Supplement now first edited. By Gotthard Lechler. 8vo. 7s.

5. LITURGIOLOGY.

Cardwell's *Two Books of Common Prayer*, set forth by authority in the Reign of King Edward VI, compared with each other. Third Edition. 8vo. 7s.

—— *History of Conferences on the Book of Common Prayer from 1551 to 1690.* 8vo. 7s. 6d.

The Gelasian Sacramentary. *Liber Sacramentorum Romanae Ecclesiae.* Edited, with Introduction, Critical Notes, and Appendix, by H. A. Wilson, M.A. Medium 8vo. 18s.

Liturgies, Eastern and Western. Edited, with Introductions and Appendices, by F. E. Brightman, M.A., on the Basis of the former Work by C. E. Hammond, M.A.

 Vol. I. Eastern Liturgies. Demy 8vo. 1l. 1s.

Helps to the Study of the Book of Common Prayer: Being a Companion to Church Worship. By the Very Rev. W. R. Stephens, B.D., Dean of Winchester. Crown 8vo. 3s. 6d.

Leofric Missal, The, as used in the Cathedral of Exeter during the Episcopate of its first Bishop, A.D. 1050-1072; together with some Account of the Red Book of Derby, the Missal of Robert of Jumièges, &c. Edited, with Introduction and Notes, by F. E. Warren, B.D., F.S.A. 4to, half-morocco, 1l. 15s.

Maskell. *Ancient Liturgy of the Church of England*, according to the uses of Sarum, York, Hereford, and Bangor, and the Roman Liturgy arranged in parallel columns, with preface and notes. By W. Maskell, M.A. Third Edition. 8vo. 15s.

—— *Monumenta Ritualia Ecclesiae Anglicanae.* The occasional Offices of the Church of England according to the old use of Salisbury, the Prymer in English, and other prayers and forms, with dissertations and notes. Second Edition. 3 vols. 8vo. 2l. 10s.

Warren. *The Liturgy and Ritual of the Celtic Church.* By F. E. Warren, B.D. 8vo. 14s.

Oxford
AT THE CLARENDON PRESS
LONDON: HENRY FROWDE
OXFORD UNIVERSITY PRESS WAREHOUSE, AMEN CORNER, E.C.

www.ingramcontent.com/pod-product-compliance
Lightning Source LLC
Chambersburg PA
CBHW030254240426
43673CB00040B/963